CHAPTER 18 ... DESPITE IT ALL, YOSHITERU ZAIMOKUZA WAILS ALONE IN THE WASTELAND. [PART ONE]

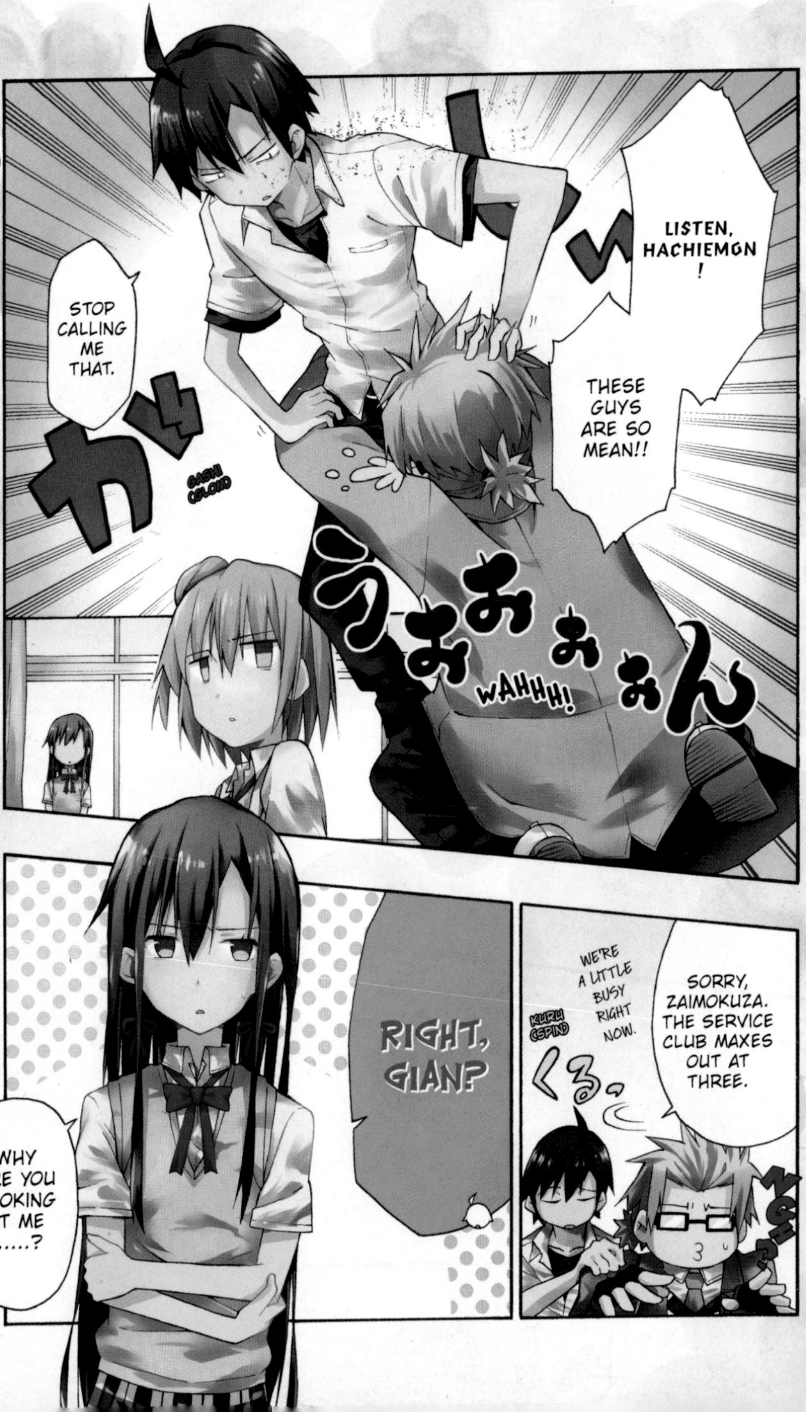
LISTEN, HACHIEMON!
THESE GUYS ARE SO MEAN!!
STOP CALLING ME THAT.
GASHI (CLONK)
WAHHH!
SORRY, ZAIMOKUZA. THE SERVICE CLUB MAXES OUT AT THREE.
WE'RE A LITTLE BUSY RIGHT NOW.
KURU (SPIN)
NGH
RIGHT, GIAN?
WHY ARE YOU LOOKING AT ME ......?

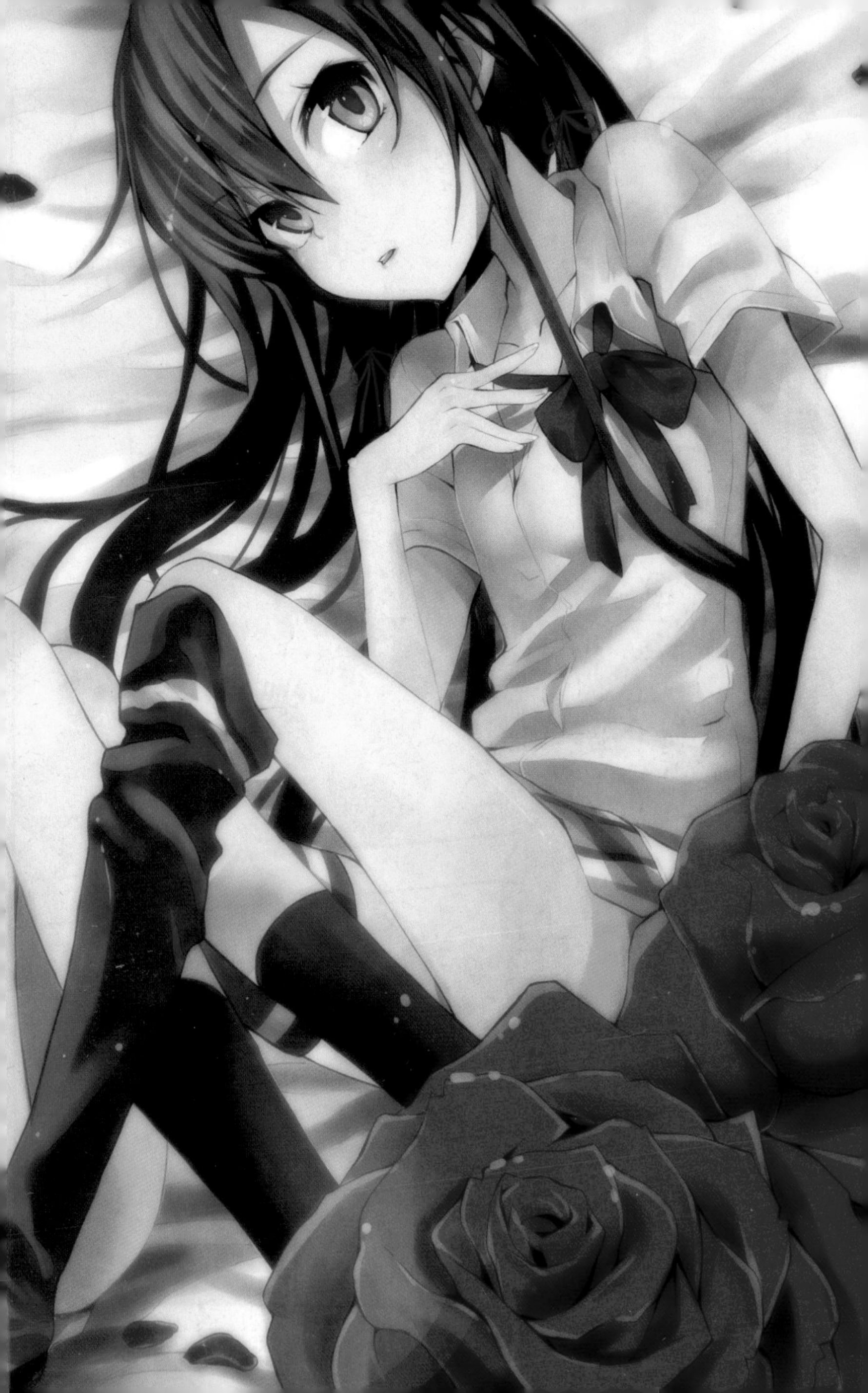

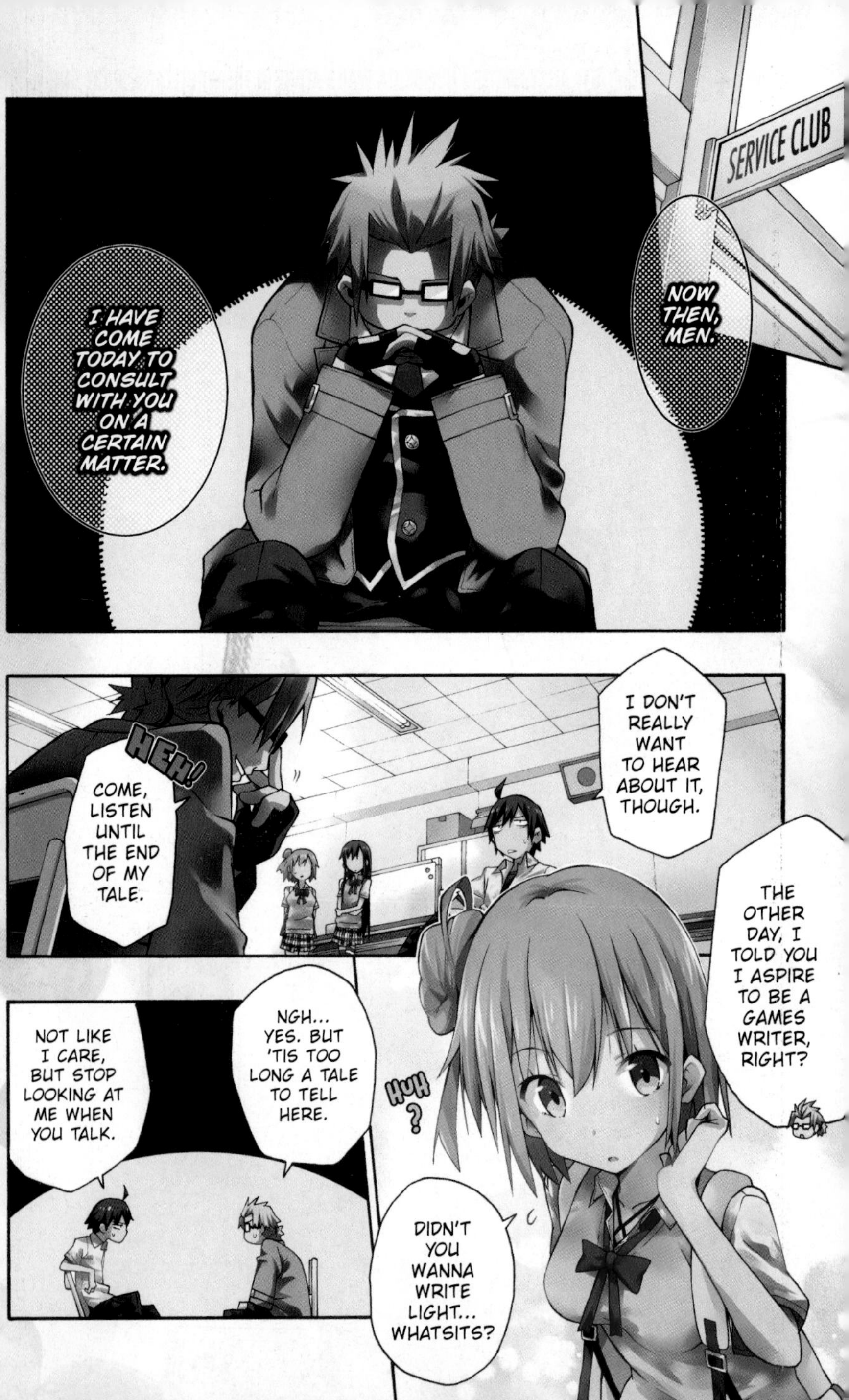
SERVICE CLUB
NOW THEN, MEN.
I HAVE COME TODAY TO CONSULT WITH YOU ON A CERTAIN MATTER.
I DON'T REALLY WANT TO HEAR ABOUT IT, THOUGH.
HEH!
COME, LISTEN UNTIL THE END OF MY TALE.
THE OTHER DAY, I TOLD YOU I ASPIRE TO BE A GAMES WRITER, RIGHT?
HUH?
DIDN'T YOU WANNA WRITE LIGHT... WHATSITS?
NGH... YES. BUT 'TIS TOO LONG A TALE TO TELL HERE.
NOT LIKE I CARE, BUT STOP LOOKING AT ME WHEN YOU TALK.

MY YOUTH ROMANTIC COMEDY is WRØNG, AS I EXPECTED @comic 04

▌Original Story
Wataru Watari
▌Art
Naomichi Io
▌Character Design
Ponkan⑧

MY YOUTH ROMANTIC COMEDY IS WRONG, AS I EXPECTED @COMIC

CHARACTERS + STORY SO FAR

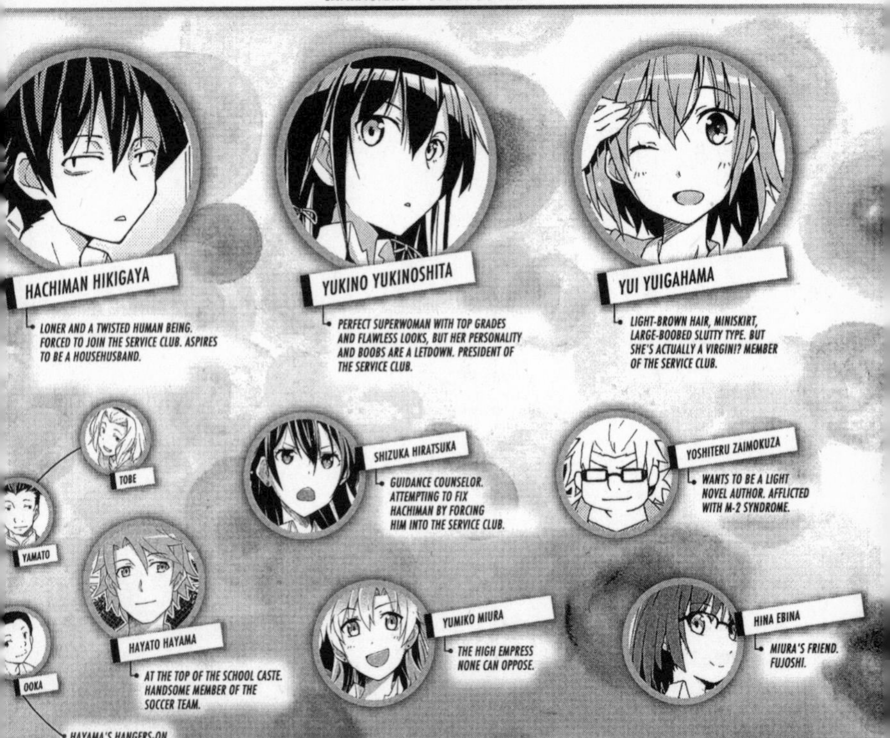
HACHIMAN HIKIGAYA
LONER AND A TWISTED HUMAN BEING. FORCED TO JOIN THE SERVICE CLUB. ASPIRES TO BE A HOUSEHUSBAND.
YUKINO YUKINOSHITA
PERFECT SUPERWOMAN WITH TOP GRADES AND FLAWLESS LOOKS, BUT HER PERSONALITY AND BOOBS ARE A LETDOWN. PRESIDENT OF THE SERVICE CLUB.
YUI YUIGAHAMA
LIGHT-BROWN HAIR, MINISKIRT, LARGE-BOOBED SLUTTY TYPE. BUT SHE'S ACTUALLY A VIRGIN!? MEMBER OF THE SERVICE CLUB.
TOBE
YAMATO
SHIZUKA HIRATSUKA
GUIDANCE COUNSELOR. ATTEMPTING TO FIX HACHIMAN BY FORCING HIM INTO THE SERVICE CLUB.
YOSHITERU ZAIMOKUZA
WANTS TO BE A LIGHT NOVEL AUTHOR. AFFLICTED WITH M-2 SYNDROME.
HAYATO HAYAMA
AT THE TOP OF THE SCHOOL CASTE. HANDSOME MEMBER OF THE SOCCER TEAM.
OOKA
HAYAMA'S HANGERS-ON.
YUMIKO MIURA
THE HIGH EMPRESS NONE CAN OPPOSE.
HINA EBINA
MIURA'S FRIEND. FUJOSHI.

THE SERVICE CLUB: A MYSTERIOUS CLUB AT CHIBA MUNICIPAL SOUBU HIGH SCHOOL. I, HACHIMAN HIKIGAYA, RUN AROUND EVERY DAY LIKE A HEADLESS CHICKEN IN AN ATTEMPT TO RESOLVE THE VARIOUS PROBLEMS THAT STUDENTS BRING TO OUR IMPROMPTU COUNSELING SERVICE...THANKS TO THE CLUB CAPTAIN, YUKINO YUKINOSHITA. I MEAN, SHE'S A SCARY GIRL. THINGS HAVE GOTTEN AWKWARD BETWEEN YUIGAHAMA AND ME, SO THE THREE OF US ATTEMPTED TO HAVE A TALK TO FIX THINGS, BUT SOMEHOW IT FELT LIKE NONE OF US WERE TALKING ABOUT THE SAME THING. SUDDENLY, ZAIMOKUZA THE TROUBLEMAKER BURSTS INTO THE CLUB ROOM, AND...!?

CONTENTS

MADE IN COOPERATION WITH THE CHIBA CITY LOCATION SERVICE

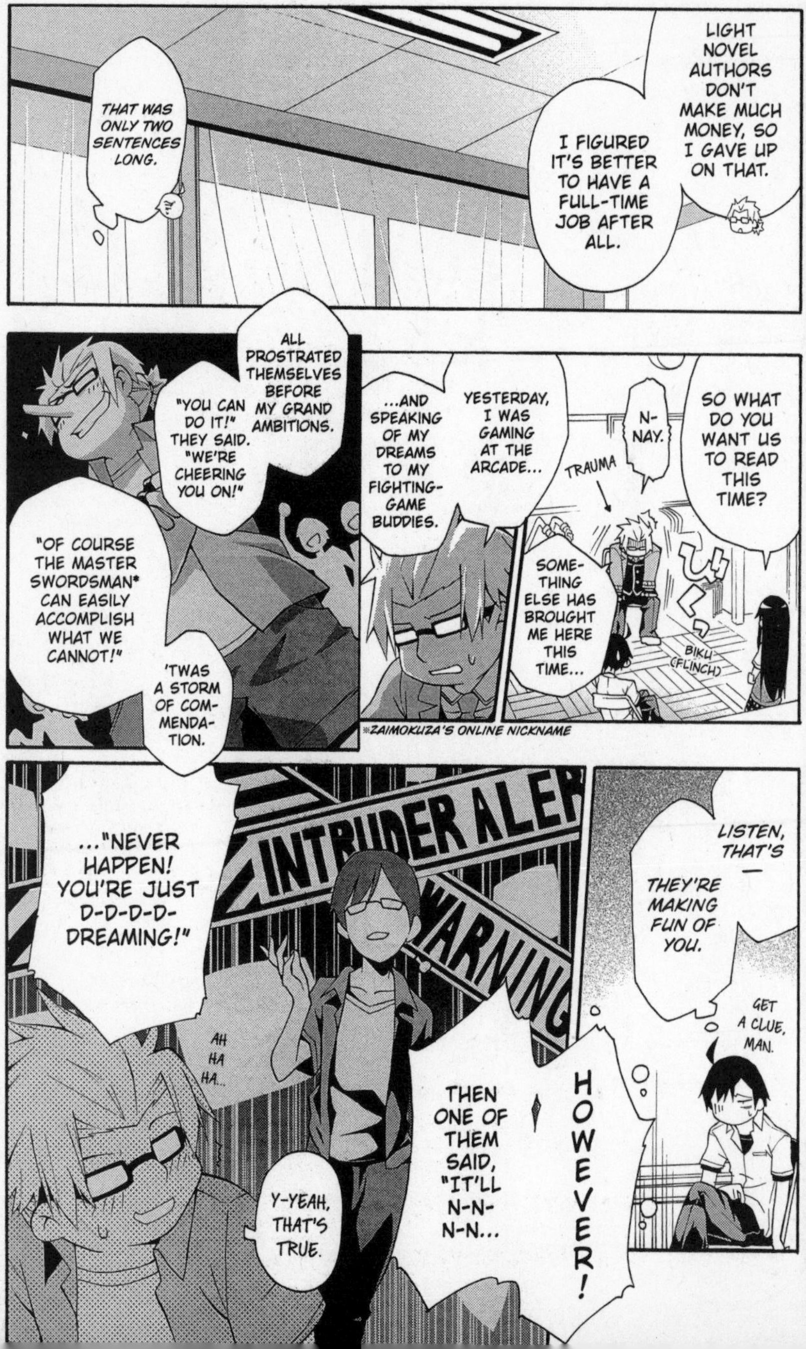
LIGHT NOVEL AUTHORS DON'T MAKE MUCH MONEY, SO I GAVE UP ON THAT.
I FIGURED IT'S BETTER TO HAVE A FULL-TIME JOB AFTER ALL.
THAT WAS ONLY TWO SENTENCES LONG.
SO WHAT DO YOU WANT US TO READ THIS TIME?
N-NAY.
TRAUMA
SOMETHING ELSE HAS BROUGHT ME HERE THIS TIME...
BIKU (FLINCH)
YESTERDAY, I WAS GAMING AT THE ARCADE...
...AND SPEAKING OF MY DREAMS TO MY FIGHTING-GAME BUDDIES.
ALL PROSTRATED THEMSELVES BEFORE MY GRAND AMBITIONS.
"YOU CAN DO IT!" THEY SAID. "WE'RE CHEERING YOU ON!"
"OF COURSE THE MASTER SWORDSMAN* CAN EASILY ACCOMPLISH WHAT WE CANNOT!"
'TWAS A STORM OF COMMENDATION.
※ZAIMOKUZA'S ONLINE NICKNAME
LISTEN, THAT'S—
THEY'RE MAKING FUN OF YOU.
GET A CLUE, MAN.
HOWEVER!
THEN ONE OF THEM SAID, "IT'LL N-N-N-N...
..."NEVER HAPPEN! YOU'RE JUST D-D-D-D-DREAMING!"
INTRUDER ALER
WARNING
AH HA HA...
Y-YEAH, THAT'S TRUE.

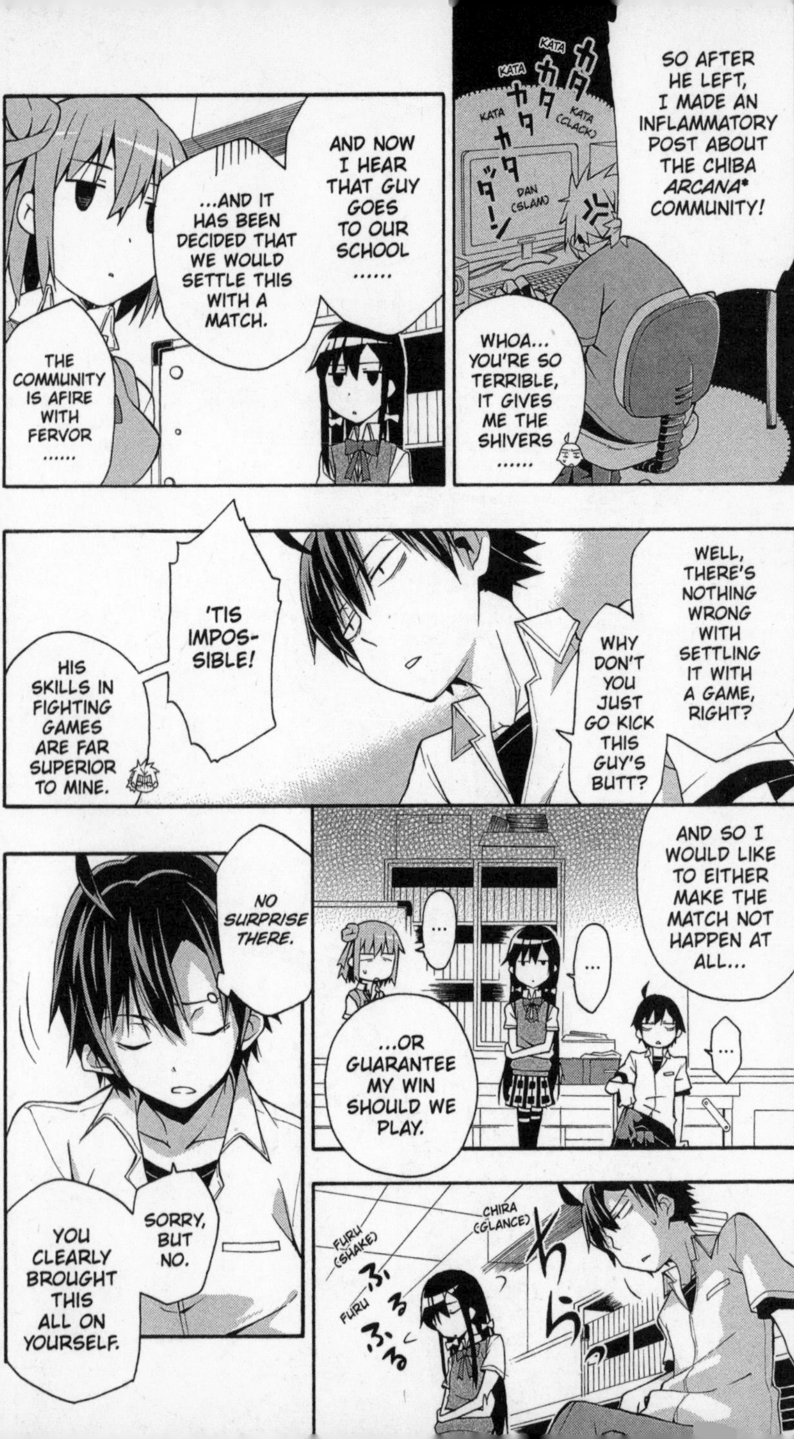
SO AFTER HE LEFT, I MADE AN INFLAMMATORY POST ABOUT THE CHIBA *ARCANA** COMMUNITY!
KATA
KATA
KATA
KATA (CLACK)
DAN (SLAM)
WHOA... YOU'RE SO TERRIBLE, IT GIVES ME THE SHIVERS ......
AND NOW I HEAR THAT GUY GOES TO OUR SCHOOL ......
...AND IT HAS BEEN DECIDED THAT WE WOULD SETTLE THIS WITH A MATCH.
THE COMMUNITY IS AFIRE WITH FERVOR ......
WELL, THERE'S NOTHING WRONG WITH SETTLING IT WITH A GAME, RIGHT?
WHY DON'T YOU JUST GO KICK THIS GUY'S BUTT?
'TIS IMPOS-SIBLE!
HIS SKILLS IN FIGHTING GAMES ARE FAR SUPERIOR TO MINE.
AND SO I WOULD LIKE TO EITHER MAKE THE MATCH NOT HAPPEN AT ALL...
...
...
...OR GUARANTEE MY WIN SHOULD WE PLAY.
...
CHIRA (GLANCE)
FURU (SHAKE)
FURU
NO SURPRISE THERE.
SORRY, BUT NO.
YOU CLEARLY BROUGHT THIS ALL ON YOURSELF.

*ZAIMOKUZA'S FAVORITE GAME (SEE V. 3, CH. 14)

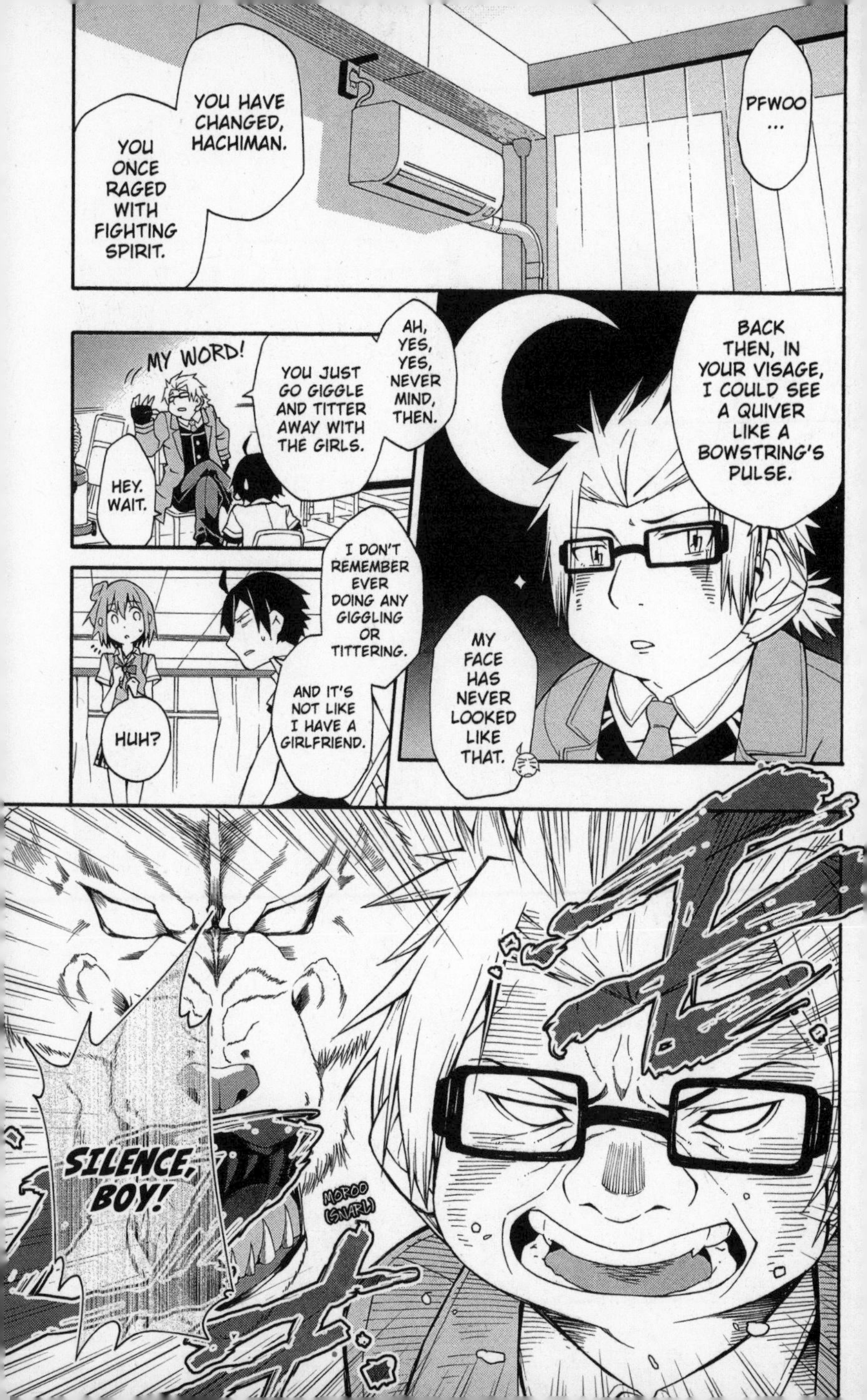
PFWOO...
YOU HAVE CHANGED, HACHIMAN.
YOU ONCE RAGED WITH FIGHTING SPIRIT.
BACK THEN, IN YOUR VISAGE, I COULD SEE A QUIVER LIKE A BOWSTRING'S PULSE.
MY FACE HAS NEVER LOOKED LIKE THAT.
AH, YES, YES, NEVER MIND, THEN.
YOU JUST GO GIGGLE AND TITTER AWAY WITH THE GIRLS.
MY WORD!
HEY. WAIT.
I DON'T REMEMBER EVER DOING ANY GIGGLING OR TITTERING.
AND IT'S NOT LIKE I HAVE A GIRLFRIEND.
HUH?
SILENCE, BOY!
MOROO (SNARL)

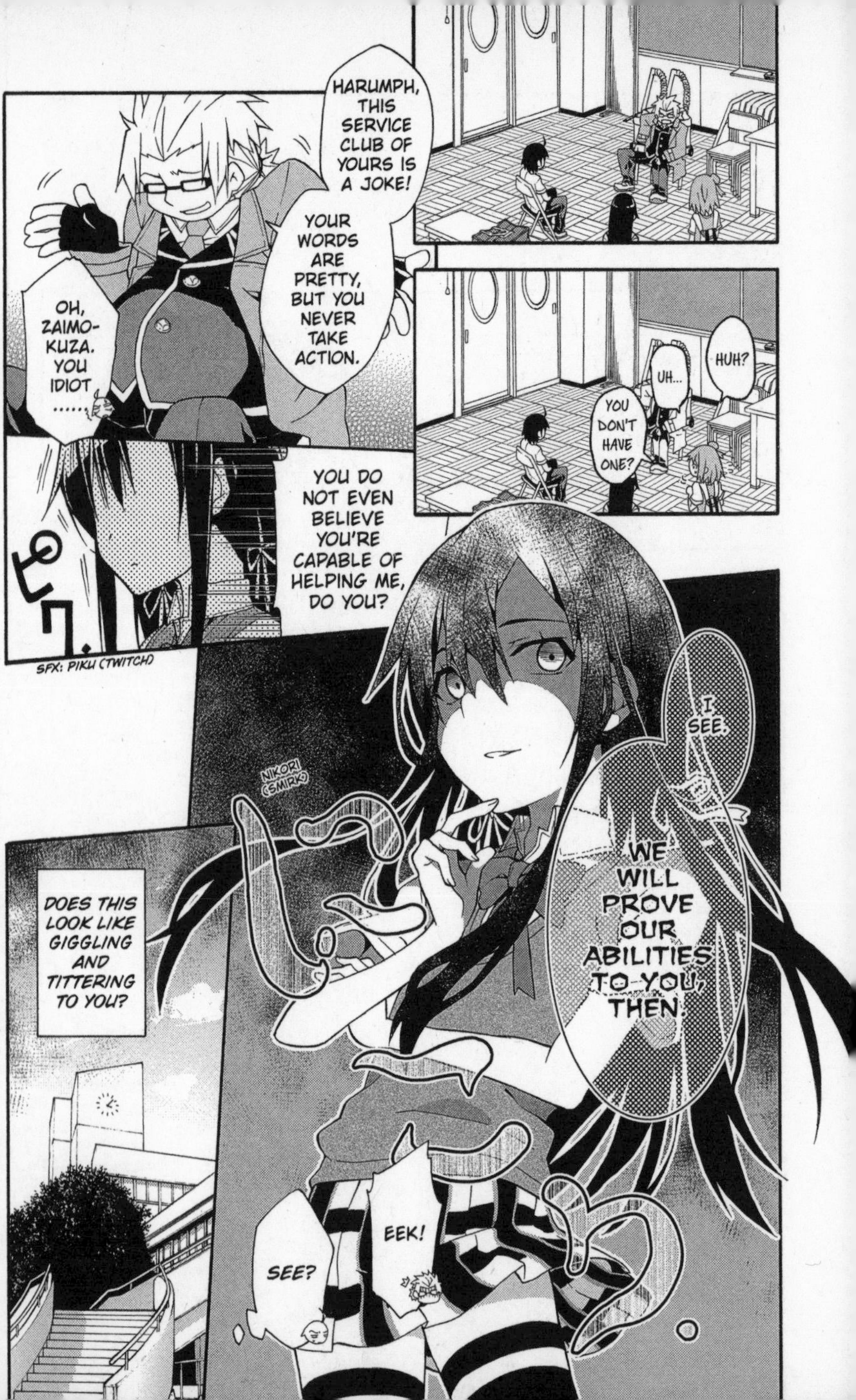
HARUMPH, THIS SERVICE CLUB OF YOURS IS A JOKE!
YOUR WORDS ARE PRETTY, BUT YOU NEVER TAKE ACTION.
OH, ZAIMOKUZA. YOU IDIOT ......
HUH?
UH...
YOU DON'T HAVE ONE?
YOU DO NOT EVEN BELIEVE YOU'RE CAPABLE OF HELPING ME, DO YOU?
SFX: PIKU (TWITCH)
I SEE.
NIKORI (SMIRK)
WE WILL PROVE OUR ABILITIES TO YOU, THEN.
EEK!
SEE?
DOES THIS LOOK LIKE GIGGLING AND TITTERING TO YOU?

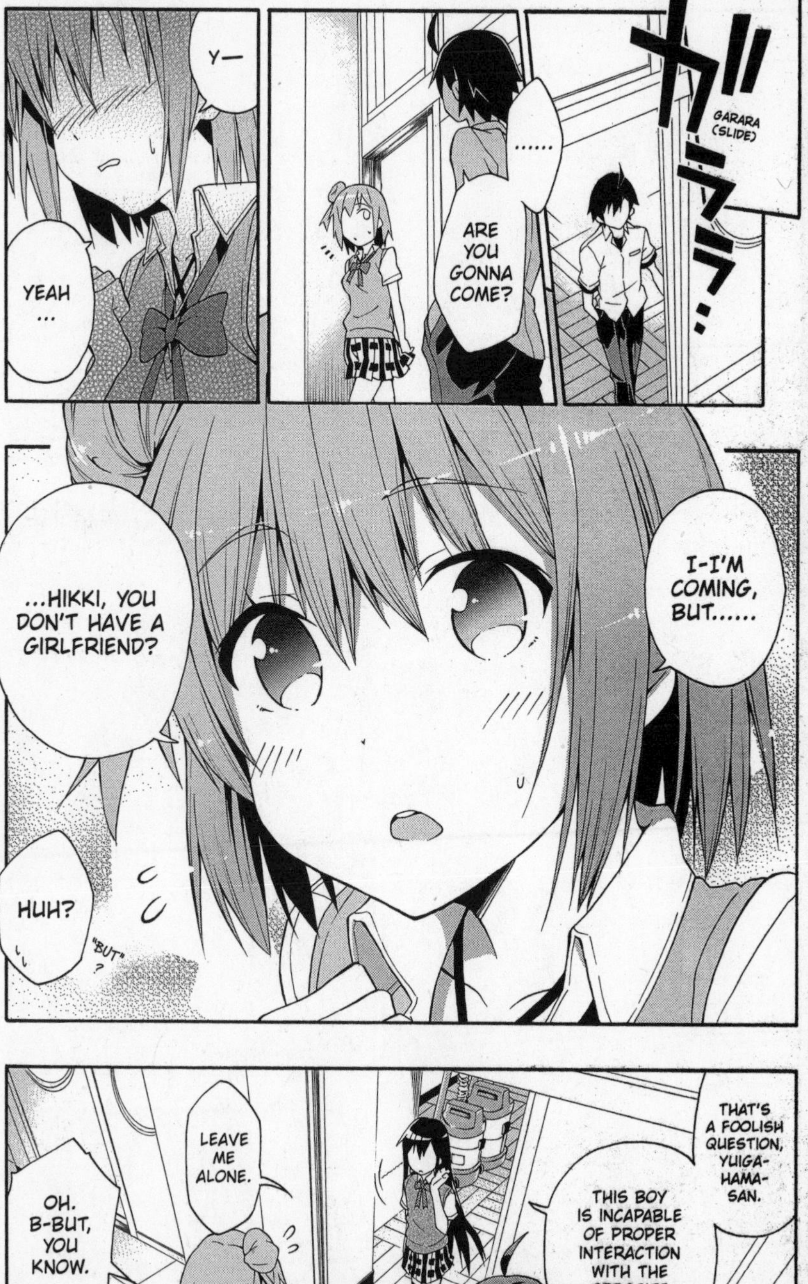
GARARA (SLIDE)
......
ARE YOU GONNA COME?
Y—
YEAH ...
I-I'M COMING, BUT......
...HIKKI, YOU DON'T HAVE A GIRLFRIEND?
HUH?
"BUT"?
THAT'S A FOOLISH QUESTION, YUIGA-HAMA-SAN.
THIS BOY IS INCAPABLE OF PROPER INTERACTION WITH THE OPPOSITE SEX.
LEAVE ME ALONE.
OH. B-BUT, YOU KNOW.

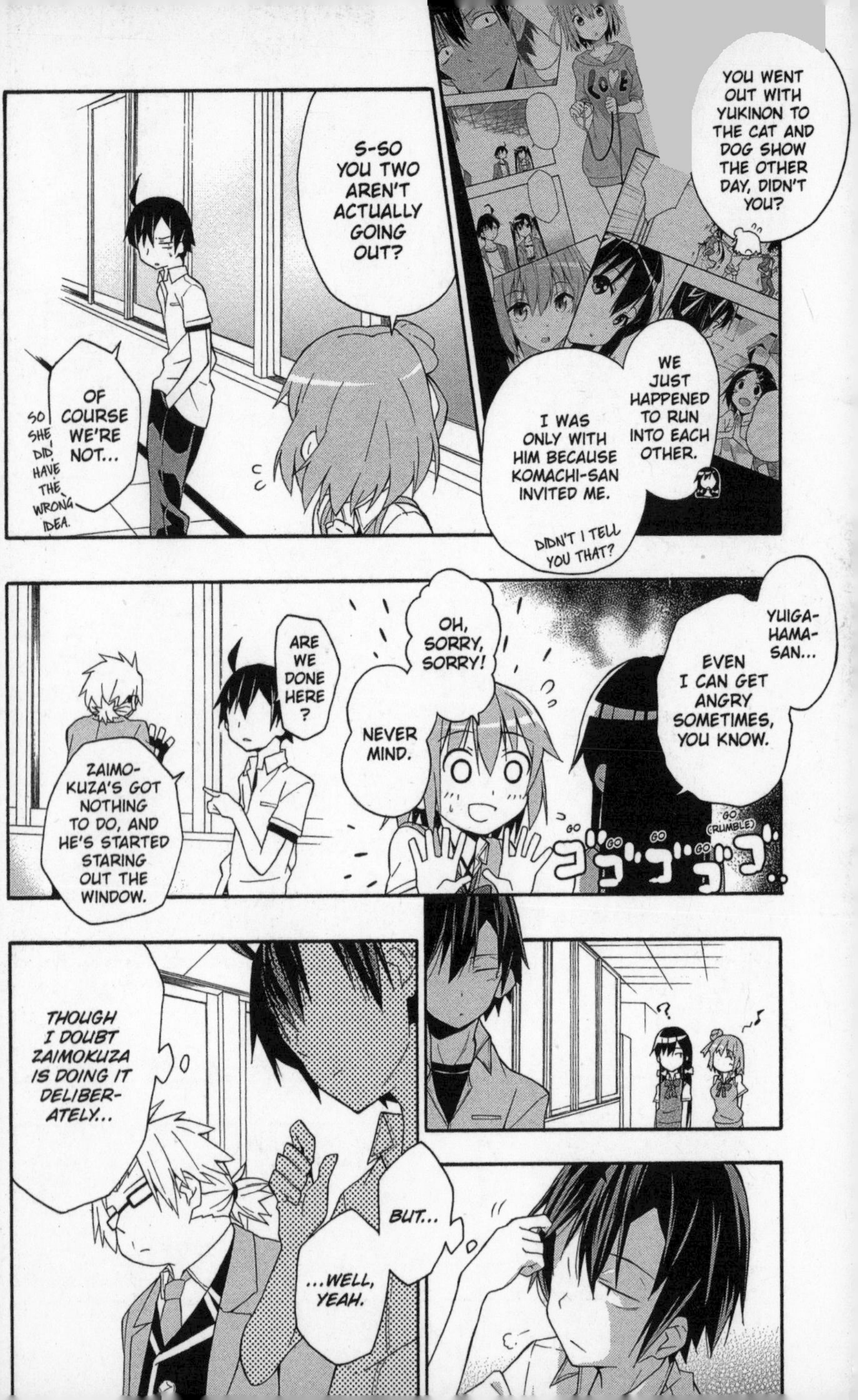
YOU WENT OUT WITH YUKINON TO THE CAT AND DOG SHOW THE OTHER DAY, DIDN'T YOU?
WE JUST HAPPENED TO RUN INTO EACH OTHER.
I WAS ONLY WITH HIM BECAUSE KOMACHI-SAN INVITED ME.
DIDN'T I TELL YOU THAT?
S-SO YOU TWO AREN'T ACTUALLY GOING OUT?
OF COURSE WE'RE NOT...
SO SHE DID HAVE THE WRONG IDEA.
YUIGA-HAMA-SAN...
EVEN I CAN GET ANGRY SOMETIMES, YOU KNOW.
GO GO GO GO (RUMBLE)
OH, SORRY, SORRY!
NEVER MIND.
ARE WE DONE HERE?
ZAIMOKUZA'S GOT NOTHING TO DO, AND HE'S STARTED STARING OUT THE WINDOW.
THOUGH I DOUBT ZAIMOKUZA IS DOING IT DELIBER-ATELY...
BUT...
...WELL, YEAH.

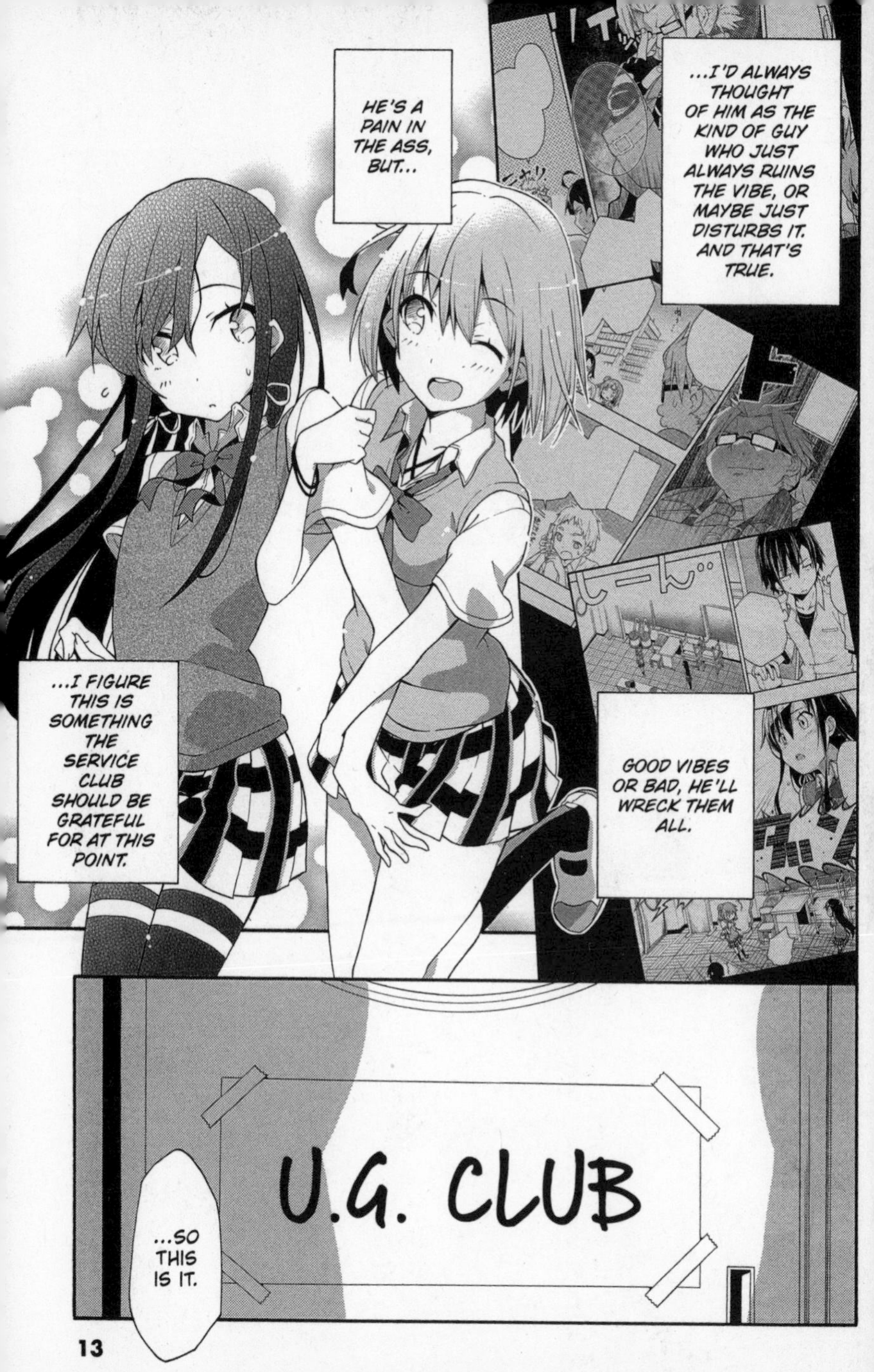
...I'D ALWAYS THOUGHT OF HIM AS THE KIND OF GUY WHO JUST ALWAYS RUINS THE VIBE, OR MAYBE JUST DISTURBS IT. AND THAT'S TRUE.
HE'S A PAIN IN THE ASS, BUT...
GOOD VIBES OR BAD, HE'LL WRECK THEM ALL.
...I FIGURE THIS IS SOMETHING THE SERVICE CLUB SHOULD BE GRATEFUL FOR AT THIS POINT.
U.G. CLUB
...SO THIS IS IT.

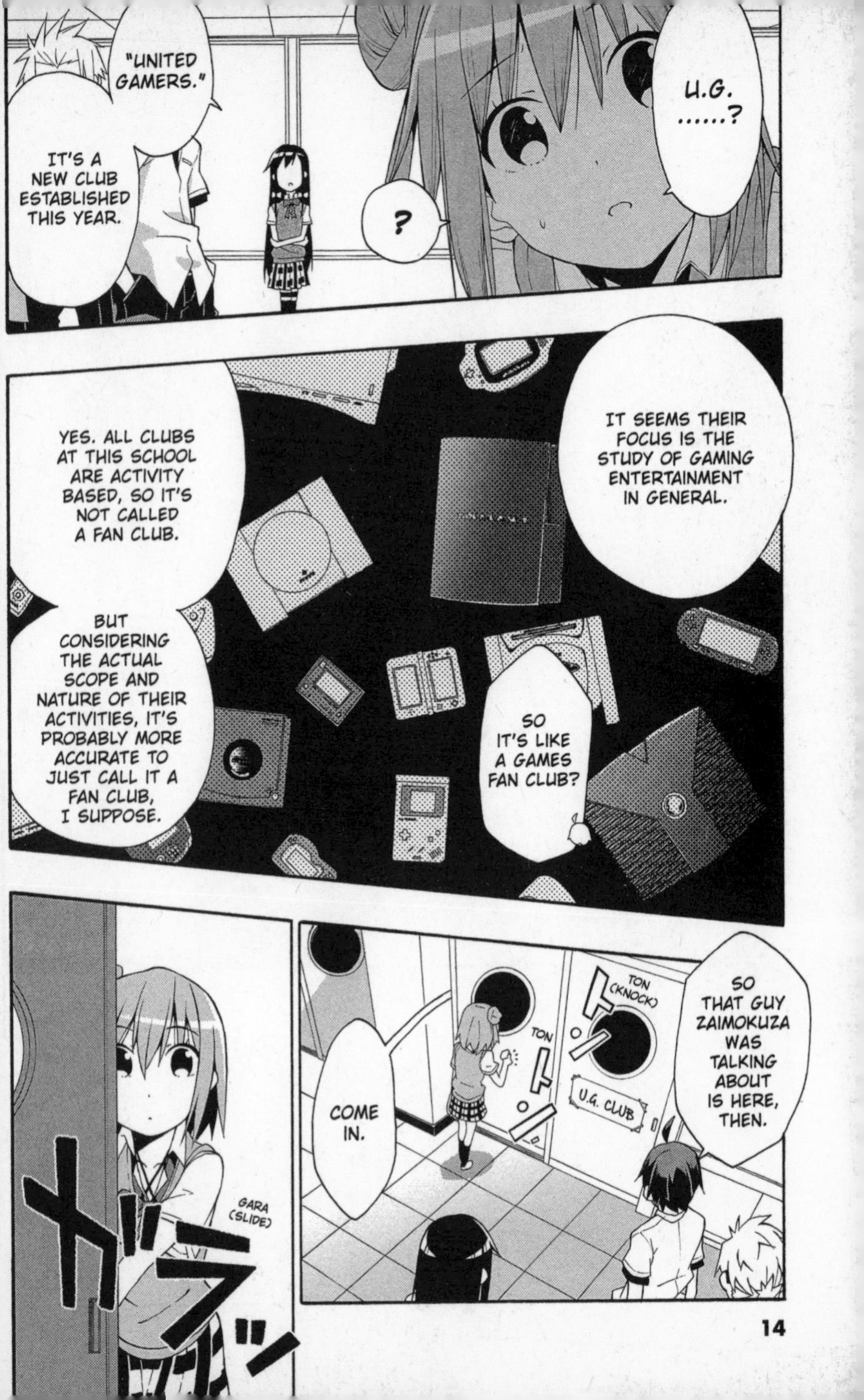
U.G. ......?
?
"UNITED GAMERS."
IT'S A NEW CLUB ESTABLISHED THIS YEAR.
IT SEEMS THEIR FOCUS IS THE STUDY OF GAMING ENTERTAINMENT IN GENERAL.
SO IT'S LIKE A GAMES FAN CLUB?
YES. ALL CLUBS AT THIS SCHOOL ARE ACTIVITY BASED, SO IT'S NOT CALLED A FAN CLUB.
BUT CONSIDERING THE ACTUAL SCOPE AND NATURE OF THEIR ACTIVITIES, IT'S PROBABLY MORE ACCURATE TO JUST CALL IT A FAN CLUB, I SUPPOSE.
SO THAT GUY ZAIMOKUZA WAS TALKING ABOUT IS HERE, THEN.
TON (KNOCK)
TON
U.G. CLUB
COME IN.
GARA (SLIDE)

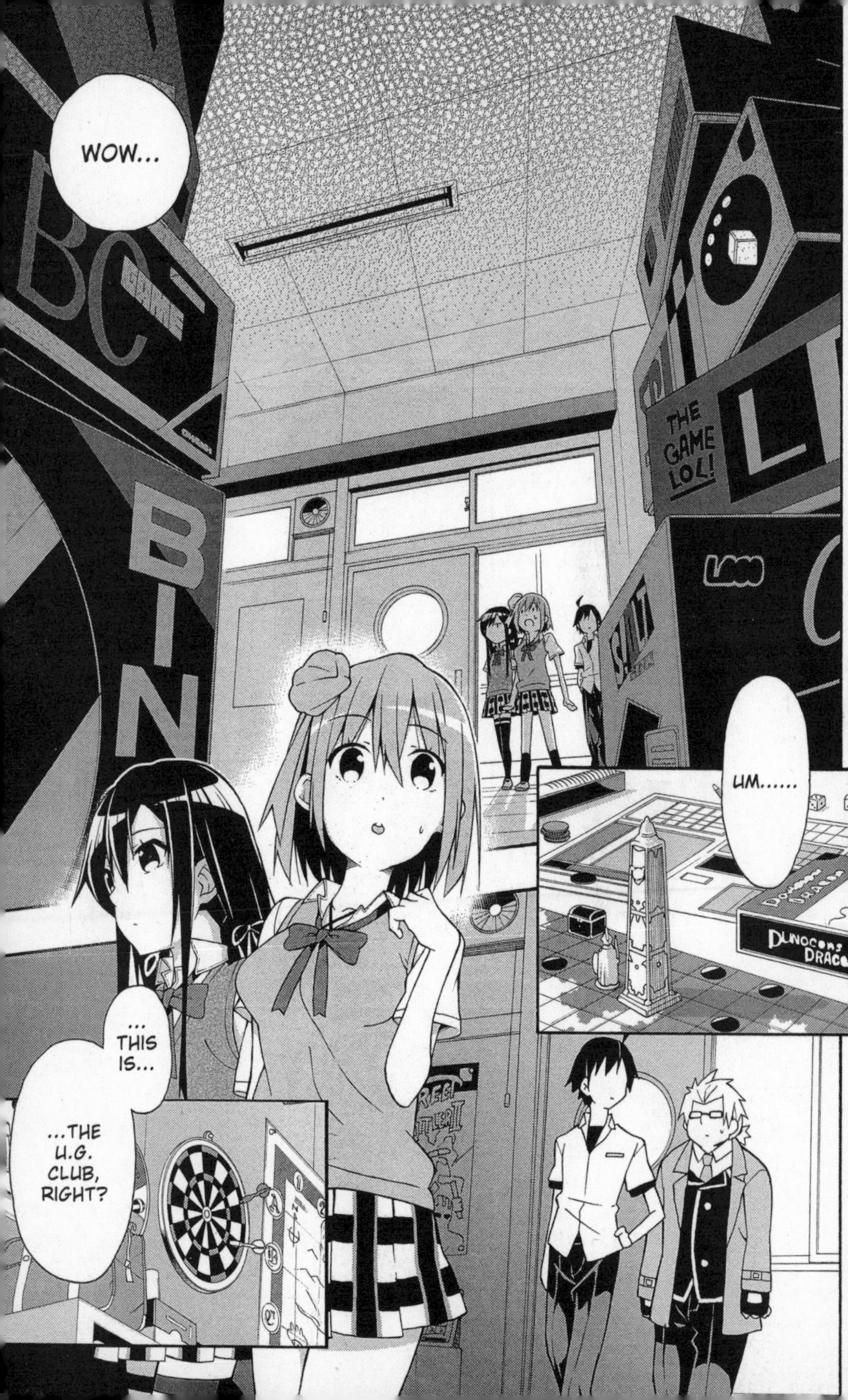
WOW...
THE GAME LOL!
UM......
...THIS IS...
...THE U.G. CLUB, RIGHT?

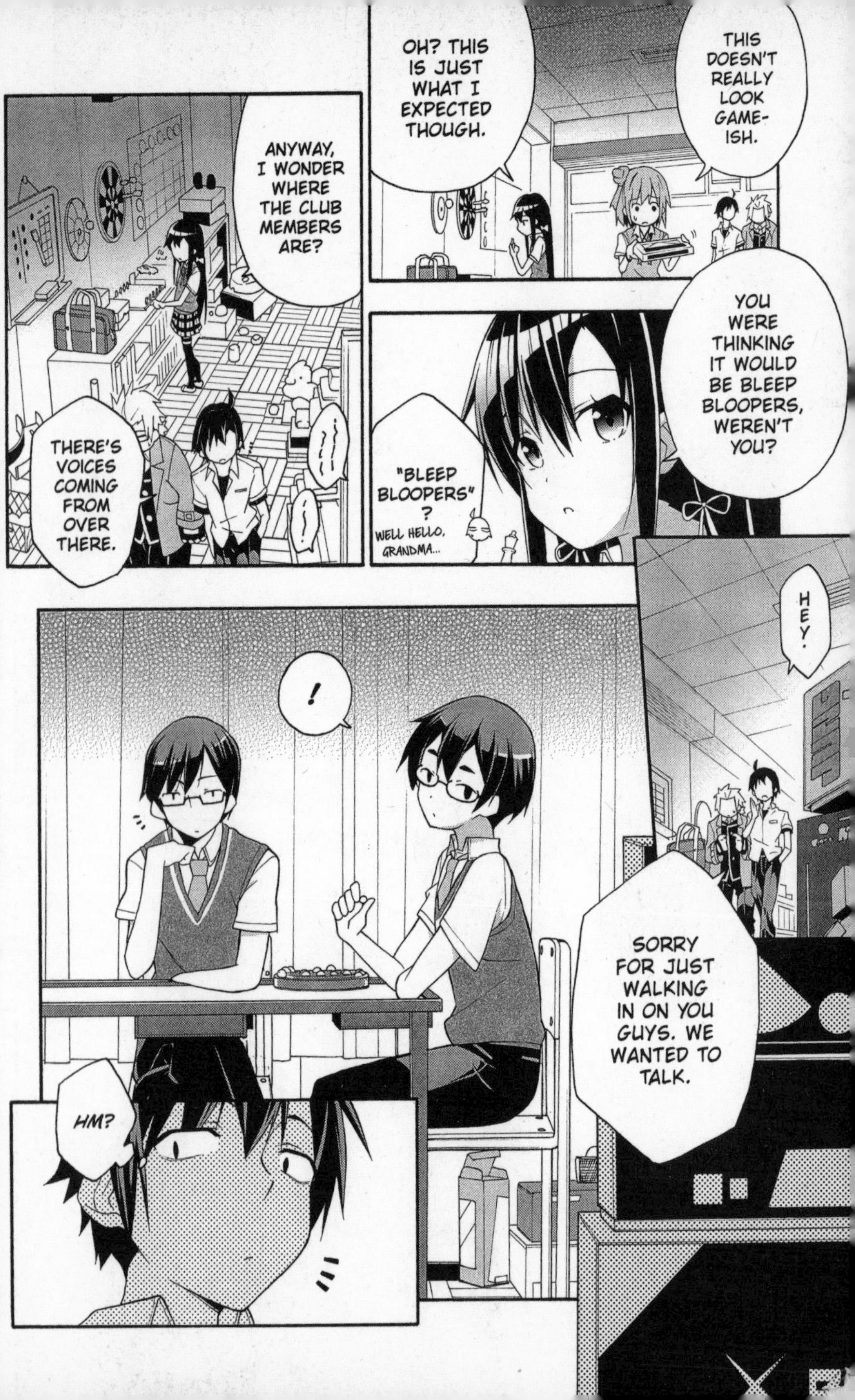
THIS DOESN'T REALLY LOOK GAME-ISH.
OH? THIS IS JUST WHAT I EXPECTED THOUGH.
YOU WERE THINKING IT WOULD BE BLEEP BLOOPERS, WEREN'T YOU?
"BLEEP BLOOPERS"?
WELL HELLO, GRANDMA...
ANYWAY, I WONDER WHERE THE CLUB MEMBERS ARE?
THERE'S VOICES COMING FROM OVER THERE.
HEY.
!
SORRY FOR JUST WALKING IN ON YOU GUYS. WE WANTED TO TALK.
HM?

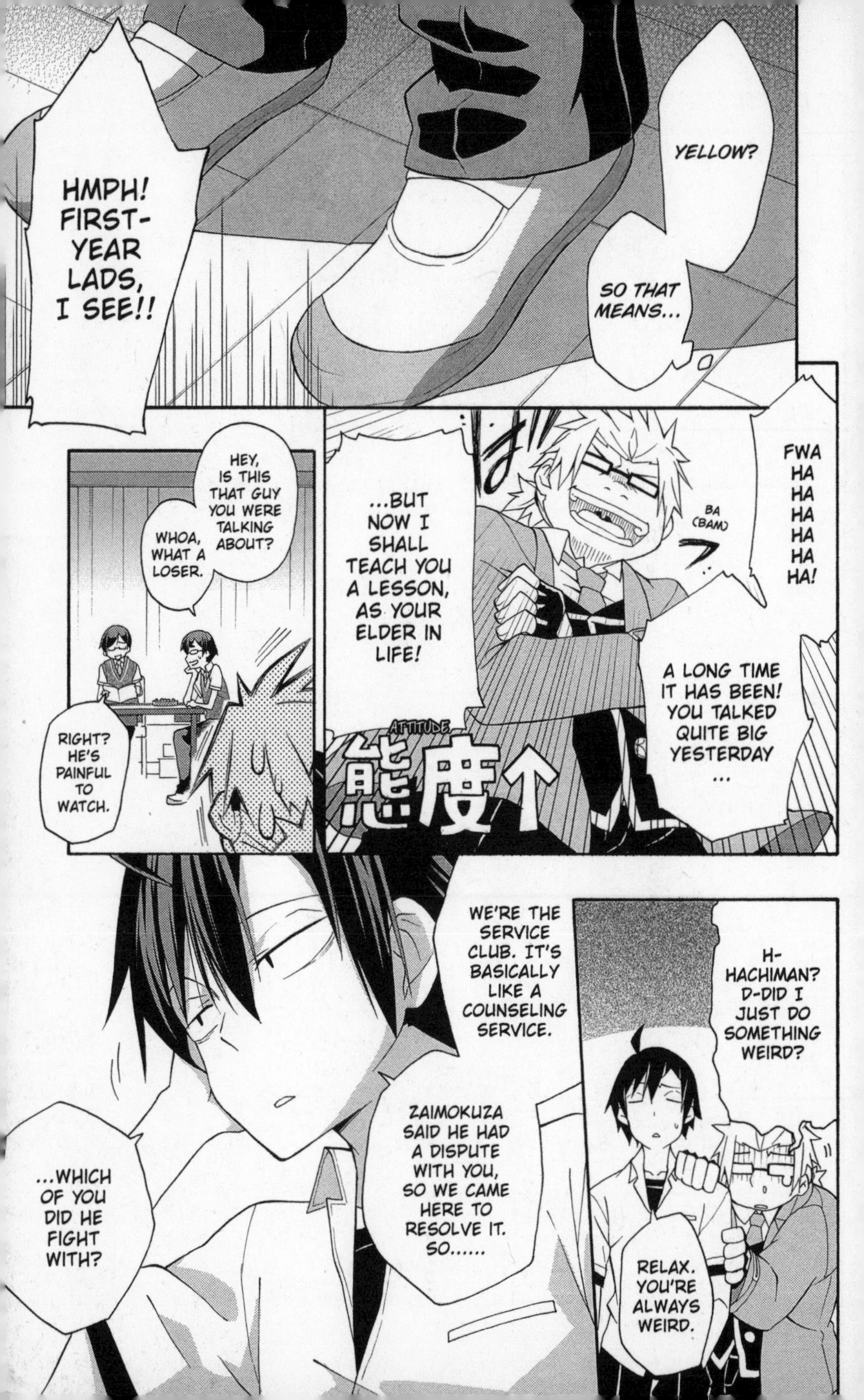
YELLOW?
SO THAT MEANS...
HMPH! FIRST-YEAR LADS, I SEE!!
FWA HA HA HA HA HA HA!
BA (BAM)
A LONG TIME IT HAS BEEN! YOU TALKED QUITE BIG YESTERDAY...
...BUT NOW I SHALL TEACH YOU A LESSON, AS YOUR ELDER IN LIFE!
ATTITUDE
態度↑
HEY, IS THIS THAT GUY YOU WERE TALKING ABOUT?
WHOA, WHAT A LOSER.
RIGHT? HE'S PAINFUL TO WATCH.
H-HACHIMAN? D-DID I JUST DO SOMETHING WEIRD?
RELAX. YOU'RE ALWAYS WEIRD.
WE'RE THE SERVICE CLUB. IT'S BASICALLY LIKE A COUNSELING SERVICE.
ZAIMOKUZA SAID HE HAD A DISPUTE WITH YOU, SO WE CAME HERE TO RESOLVE IT. SO......
...WHICH OF YOU DID HE FIGHT WITH?

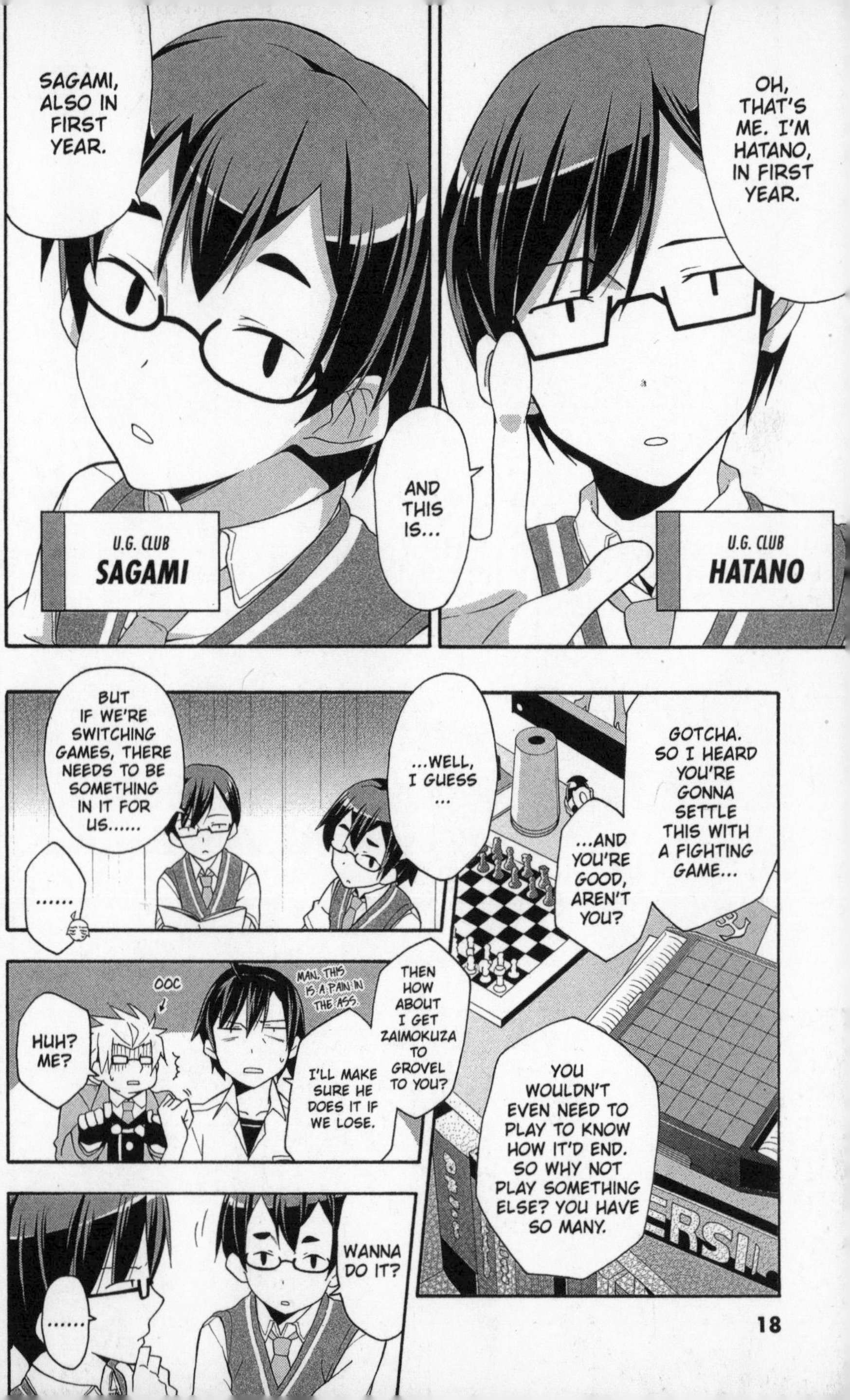
OH, THAT'S ME. I'M HATANO, IN FIRST YEAR.
U.G. CLUB HATANO
AND THIS IS...
SAGAMI, ALSO IN FIRST YEAR.
U.G. CLUB SAGAMI
GOTCHA. SO I HEARD YOU'RE GONNA SETTLE THIS WITH A FIGHTING GAME...
...AND YOU'RE GOOD, AREN'T YOU?
YOU WOULDN'T EVEN NEED TO PLAY TO KNOW HOW IT'D END. SO WHY NOT PLAY SOMETHING ELSE? YOU HAVE SO MANY.
...WELL, I GUESS...
BUT IF WE'RE SWITCHING GAMES, THERE NEEDS TO BE SOMETHING IN IT FOR US......
......
THEN HOW ABOUT I GET ZAIMOKUZA TO GROVEL TO YOU?
I'LL MAKE SURE HE DOES IT IF WE LOSE.
MAN, THIS IS A PAIN IN THE ASS.
OOC
HUH? ME?
WANNA DO IT?
....

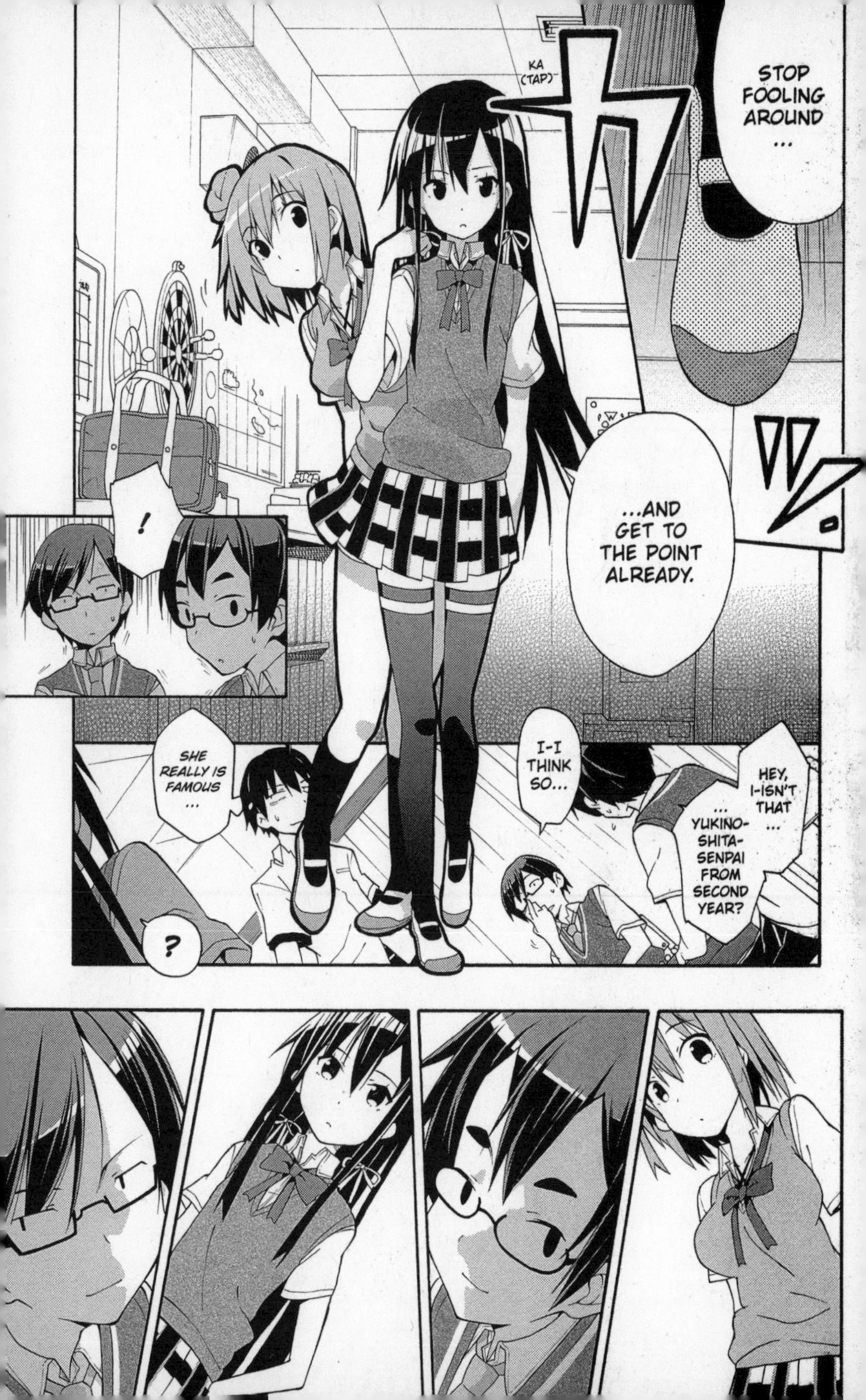

STOP FOOLING AROUND ...
KA (TAP)
...AND GET TO THE POINT ALREADY.
!
HEY, I-ISN'T THAT ...
... YUKINO-SHITA-SENPAI FROM SECOND YEAR?
I-I THINK SO...
SHE REALLY IS FAMOUS ...
?

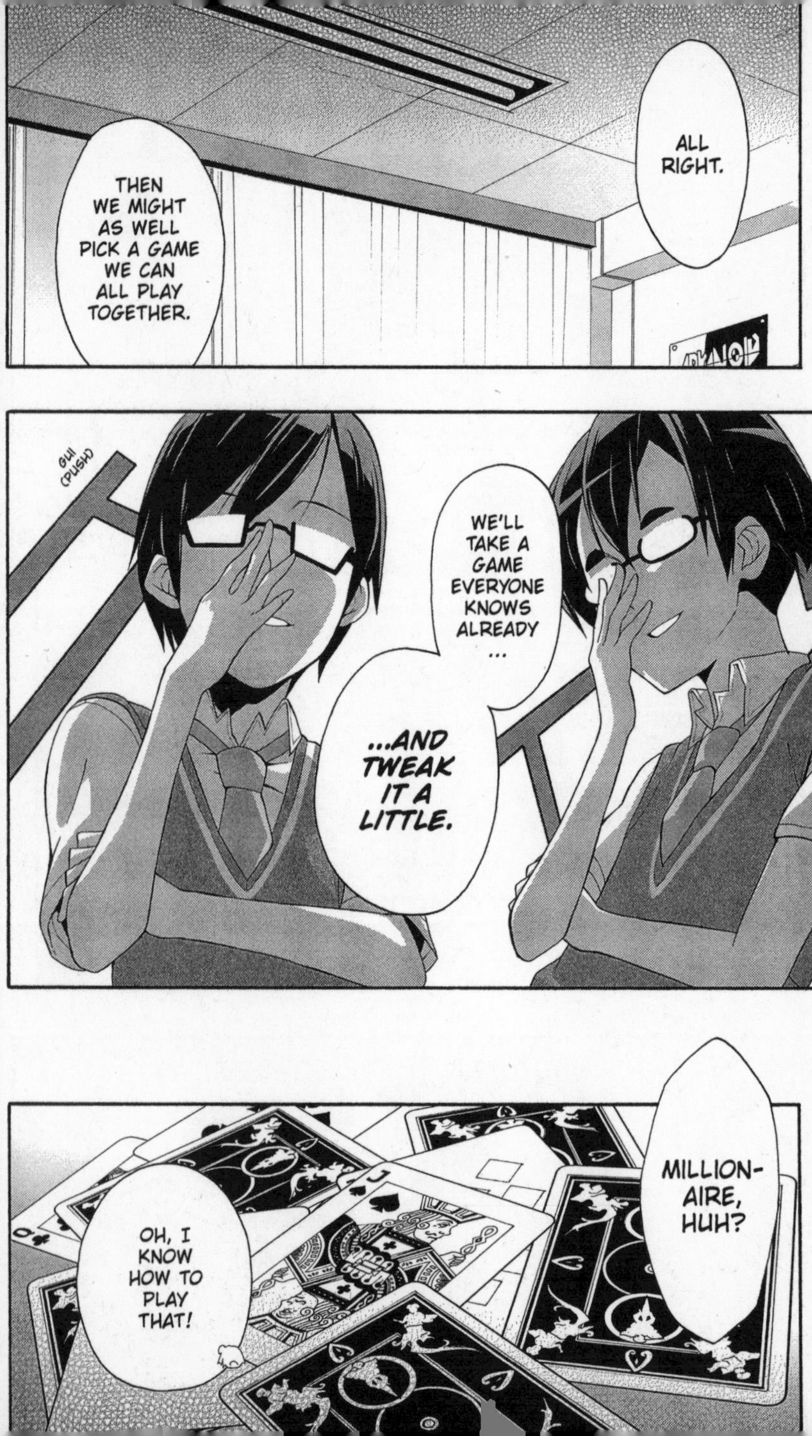
ALL RIGHT.
THEN WE MIGHT AS WELL PICK A GAME WE CAN ALL PLAY TOGETHER.
WE'LL TAKE A GAME EVERYONE KNOWS ALREADY ...
...AND TWEAK IT A LITTLE.
GUI (PUSH)
MILLION-AIRE, HUH?
OH, I KNOW HOW TO PLAY THAT!

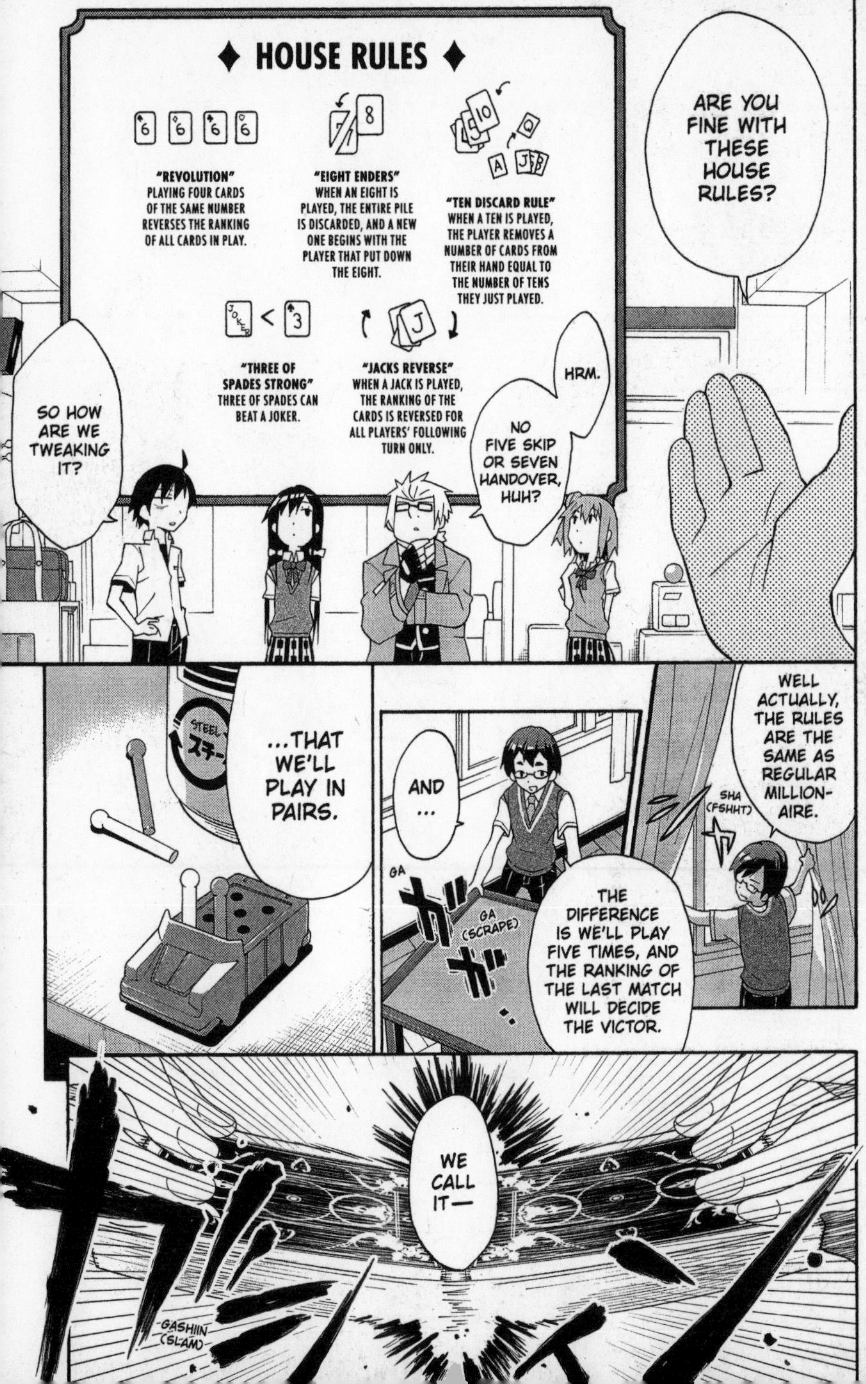
ARE YOU FINE WITH THESE HOUSE RULES?
HOUSE RULES
"REVOLUTION" PLAYING FOUR CARDS OF THE SAME NUMBER REVERSES THE RANKING OF ALL CARDS IN PLAY.
"EIGHT ENDERS" WHEN AN EIGHT IS PLAYED, THE ENTIRE PILE IS DISCARDED, AND A NEW ONE BEGINS WITH THE PLAYER THAT PUT DOWN THE EIGHT.
"TEN DISCARD RULE" WHEN A TEN IS PLAYED, THE PLAYER REMOVES A NUMBER OF CARDS FROM THEIR HAND EQUAL TO THE NUMBER OF TENS THEY JUST PLAYED.
"THREE OF SPADES STRONG" THREE OF SPADES CAN BEAT A JOKER.
"JACKS REVERSE" WHEN A JACK IS PLAYED, THE RANKING OF THE CARDS IS REVERSED FOR ALL PLAYERS' FOLLOWING TURN ONLY.
HRM.
NO FIVE SKIP OR SEVEN HANDOVER, HUH?
SO HOW ARE WE TWEAKING IT?
WELL ACTUALLY, THE RULES ARE THE SAME AS REGULAR MILLION-AIRE.
SHA (FSHHT)
THE DIFFERENCE IS WE'LL PLAY FIVE TIMES, AND THE RANKING OF THE LAST MATCH WILL DECIDE THE VICTOR.
GA
GA (SCRAPE)
AND ...
...THAT WE'LL PLAY IN PAIRS.
STEEL
WE CALL IT—
GASHIIN (SLAM)

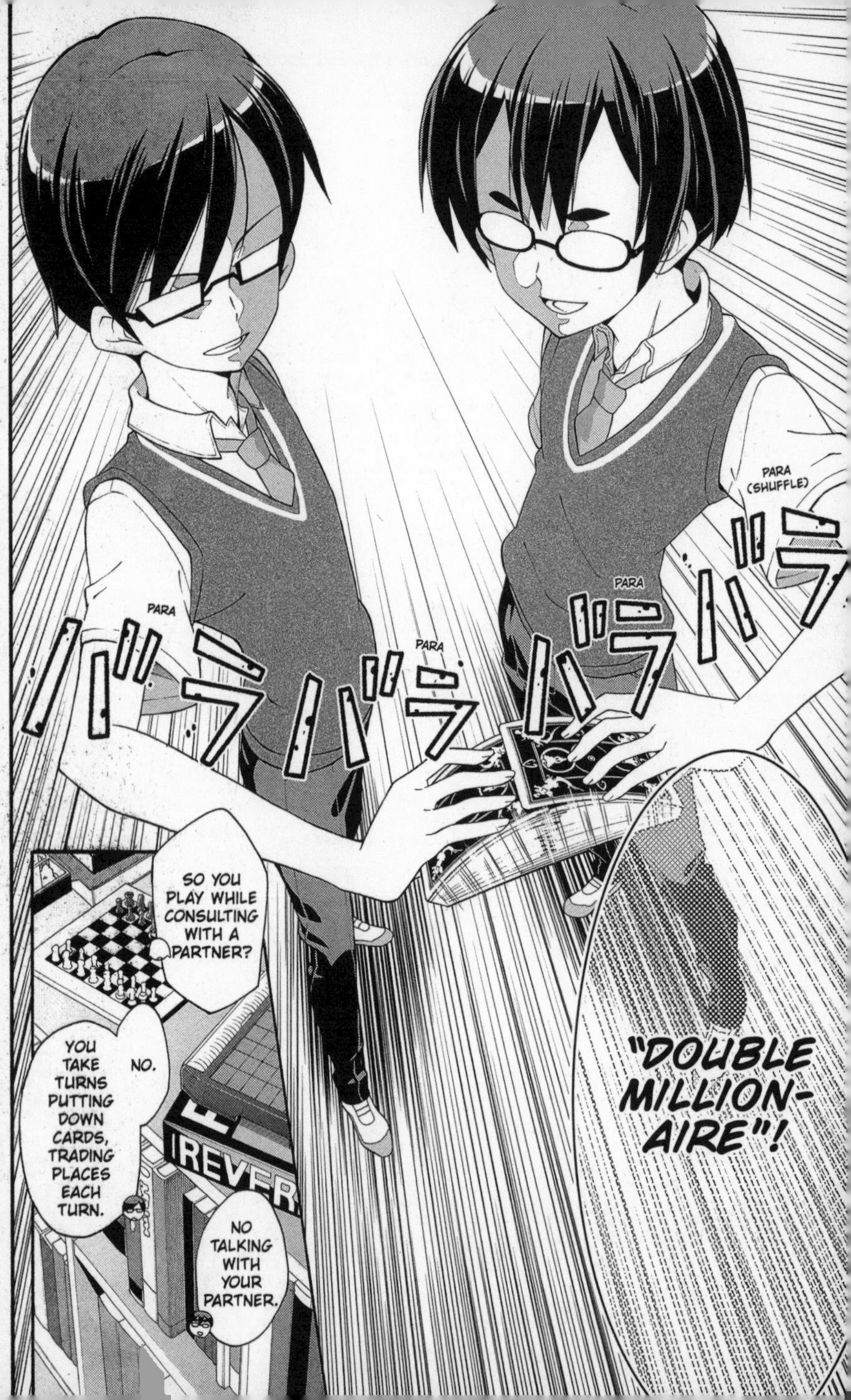
PARA (SHUFFLE)
バラバラ
PARA
PARA
PARA
バラバラ
"DOUBLE MILLION-AIRE"!
SO YOU PLAY WHILE CONSULTING WITH A PARTNER?
NO.
YOU TAKE TURNS PUTTING DOWN CARDS, TRADING PLACES EACH TURN.
NO TALKING WITH YOUR PARTNER.
IREVER

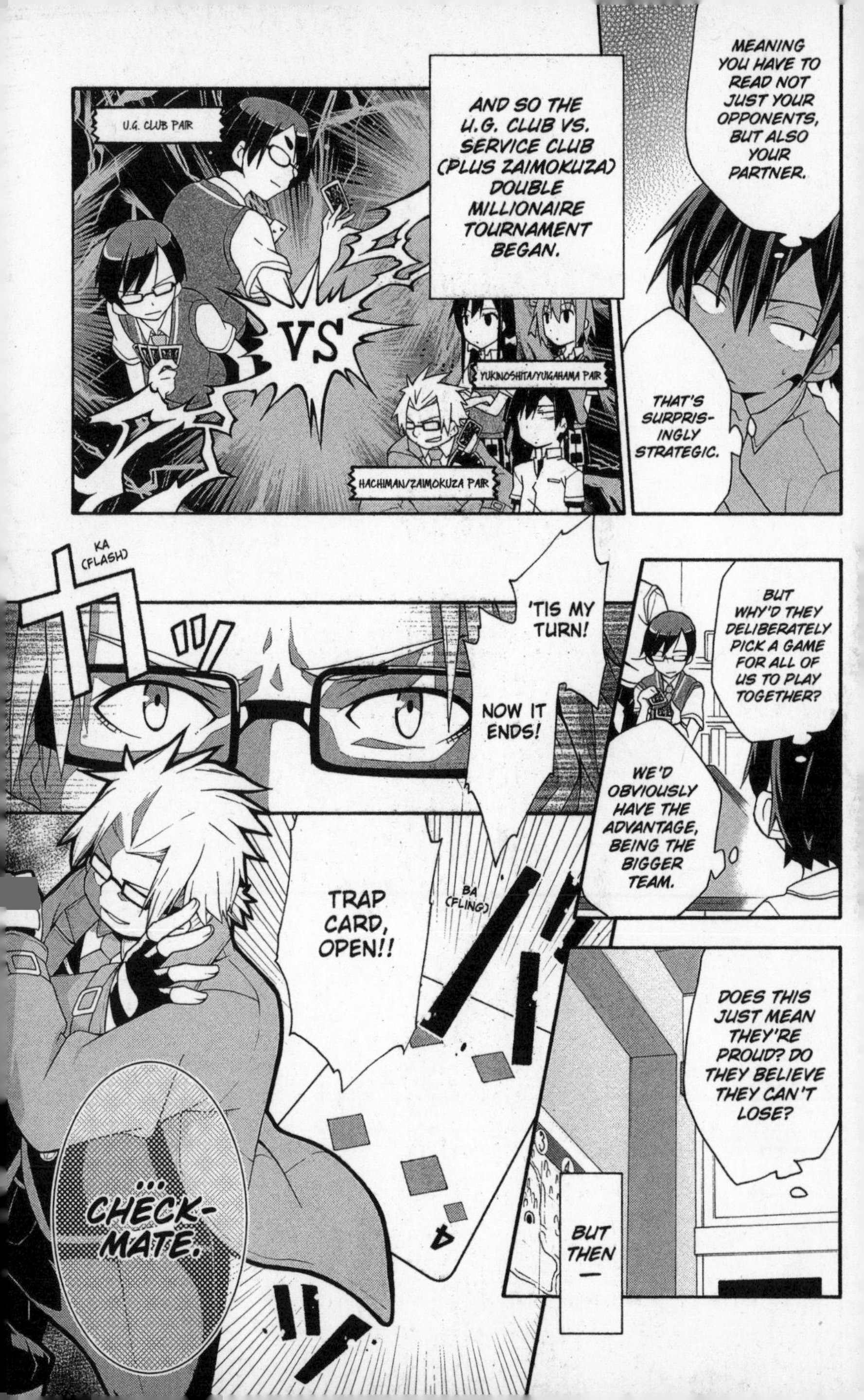
MEANING YOU HAVE TO READ NOT JUST YOUR OPPONENTS, BUT ALSO YOUR PARTNER.
THAT'S SURPRISINGLY STRATEGIC.
AND SO THE U.G. CLUB VS. SERVICE CLUB (PLUS ZAIMOKUZA) DOUBLE MILLIONAIRE TOURNAMENT BEGAN.
U.G. CLUB PAIR
VS
YUKINOSHITA/YUIGAHAMA PAIR
HACHIMAN/ZAIMOKUZA PAIR
BUT WHY'D THEY DELIBERATELY PICK A GAME FOR ALL OF US TO PLAY TOGETHER?
WE'D OBVIOUSLY HAVE THE ADVANTAGE, BEING THE BIGGER TEAM.
KA (FLASH)
'TIS MY TURN!
NOW IT ENDS!
DOES THIS JUST MEAN THEY'RE PROUD? DO THEY BELIEVE THEY CAN'T LOSE?
BUT THEN—
TRAP CARD, OPEN!!
BA (FLING)
...CHECKMATE.

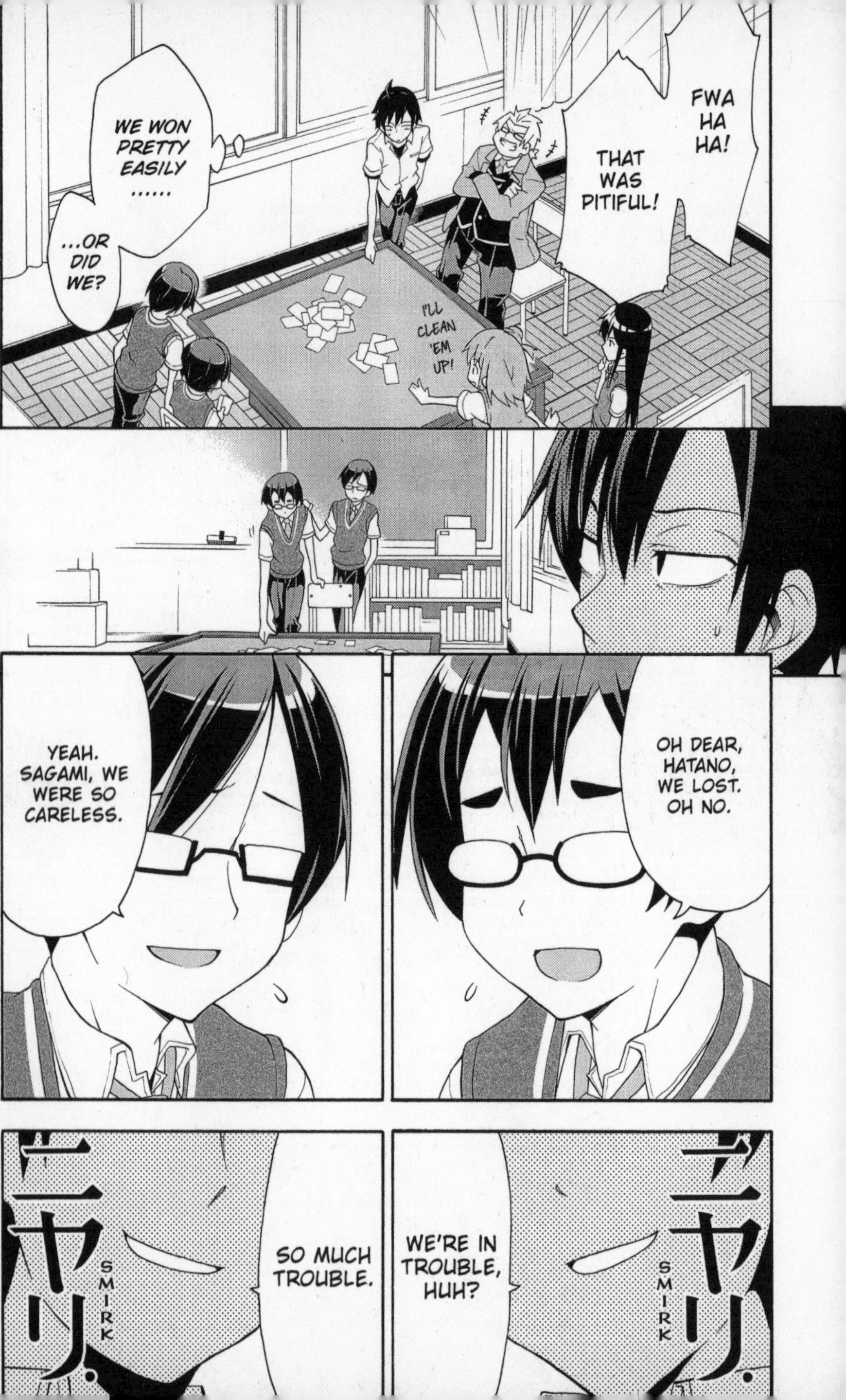
FWA HA HA!
THAT WAS PITIFUL!
WE WON PRETTY EASILY ......
...OR DID WE?
I'LL CLEAN 'EM UP!
OH DEAR, HATANO, WE LOST. OH NO.
YEAH. SAGAMI, WE WERE SO CARELESS.
ニヤリ.
SMIRK
WE'RE IN TROUBLE, HUH?
SO MUCH TROUBLE.
SMIRK
ニヤリ.

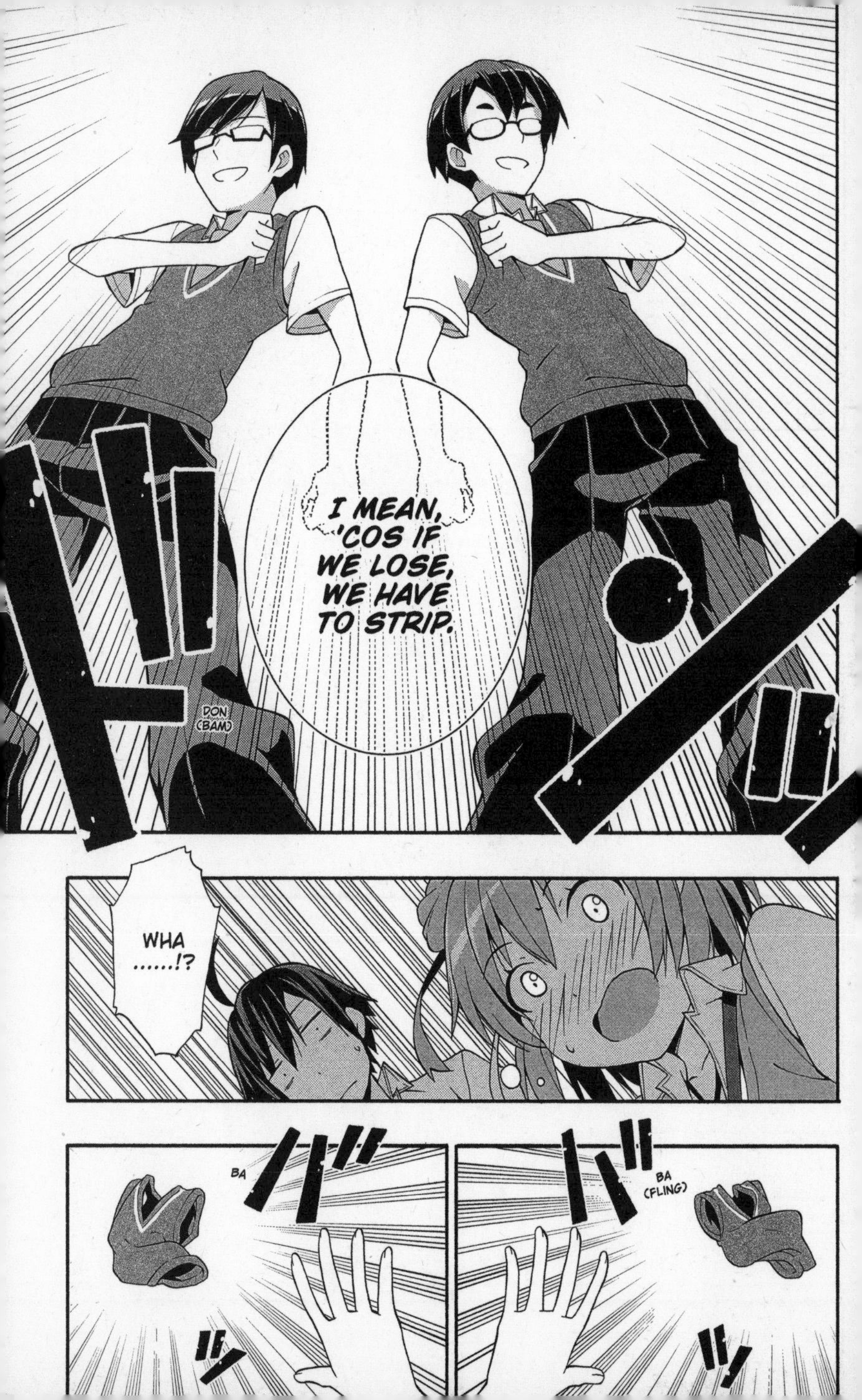
I MEAN, 'COS IF WE LOSE, WE HAVE TO STRIP.
DON (BAM)
WHA ......!?
BA (FLING)
BA

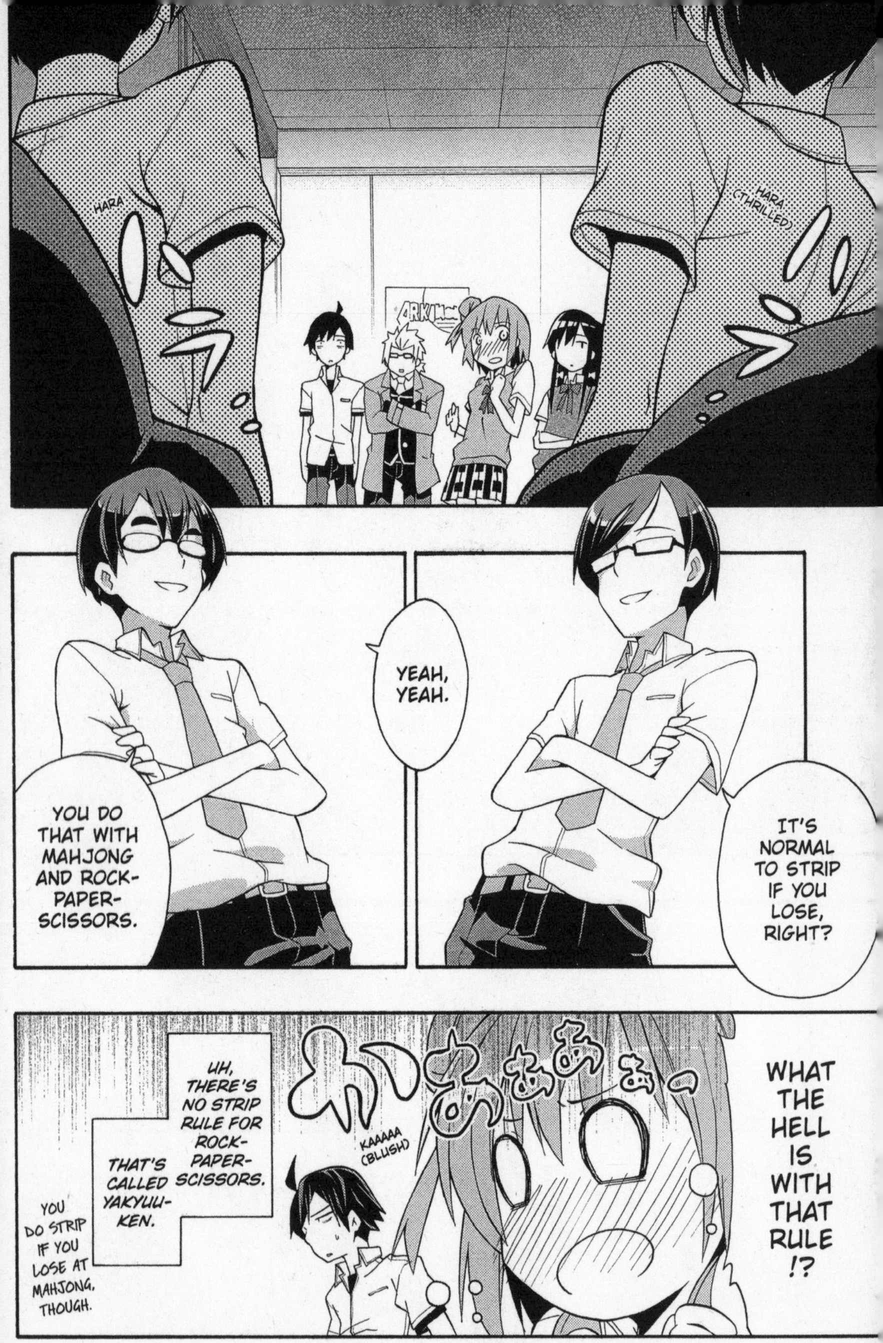
HARA (THRILLED)
HARA
IT'S NORMAL TO STRIP IF YOU LOSE, RIGHT?
YEAH, YEAH.
YOU DO THAT WITH MAHJONG AND ROCK-PAPER-SCISSORS.
WHAT THE HELL IS WITH THAT RULE!?
KAAAAA (BLUSH)
UH, THERE'S NO STRIP RULE FOR ROCK-PAPER-SCISSORS.
THAT'S CALLED YAKYUUKEN.
YOU DO STRIP IF YOU LOSE AT MAHJONG, THOUGH.

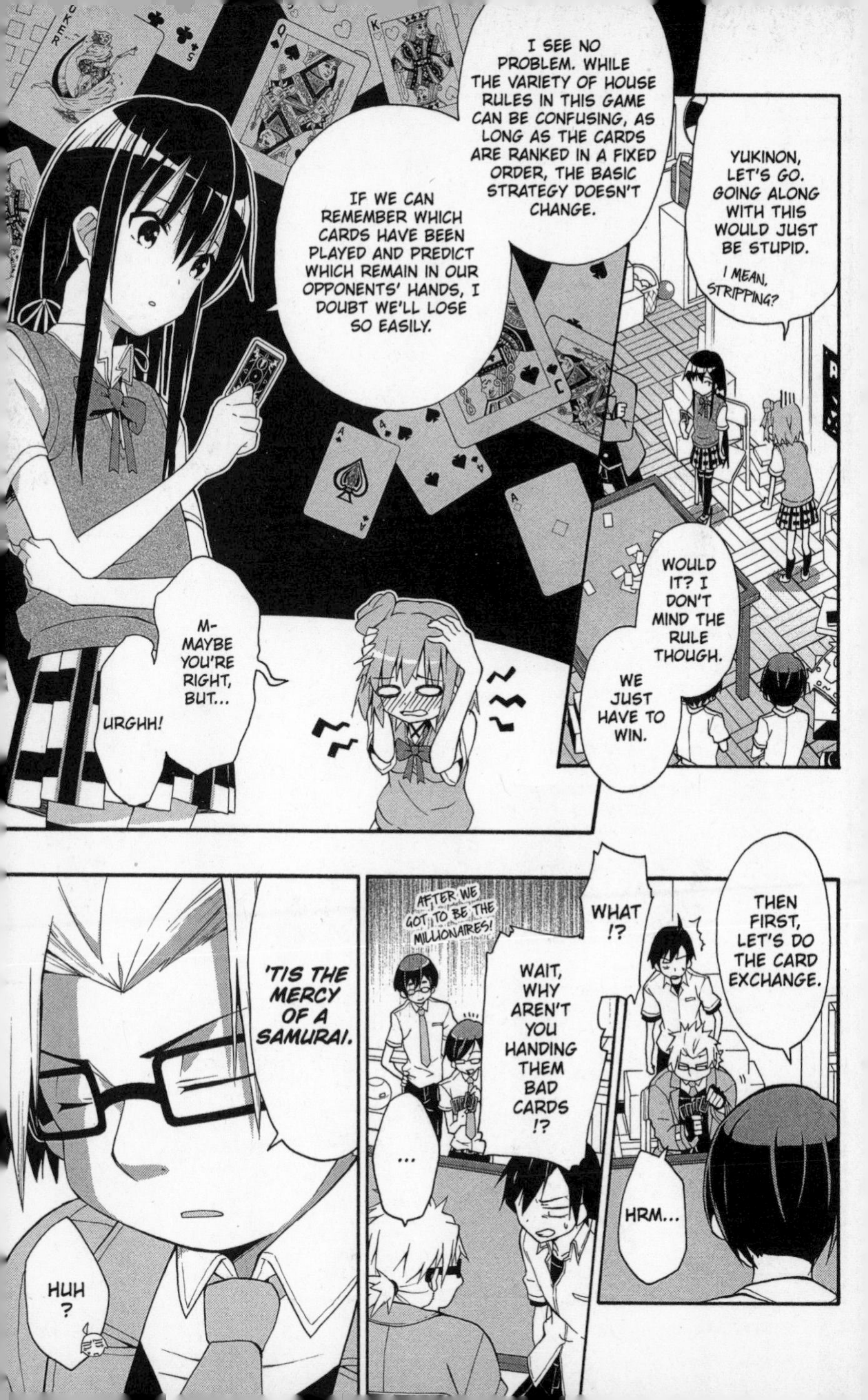
YUKINON, LET'S GO. GOING ALONG WITH THIS WOULD JUST BE STUPID.
I MEAN, STRIPPING?
WOULD IT? I DON'T MIND THE RULE THOUGH.
WE JUST HAVE TO WIN.
I SEE NO PROBLEM. WHILE THE VARIETY OF HOUSE RULES IN THIS GAME CAN BE CONFUSING, AS LONG AS THE CARDS ARE RANKED IN A FIXED ORDER, THE BASIC STRATEGY DOESN'T CHANGE.
IF WE CAN REMEMBER WHICH CARDS HAVE BEEN PLAYED AND PREDICT WHICH REMAIN IN OUR OPPONENTS' HANDS, I DOUBT WE'LL LOSE SO EASILY.
M-MAYBE YOU'RE RIGHT, BUT...
URGHH!
THEN FIRST, LET'S DO THE CARD EXCHANGE.
WHAT!?
AFTER WE GOT TO BE THE MILLIONAIRES!
WAIT, WHY AREN'T YOU HANDING THEM BAD CARDS!?
HRM...
...
'TIS THE MERCY OF A SAMURAI.
HUH?

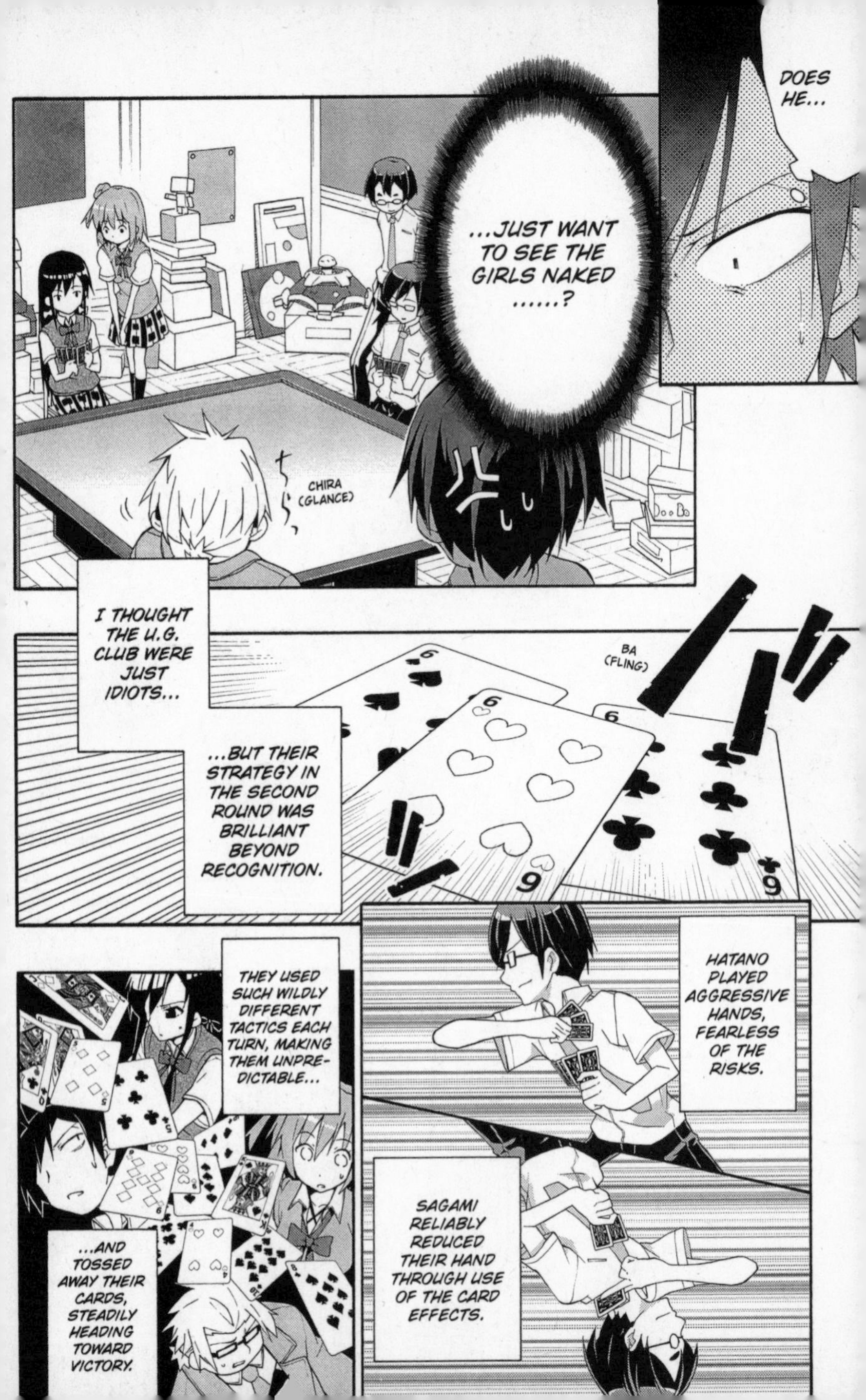
DOES HE...
...JUST WANT TO SEE THE GIRLS NAKED ......?
CHIRA (GLANCE)
I THOUGHT THE U.G. CLUB WERE JUST IDIOTS...
BA (FLING)
...BUT THEIR STRATEGY IN THE SECOND ROUND WAS BRILLIANT BEYOND RECOGNITION.
HATANO PLAYED AGGRESSIVE HANDS, FEARLESS OF THE RISKS.
SAGAMI RELIABLY REDUCED THEIR HAND THROUGH USE OF THE CARD EFFECTS.
THEY USED SUCH WILDLY DIFFERENT TACTICS EACH TURN, MAKING THEM UNPREDICTABLE...
...AND TOSSED AWAY THEIR CARDS, STEADILY HEADING TOWARD VICTORY.

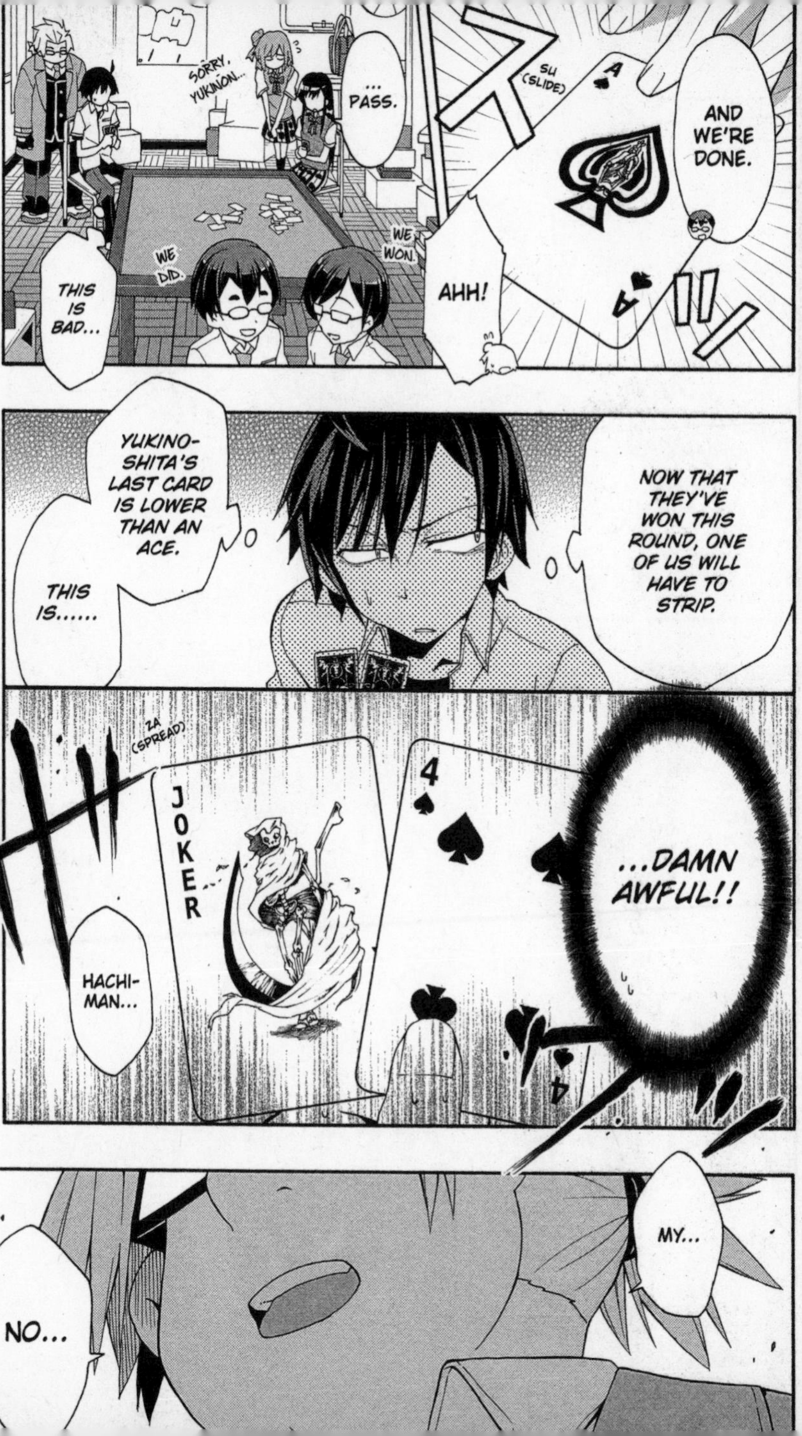
SU (SLIDE)
A
AND WE'RE DONE.
AHH!
... PASS.
SORRY, YUKINON...
WE WON.
WE DID.
THIS IS BAD...
NOW THAT THEY'VE WON THIS ROUND, ONE OF US WILL HAVE TO STRIP.
YUKINOSHITA'S LAST CARD IS LOWER THAN AN ACE.
THIS IS......
...DAMN AWFUL!!
4
JOKER
ZA (SPREAD)
HACHIMAN...
MY...
NO...

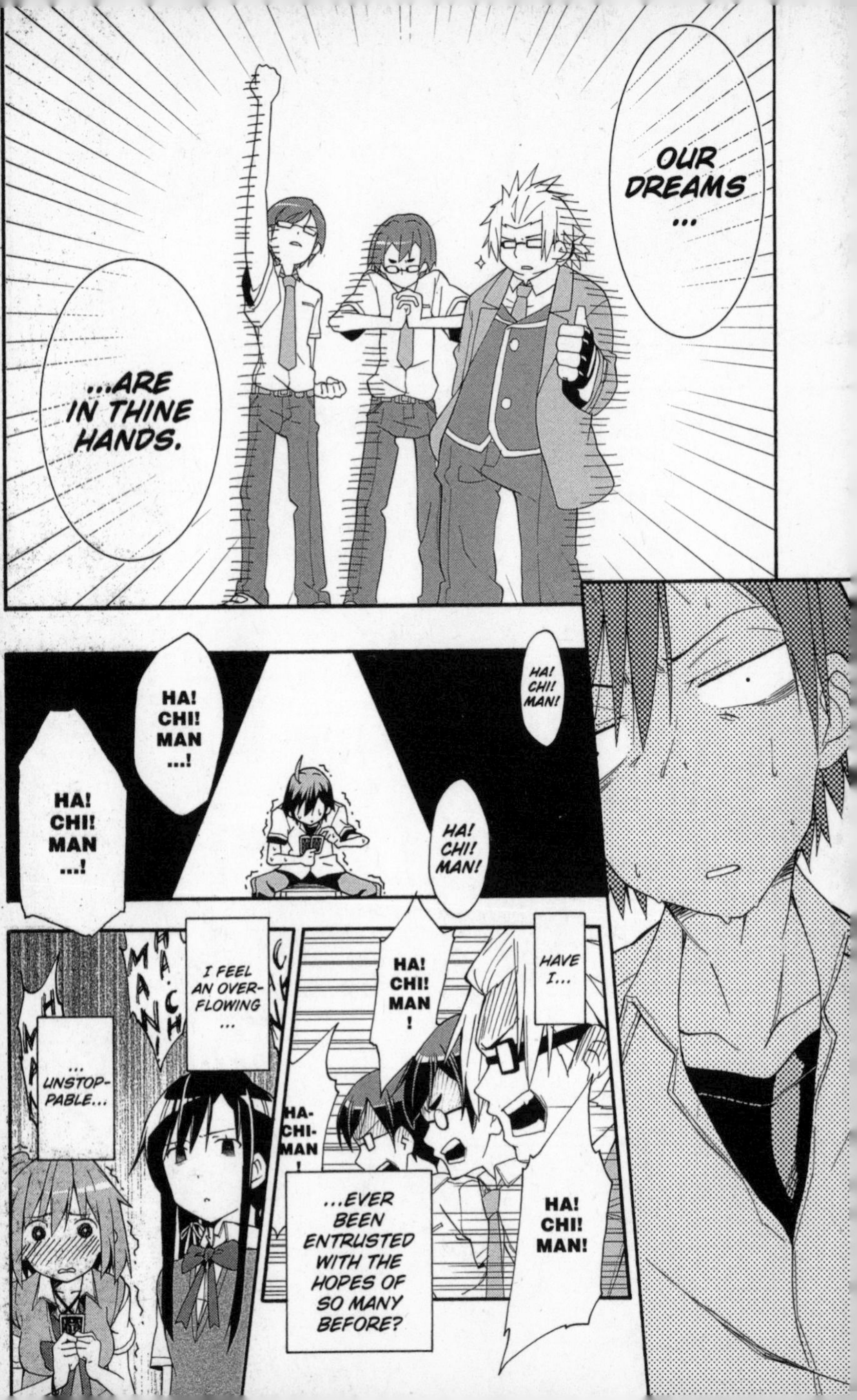
OUR DREAMS ...
...ARE IN THINE HANDS.
HA! CHI! MAN!
HA! CHI! MAN!
HA! CHI! MAN ...!
HA! CHI! MAN ...!
HAVE I...
HA! CHI! MAN!
HA! CHI! MAN !
...EVER BEEN ENTRUSTED WITH THE HOPES OF SO MANY BEFORE?
HA-CHI-MAN !
I FEEL AN OVER-FLOWING ...
... UNSTOPPABLE...
HA CHI MAN
HA CHI MAN

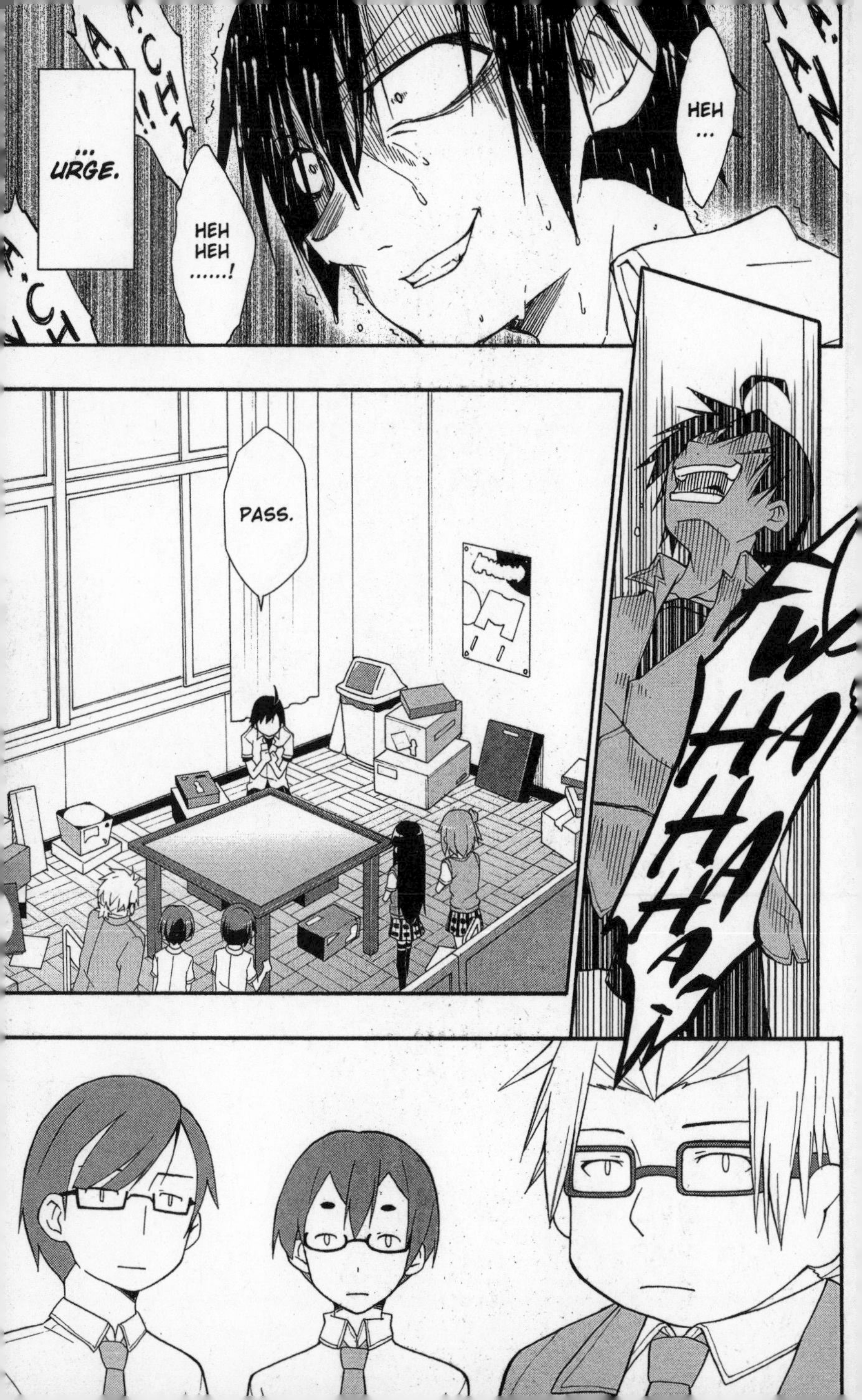
HEH ...
HEH HEH ......!
... URGE.
A.CHI!!
FWAHAHAHAHA
PASS.

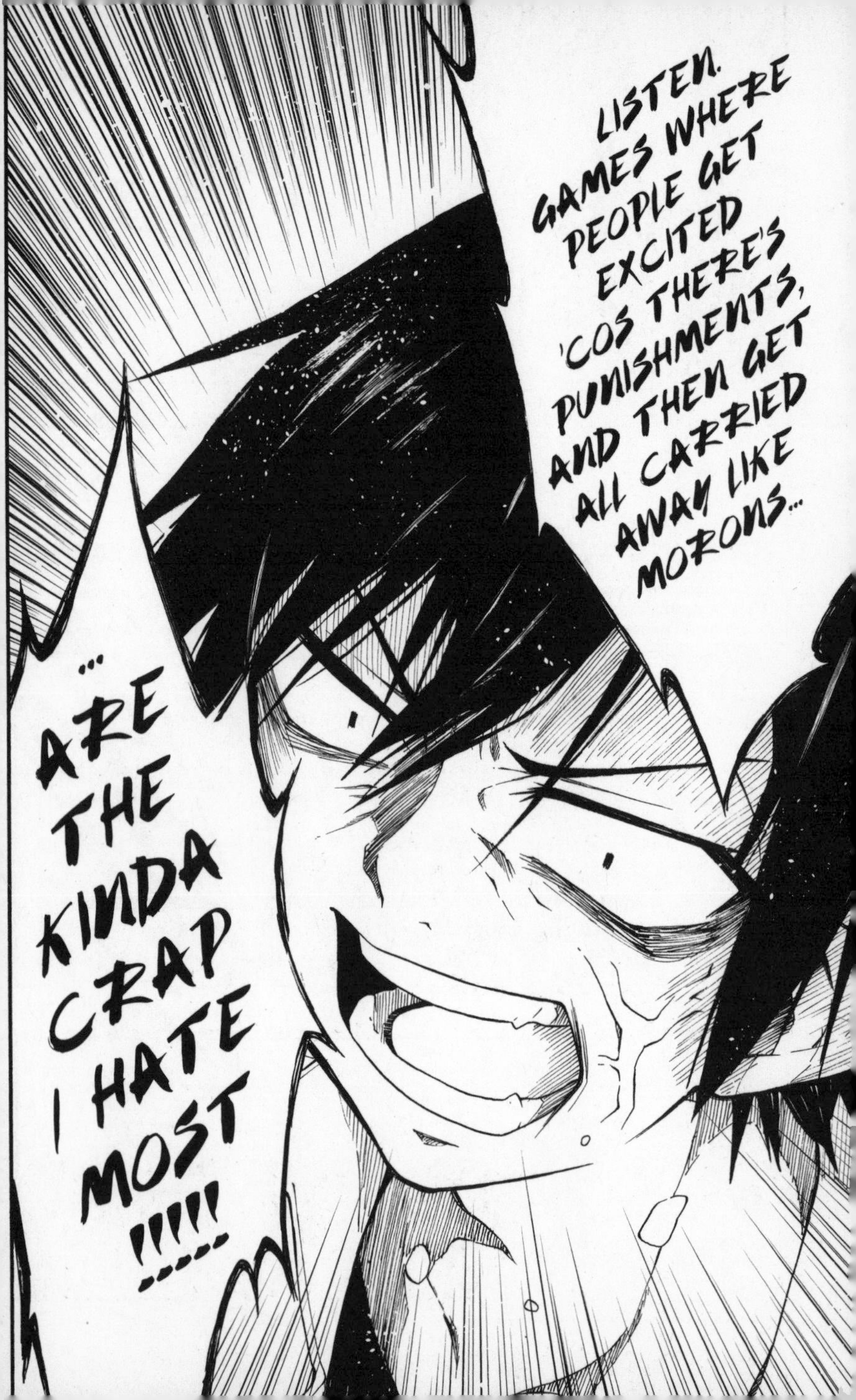
LISTEN. GAMES WHERE PEOPLE GET EXCITED 'COS THERE'S PUNISHMENTS, AND THEN GET ALL CARRIED AWAY LIKE MORONS...
...ARE THE KINDA CRAP I HATE MOST!!!!!

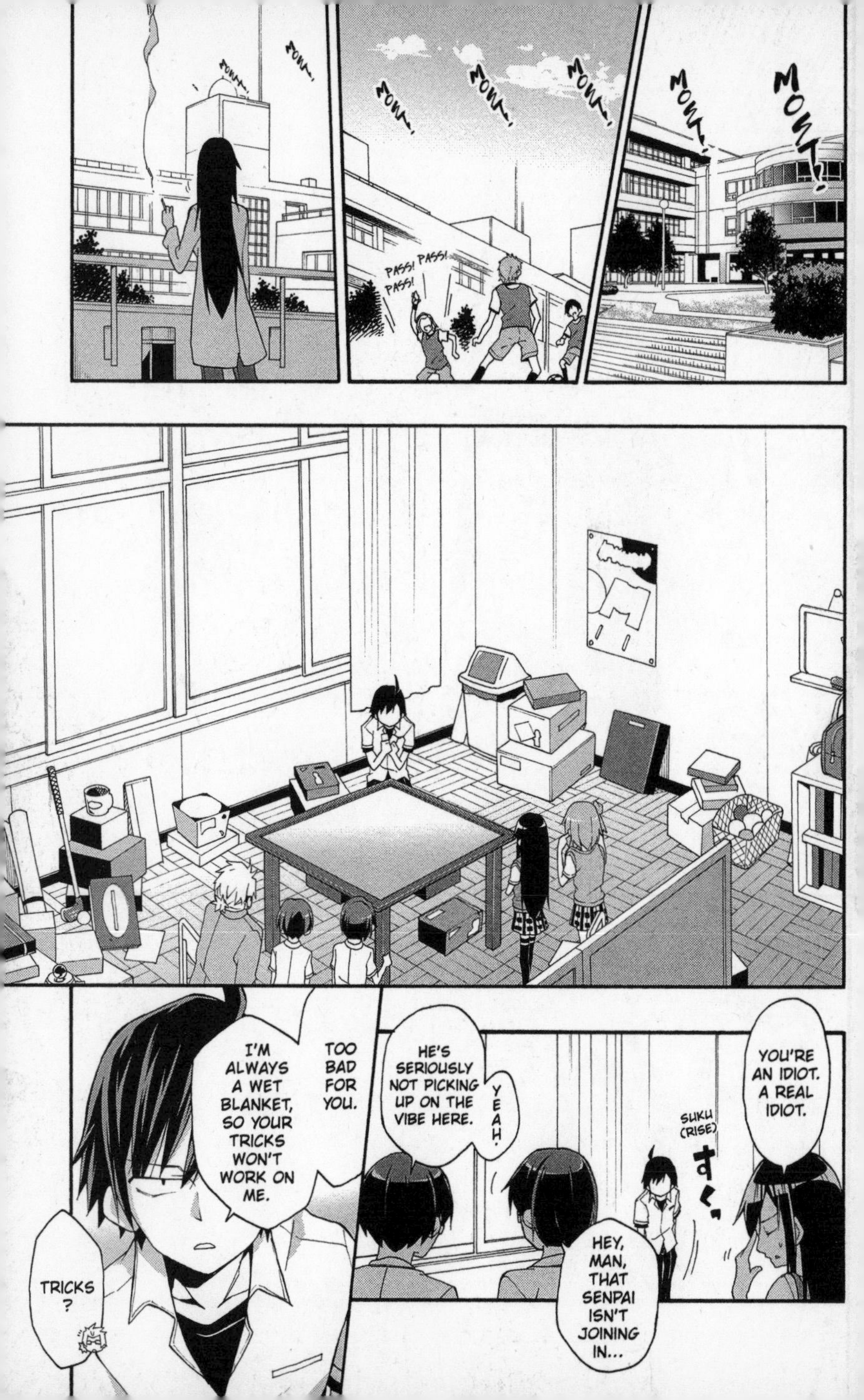
PASS! PASS! PASS!
YOU'RE AN IDIOT. A REAL IDIOT.
SUKU (RISE)
すく
HEY, MAN, THAT SENPAI ISN'T JOINING IN...
HE'S SERIOUSLY NOT PICKING UP ON THE VIBE HERE.
YEAH.
TOO BAD FOR YOU.
I'M ALWAYS A WET BLANKET, SO YOUR TRICKS WON'T WORK ON ME.
TRICKS?

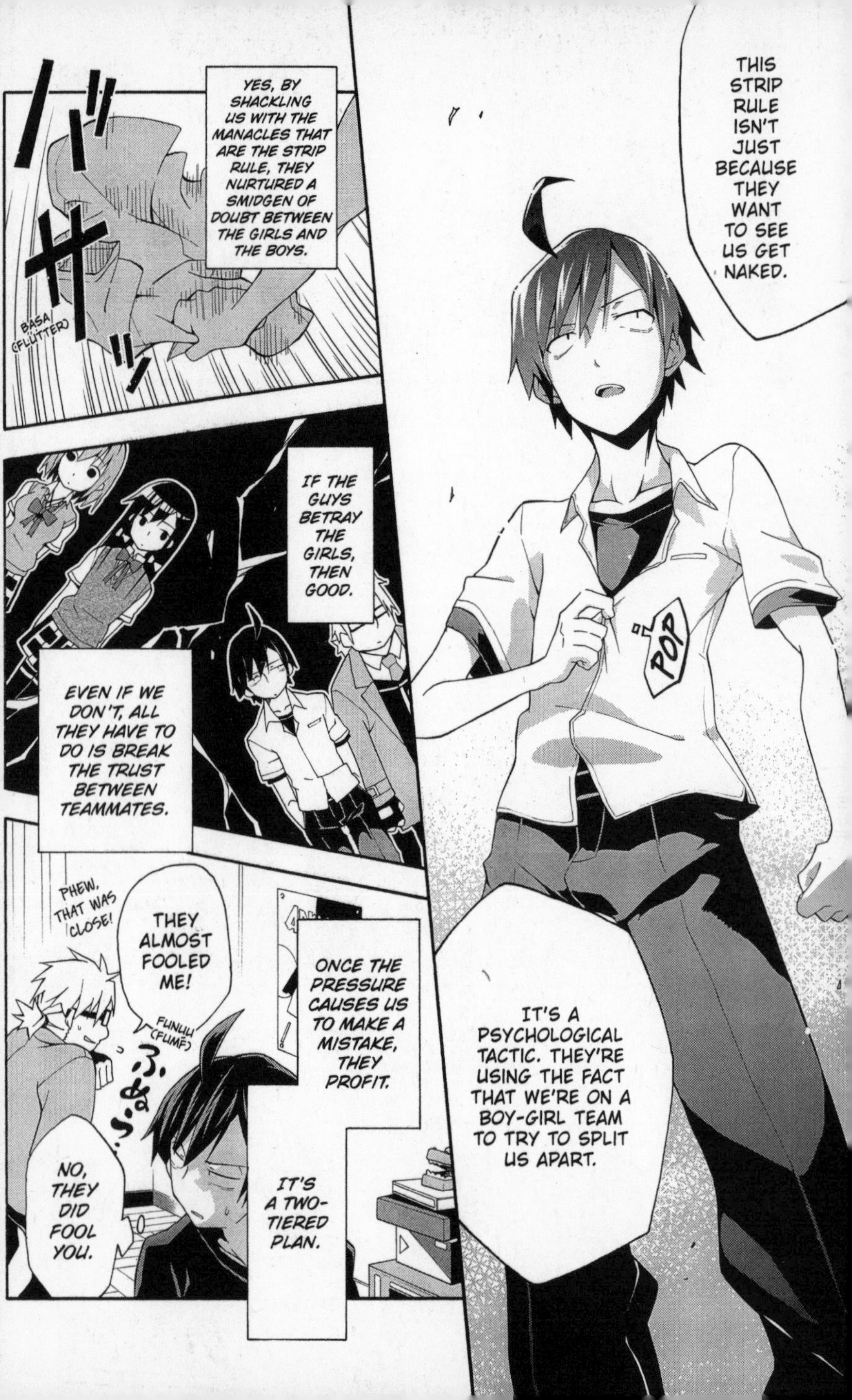
THIS STRIP RULE ISN'T JUST BECAUSE THEY WANT TO SEE US GET NAKED.
POP
IT'S A PSYCHOLOGICAL TACTIC. THEY'RE USING THE FACT THAT WE'RE ON A BOY-GIRL TEAM TO TRY TO SPLIT US APART.
YES, BY SHACKLING US WITH THE MANACLES THAT ARE THE STRIP RULE, THEY NURTURED A SMIDGEN OF DOUBT BETWEEN THE GIRLS AND THE BOYS.
BASA (FLUTTER)
IF THE GUYS BETRAY THE GIRLS, THEN GOOD.
EVEN IF WE DON'T, ALL THEY HAVE TO DO IS BREAK THE TRUST BETWEEN TEAMMATES.
ONCE THE PRESSURE CAUSES US TO MAKE A MISTAKE, THEY PROFIT.
IT'S A TWO-TIERED PLAN.
THEY ALMOST FOOLED ME!
PHEW, THAT WAS CLOSE!
FUNUU (FUME)
ふぬぅ
NO, THEY DID FOOL YOU.

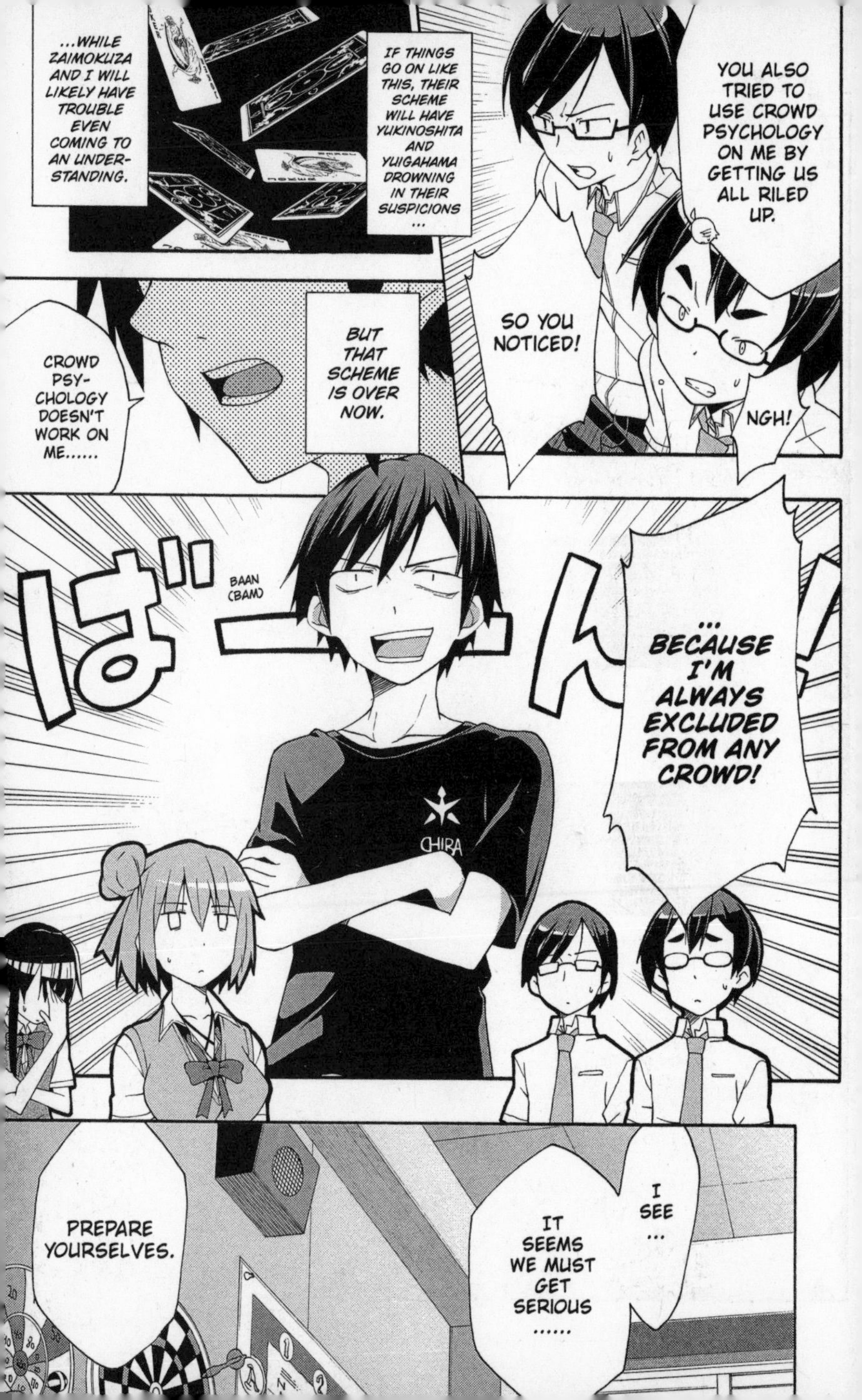

YOU ALSO TRIED TO USE CROWD PSYCHOLOGY ON ME BY GETTING US ALL RILED UP.
SO YOU NOTICED!
NGH!
IF THINGS GO ON LIKE THIS, THEIR SCHEME WILL HAVE YUKINOSHITA AND YUIGAHAMA DROWNING IN THEIR SUSPICIONS ...
...WHILE ZAIMOKUZA AND I WILL LIKELY HAVE TROUBLE EVEN COMING TO AN UNDER-STANDING.
BUT THAT SCHEME IS OVER NOW.
CROWD PSY-CHOLOGY DOESN'T WORK ON ME......
... BECAUSE I'M ALWAYS EXCLUDED FROM ANY CROWD!
ばーん!
BAAN (BAM)
CHIBA
I SEE ...
IT SEEMS WE MUST GET SERIOUS ......
PREPARE YOURSELVES.

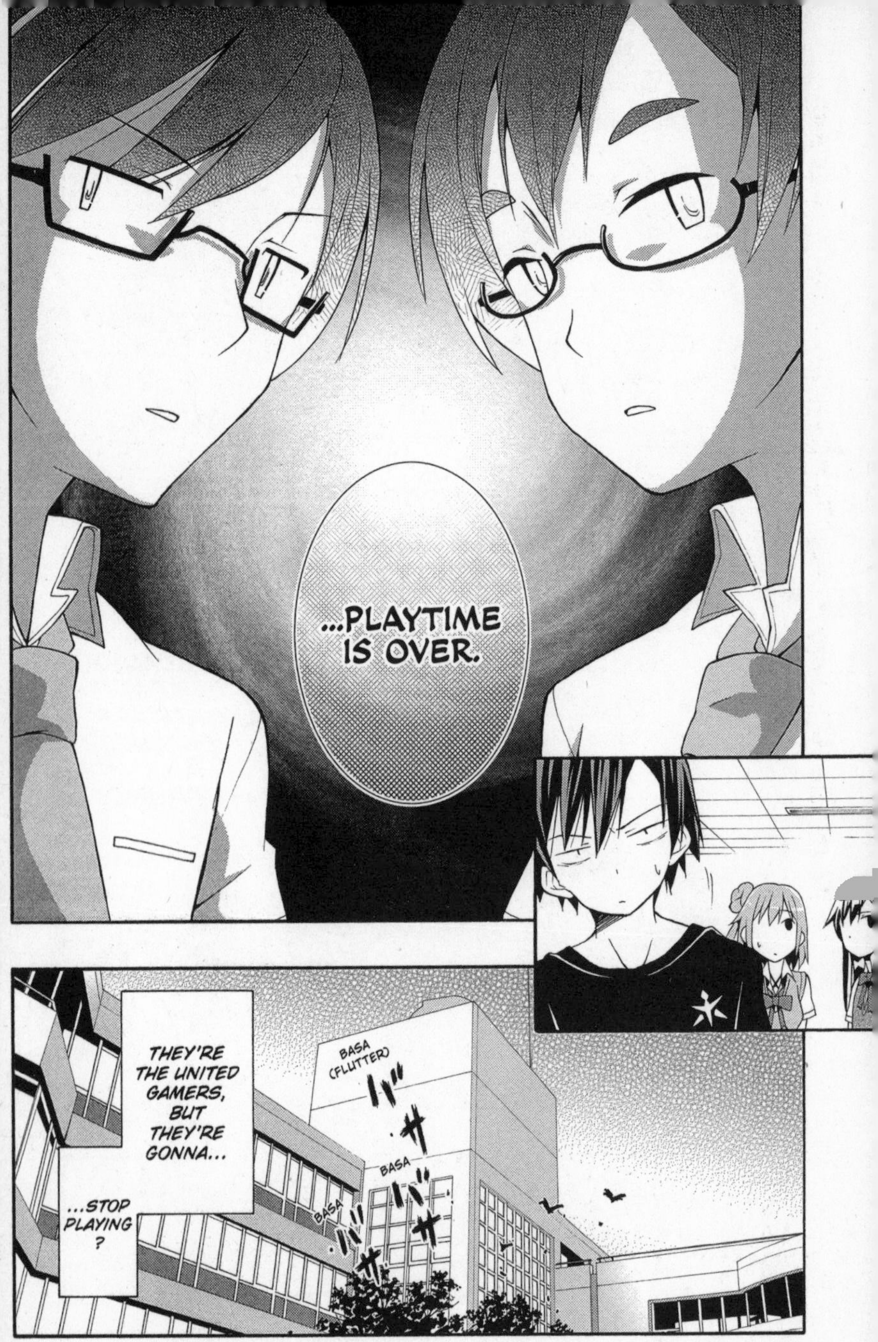

...PLAYTIME IS OVER.
BASA (FLUTTER)
THEY'RE THE UNITED GAMERS, BUT THEY'RE GONNA...
BASA
BASA
...STOP PLAYING?

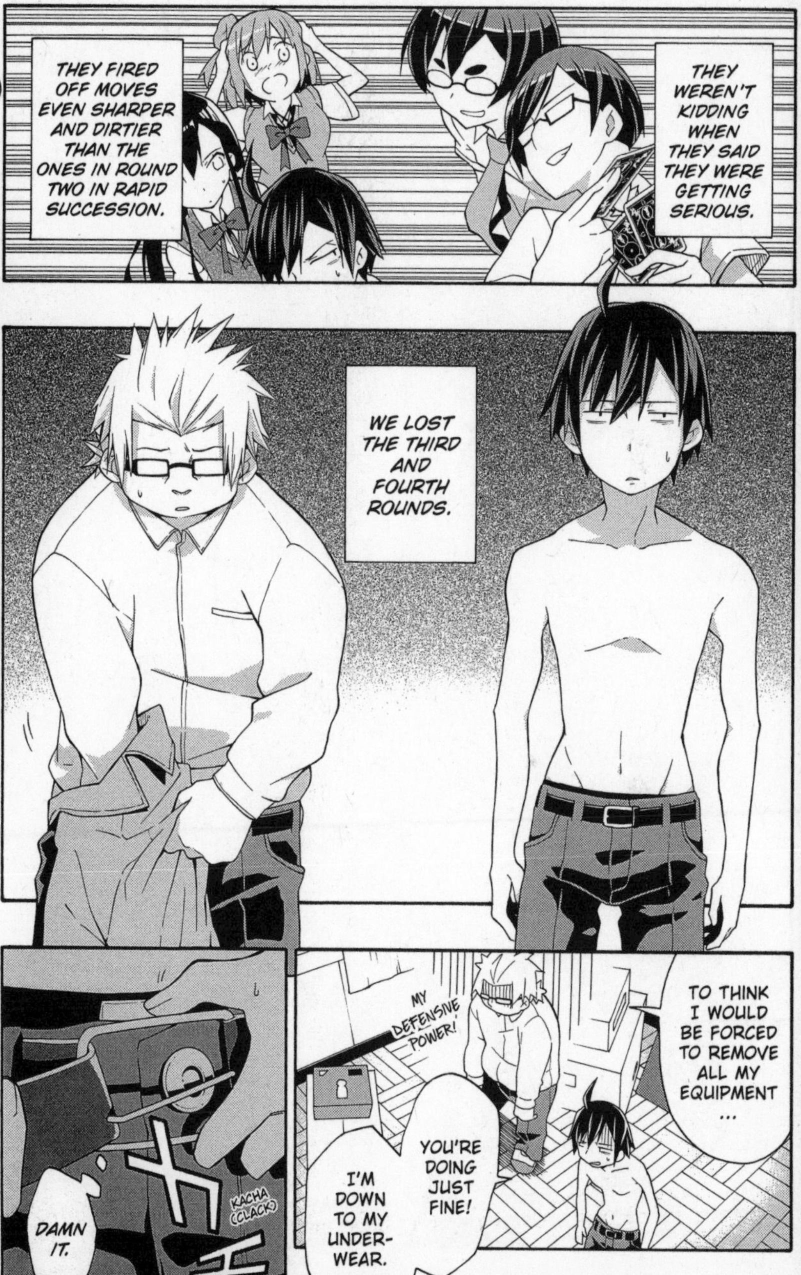
THEY WEREN'T KIDDING WHEN THEY SAID THEY WERE GETTING SERIOUS.
THEY FIRED OFF MOVES EVEN SHARPER AND DIRTIER THAN THE ONES IN ROUND TWO IN RAPID SUCCESSION.
WE LOST THE THIRD AND FOURTH ROUNDS.
TO THINK I WOULD BE FORCED TO REMOVE ALL MY EQUIPMENT ...
MY DEFENSIVE POWER!
YOU'RE DOING JUST FINE!
I'M DOWN TO MY UNDER-WEAR.
KACHA (CLACK)
DAMN IT.

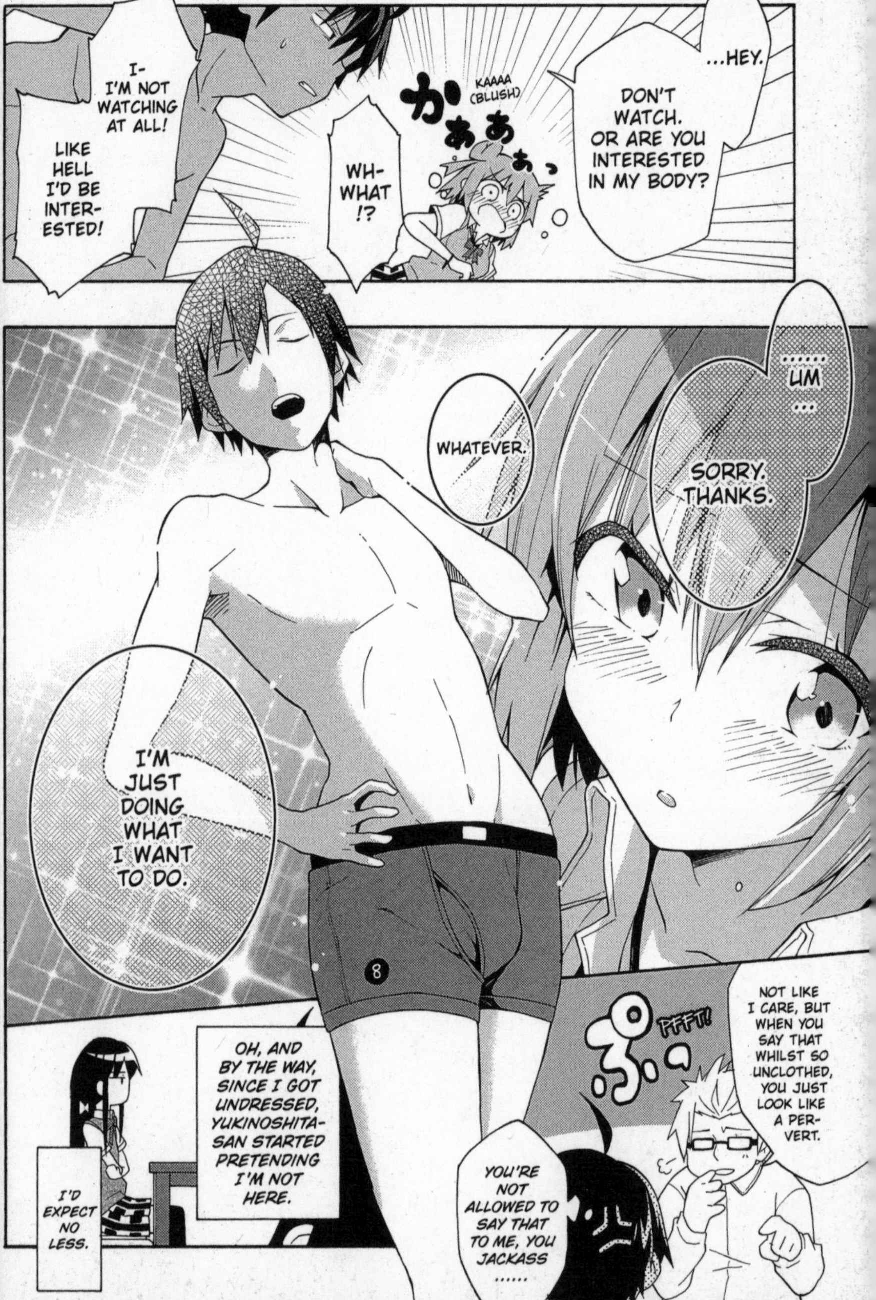
...HEY.
DON'T WATCH. OR ARE YOU INTERESTED IN MY BODY?
かあああ
KAAAA (BLUSH)
WH- WHAT !?
I- I'M NOT WATCHING AT ALL!
LIKE HELL I'D BE INTERESTED!
......UM ...
SORRY. THANKS.
WHATEVER.
I'M JUST DOING WHAT I WANT TO DO.
NOT LIKE I CARE, BUT WHEN YOU SAY THAT WHILST SO UNCLOTHED, YOU JUST LOOK LIKE A PERVERT.
ぷっ
PFFT!
YOU'RE NOT ALLOWED TO SAY THAT TO ME, YOU JACKASS ......
OH, AND BY THE WAY, SINCE I GOT UNDRESSED, YUKINOSHITA-SAN STARTED PRETENDING I'M NOT HERE.
I'D EXPECT NO LESS.

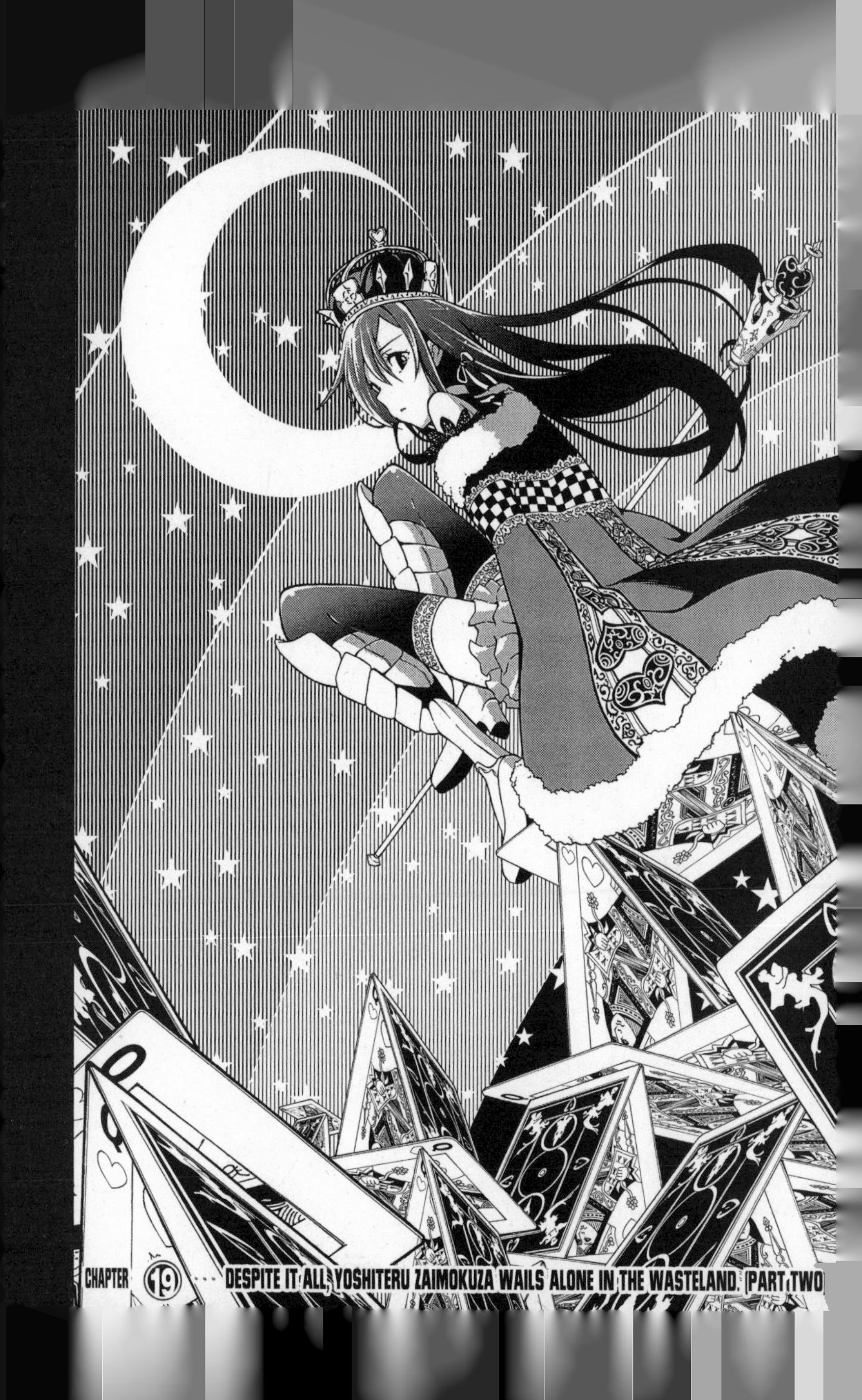

CHAPTER 19 … DESPITE IT ALL, YOSHITERU ZAIMOKUZA WAILS ALONE IN THE WASTELAND. (PART TWO)

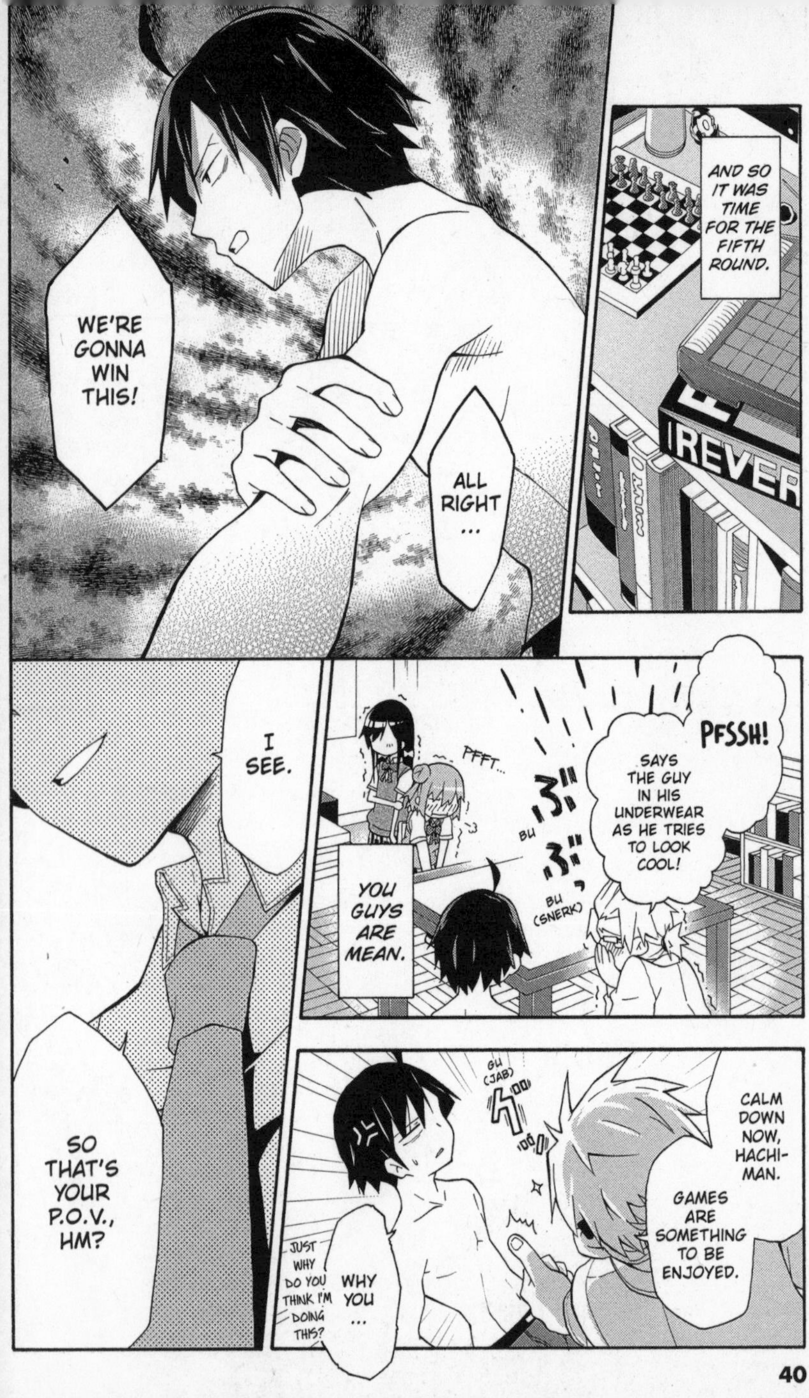
AND SO IT WAS TIME FOR THE FIFTH ROUND.
REVER
ALL RIGHT ...
WE'RE GONNA WIN THIS!
PFSSH!
SAYS THE GUY IN HIS UNDERWEAR AS HE TRIES TO LOOK COOL!
BU
BU (SNERK)
PFFT...
YOU GUYS ARE MEAN.
CALM DOWN NOW, HACHI-MAN.
GAMES ARE SOMETHING TO BE ENJOYED.
GU (JAB)
WHY YOU ...
JUST WHY DO YOU THINK I'M DOING THIS?
I SEE.
SO THAT'S YOUR P.O.V., HM?

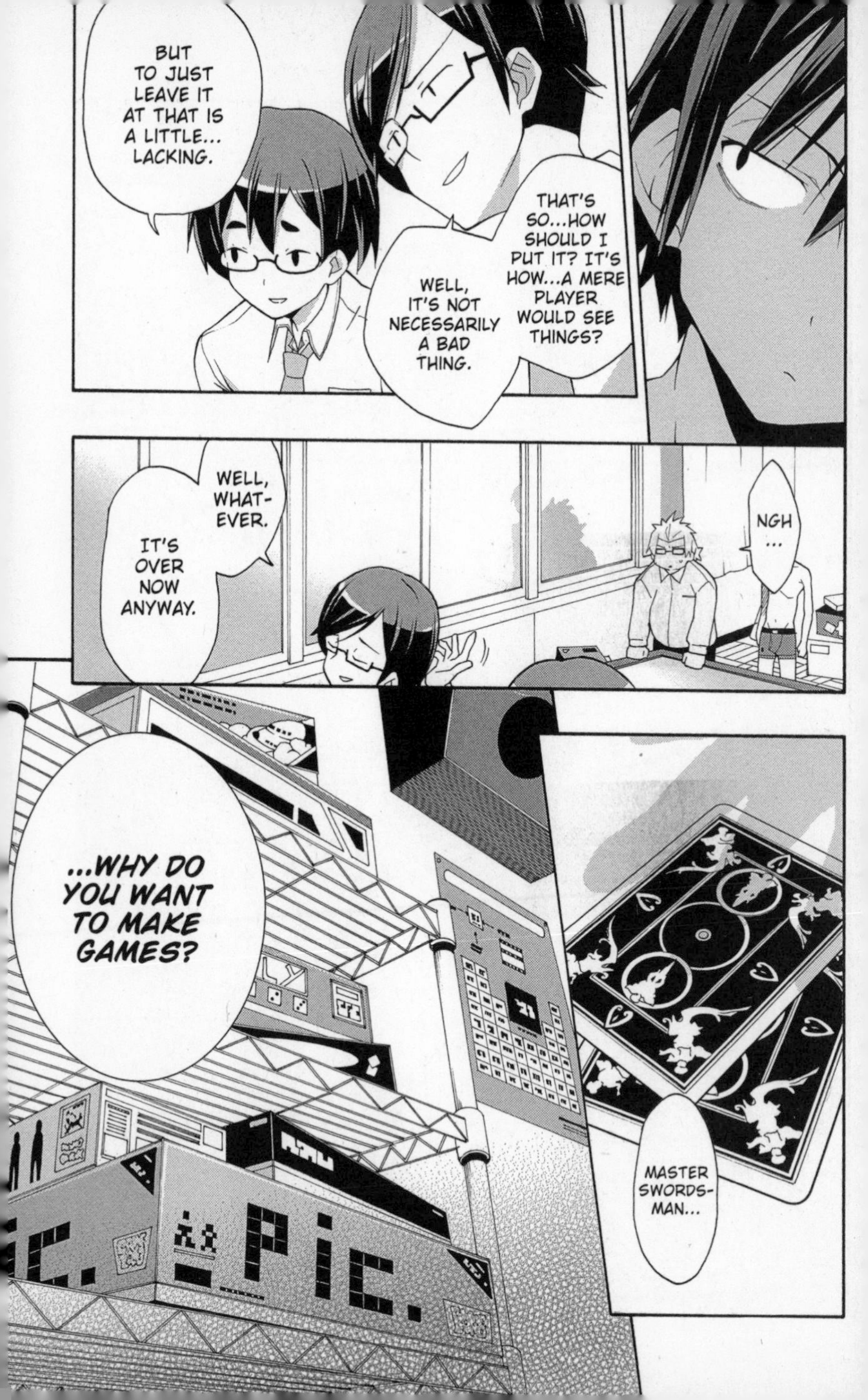
THAT'S SO...HOW SHOULD I PUT IT? IT'S HOW...A MERE PLAYER WOULD SEE THINGS?
WELL, IT'S NOT NECESSARILY A BAD THING.
BUT TO JUST LEAVE IT AT THAT IS A LITTLE... LACKING.
NGH...
WELL, WHAT-EVER.
IT'S OVER NOW ANYWAY.
MASTER SWORDS-MAN...
...WHY DO YOU WANT TO MAKE GAMES?

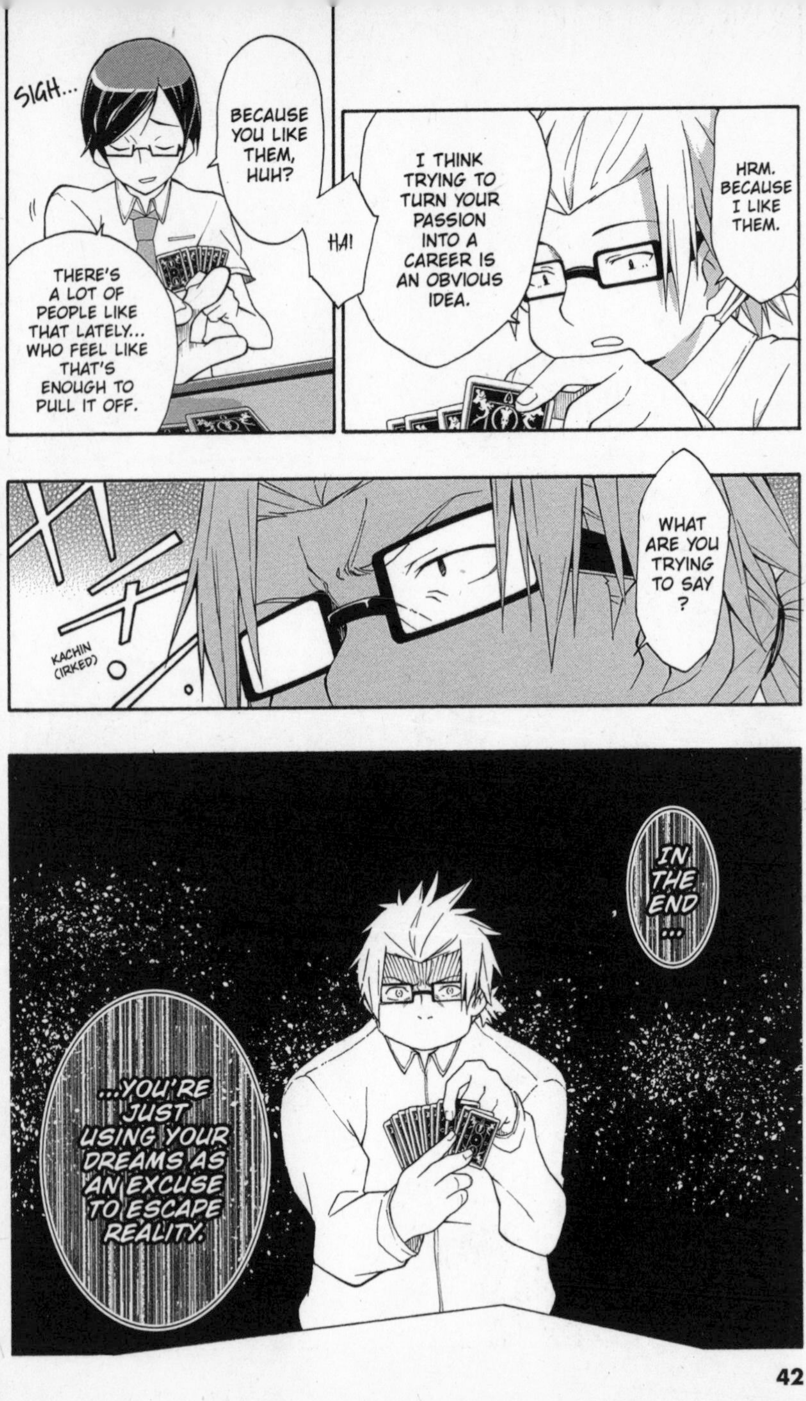
HRM. BECAUSE I LIKE THEM.
I THINK TRYING TO TURN YOUR PASSION INTO A CAREER IS AN OBVIOUS IDEA.
SIGH...
BECAUSE YOU LIKE THEM, HUH?
THERE'S A LOT OF PEOPLE LIKE THAT LATELY... WHO FEEL LIKE THAT'S ENOUGH TO PULL IT OFF.
HA!
WHAT ARE YOU TRYING TO SAY?
KACHIN (IRKED)
IN THE END...
...YOU'RE JUST USING YOUR DREAMS AS AN EXCUSE TO ESCAPE REALITY.

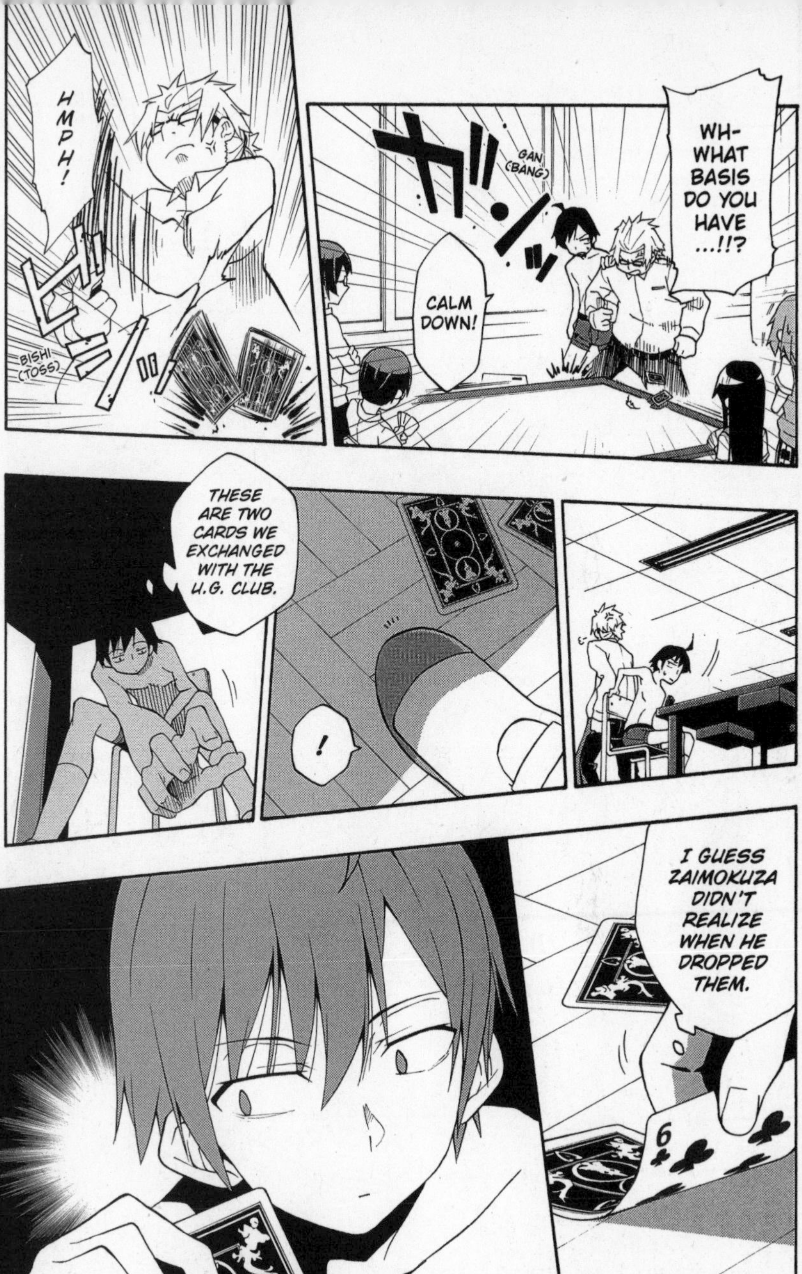
WH-WHAT BASIS DO YOU HAVE ...!!?
GAN (BANG)
CALM DOWN!
HMPH!
BISHI (TOSS)
THESE ARE TWO CARDS WE EXCHANGED WITH THE U.G. CLUB.
!
I GUESS ZAIMOKUZA DIDN'T REALIZE WHEN HE DROPPED THEM.

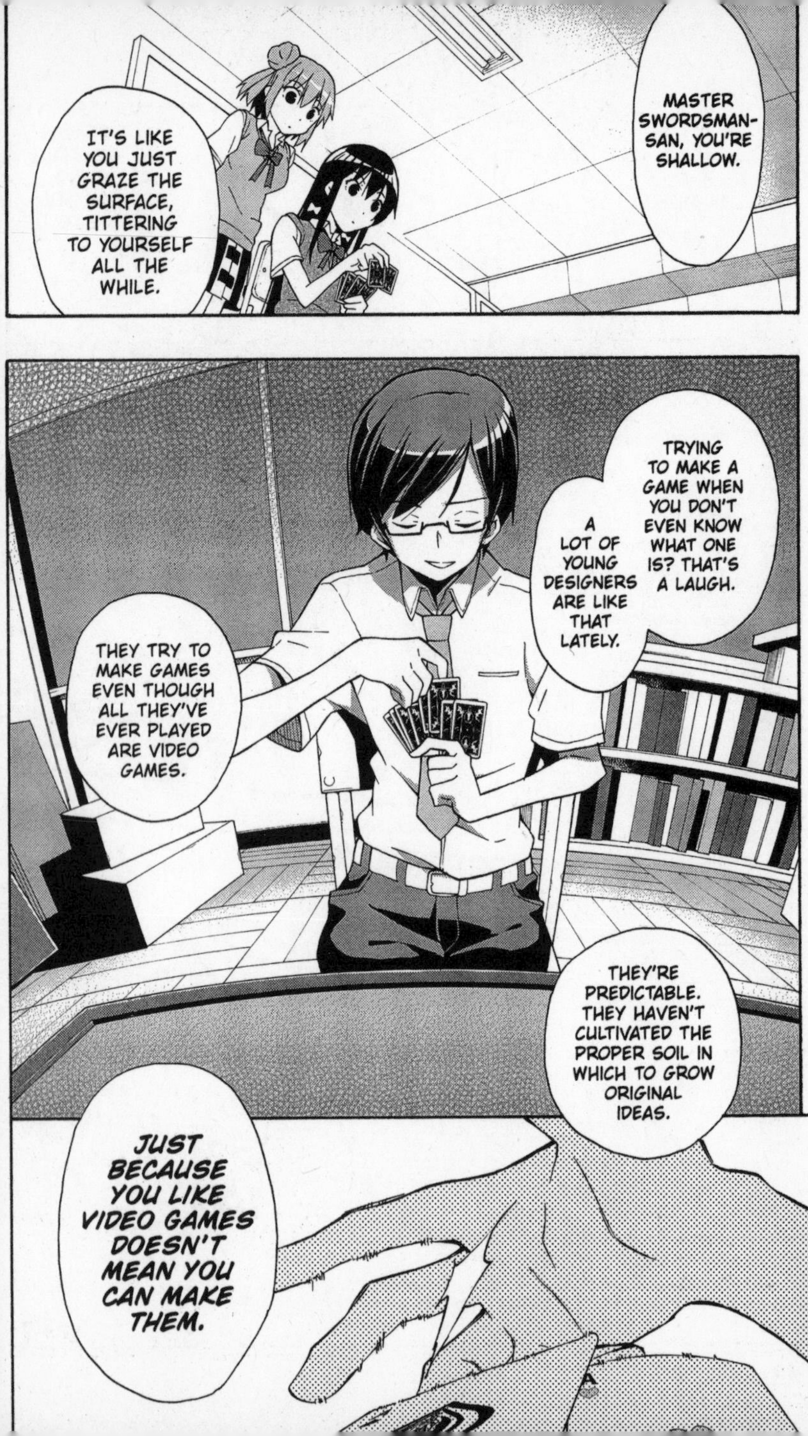
MASTER SWORDSMAN-SAN, YOU'RE SHALLOW.
IT'S LIKE YOU JUST GRAZE THE SURFACE, TITTERING TO YOURSELF ALL THE WHILE.
TRYING TO MAKE A GAME WHEN YOU DON'T EVEN KNOW WHAT ONE IS? THAT'S A LAUGH.
A LOT OF YOUNG DESIGNERS ARE LIKE THAT LATELY.
THEY TRY TO MAKE GAMES EVEN THOUGH ALL THEY'VE EVER PLAYED ARE VIDEO GAMES.
THEY'RE PREDICTABLE. THEY HAVEN'T CULTIVATED THE PROPER SOIL IN WHICH TO GROW ORIGINAL IDEAS.
JUST BECAUSE YOU LIKE VIDEO GAMES DOESN'T MEAN YOU CAN MAKE THEM.

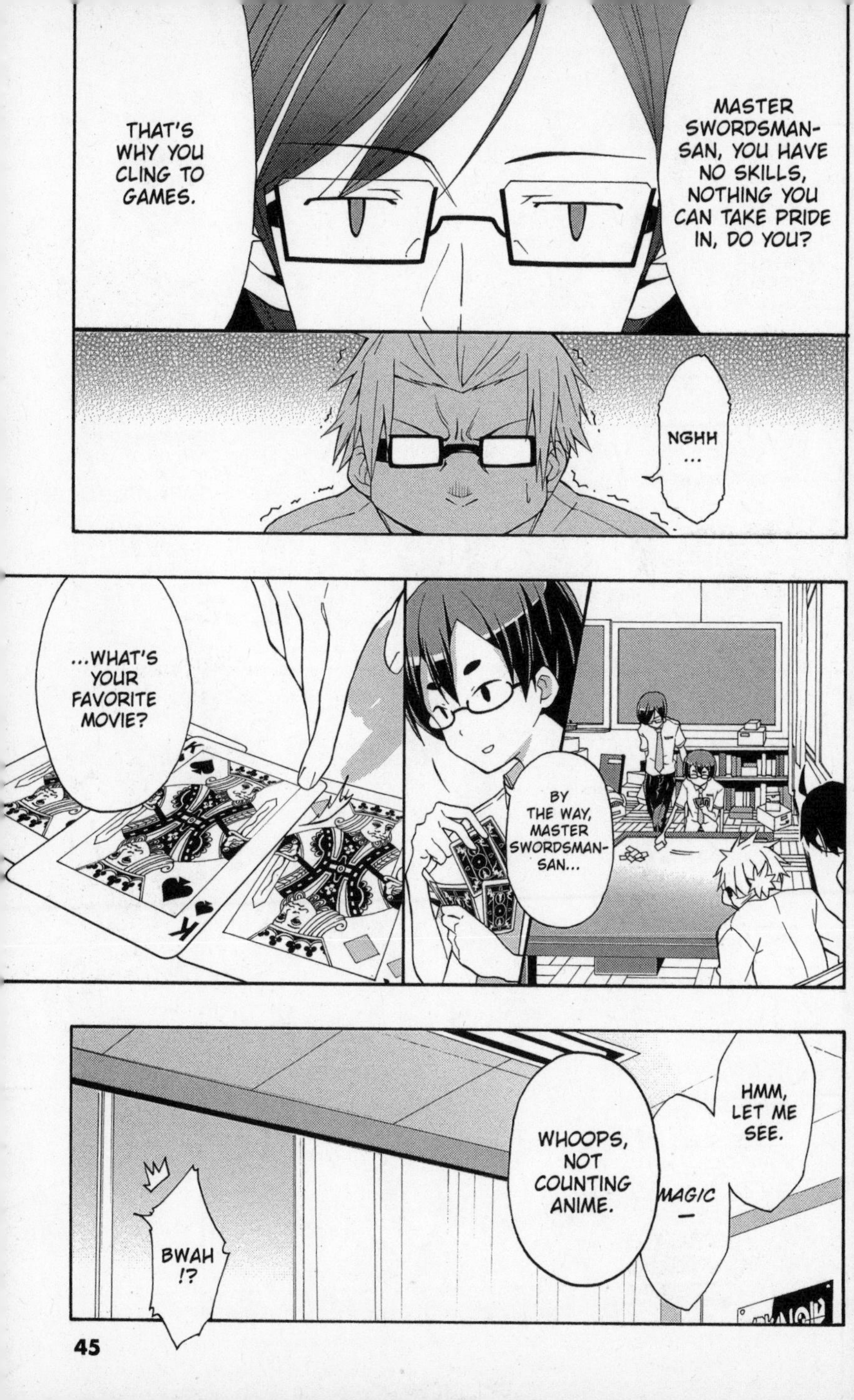
MASTER SWORDSMAN-SAN, YOU HAVE NO SKILLS, NOTHING YOU CAN TAKE PRIDE IN, DO YOU?
THAT'S WHY YOU CLING TO GAMES.
NGHH...
BY THE WAY, MASTER SWORDSMAN-SAN...
...WHAT'S YOUR FAVORITE MOVIE?
HMM, LET ME SEE.
MAGIC—
WHOOPS, NOT COUNTING ANIME.
BWAH!?

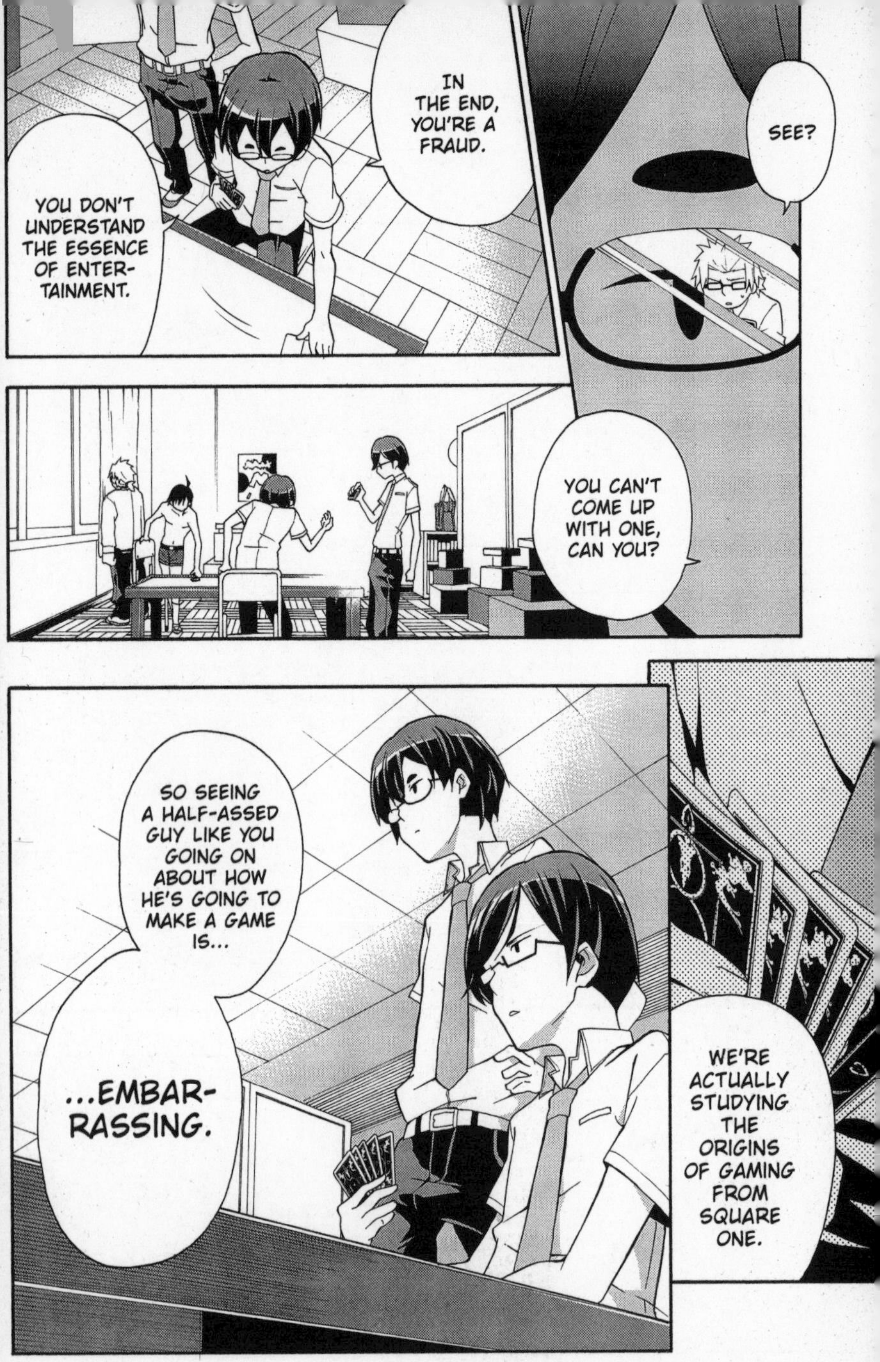
SEE?
YOU CAN'T COME UP WITH ONE, CAN YOU?
IN THE END, YOU'RE A FRAUD.
YOU DON'T UNDERSTAND THE ESSENCE OF ENTER-TAINMENT.
WE'RE ACTUALLY STUDYING THE ORIGINS OF GAMING FROM SQUARE ONE.
SO SEEING A HALF-ASSED GUY LIKE YOU GOING ON ABOUT HOW HE'S GOING TO MAKE A GAME IS...
...EMBAR-RASSING.

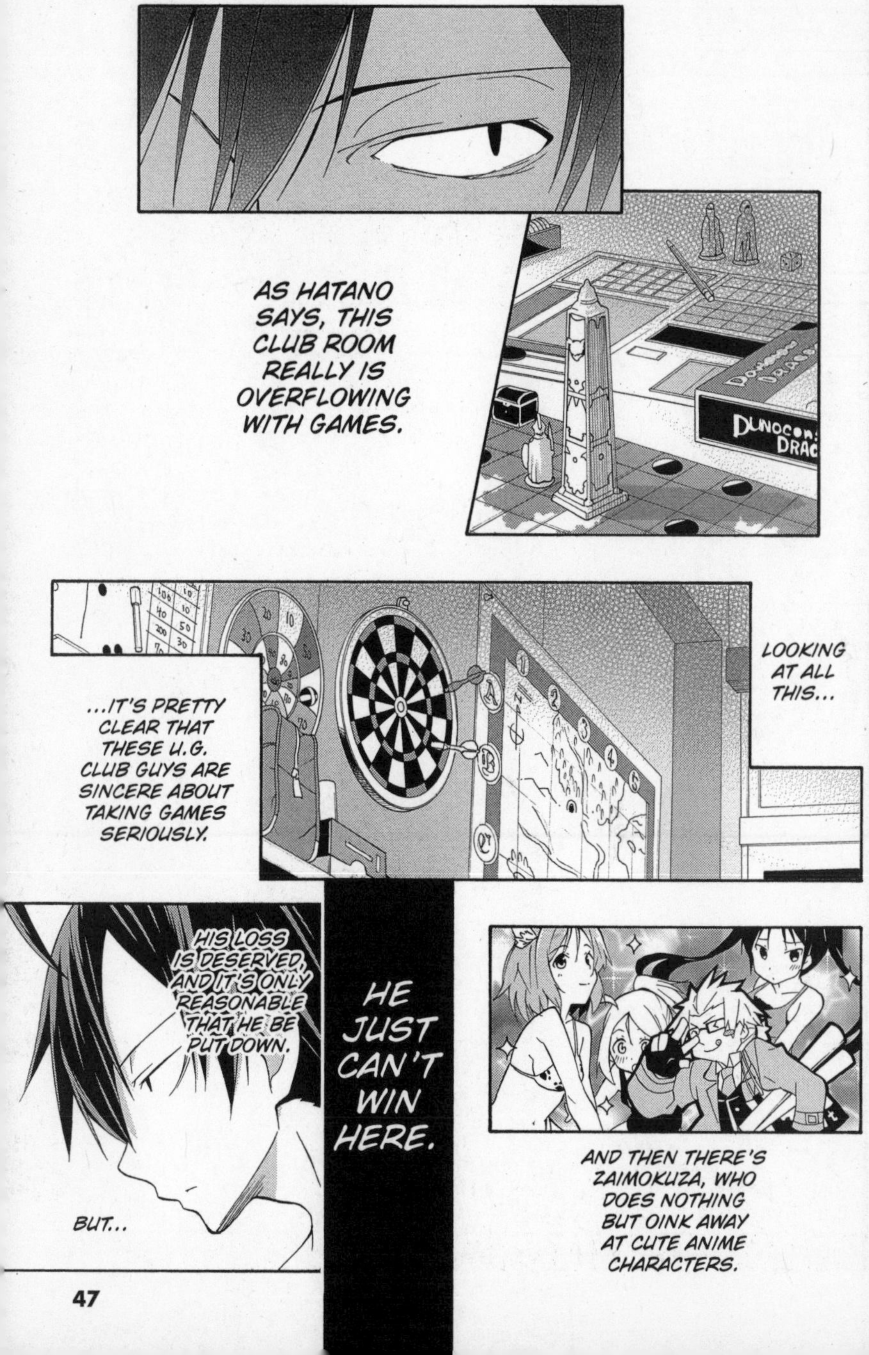
AS HATANO SAYS, THIS CLUB ROOM REALLY IS OVERFLOWING WITH GAMES.
DUNGEONS DRAC
LOOKING AT ALL THIS...
...IT'S PRETTY CLEAR THAT THESE U.G. CLUB GUYS ARE SINCERE ABOUT TAKING GAMES SERIOUSLY.
AND THEN THERE'S ZAIMOKUZA, WHO DOES NOTHING BUT OINK AWAY AT CUTE ANIME CHARACTERS.
HE JUST CAN'T WIN HERE.
HIS LOSS IS DESERVED, AND IT'S ONLY REASONABLE THAT HE BE PUT DOWN.
BUT...

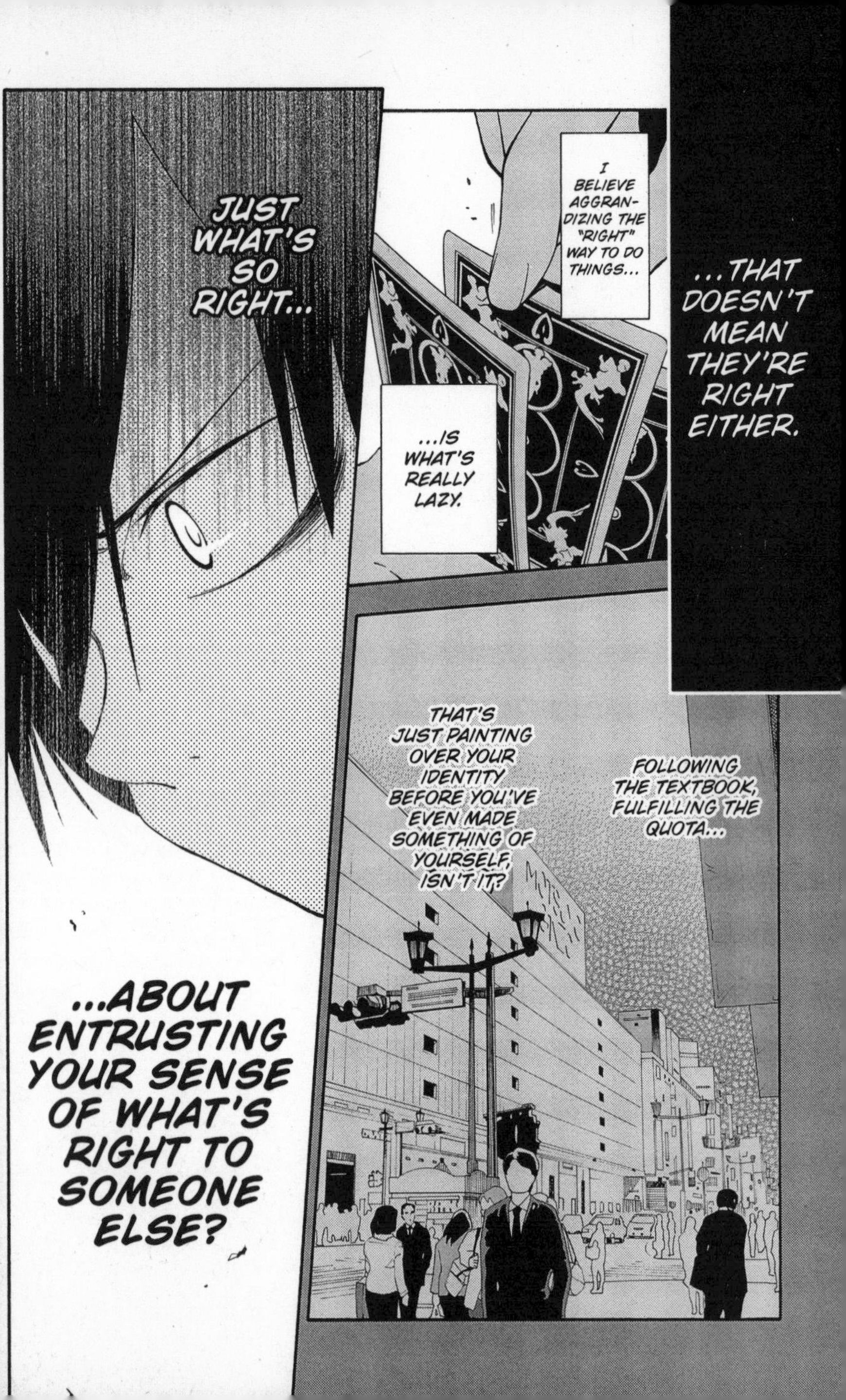

...THAT DOESN'T MEAN THEY'RE RIGHT EITHER.
I BELIEVE AGGRAN-DIZING THE "RIGHT" WAY TO DO THINGS...
...IS WHAT'S REALLY LAZY.
FOLLOWING THE TEXTBOOK, FULFILLING THE QUOTA...
THAT'S JUST PAINTING OVER YOUR IDENTITY BEFORE YOU'VE EVEN MADE SOMETHING OF YOURSELF, ISN'T IT?
JUST WHAT'S SO RIGHT...
...ABOUT ENTRUSTING YOUR SENSE OF WHAT'S RIGHT TO SOMEONE ELSE?

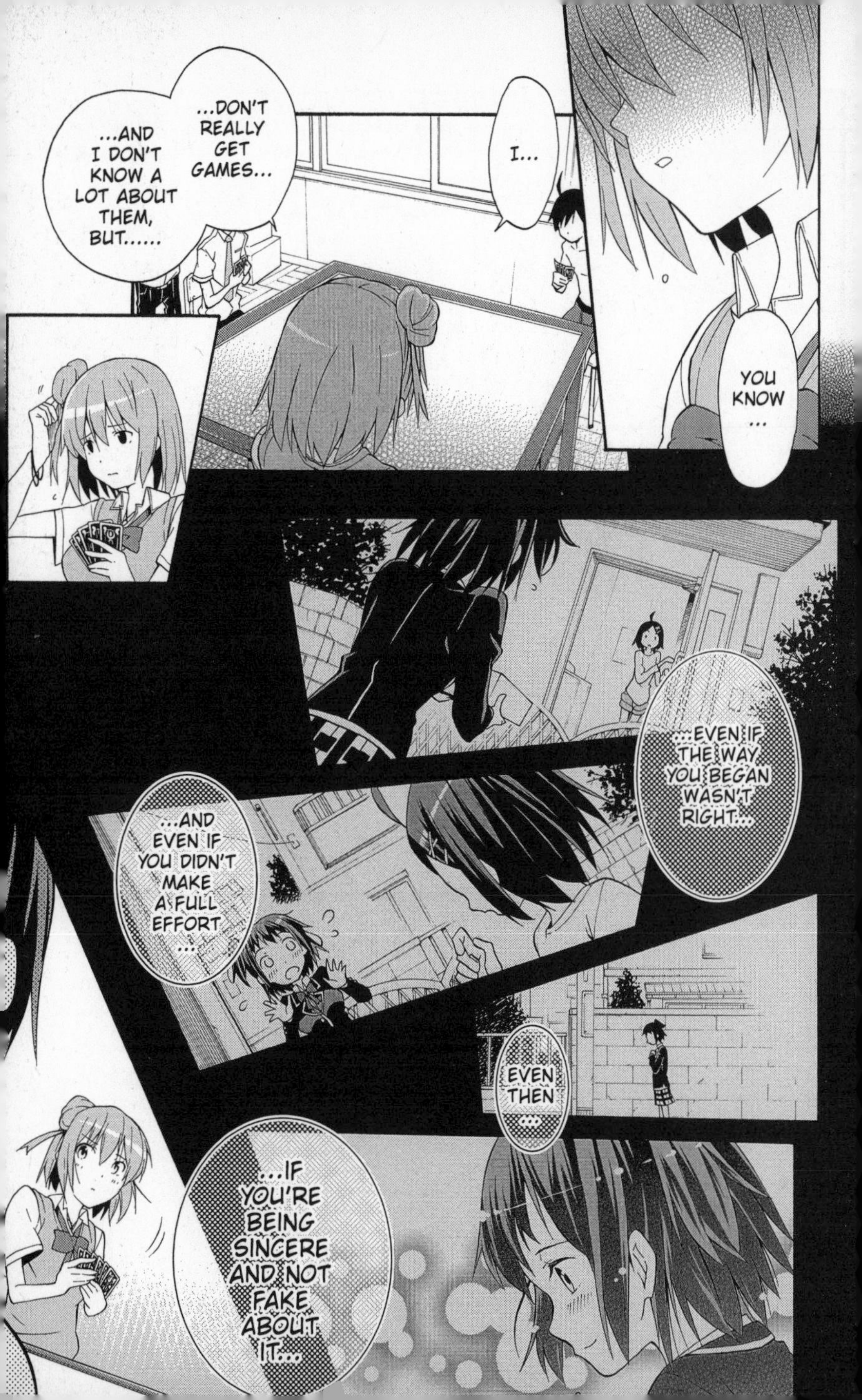
YOU KNOW ...
I...
...DON'T REALLY GET GAMES...
...AND I DON'T KNOW A LOT ABOUT THEM, BUT......
...EVEN IF THE WAY YOU BEGAN WASN'T RIGHT...
...AND EVEN IF YOU DIDN'T MAKE A FULL EFFORT ...
EVEN THEN ...
...IF YOU'RE BEING SINCERE AND NOT FAKE ABOUT IT...

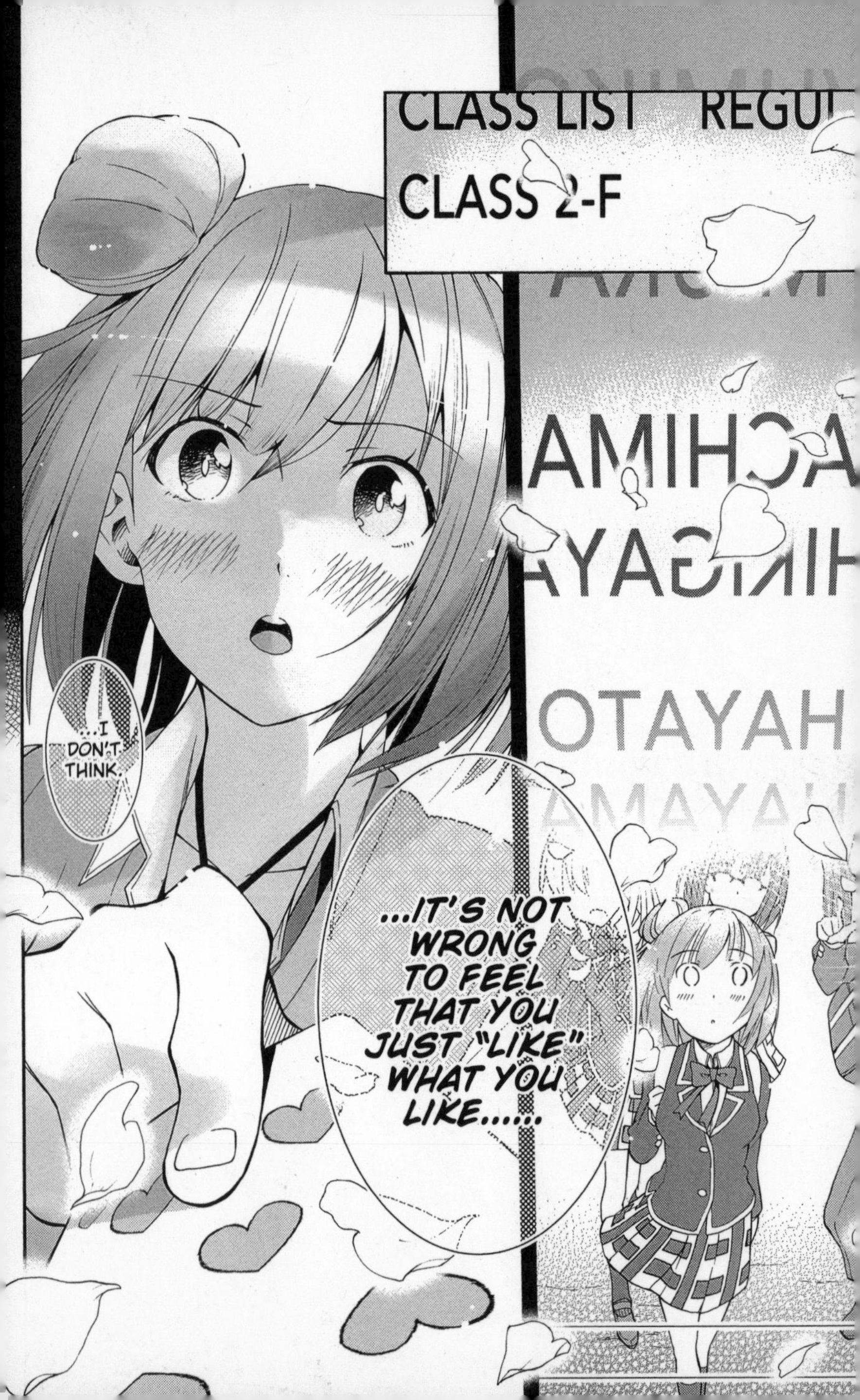
CLASS LIST REGU
CLASS 2-F
...IT'S NOT WRONG TO FEEL THAT YOU JUST "LIKE" WHAT YOU LIKE......
...I DON'T THINK.

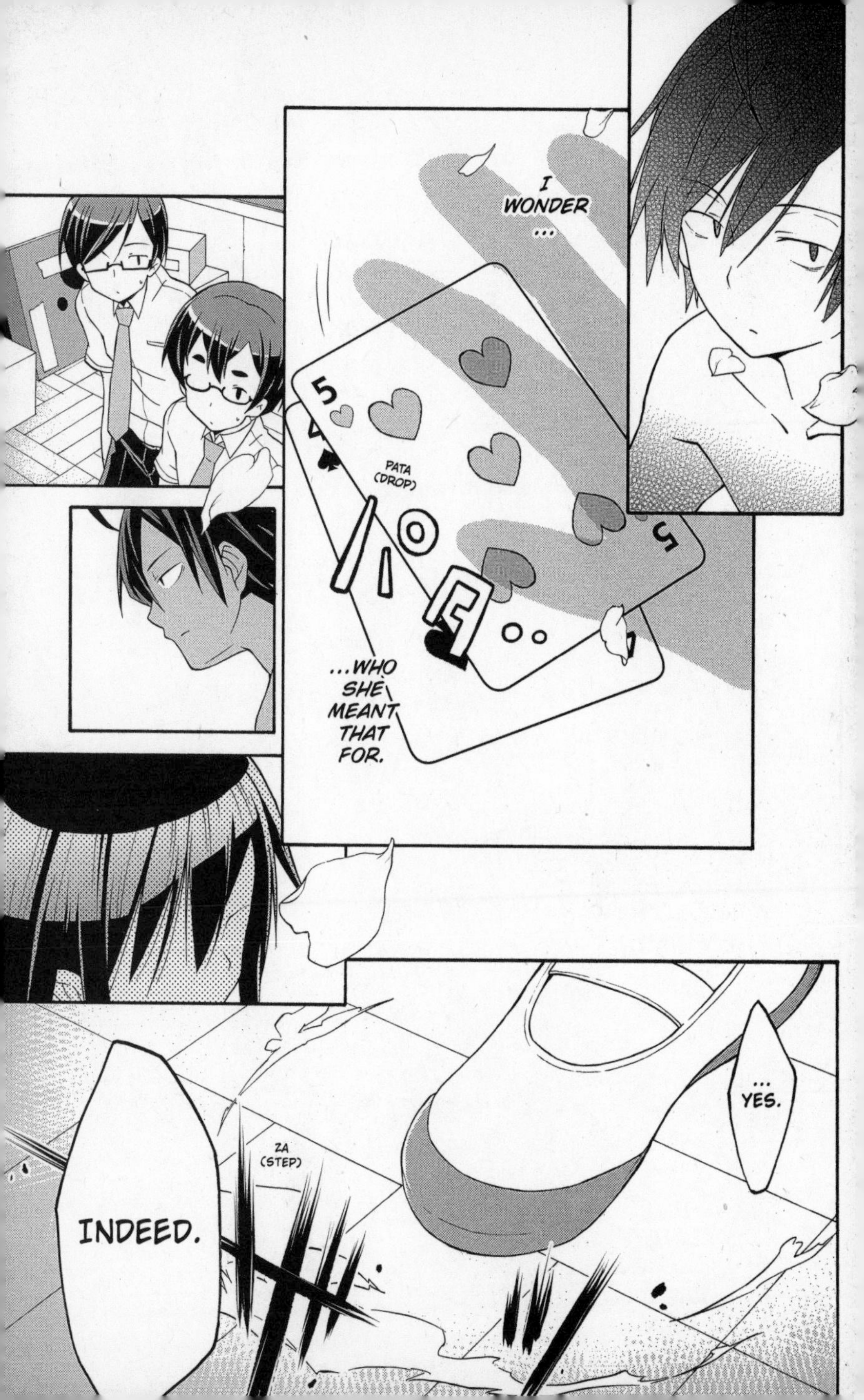
I WONDER ...
PATA (DROP)
...WHO SHE MEANT THAT FOR.
...YES.
ZA (STEP)
INDEED.

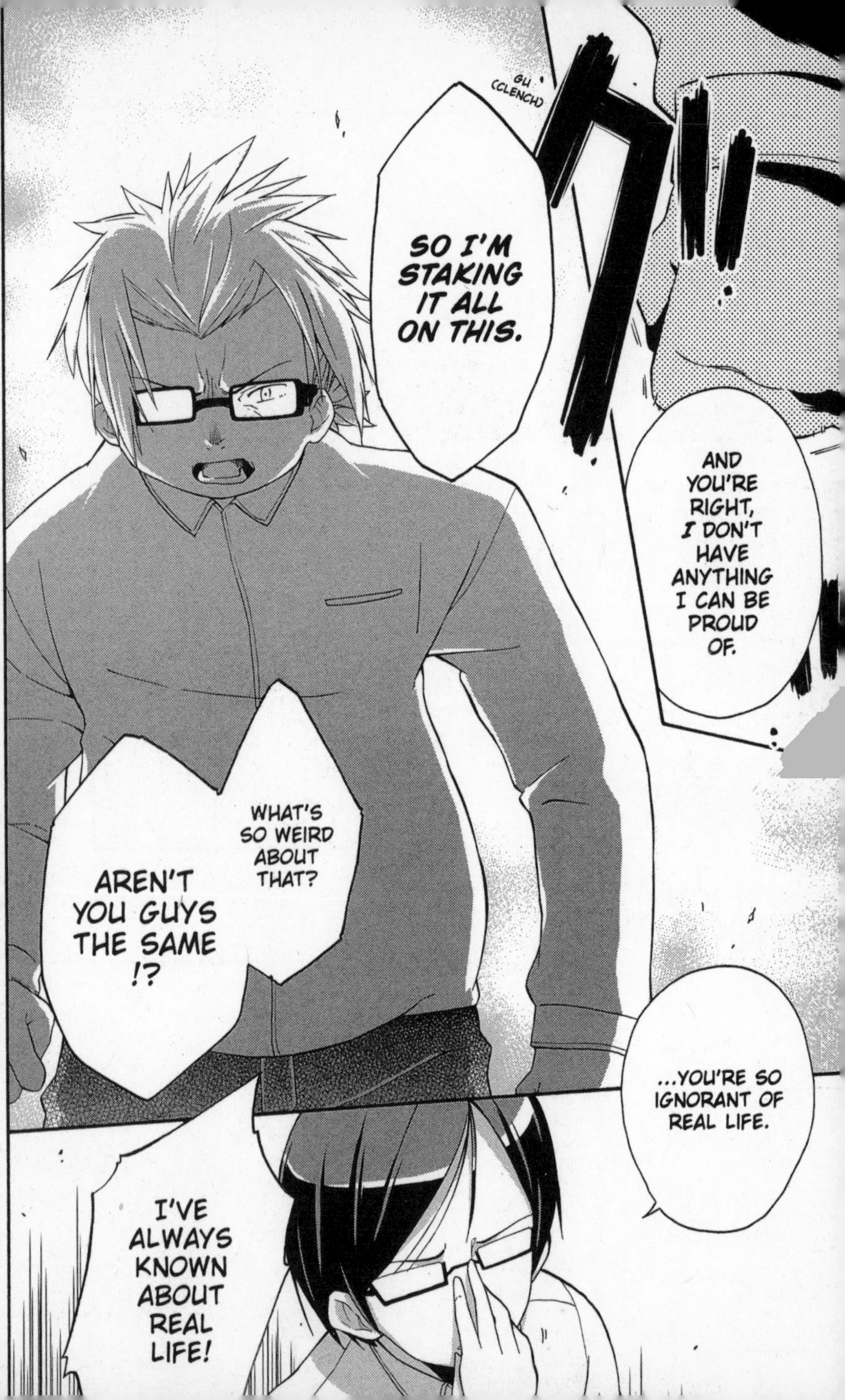
GU (CLENCH)
AND YOU'RE RIGHT, I DON'T HAVE ANYTHING I CAN BE PROUD OF.
SO I'M STAKING IT ALL ON THIS.
WHAT'S SO WEIRD ABOUT THAT?
AREN'T YOU GUYS THE SAME !?
...YOU'RE SO IGNORANT OF REAL LIFE.
I'VE ALWAYS KNOWN ABOUT REAL LIFE!

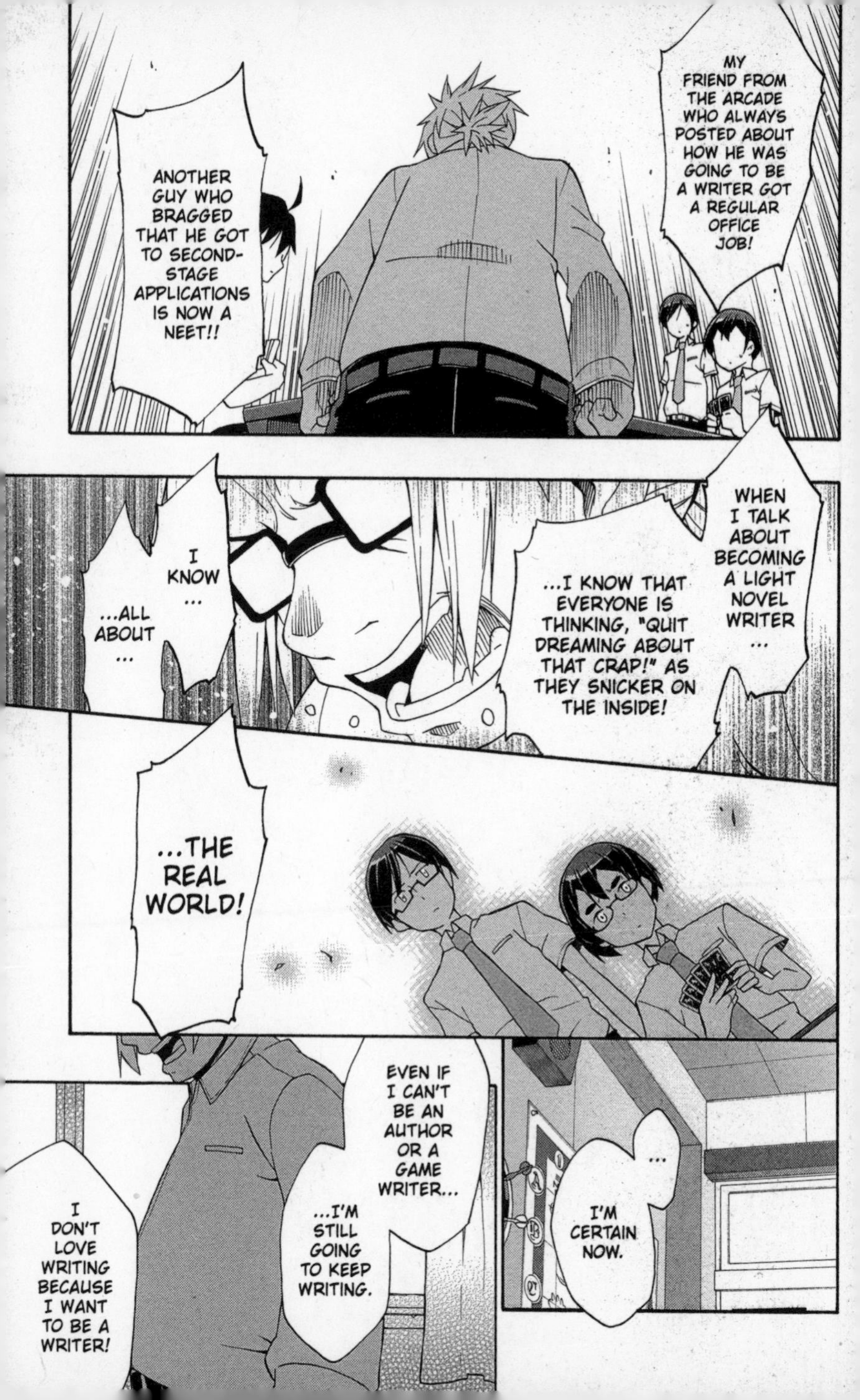
MY FRIEND FROM THE ARCADE WHO ALWAYS POSTED ABOUT HOW HE WAS GOING TO BE A WRITER GOT A REGULAR OFFICE JOB!
ANOTHER GUY WHO BRAGGED THAT HE GOT TO SECOND-STAGE APPLICATIONS IS NOW A NEET!!
WHEN I TALK ABOUT BECOMING A LIGHT NOVEL WRITER ...
...I KNOW THAT EVERYONE IS THINKING, "QUIT DREAMING ABOUT THAT CRAP!" AS THEY SNICKER ON THE INSIDE!
I KNOW ...
...ALL ABOUT ...
...THE REAL WORLD!
...
I'M CERTAIN NOW.
EVEN IF I CAN'T BE AN AUTHOR OR A GAME WRITER...
...I'M STILL GOING TO KEEP WRITING.
I DON'T LOVE WRITING BECAUSE I WANT TO BE A WRITER!

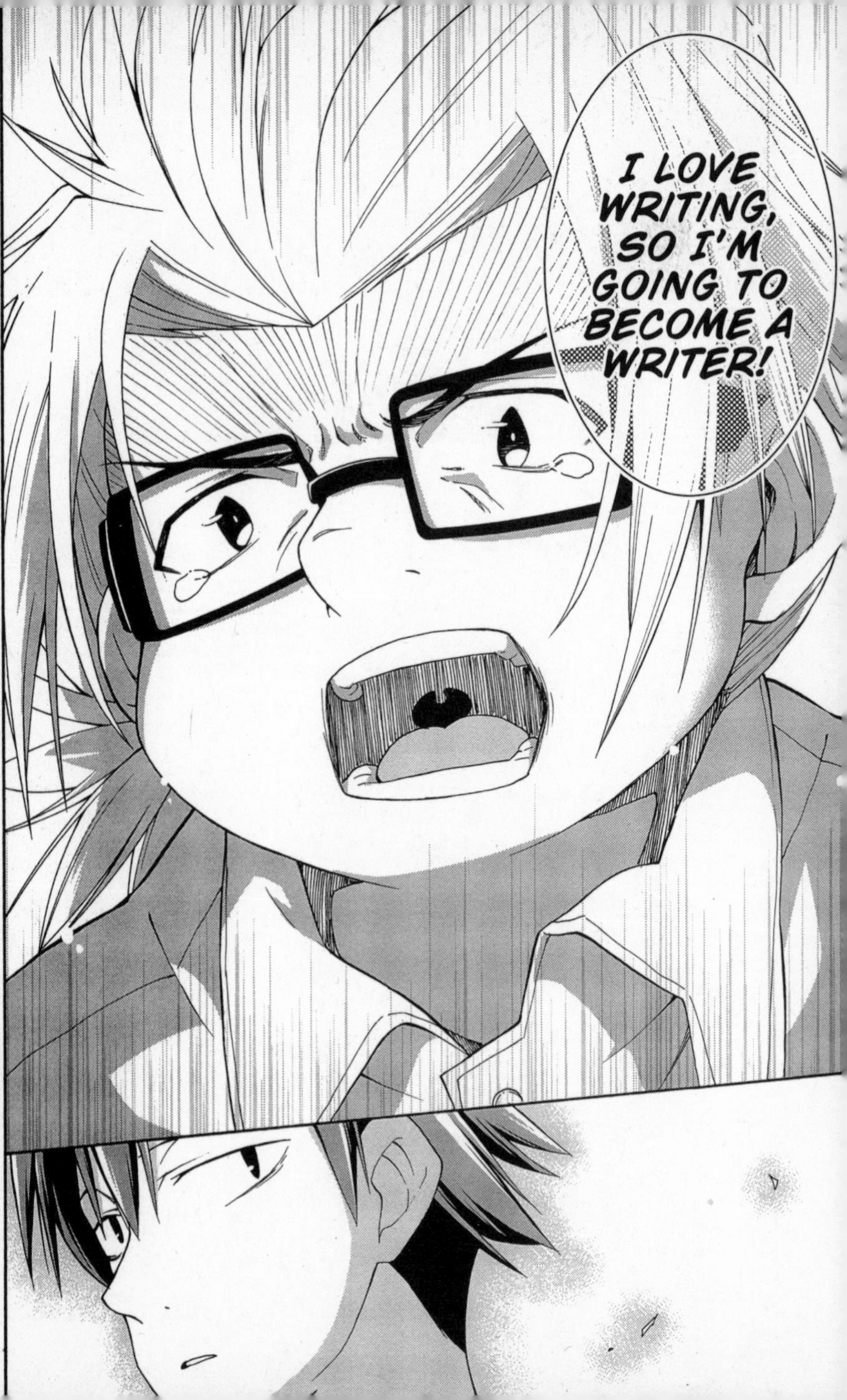
I LOVE WRITING, SO I'M GOING TO BECOME A WRITER!

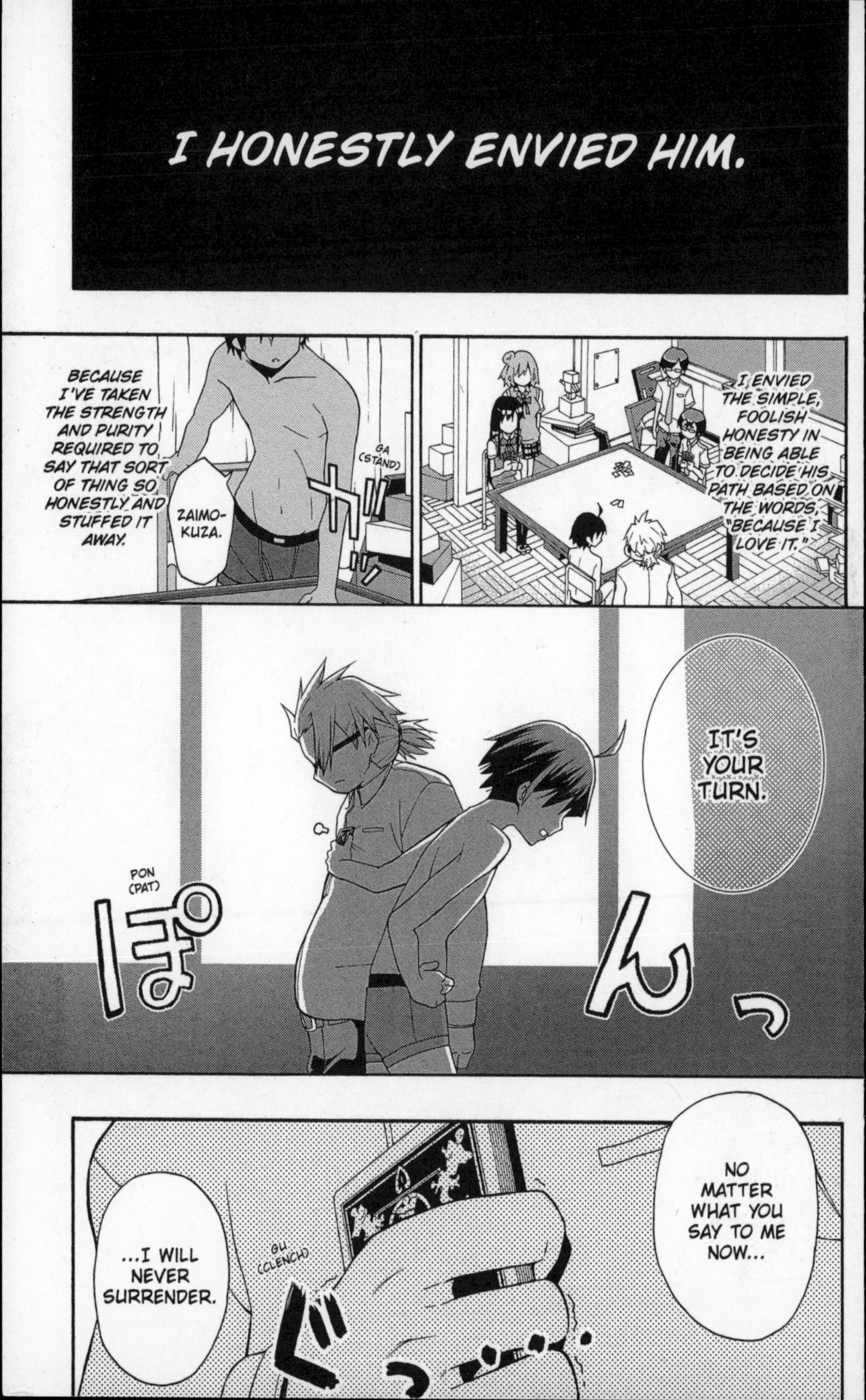
I HONESTLY ENVIED HIM.
I ENVIED THE SIMPLE, FOOLISH HONESTY IN BEING ABLE TO DECIDE HIS PATH BASED ON THE WORDS, "BECAUSE I LOVE IT."
BECAUSE I'VE TAKEN THE STRENGTH AND PURITY REQUIRED TO SAY THAT SORT OF THING SO HONESTLY AND STUFFED IT AWAY.
GA (STAND)
ZAIMOKUZA.
IT'S YOUR TURN.
PON (PAT)
ぽんっ
NO MATTER WHAT YOU SAY TO ME NOW...
GU (CLENCH)
...I WILL NEVER SURRENDER.

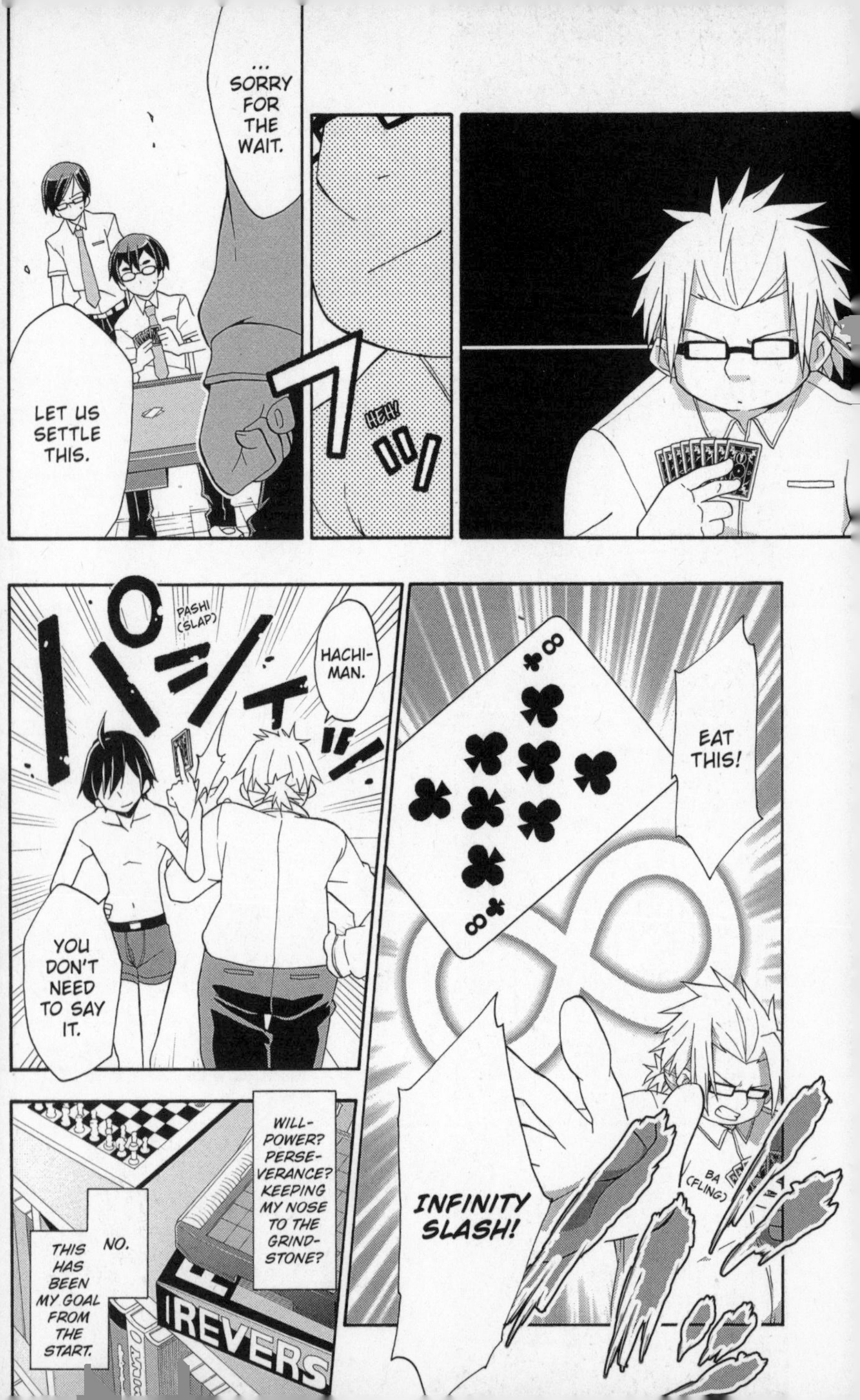
HEH!
... SORRY FOR THE WAIT.
LET US SETTLE THIS.
EAT THIS!
INFINITY SLASH!
BA (FLING)
HACHI-MAN.
PASHI (SLAP)
YOU DON'T NEED TO SAY IT.
WILL-POWER? PERSE-VERANCE? KEEPING MY NOSE TO THE GRIND-STONE?
NO.
THIS HAS BEEN MY GOAL FROM THE START.
REVERS

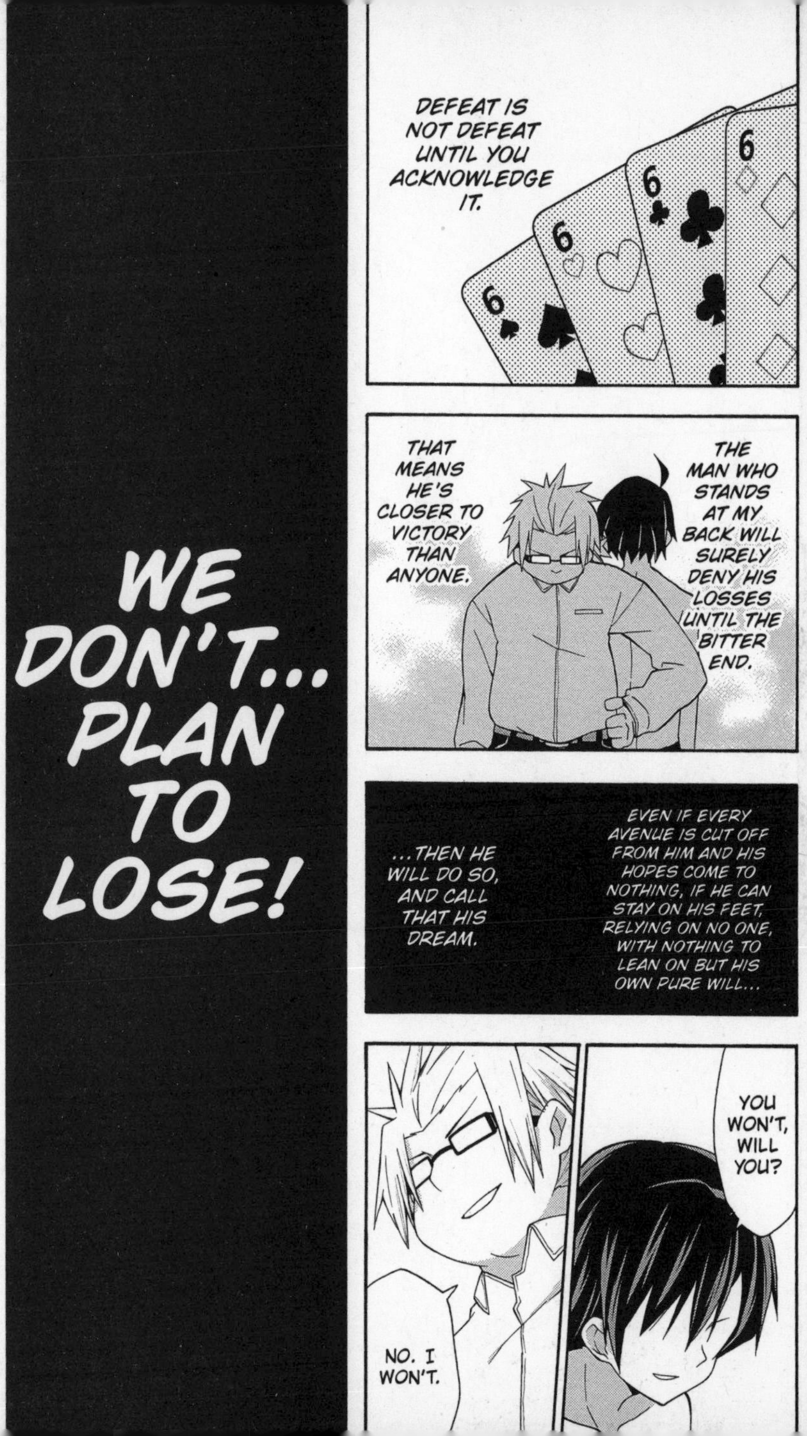
DEFEAT IS NOT DEFEAT UNTIL YOU ACKNOWLEDGE IT.
THE MAN WHO STANDS AT MY BACK WILL SURELY DENY HIS LOSSES UNTIL THE BITTER END.
THAT MEANS HE'S CLOSER TO VICTORY THAN ANYONE.
EVEN IF EVERY AVENUE IS CUT OFF FROM HIM AND HIS HOPES COME TO NOTHING, IF HE CAN STAY ON HIS FEET, RELYING ON NO ONE, WITH NOTHING TO LEAN ON BUT HIS OWN PURE WILL...
...THEN HE WILL DO SO, AND CALL THAT HIS DREAM.
YOU WON'T, WILL YOU?
NO. I WON'T.
WE DON'T... PLAN TO LOSE!

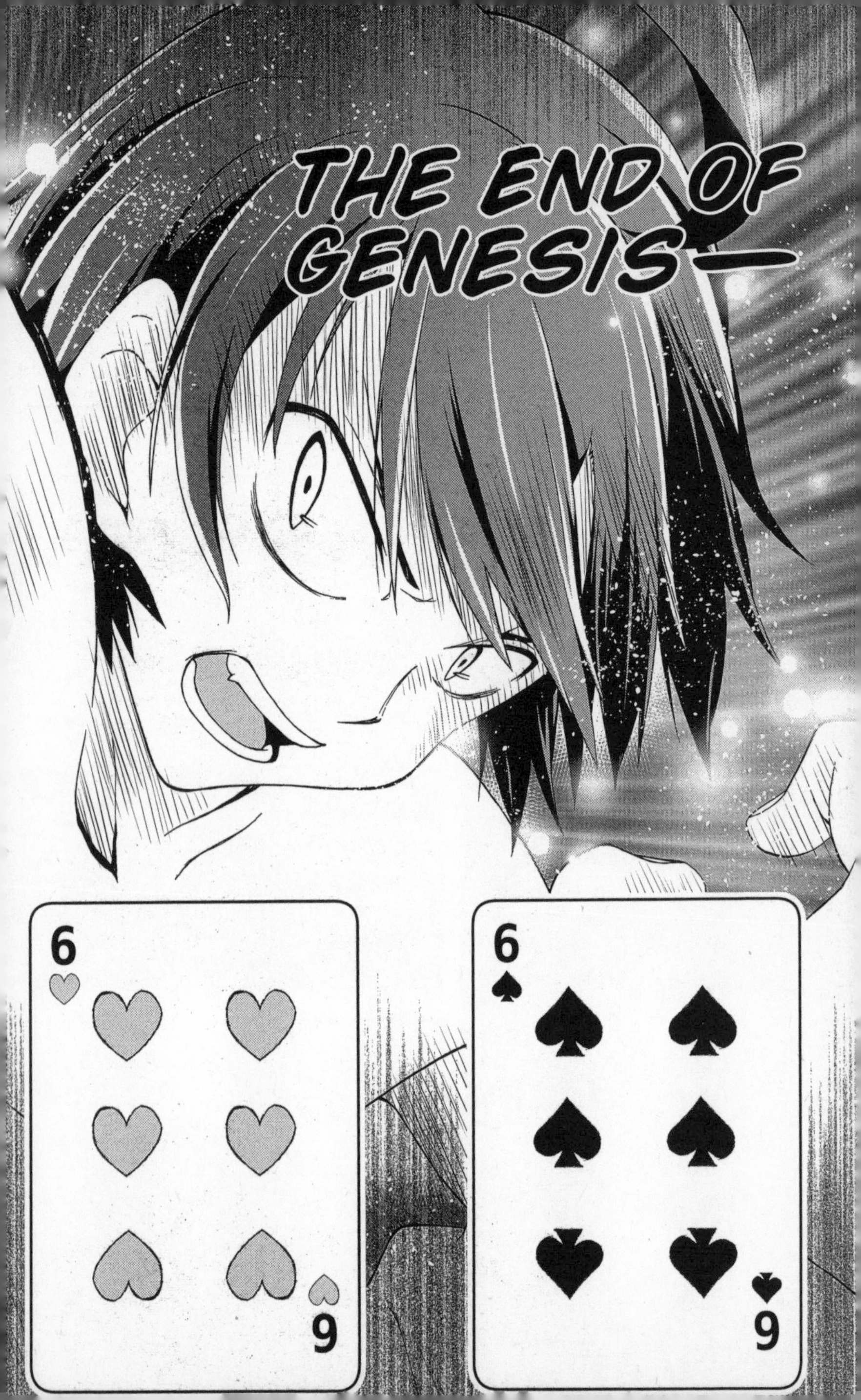
THE END OF GENESIS—
6
9
6
9

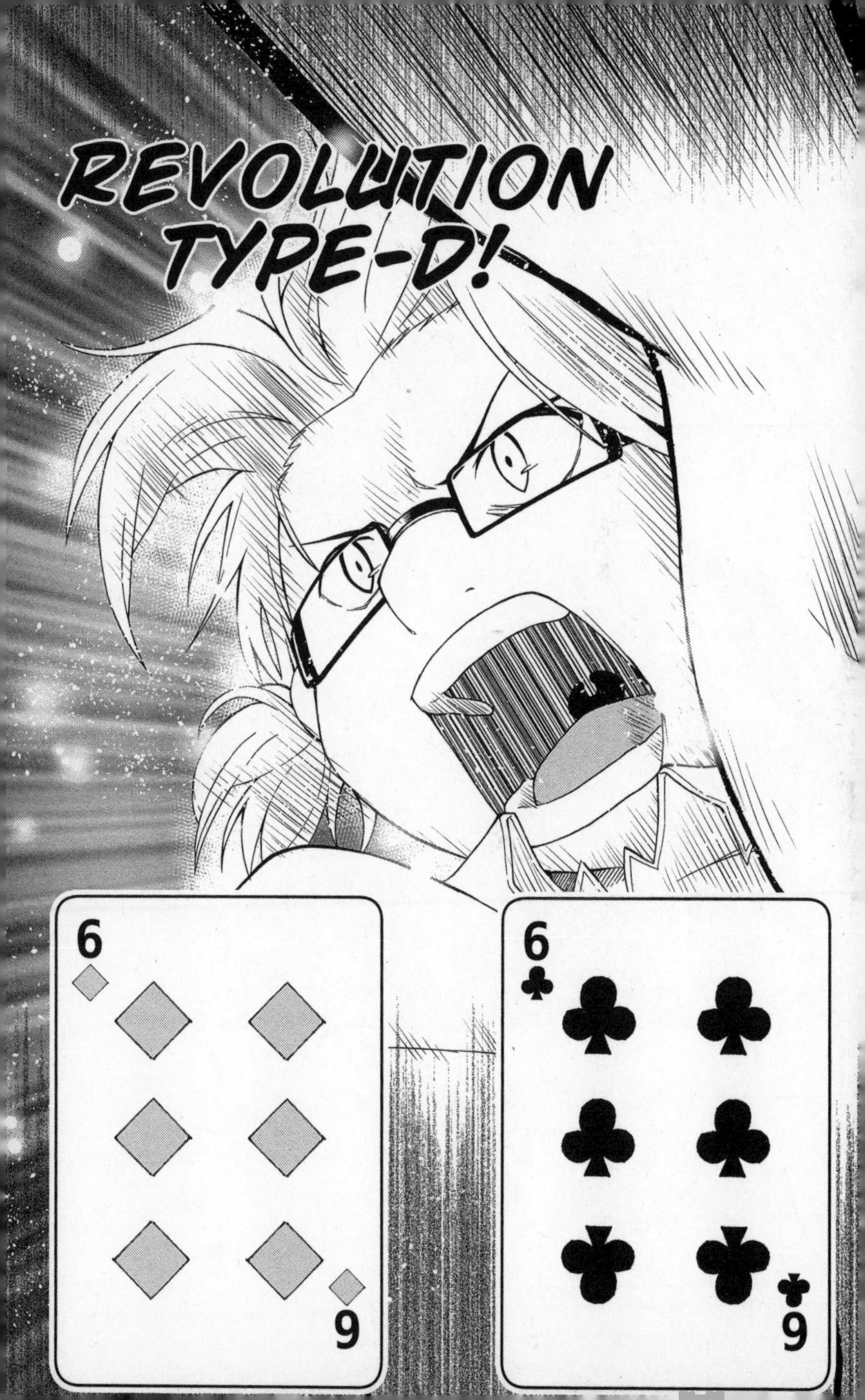
REVOLUTION TYPE-D!
6
9
6
9

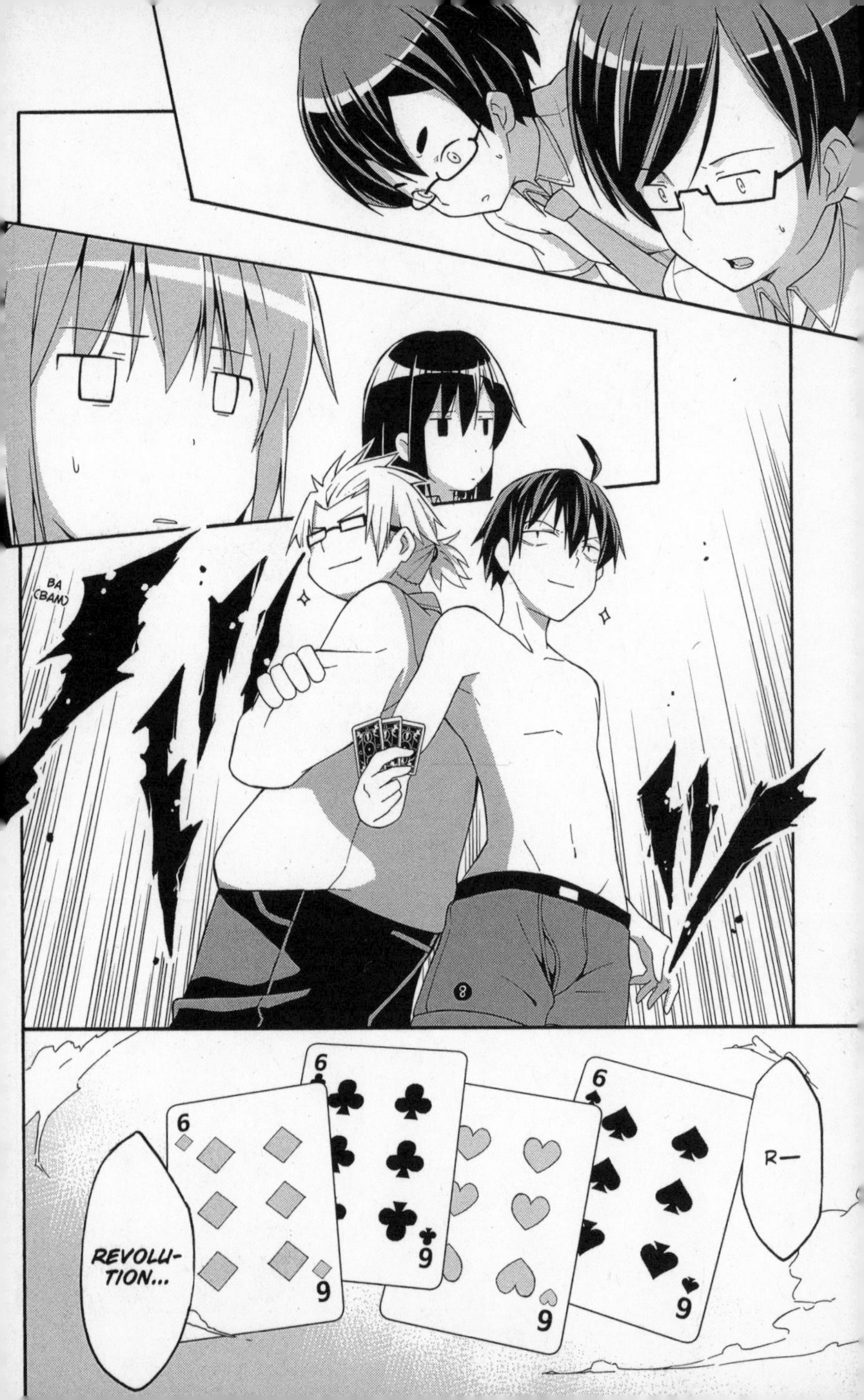
BA (BAM)
R—
REVOLU-TION...

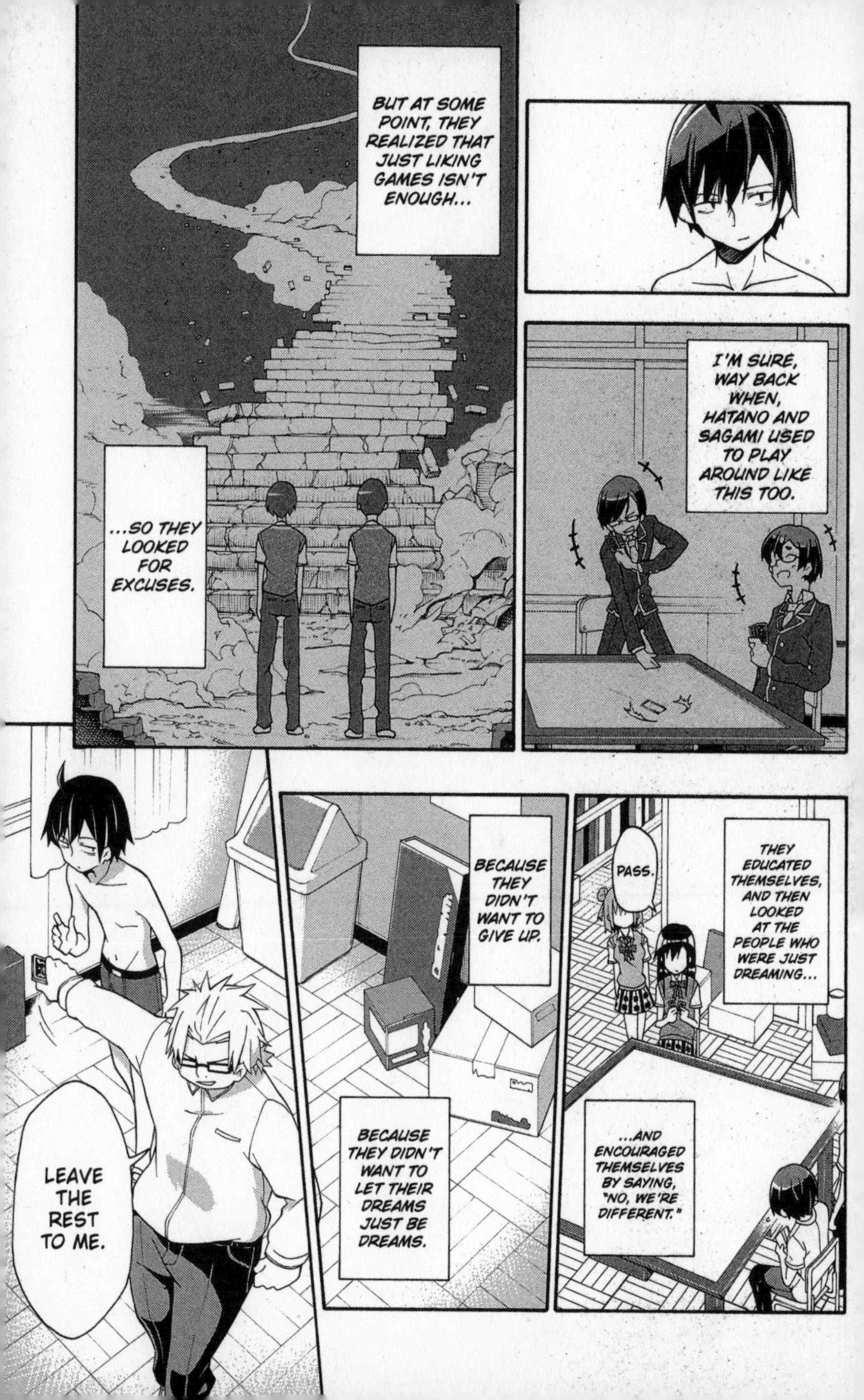
I'M SURE, WAY BACK WHEN, HATANO AND SAGAMI USED TO PLAY AROUND LIKE THIS TOO.
BUT AT SOME POINT, THEY REALIZED THAT JUST LIKING GAMES ISN'T ENOUGH...
...SO THEY LOOKED FOR EXCUSES.
THEY EDUCATED THEMSELVES, AND THEN LOOKED AT THE PEOPLE WHO WERE JUST DREAMING...
PASS.
...AND ENCOURAGED THEMSELVES BY SAYING, "NO, WE'RE DIFFERENT."
BECAUSE THEY DIDN'T WANT TO GIVE UP.
BECAUSE THEY DIDN'T WANT TO LET THEIR DREAMS JUST BE DREAMS.
LEAVE THE REST TO ME.

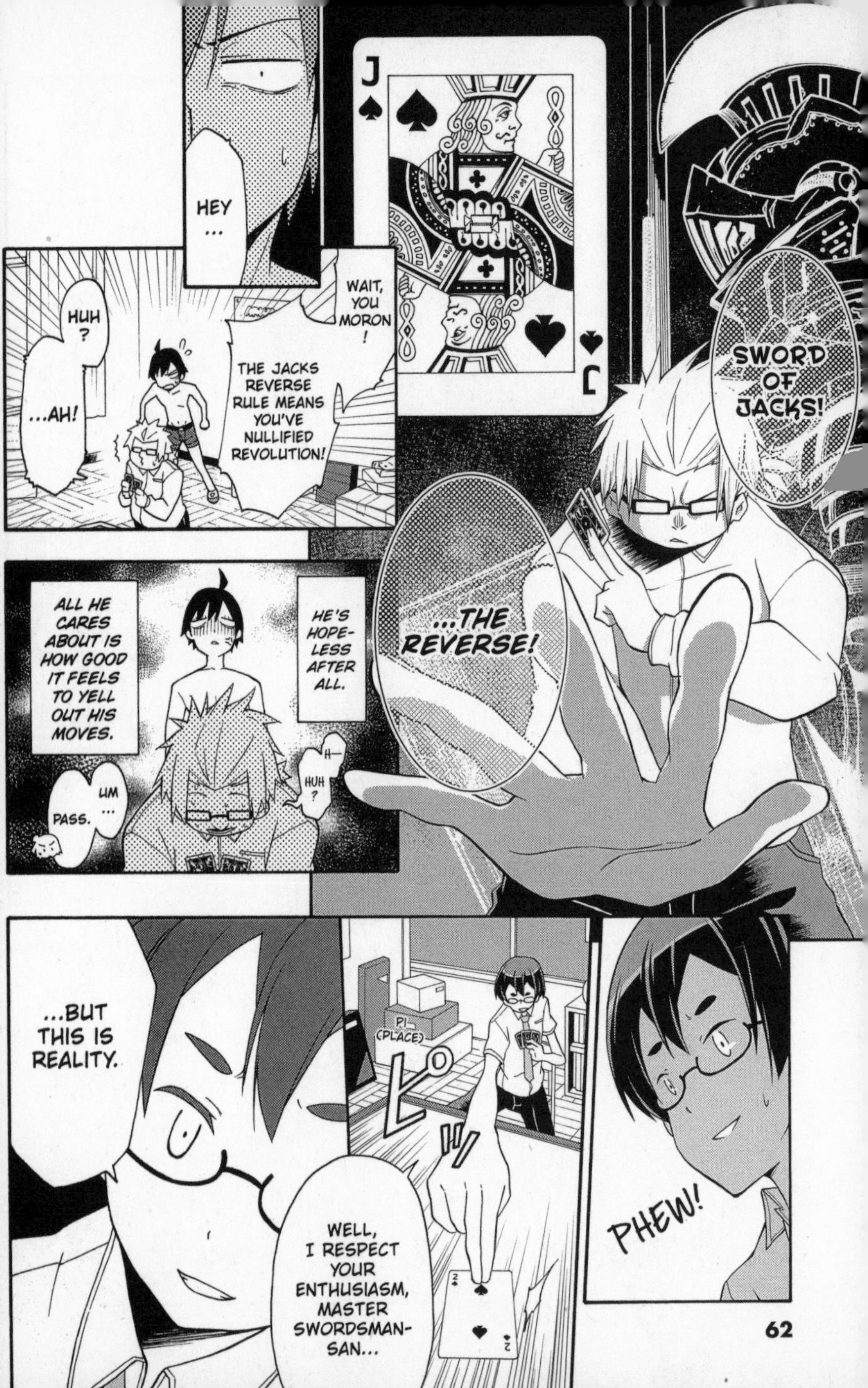
SWORD OF JACKS!
...THE REVERSE!
HEY ...
WAIT, YOU MORON!
THE JACKS REVERSE RULE MEANS YOU'VE NULLIFIED REVOLUTION!
HUH?
...AH!
HE'S HOPELESS AFTER ALL.
ALL HE CARES ABOUT IS HOW GOOD IT FEELS TO YELL OUT HIS MOVES.
H— HUH?
UM ... PASS.
PHEW!
PI_ (PLACE)
WELL, I RESPECT YOUR ENTHUSIASM, MASTER SWORDSMAN-SAN...
...BUT THIS IS REALITY.

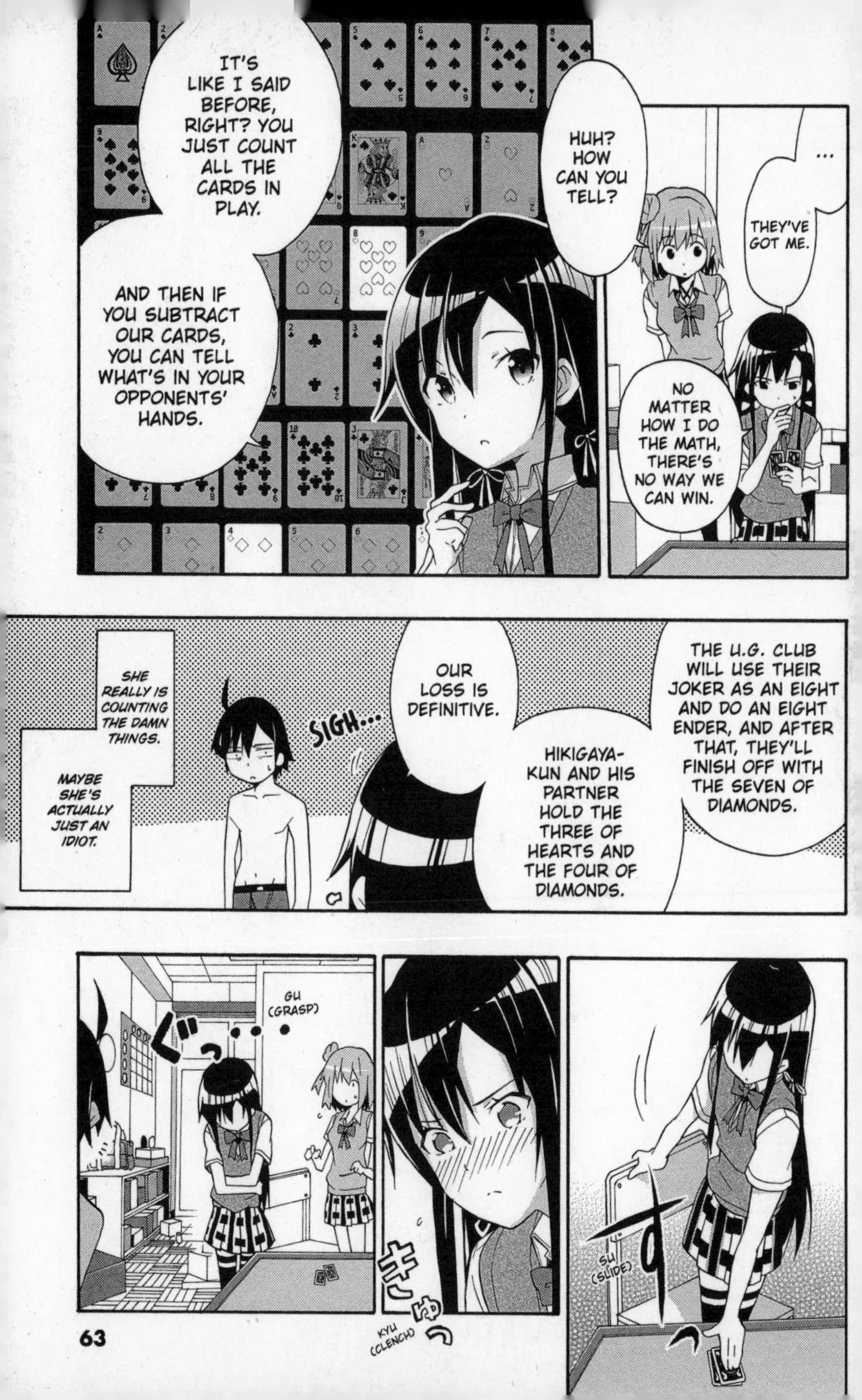
...
THEY'VE GOT ME.
NO MATTER HOW I DO THE MATH, THERE'S NO WAY WE CAN WIN.
HUH? HOW CAN YOU TELL?
IT'S LIKE I SAID BEFORE, RIGHT? YOU JUST COUNT ALL THE CARDS IN PLAY.
AND THEN IF YOU SUBTRACT OUR CARDS, YOU CAN TELL WHAT'S IN YOUR OPPONENTS' HANDS.
THE U.G. CLUB WILL USE THEIR JOKER AS AN EIGHT AND DO AN EIGHT ENDER, AND AFTER THAT, THEY'LL FINISH OFF WITH THE SEVEN OF DIAMONDS.
HIKIGAYA-KUN AND HIS PARTNER HOLD THE THREE OF HEARTS AND THE FOUR OF DIAMONDS.
OUR LOSS IS DEFINITIVE.
SIGH...
SHE REALLY IS COUNTING THE DAMN THINGS.
MAYBE SHE'S ACTUALLY JUST AN IDIOT.
SU (SLIDE)
KYU (CLENCH)
GU (GRASP)

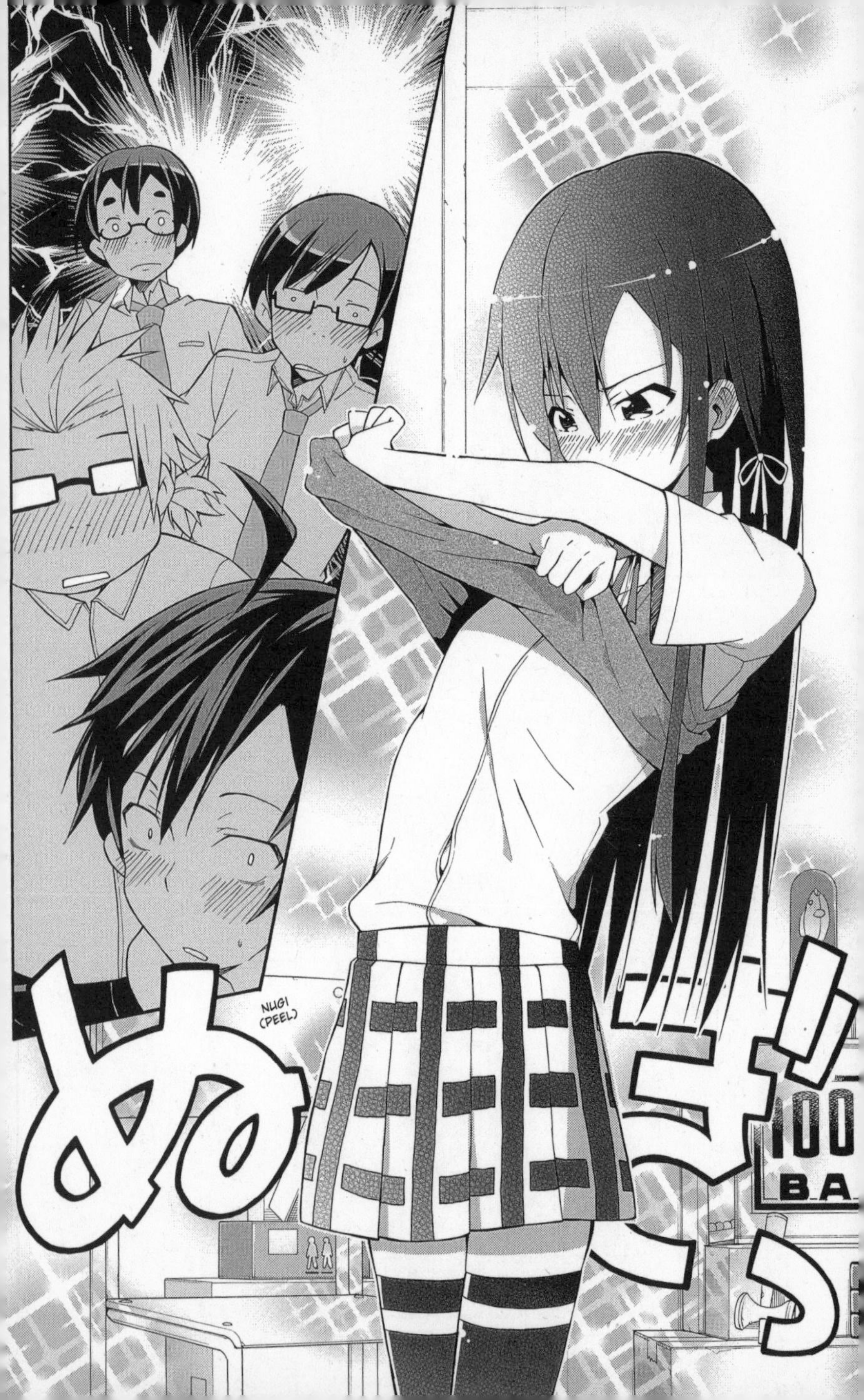
ぬぎっ
NUGI
(PEEL)

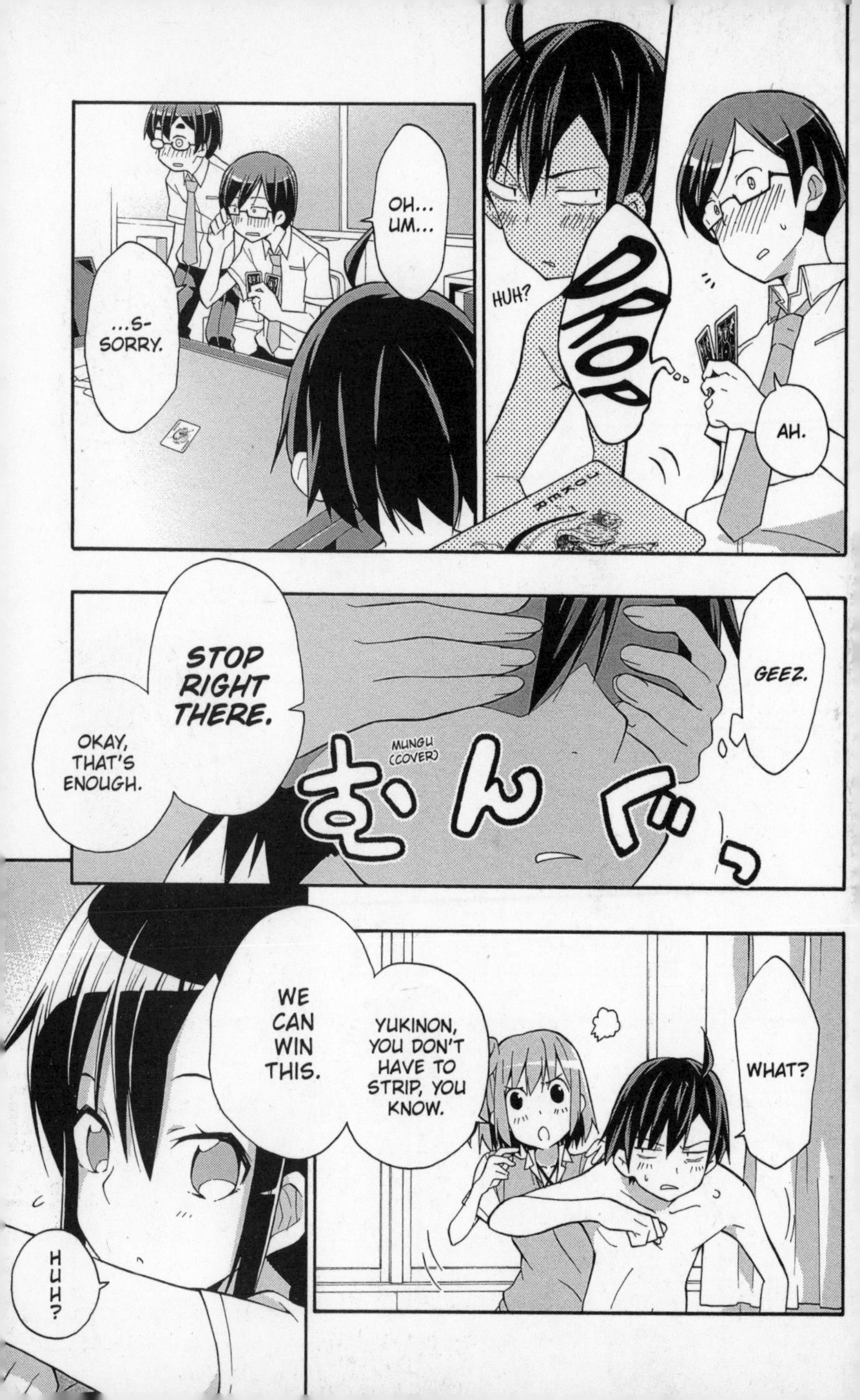
DROP
HUH?
AH.
OH... UM...
...S- SORRY.
GEEZ.
MUNGU (COVER)
STOP RIGHT THERE.
OKAY, THAT'S ENOUGH.
WHAT?
YUKINON, YOU DON'T HAVE TO STRIP, YOU KNOW.
WE CAN WIN THIS.
HUH?

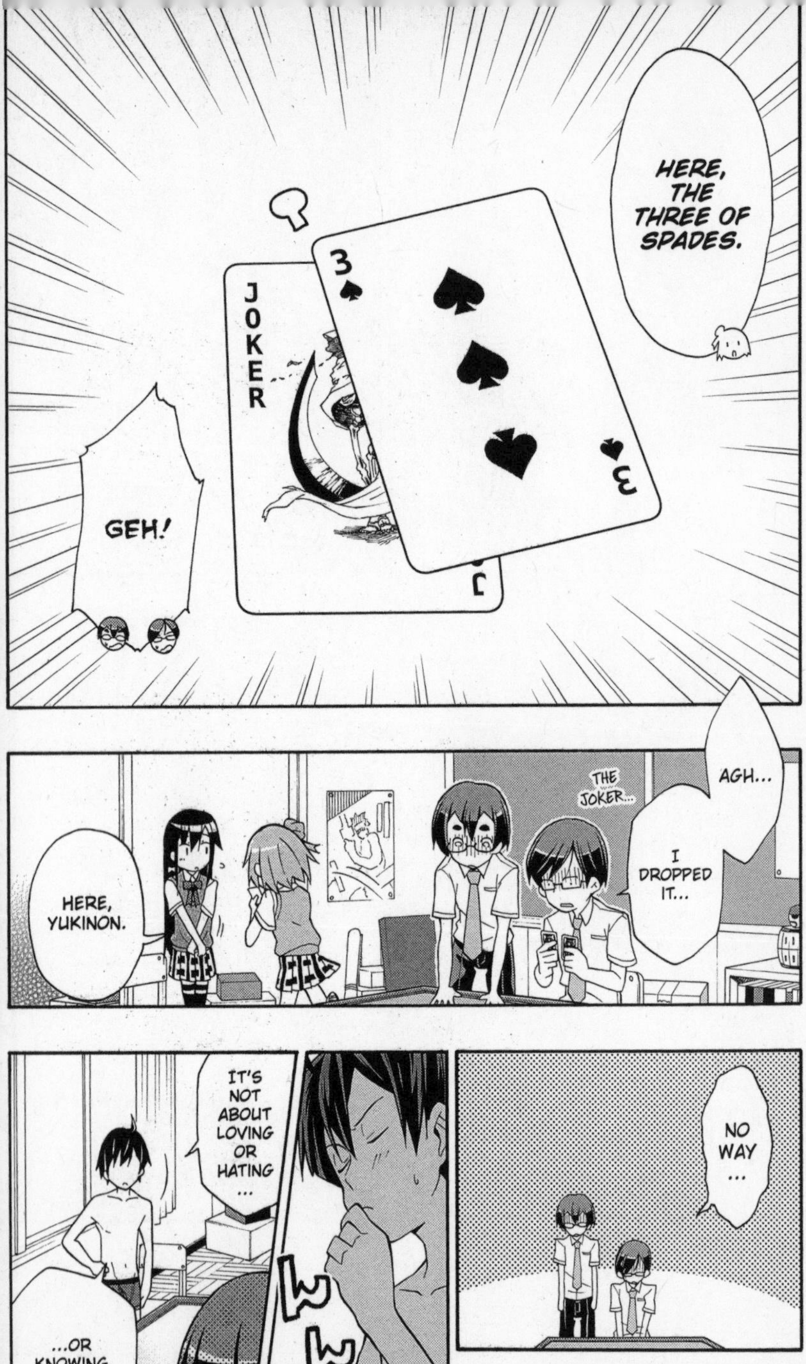
HERE, THE THREE OF SPADES.
JOKER
GEH!
AGH...
THE JOKER...
I DROPPED IT...
HERE, YUKINON.
NO WAY...
IT'S NOT ABOUT LOVING OR HATING...
NN (AHEM)
...OR KNOWING THE GAME OR NOT.

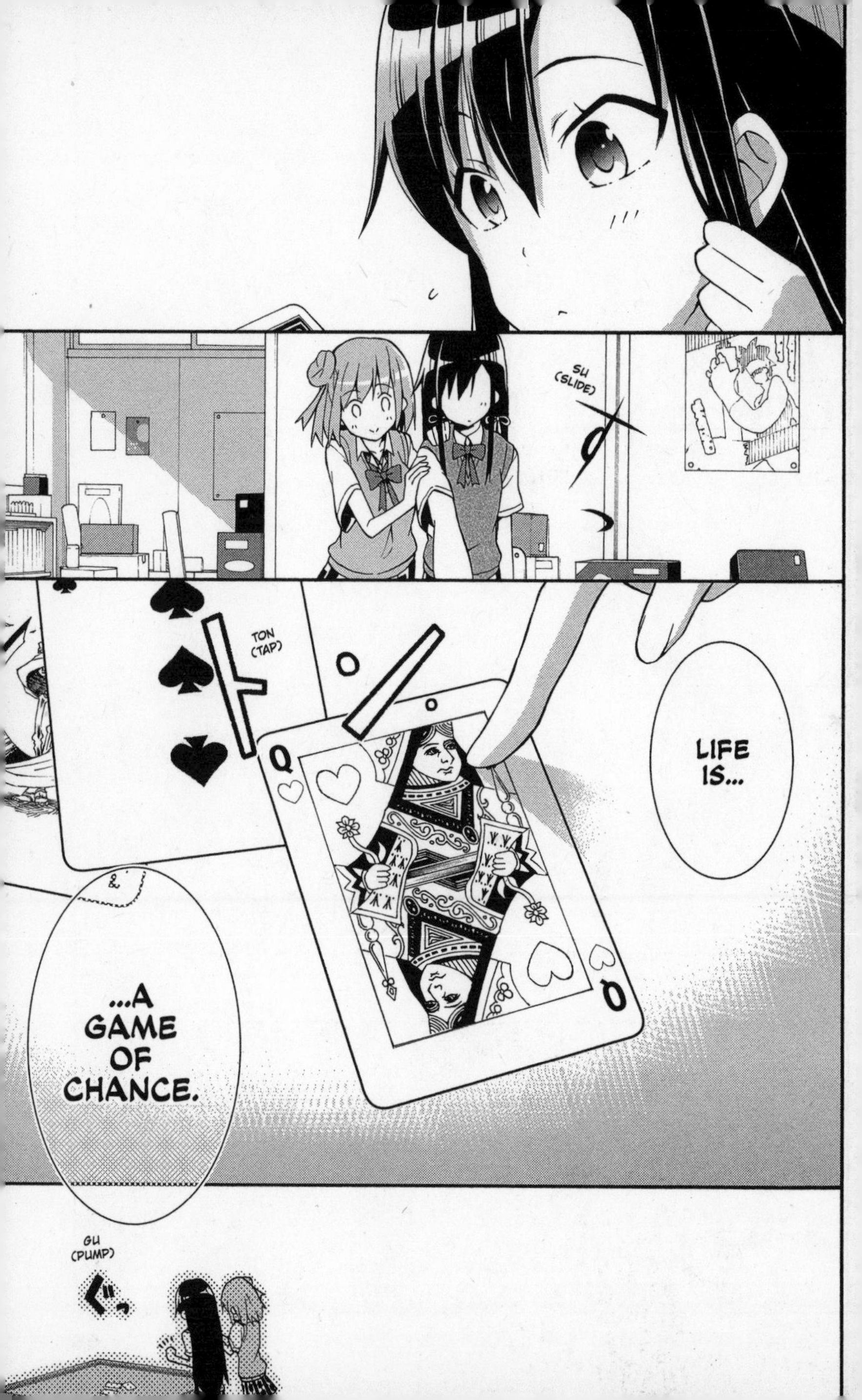
SU (SLIDE)
TON (TAP)
LIFE IS...
...A GAME OF CHANCE.
GU (PUMP)

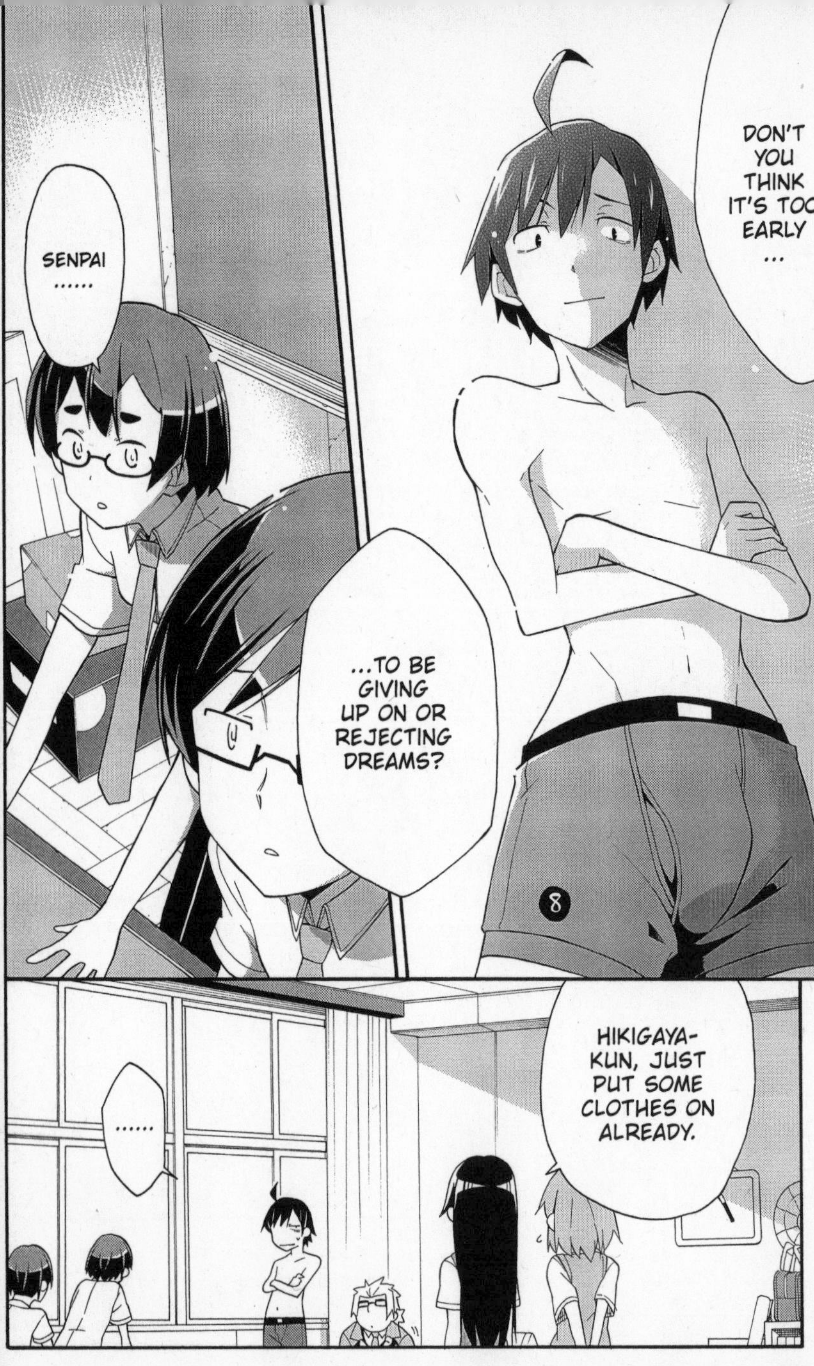
DON'T YOU THINK IT'S TOO EARLY ...
...TO BE GIVING UP ON OR REJECTING DREAMS?
SENPAI ......
HIKIGAYA-KUN, JUST PUT SOME CLOTHES ON ALREADY.
......

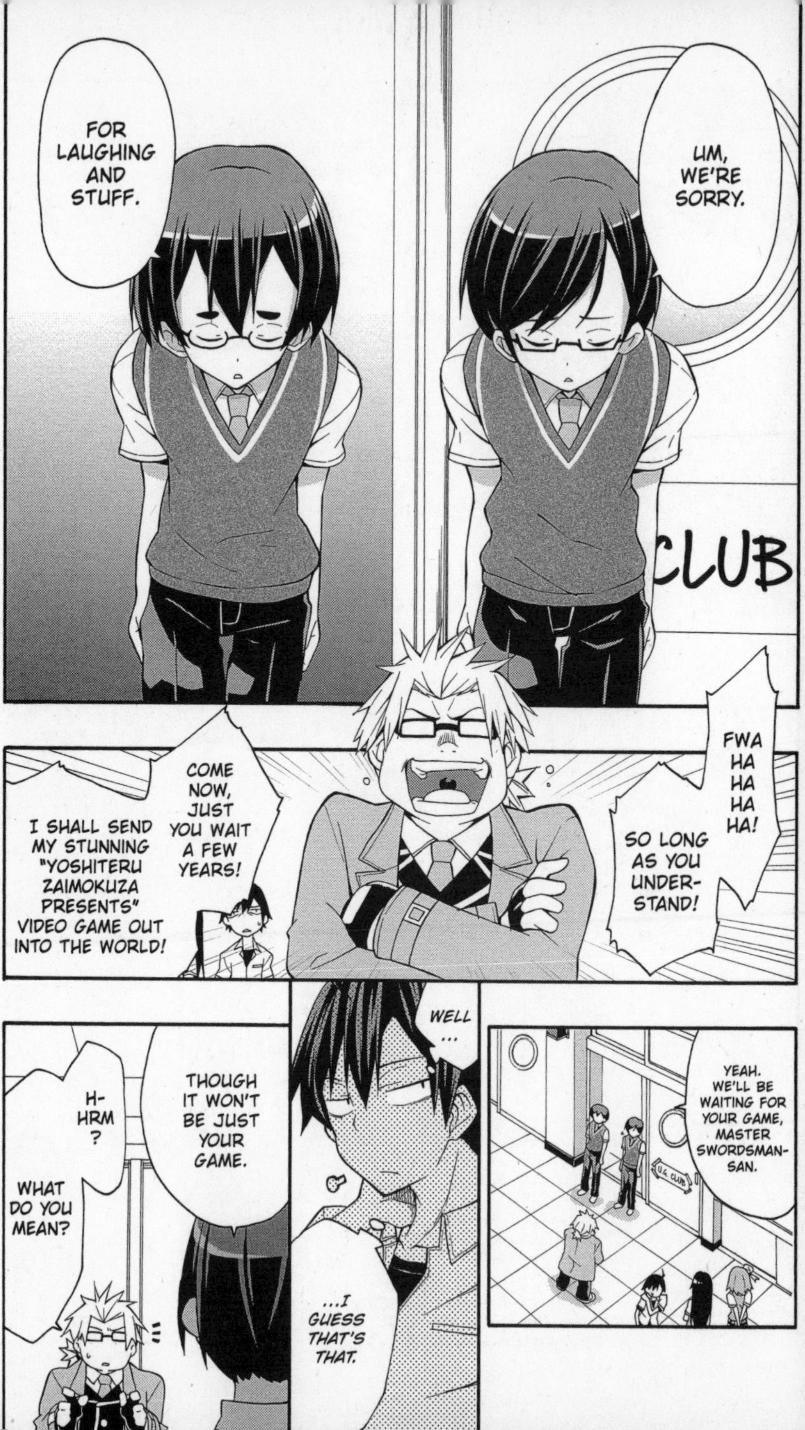
UM, WE'RE SORRY.
CLUB
FOR LAUGHING AND STUFF.
FWA HA HA HA HA!
SO LONG AS YOU UNDERSTAND!
COME NOW, JUST YOU WAIT A FEW YEARS!
I SHALL SEND MY STUNNING "YOSHITERU ZAIMOKUZA PRESENTS" VIDEO GAME OUT INTO THE WORLD!
YEAH. WE'LL BE WAITING FOR YOUR GAME, MASTER SWORDSMAN-SAN.
U.G. CLUB
WELL...
...I GUESS THAT'S THAT.
THOUGH IT WON'T BE JUST YOUR GAME.
H-HRM?
WHAT DO YOU MEAN?

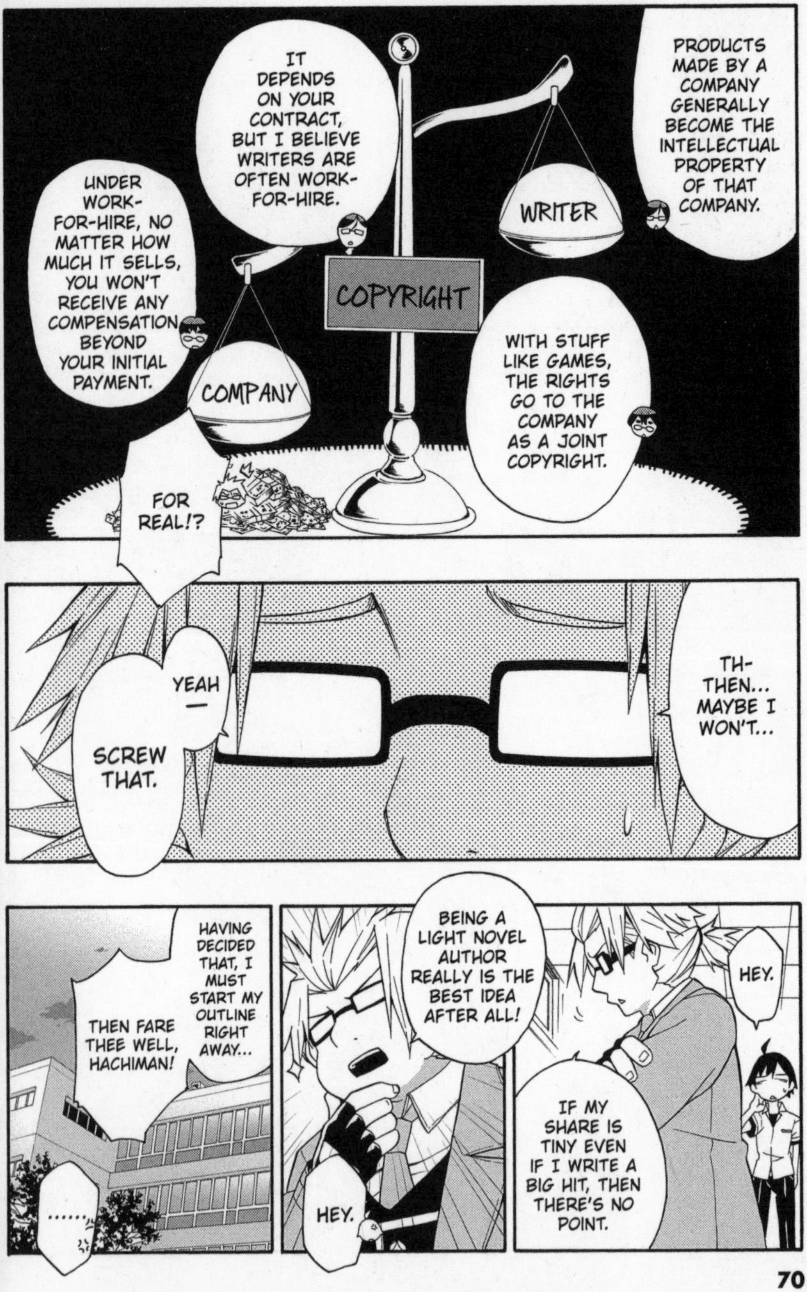
PRODUCTS MADE BY A COMPANY GENERALLY BECOME THE INTELLECTUAL PROPERTY OF THAT COMPANY.
WRITER
WITH STUFF LIKE GAMES, THE RIGHTS GO TO THE COMPANY AS A JOINT COPYRIGHT.
IT DEPENDS ON YOUR CONTRACT, BUT I BELIEVE WRITERS ARE OFTEN WORK-FOR-HIRE.
COPYRIGHT
UNDER WORK-FOR-HIRE, NO MATTER HOW MUCH IT SELLS, YOU WON'T RECEIVE ANY COMPENSATION BEYOND YOUR INITIAL PAYMENT.
COMPANY
FOR REAL!?
TH-THEN... MAYBE I WON'T...
YEAH — SCREW THAT.
HEY.
IF MY SHARE IS TINY EVEN IF I WRITE A BIG HIT, THEN THERE'S NO POINT.
BEING A LIGHT NOVEL AUTHOR REALLY IS THE BEST IDEA AFTER ALL!
HEY.
HAVING DECIDED THAT, I MUST START MY OUTLINE RIGHT AWAY...
THEN FARE THEE WELL, HACHIMAN!
......

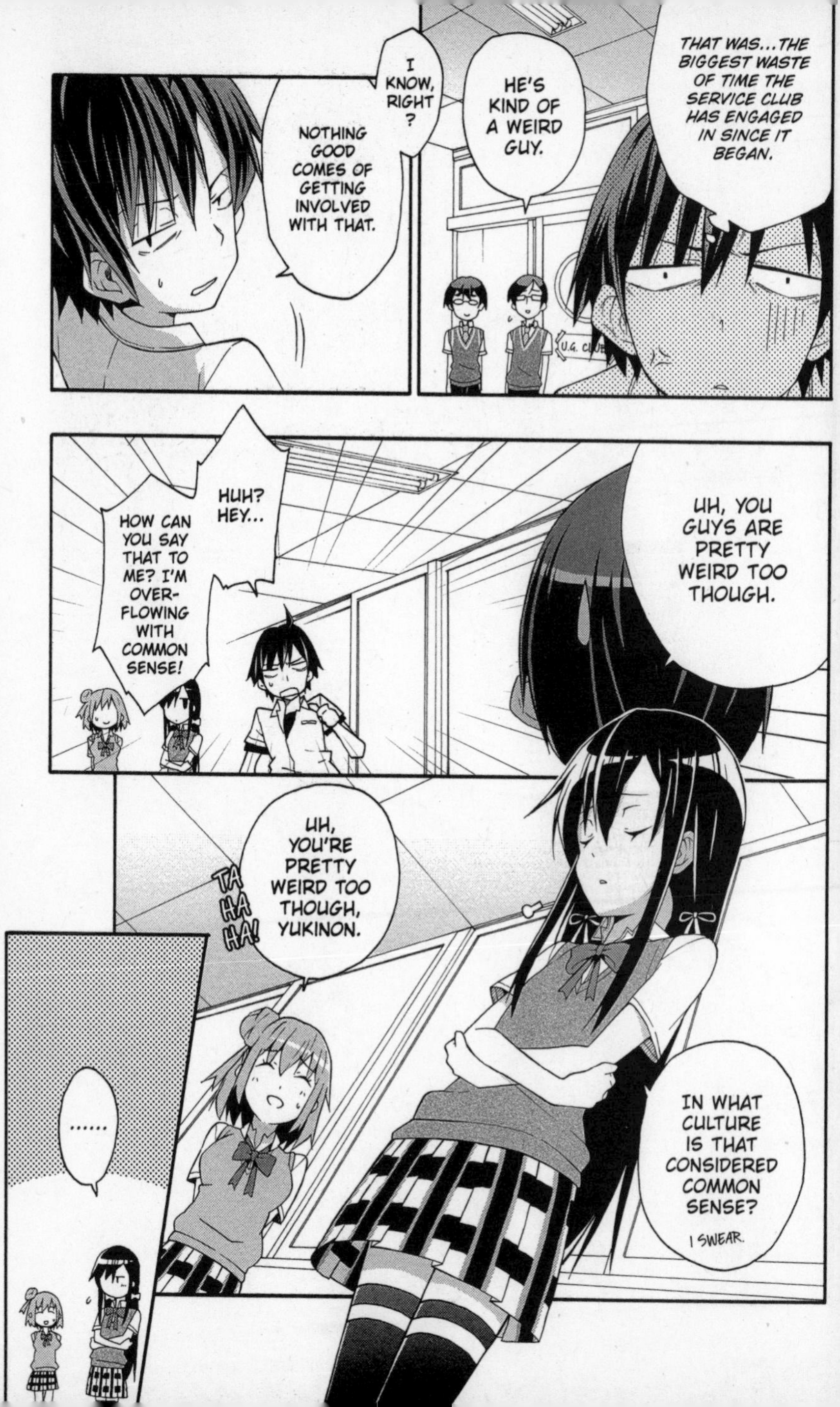
THAT WAS...THE BIGGEST WASTE OF TIME THE SERVICE CLUB HAS ENGAGED IN SINCE IT BEGAN.
HE'S KIND OF A WEIRD GUY.
U.G. CLUB
I KNOW, RIGHT?
NOTHING GOOD COMES OF GETTING INVOLVED WITH THAT.
UH, YOU GUYS ARE PRETTY WEIRD TOO THOUGH.
HUH? HEY...
HOW CAN YOU SAY THAT TO ME? I'M OVER-FLOWING WITH COMMON SENSE!
UH, YOU'RE PRETTY WEIRD TOO THOUGH, YUKINON.
TA HA HA!
IN WHAT CULTURE IS THAT CONSIDERED COMMON SENSE?
I SWEAR.
......

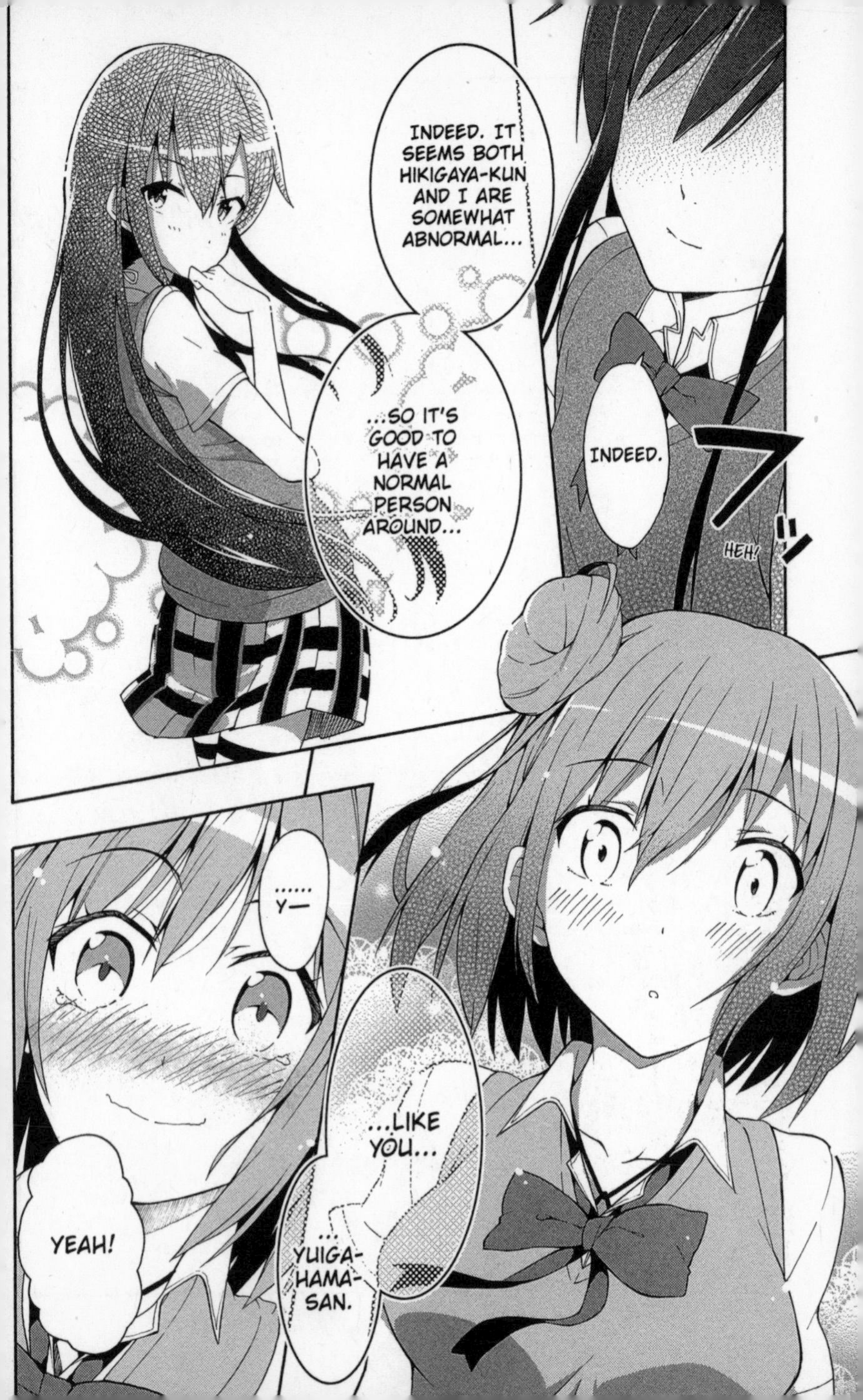

INDEED. IT SEEMS BOTH HIKIGAYA-KUN AND I ARE SOMEWHAT ABNORMAL...
...SO IT'S GOOD TO HAVE A NORMAL PERSON AROUND...
INDEED.
HEH!
...LIKE YOU...
...YUIGA-HAMA-SAN.
......Y—
YEAH!

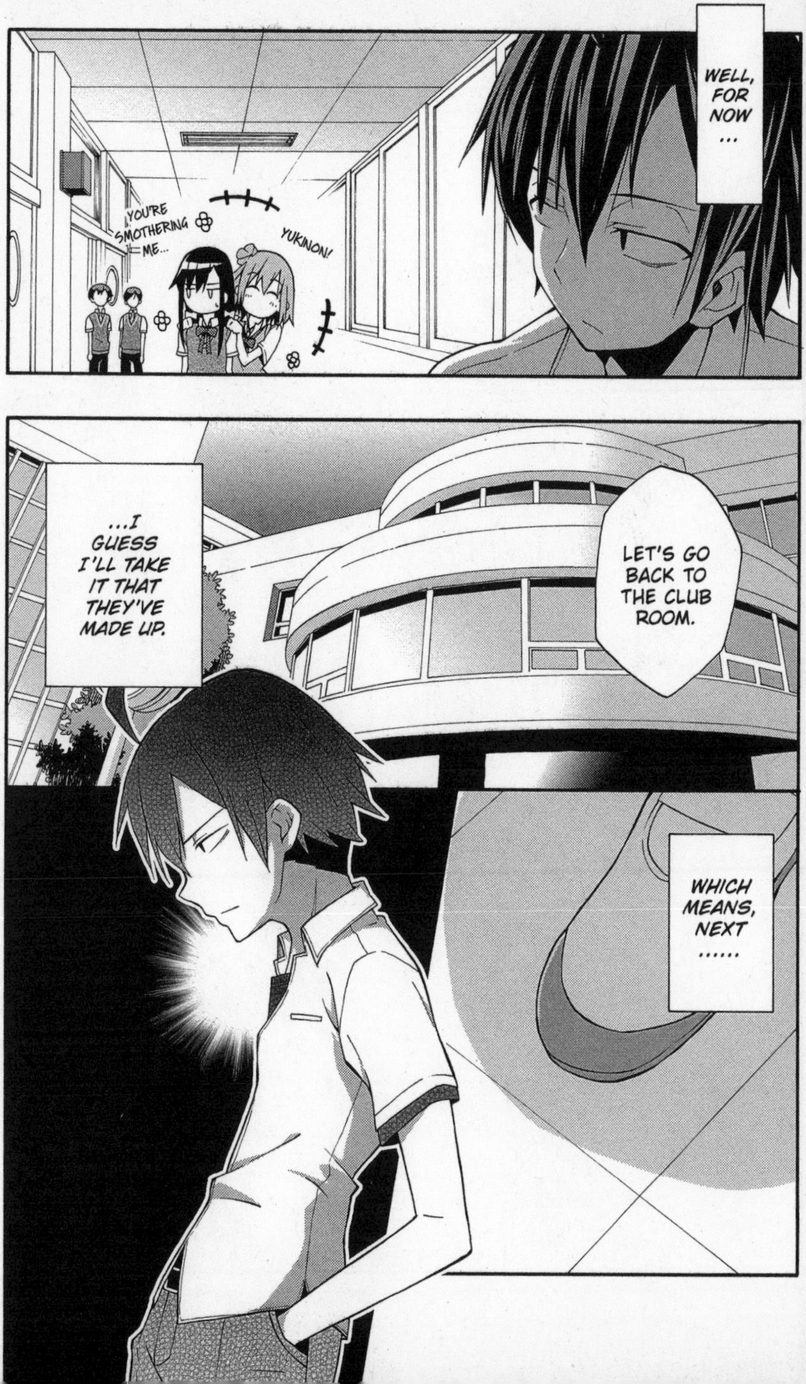
WELL, FOR NOW ...
YUKINON!
YOU'RE SMOTHERING ME...
LET'S GO BACK TO THE CLUB ROOM.
...I GUESS I'LL TAKE IT THAT THEY'VE MADE UP.
WHICH MEANS, NEXT ......

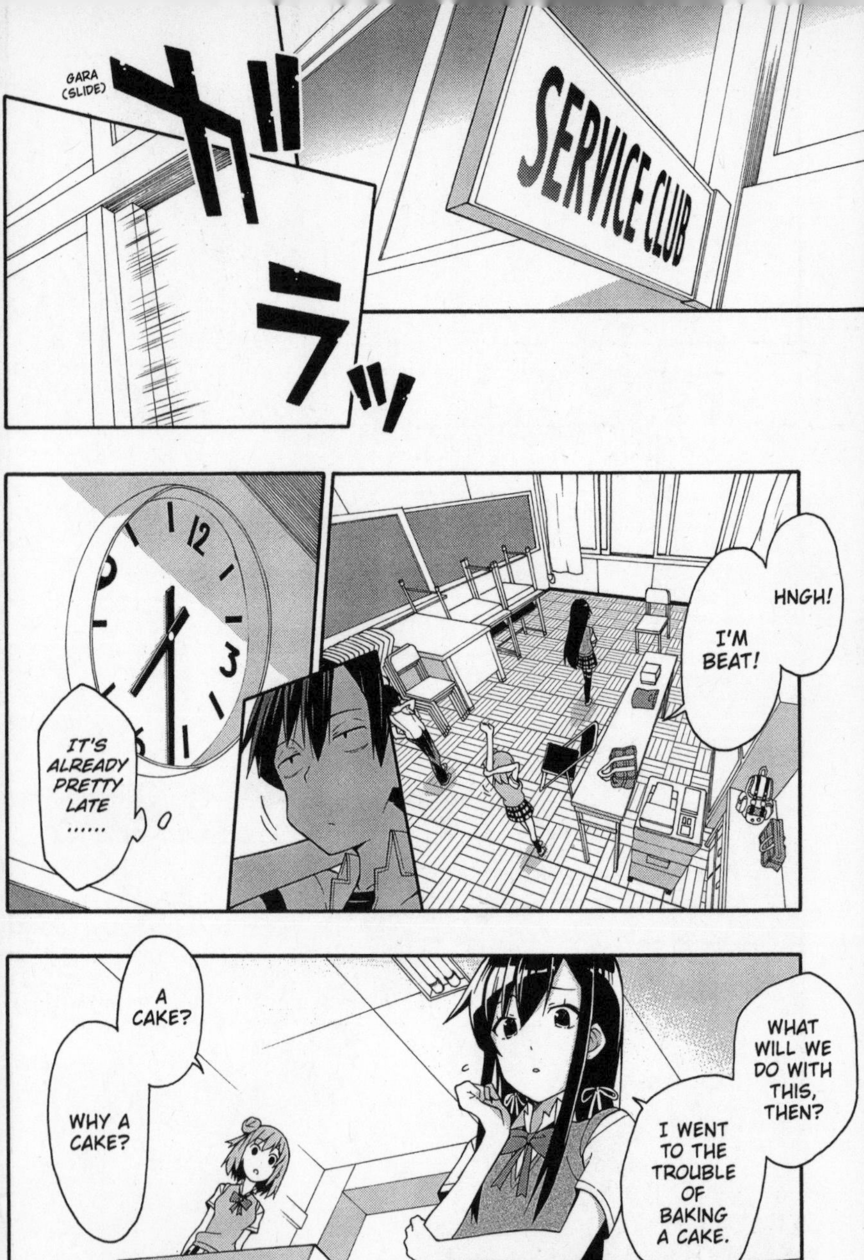
SERVICE CLUB
GARA (SLIDE)
HNGH!
I'M BEAT!
IT'S ALREADY PRETTY LATE......
WHAT WILL WE DO WITH THIS, THEN?
I WENT TO THE TROUBLE OF BAKING A CAKE.
A CAKE?
WHY A CAKE?

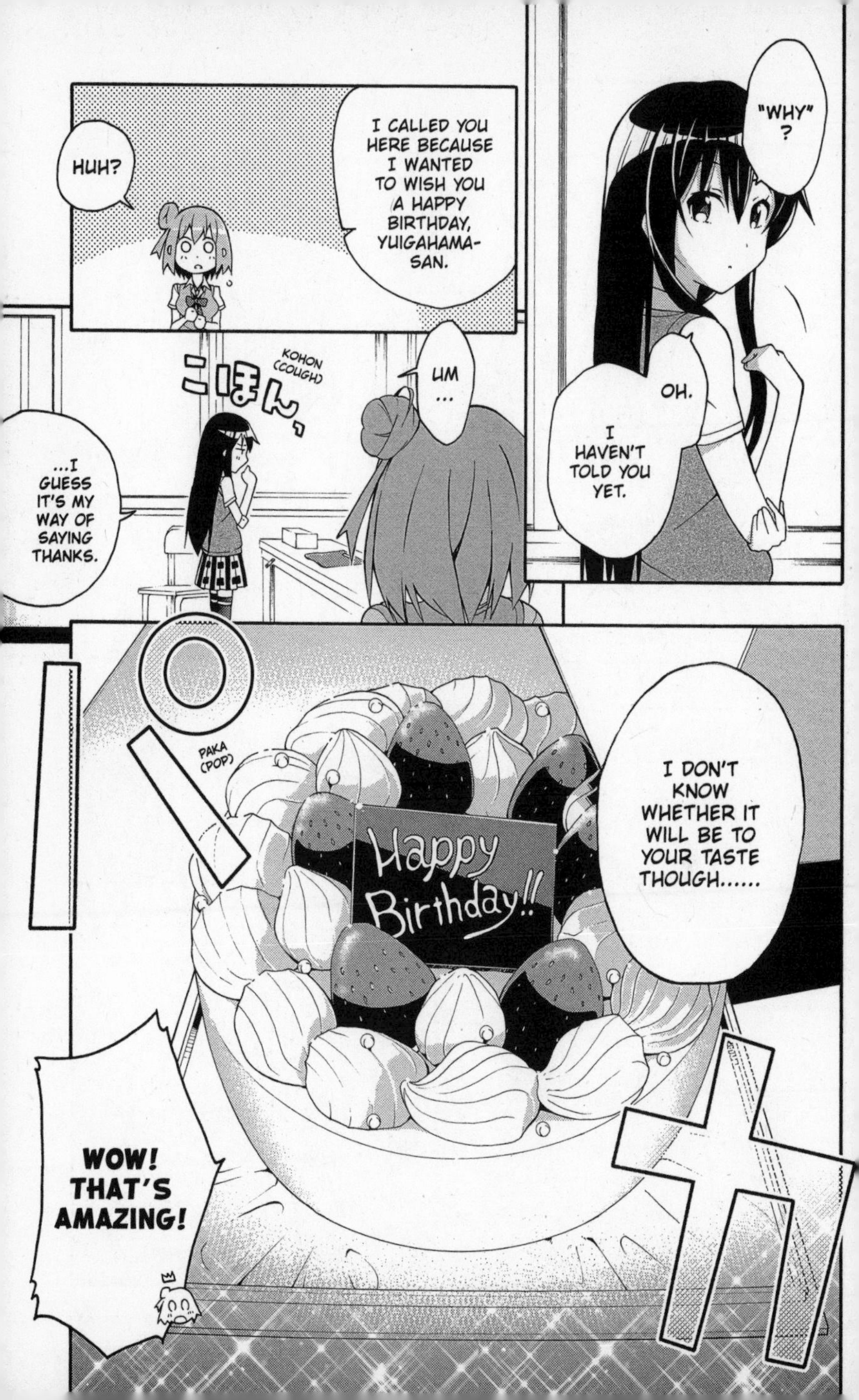
"WHY"?
OH.
I HAVEN'T TOLD YOU YET.
I CALLED YOU HERE BECAUSE I WANTED TO WISH YOU A HAPPY BIRTHDAY, YUIGAHAMA-SAN.
HUH?
UM ...
こほん、
KOHON (COUGH)
...I GUESS IT'S MY WAY OF SAYING THANKS.
I DON'T KNOW WHETHER IT WILL BE TO YOUR TASTE THOUGH......
PAKA (POP)
Happy Birthday!!
WOW! THAT'S AMAZING!

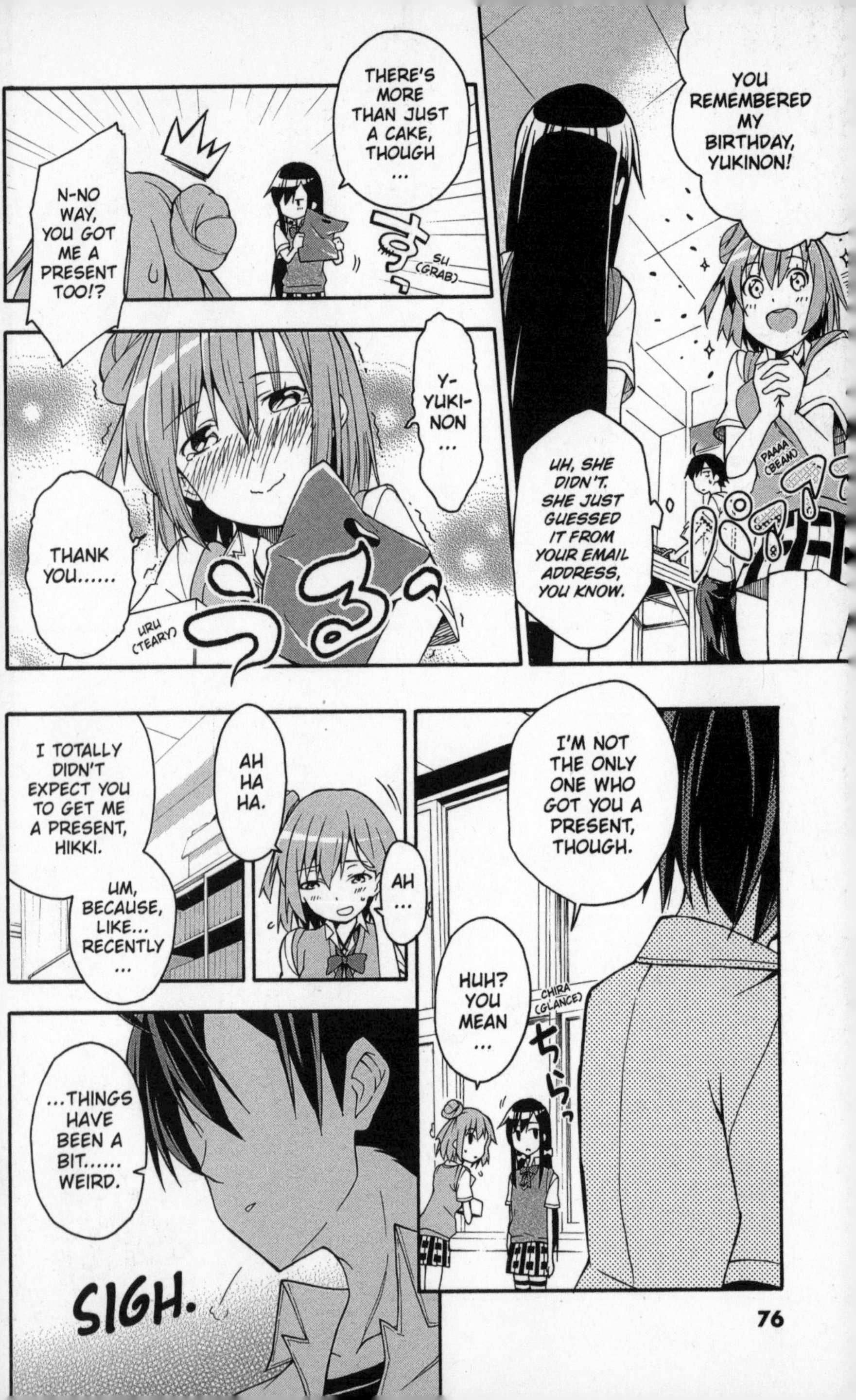
YOU REMEMBERED MY BIRTHDAY, YUKINON!
PAAAA (BEAM)
UH, SHE DIDN'T. SHE JUST GUESSED IT FROM YOUR EMAIL ADDRESS, YOU KNOW.
THERE'S MORE THAN JUST A CAKE, THOUGH ...
SU (GRAB)
N-NO WAY, YOU GOT ME A PRESENT TOO!?
Y-YUKI-NON ...
THANK YOU......
URU (TEARY)
I'M NOT THE ONLY ONE WHO GOT YOU A PRESENT, THOUGH.
HUH? YOU MEAN ...
CHIRA (GLANCE)
AH HA HA.
AH ...
I TOTALLY DIDN'T EXPECT YOU TO GET ME A PRESENT, HIKKI.
UM, BECAUSE, LIKE... RECENTLY ...
...THINGS HAVE BEEN A BIT...... WEIRD.
SIGH.

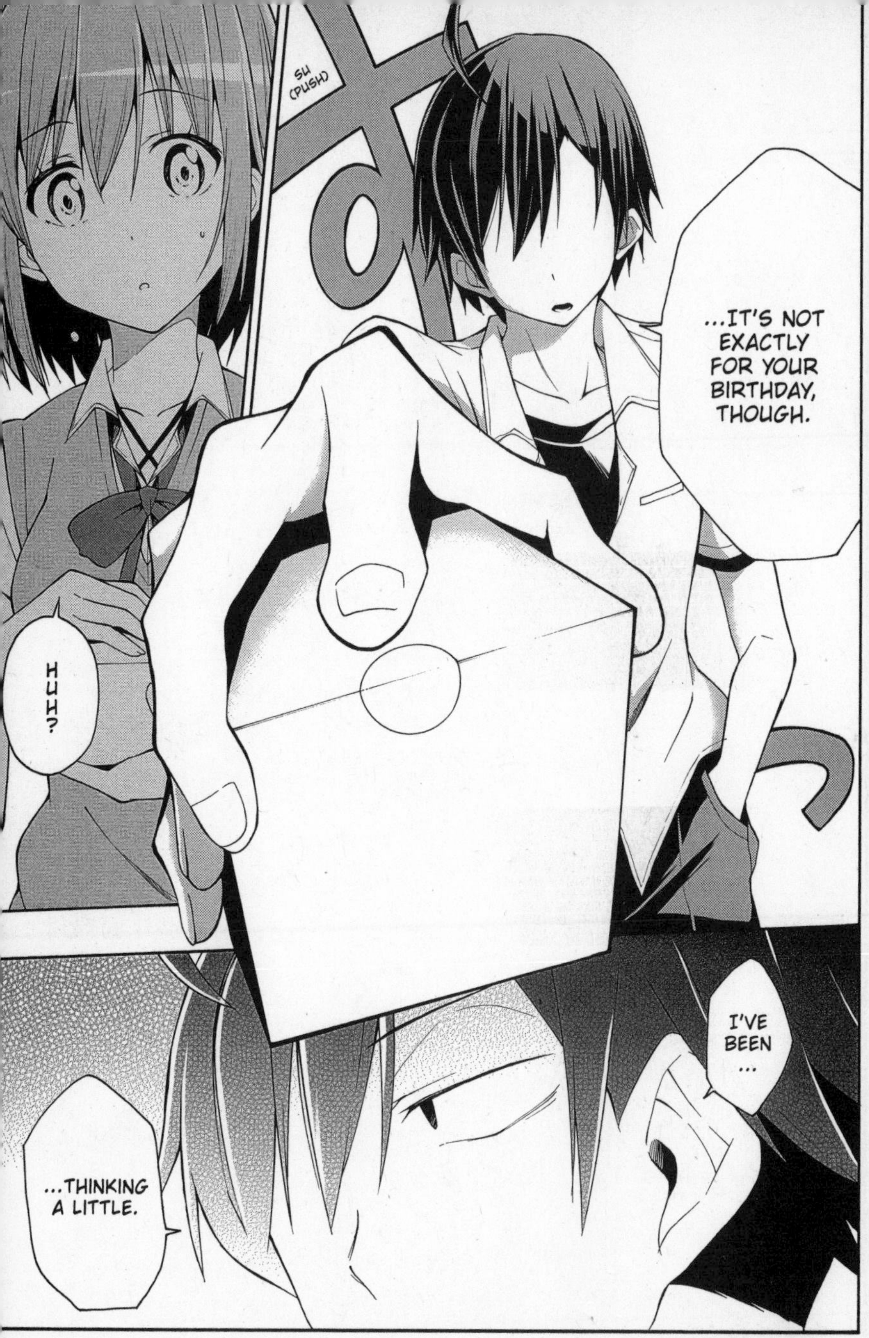
SU (PUSH)
...IT'S NOT EXACTLY FOR YOUR BIRTHDAY, THOUGH.
HUH?
I'VE BEEN ...
...THINKING A LITTLE.

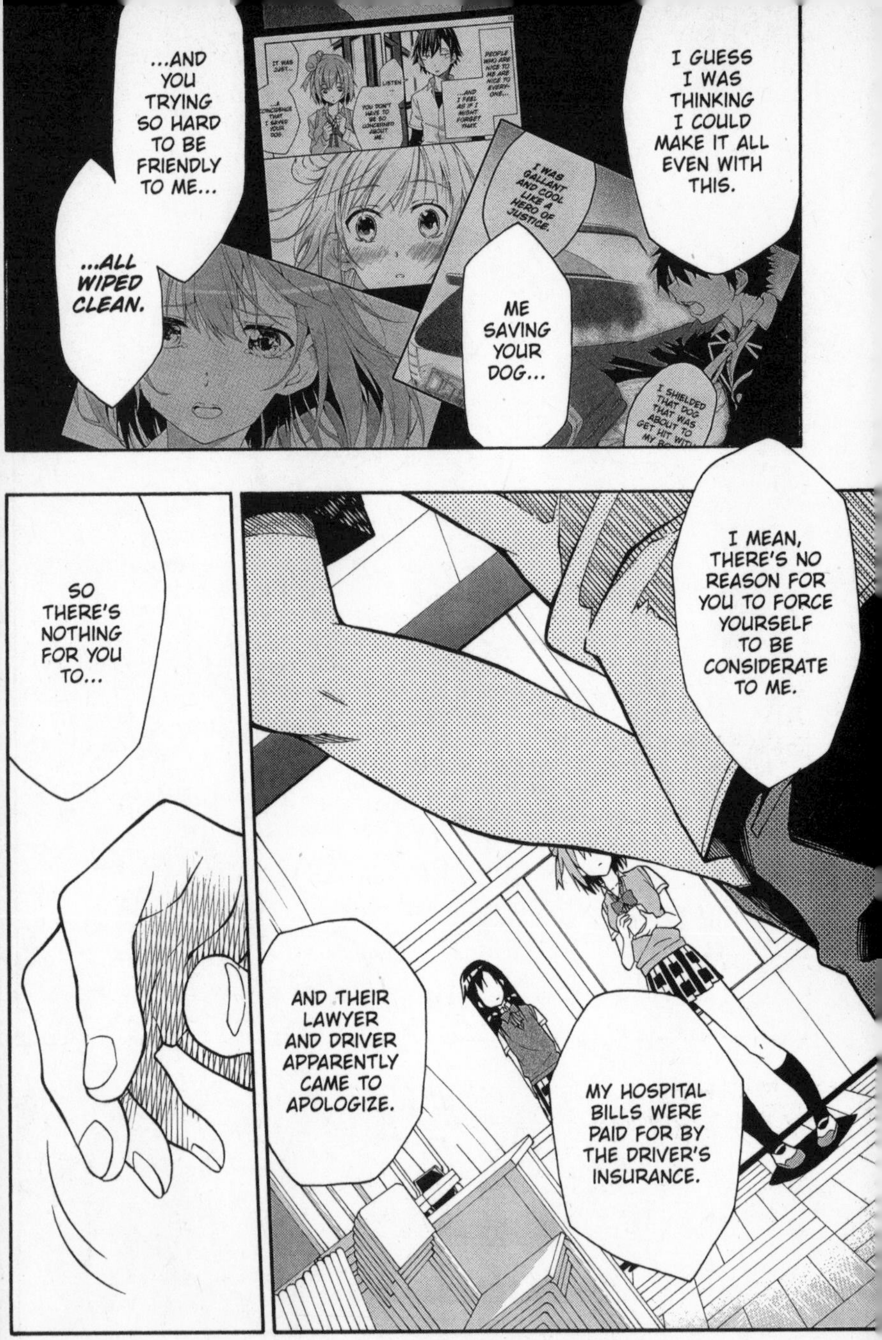
I GUESS I WAS THINKING I COULD MAKE IT ALL EVEN WITH THIS.
PEOPLE WHO ARE NICE TO ME ARE NICE TO EVERYONE...
...AND I FEEL AS IF I MIGHT FORGET THAT.
LISTEN...
YOU DON'T HAVE TO BE SO CONCERNED ABOUT ME.
IT WAS JUST...
...A COINCIDENCE THAT I SAVED YOUR DOG.
I WAS GALLANT AND COOL LIKE A HERO OF JUSTICE.
I SHIELDED THAT DOG THAT WAS ABOUT TO GET HIT WITH MY
ME SAVING YOUR DOG...
...AND YOU TRYING SO HARD TO BE FRIENDLY TO ME...
...ALL WIPED CLEAN.
I MEAN, THERE'S NO REASON FOR YOU TO FORCE YOURSELF TO BE CONSIDERATE TO ME.
MY HOSPITAL BILLS WERE PAID FOR BY THE DRIVER'S INSURANCE.
AND THEIR LAWYER AND DRIVER APPARENTLY CAME TO APOLOGIZE.
SO THERE'S NOTHING FOR YOU TO...

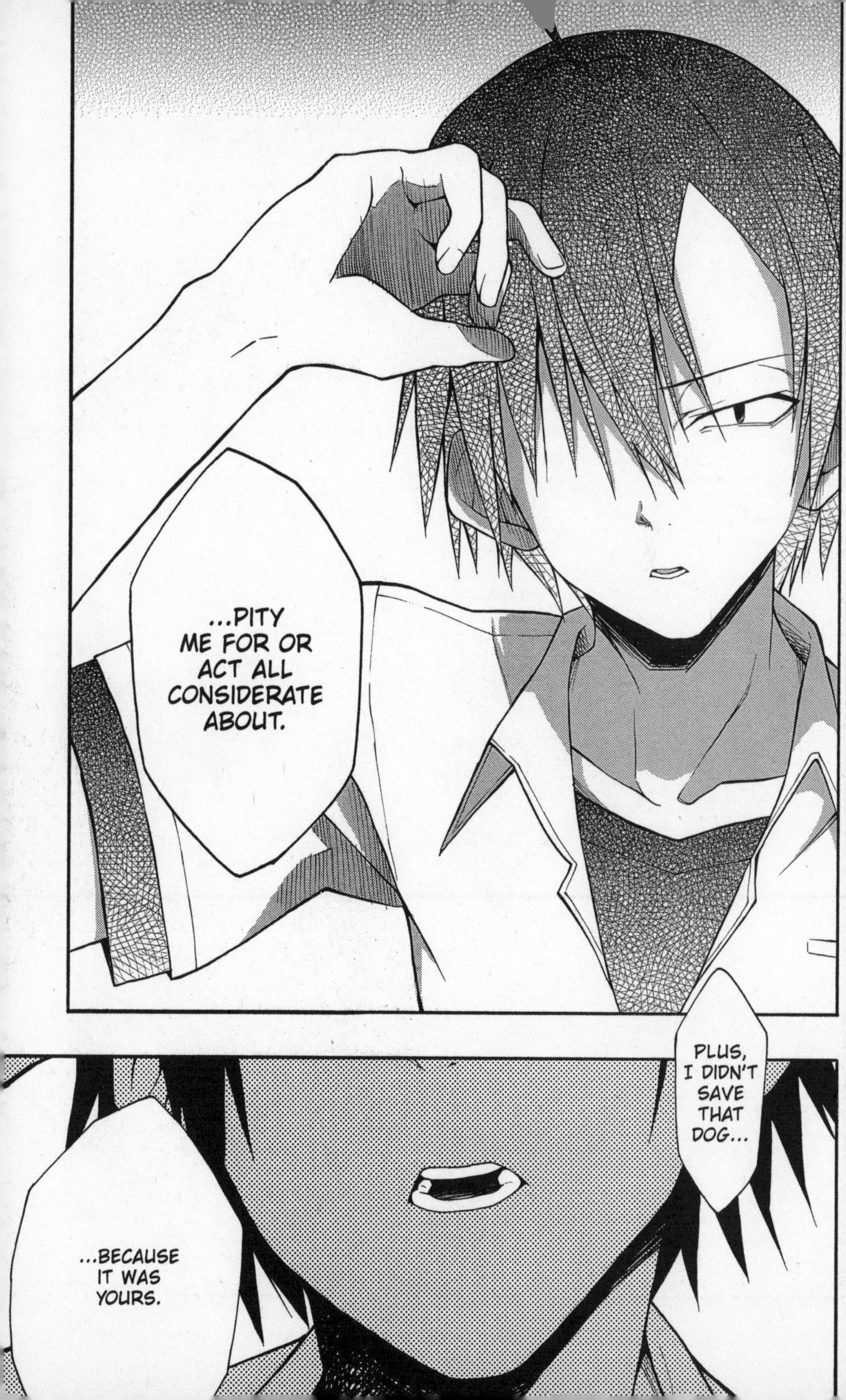
...PITY ME FOR OR ACT ALL CONSIDERATE ABOUT.
PLUS, I DIDN'T SAVE THAT DOG...
...BECAUSE IT WAS YOURS.

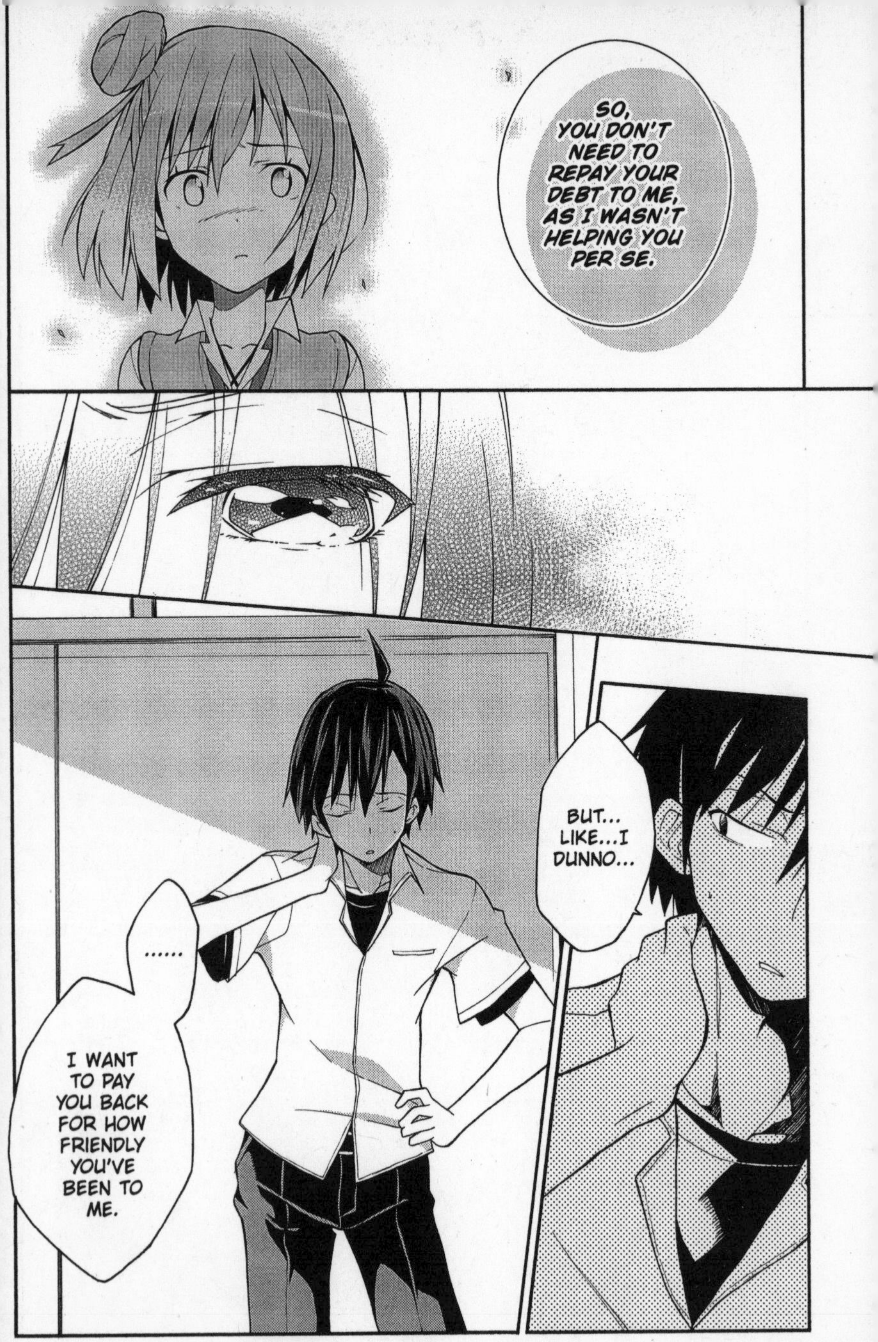
SO, YOU DON'T NEED TO REPAY YOUR DEBT TO ME, AS I WASN'T HELPING YOU PER SE.
BUT... LIKE...I DUNNO...
......
I WANT TO PAY YOU BACK FOR HOW FRIENDLY YOU'VE BEEN TO ME.

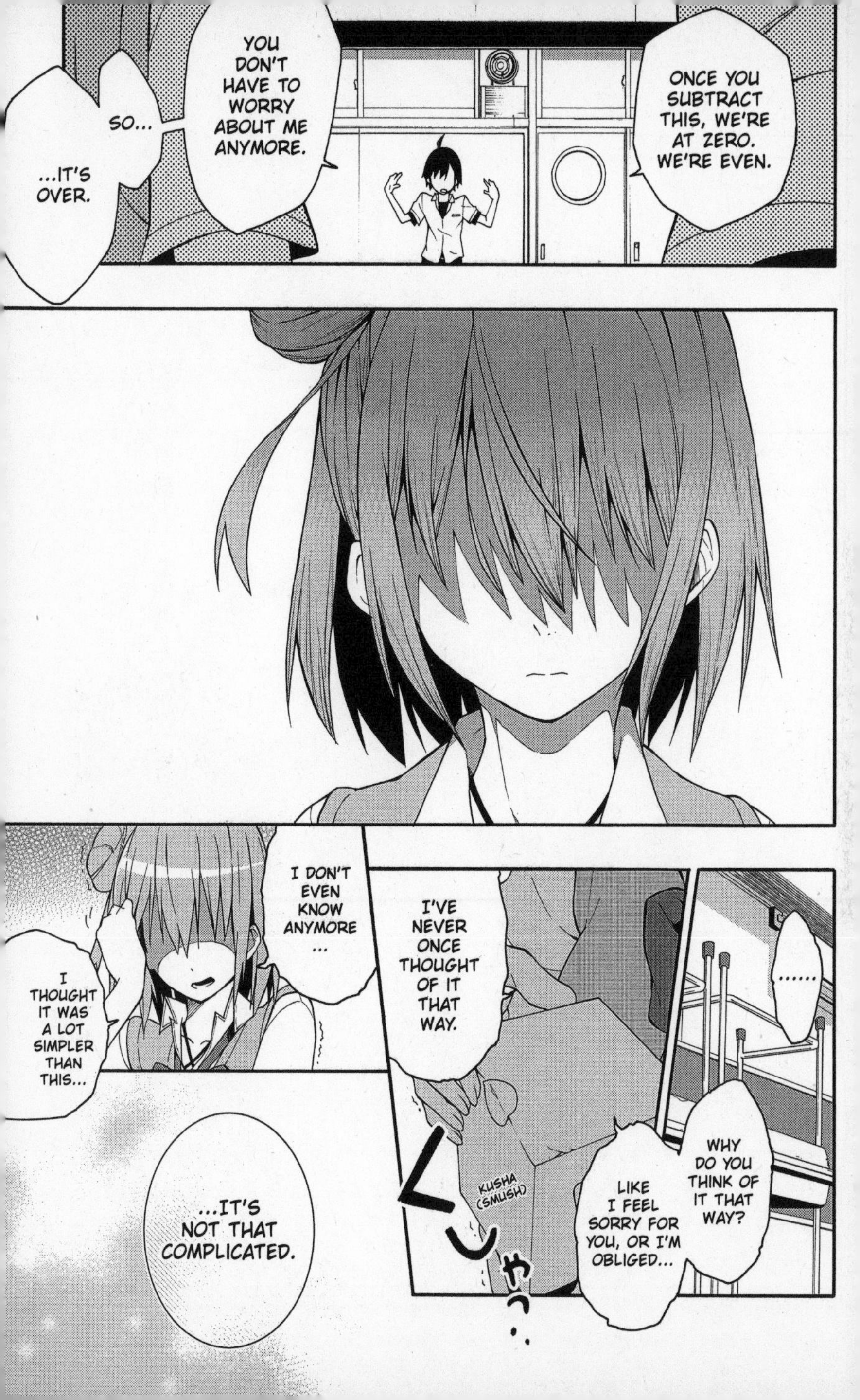
ONCE YOU SUBTRACT THIS, WE'RE AT ZERO. WE'RE EVEN.
YOU DON'T HAVE TO WORRY ABOUT ME ANYMORE.
SO...
...IT'S OVER.
......
WHY DO YOU THINK OF IT THAT WAY?
LIKE I FEEL SORRY FOR YOU, OR I'M OBLIGED...
I'VE NEVER ONCE THOUGHT OF IT THAT WAY.
KUSHA (SMUSH)
くしゃっ..
I DON'T EVEN KNOW ANYMORE...
I THOUGHT IT WAS A LOT SIMPLER THAN THIS...
...IT'S NOT THAT COMPLICATED.

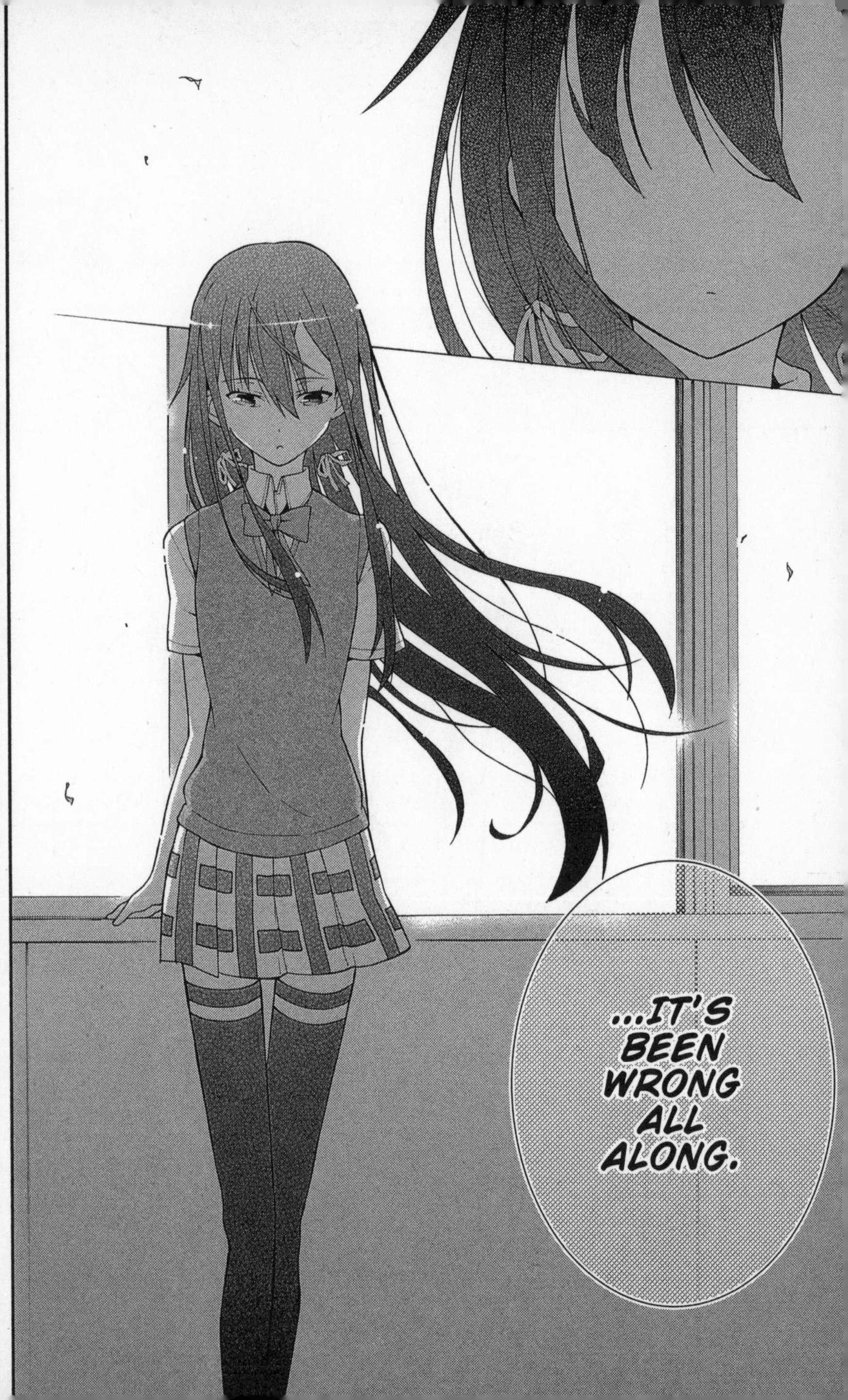
...IT'S BEEN WRONG ALL ALONG.

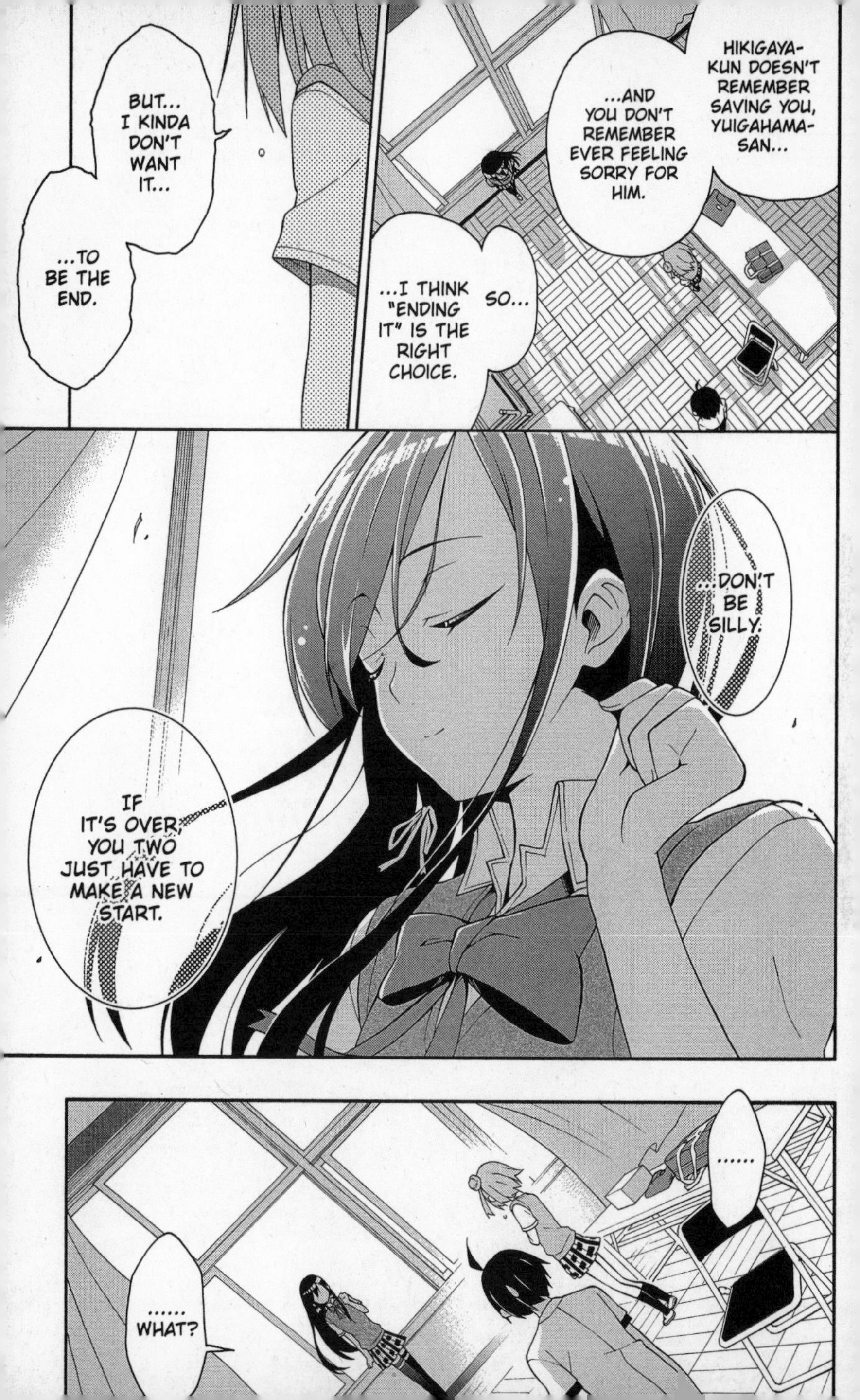
HIKIGAYA-KUN DOESN'T REMEMBER SAVING YOU, YUIGAHAMA-SAN...
...AND YOU DON'T REMEMBER EVER FEELING SORRY FOR HIM.
SO...
...I THINK "ENDING IT" IS THE RIGHT CHOICE.
BUT... I KINDA DON'T WANT IT...
...TO BE THE END.
...DON'T BE SILLY.
IF IT'S OVER, YOU TWO JUST HAVE TO MAKE A NEW START.
......
......WHAT?

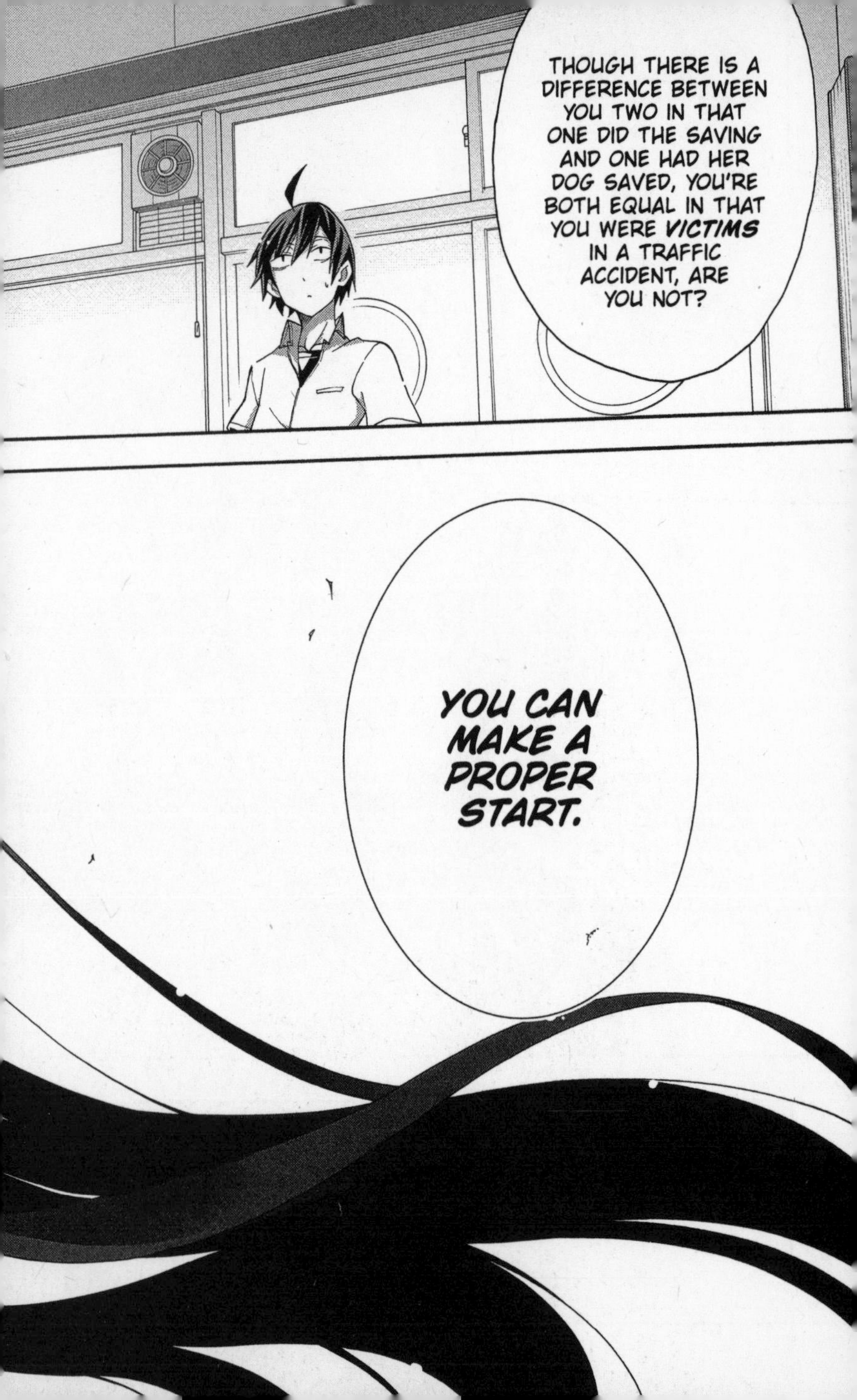
THOUGH THERE IS A DIFFERENCE BETWEEN YOU TWO IN THAT ONE DID THE SAVING AND ONE HAD HER DOG SAVED, YOU'RE BOTH EQUAL IN THAT YOU WERE *VICTIMS* IN A TRAFFIC ACCIDENT, ARE YOU NOT?
YOU CAN MAKE A PROPER START.

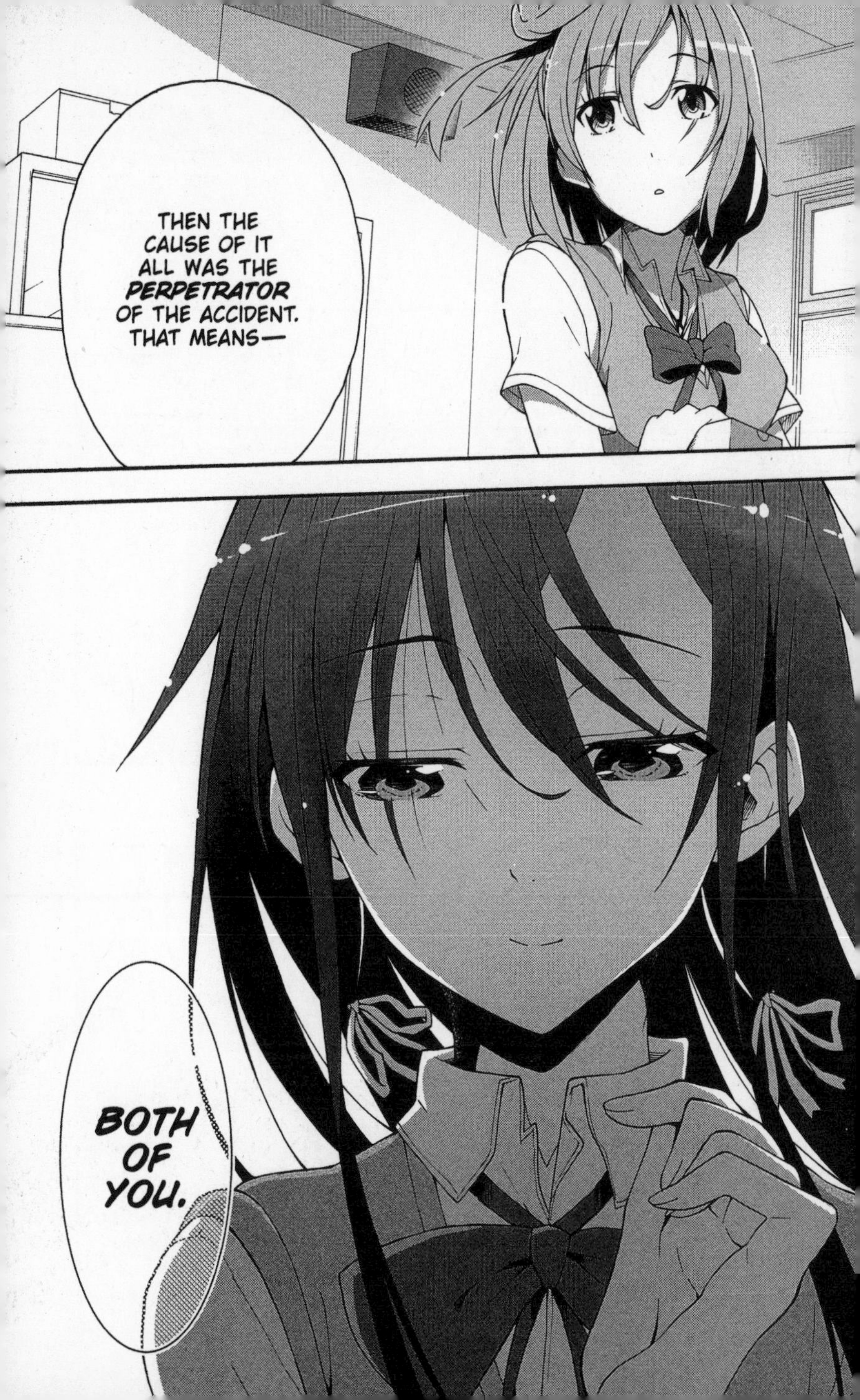
THEN THE CAUSE OF IT ALL WAS THE PERPETRATOR OF THE ACCIDENT. THAT MEANS—
BOTH OF YOU.

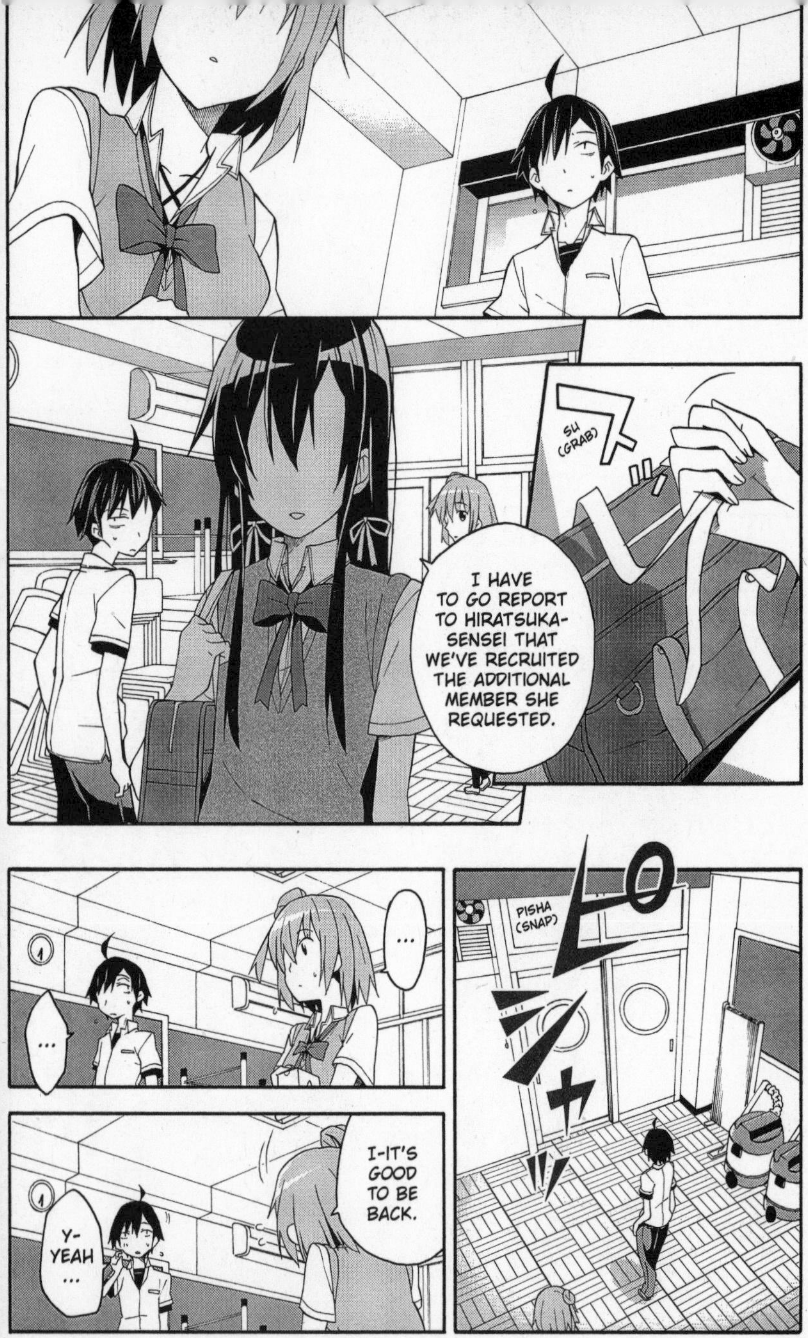
SU (GRAB)
I HAVE TO GO REPORT TO HIRATSUKA-SENSEI THAT WE'VE RECRUITED THE ADDITIONAL MEMBER SHE REQUESTED.
PISHA (SNAP)
...
...
I-IT'S GOOD TO BE BACK.
Y-YEAH ...

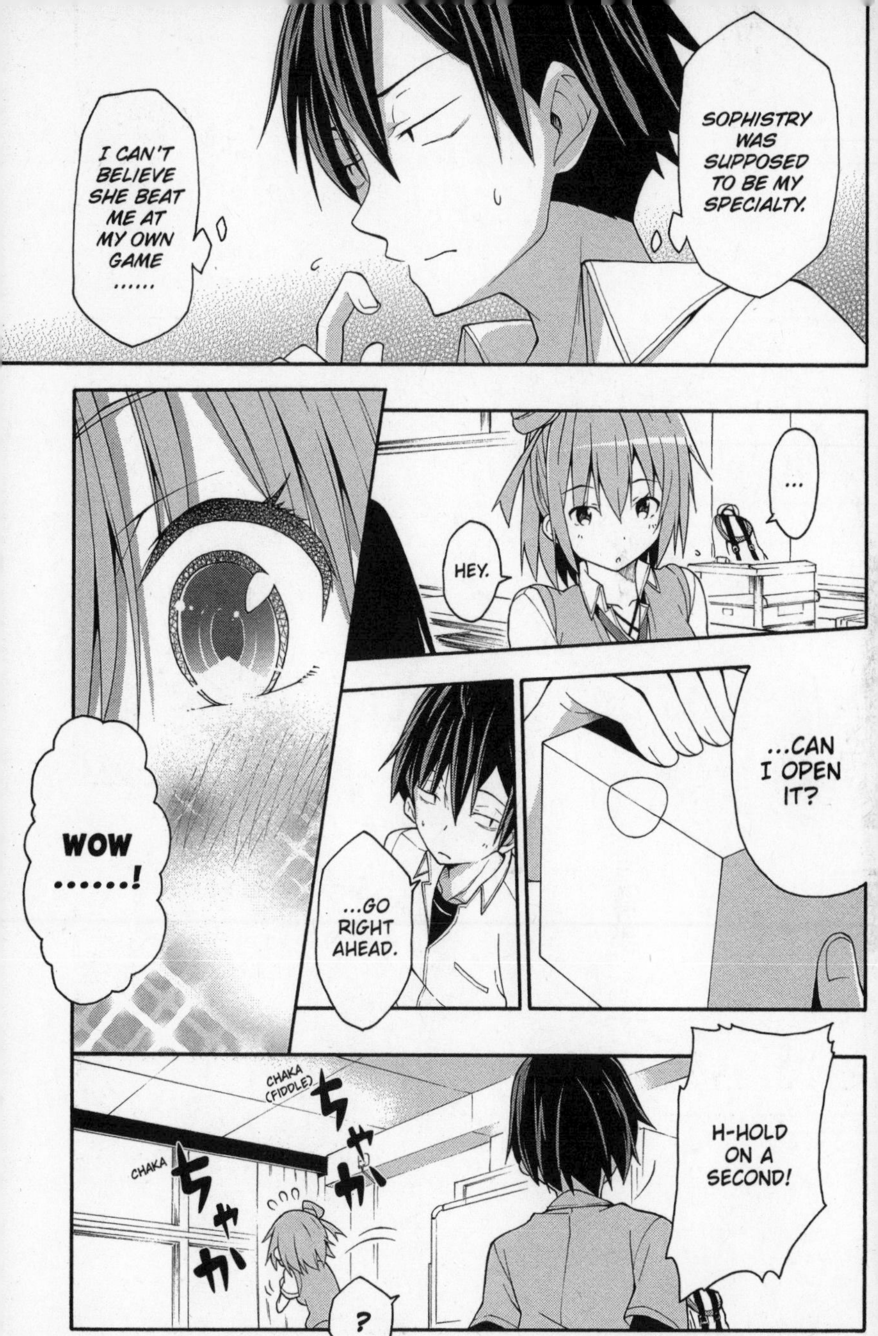
SOPHISTRY WAS SUPPOSED TO BE MY SPECIALTY.
I CAN'T BELIEVE SHE BEAT ME AT MY OWN GAME ......
...
HEY.
...CAN I OPEN IT?
...GO RIGHT AHEAD.
WOW ......!
H-HOLD ON A SECOND!
ちゃか
CHAKA (FIDDLE)
ちゃか
CHAKA
?

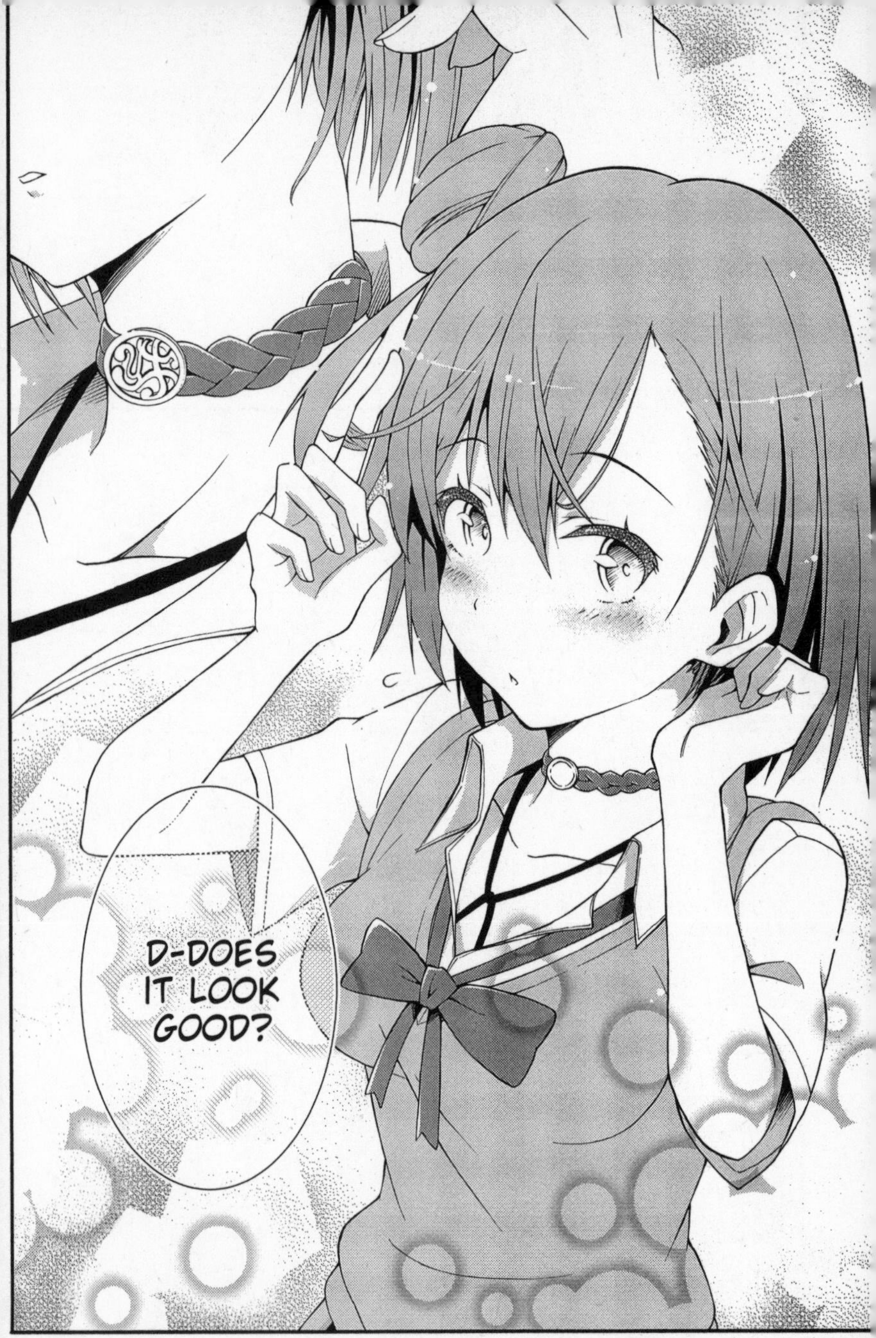
D-DOES IT LOOK GOOD?

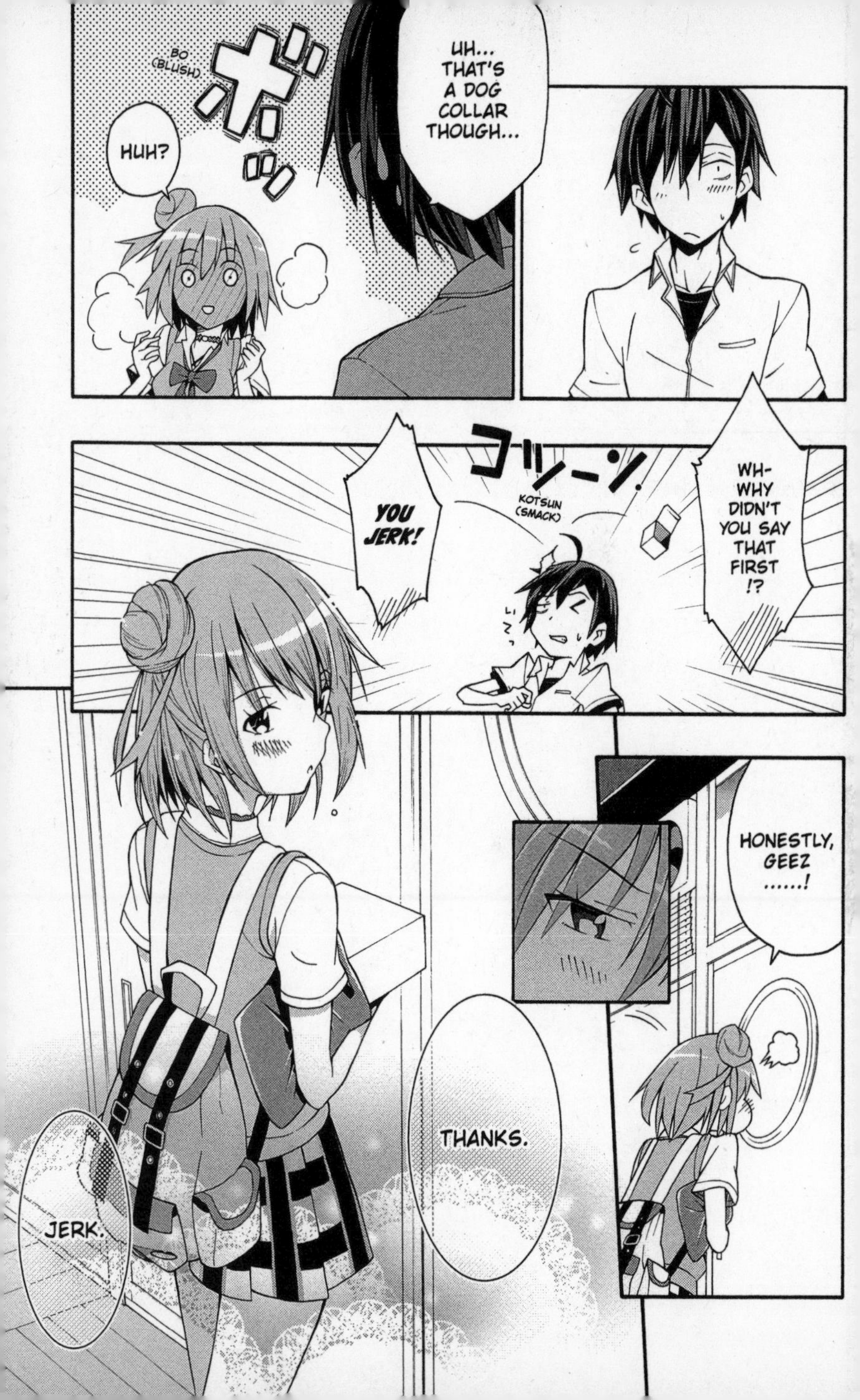
UH... THAT'S A DOG COLLAR THOUGH...
BO (BLUSH)
HUH?
WH- WHY DIDN'T YOU SAY THAT FIRST!?
KOTSUN (SMACK)
YOU JERK!
HONESTLY, GEEZ ......!
THANKS.
JERK.

YUKINOSHITA
SAID, "IF IT'S
OVER, YOU
JUST HAVE TO
MAKE A NEW
START."

CRUMPLE

SNAP

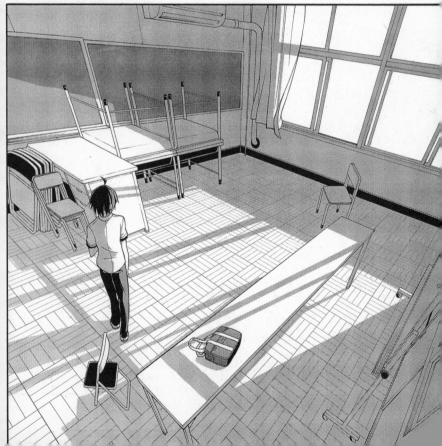

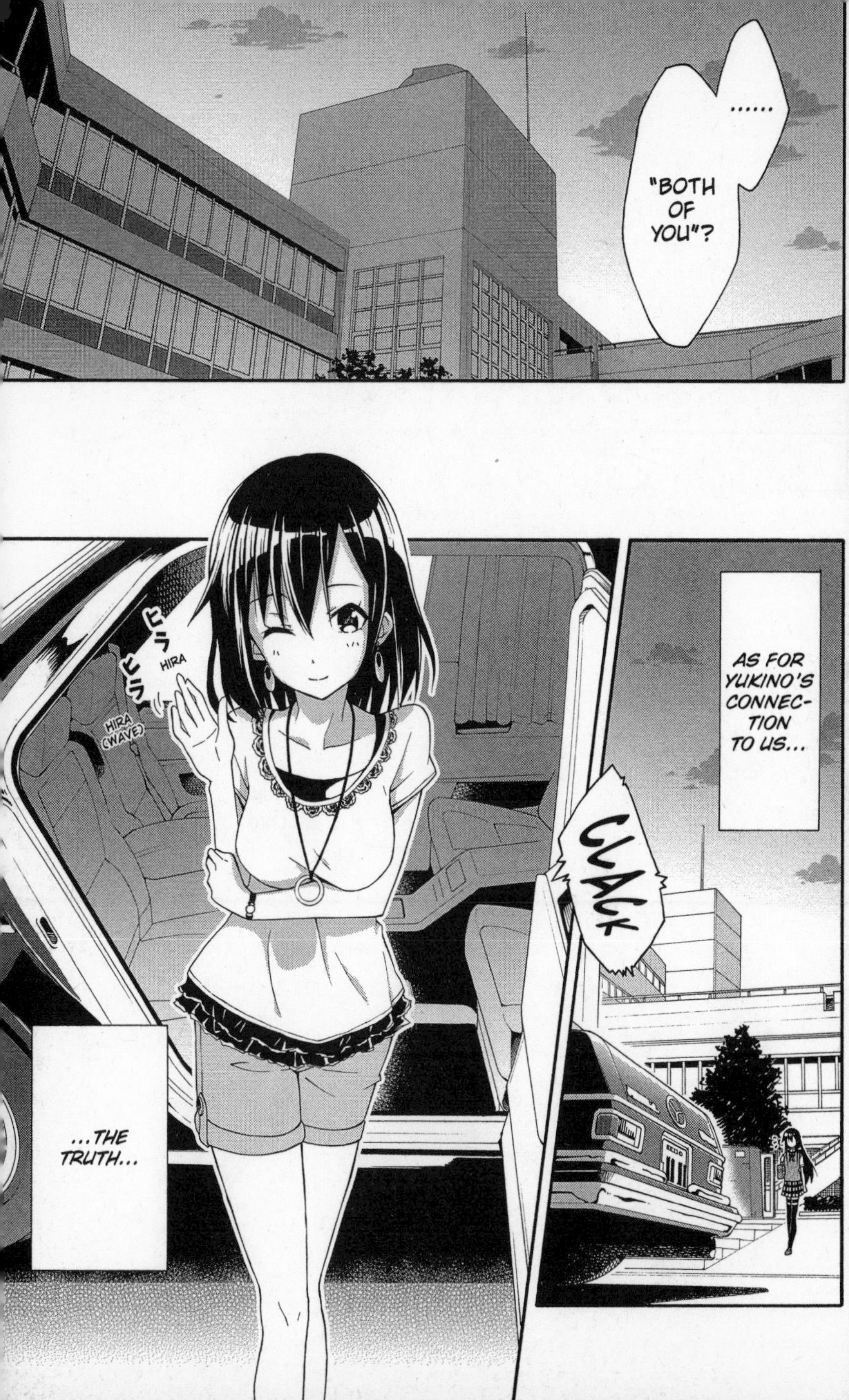
......
"BOTH OF YOU"?
AS FOR YUKINO'S CONNECTION TO US...
CLACK
ヒラ HIRA
ヒラ HIRA (WAVE)
...THE TRUTH...

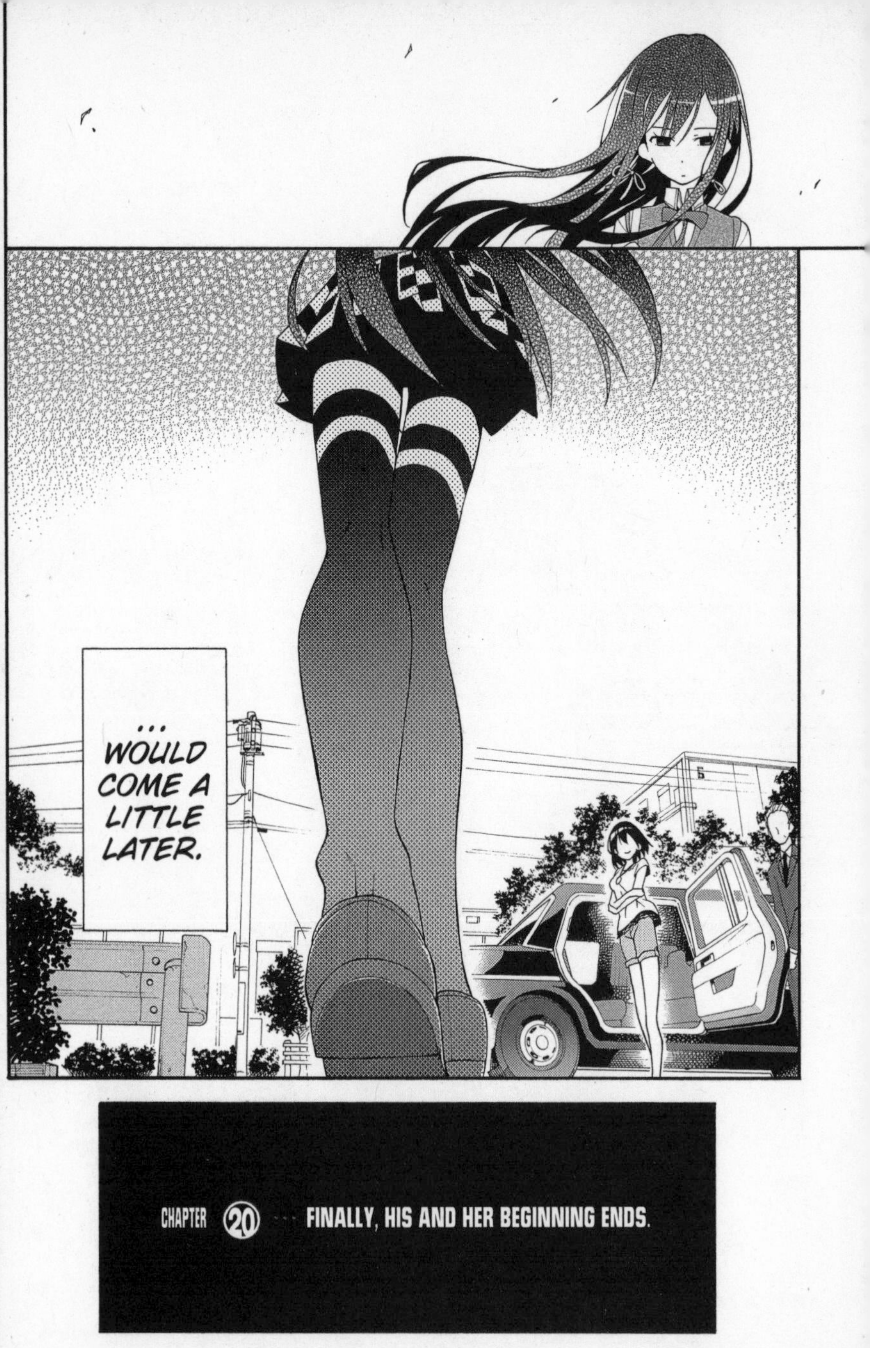
...WOULD COME A LITTLE LATER.

CHAPTER 20 ··· FINALLY, HIS AND HER BEGINNING ENDS.

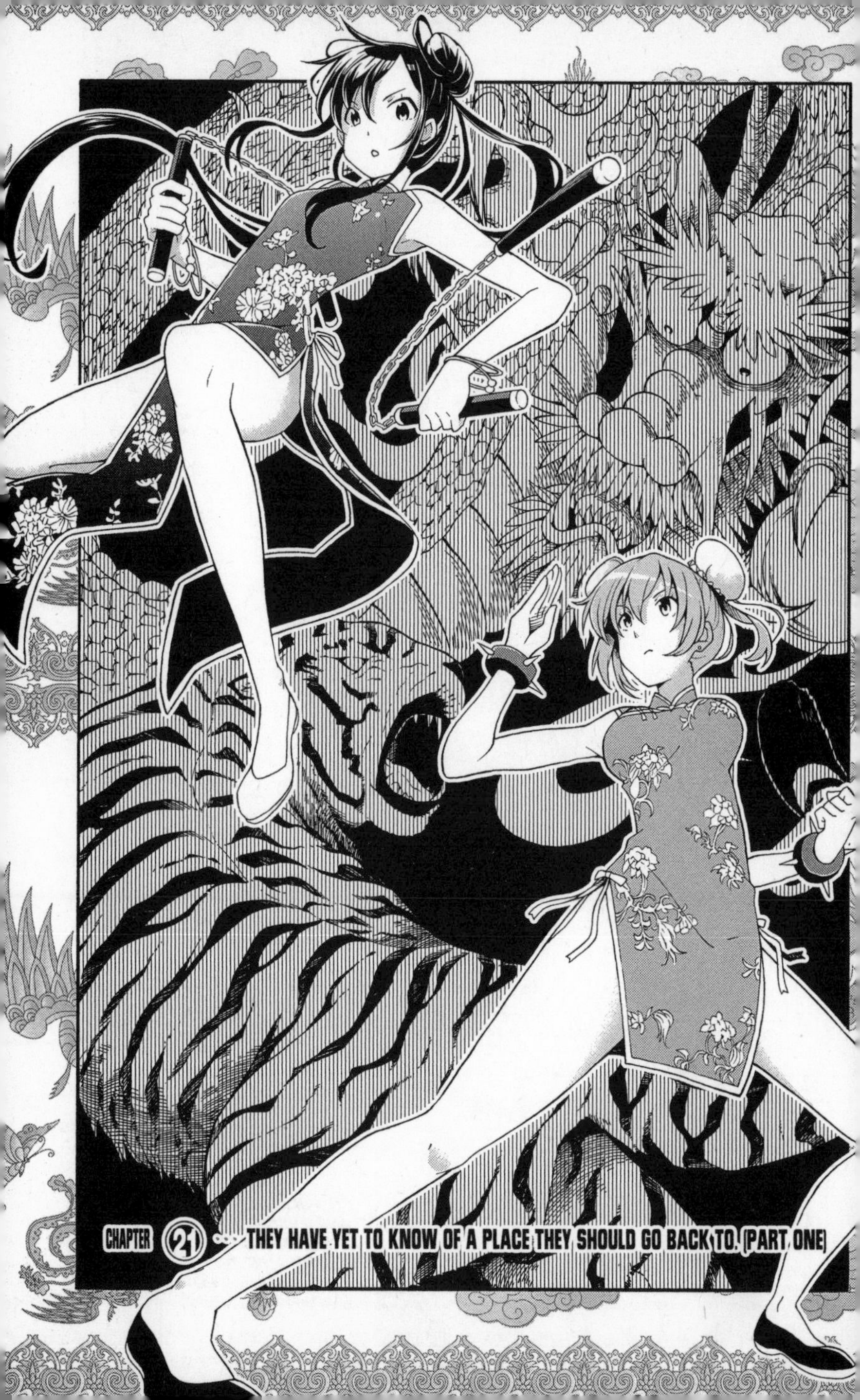
CHAPTER 21 ··· THEY HAVE YET TO KNOW OF A PLACE THEY SHOULD GO BACK TO. (PART ONE)

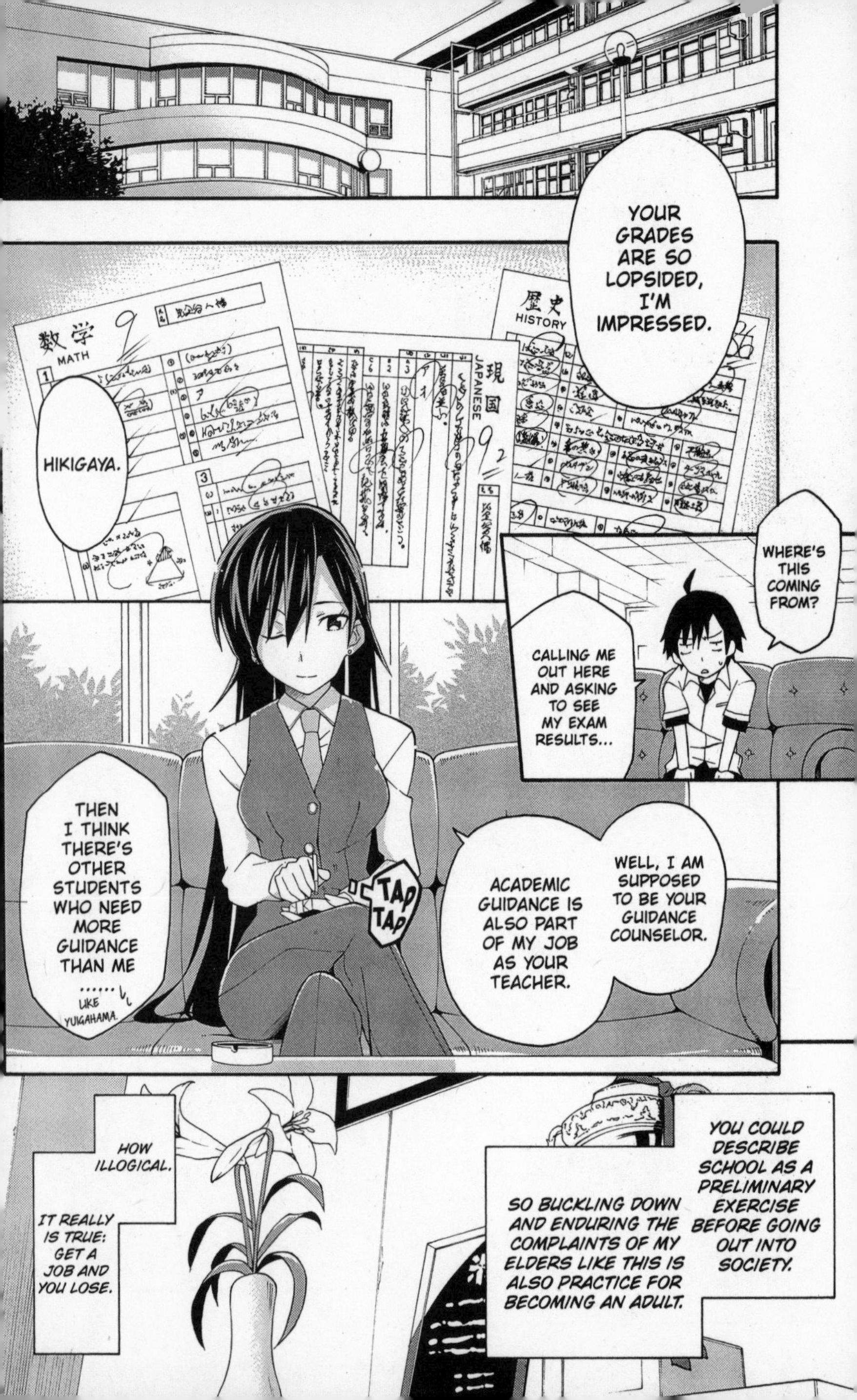
YOUR GRADES ARE SO LOPSIDED, I'M IMPRESSED.
歴史 HISTORY
現国 JAPANESE
数学 MATH
HIKIGAYA.
WHERE'S THIS COMING FROM?
CALLING ME OUT HERE AND ASKING TO SEE MY EXAM RESULTS...
WELL, I AM SUPPOSED TO BE YOUR GUIDANCE COUNSELOR.
ACADEMIC GUIDANCE IS ALSO PART OF MY JOB AS YOUR TEACHER.
TAP TAP
THEN I THINK THERE'S OTHER STUDENTS WHO NEED MORE GUIDANCE THAN ME ......
LIKE YUIGAHAMA.
YOU COULD DESCRIBE SCHOOL AS A PRELIMINARY EXERCISE BEFORE GOING OUT INTO SOCIETY.
SO BUCKLING DOWN AND ENDURING THE COMPLAINTS OF MY ELDERS LIKE THIS IS ALSO PRACTICE FOR BECOMING AN ADULT.
HOW ILLOGICAL.
IT REALLY IS TRUE: GET A JOB AND YOU LOSE.

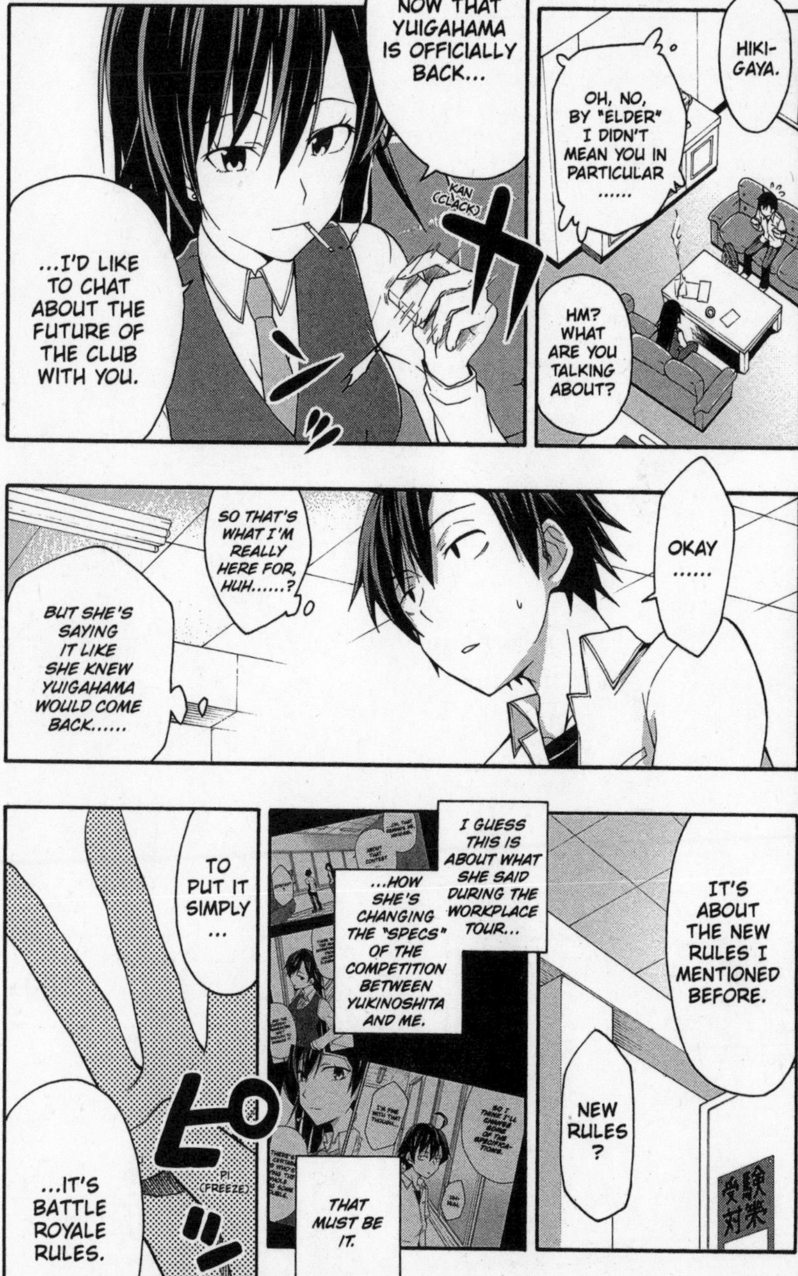
HIKI-GAYA.
OH, NO, BY "ELDER" I DIDN'T MEAN YOU IN PARTICULAR......
HM? WHAT ARE YOU TALKING ABOUT?
NOW THAT YUIGAHAMA IS OFFICIALLY BACK...
KAN (CLACK)
...I'D LIKE TO CHAT ABOUT THE FUTURE OF THE CLUB WITH YOU.
OKAY......
SO THAT'S WHAT I'M REALLY HERE FOR, HUH......?
BUT SHE'S SAYING IT LIKE SHE KNEW YUIGAHAMA WOULD COME BACK......
IT'S ABOUT THE NEW RULES I MENTIONED BEFORE.
NEW RULES?
I GUESS THIS IS ABOUT WHAT SHE SAID DURING THE WORKPLACE TOUR...
...HOW SHE'S CHANGING THE "SPECS" OF THE COMPETITION BETWEEN YUKINOSHITA AND ME.
THAT MUST BE IT.
TO PUT IT SIMPLY...
PI (FREEZE)
...IT'S BATTLE ROYALE RULES.

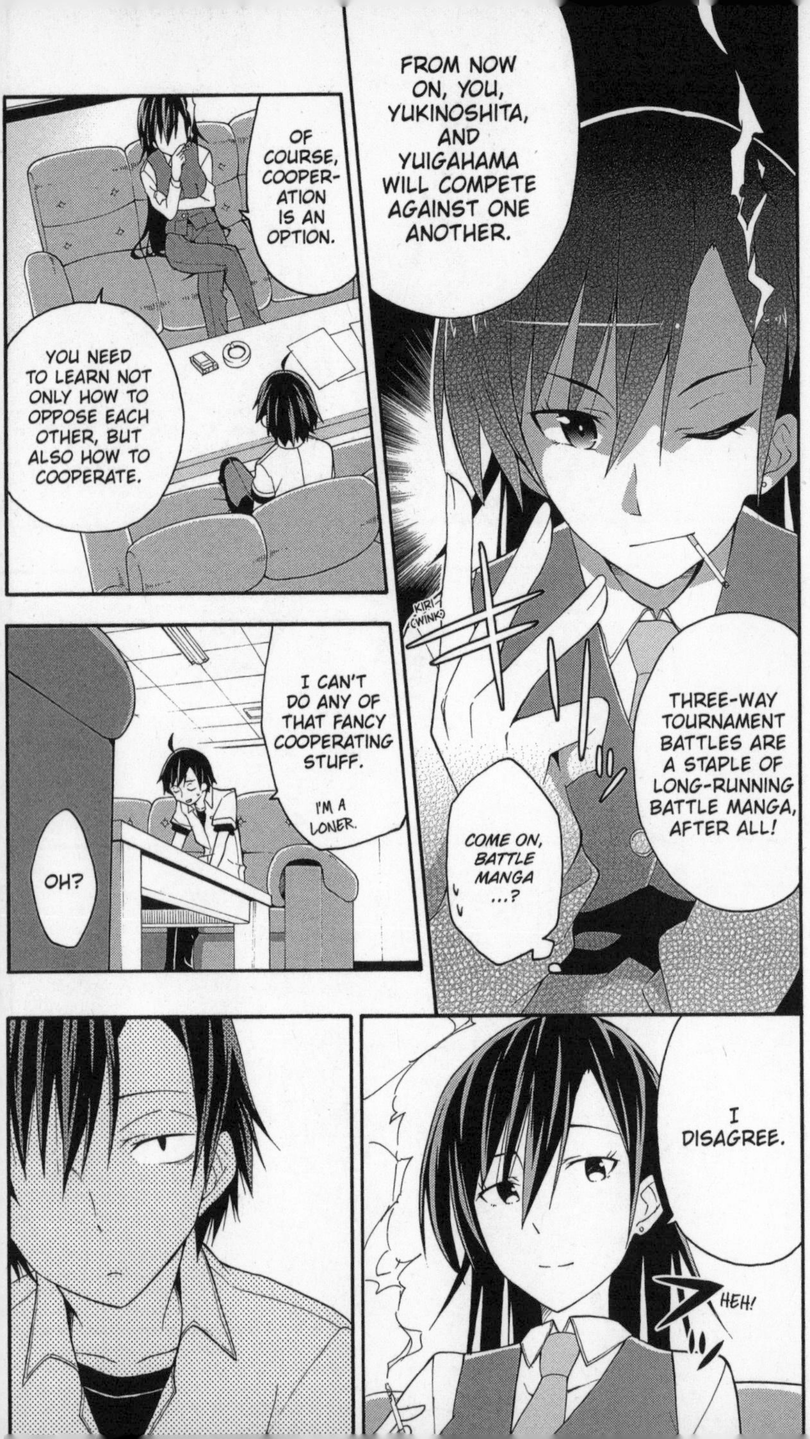
FROM NOW ON, YOU, YUKINOSHITA, AND YUIGAHAMA WILL COMPETE AGAINST ONE ANOTHER.
KIRI (WINK)
THREE-WAY TOURNAMENT BATTLES ARE A STAPLE OF LONG-RUNNING BATTLE MANGA, AFTER ALL!
COME ON, BATTLE MANGA ...?
OF COURSE, COOPER-ATION IS AN OPTION.
YOU NEED TO LEARN NOT ONLY HOW TO OPPOSE EACH OTHER, BUT ALSO HOW TO COOPERATE.
I CAN'T DO ANY OF THAT FANCY COOPERATING STUFF.
I'M A LONER.
OH?
I DISAGREE.
HEH!

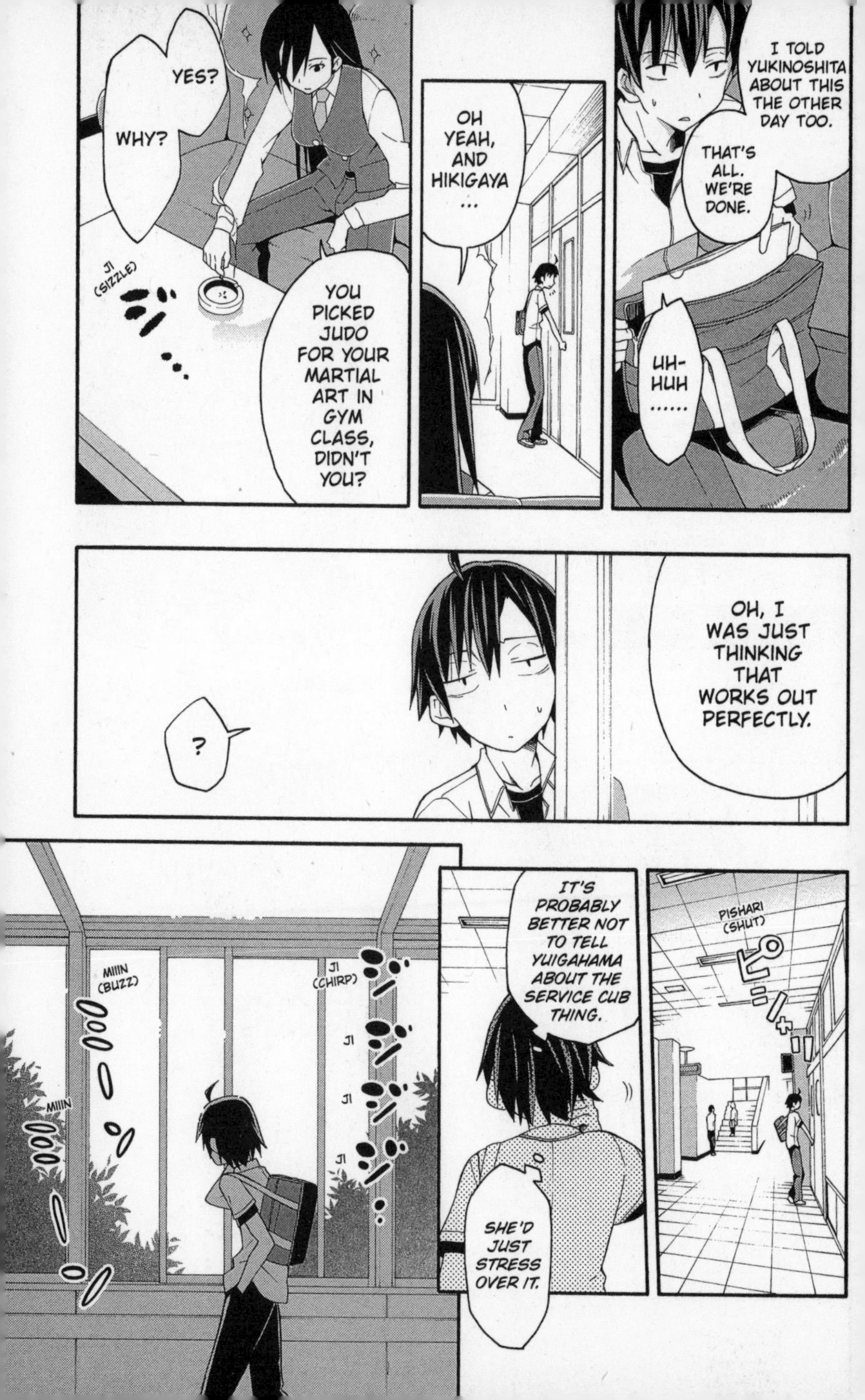
I TOLD YUKINOSHITA ABOUT THIS THE OTHER DAY TOO.
THAT'S ALL. WE'RE DONE.
UH-HUH ......
OH YEAH, AND HIKIGAYA ...
YES?
WHY?
JI (SIZZLE)
YOU PICKED JUDO FOR YOUR MARTIAL ART IN GYM CLASS, DIDN'T YOU?
OH, I WAS JUST THINKING THAT WORKS OUT PERFECTLY.
?
PISHARI (SHUT)
IT'S PROBABLY BETTER NOT TO TELL YUIGAHAMA ABOUT THE SERVICE CUB THING.
SHE'D JUST STRESS OVER IT.
JI (CHIRP)
MIIIN (BUZZ)
JI
JI
MIIIN
JI

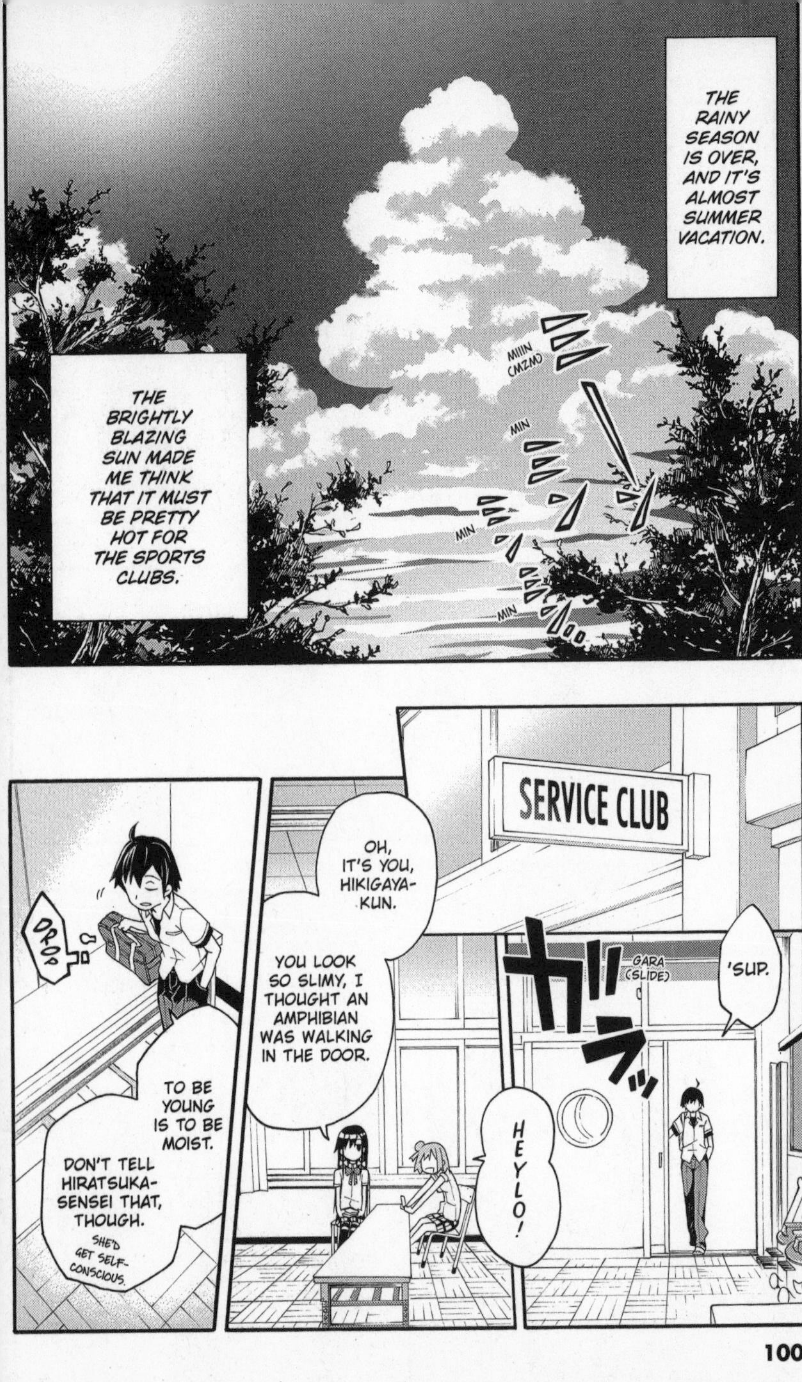
THE RAINY SEASON IS OVER, AND IT'S ALMOST SUMMER VACATION.
MIIIN (MZM)
MIN
MIN
MIN
THE BRIGHTLY BLAZING SUN MADE ME THINK THAT IT MUST BE PRETTY HOT FOR THE SPORTS CLUBS.
SERVICE CLUB
GARA (SLIDE)
'SUP.
HEYLO!
OH, IT'S YOU, HIKIGAYA-KUN.
YOU LOOK SO SLIMY, I THOUGHT AN AMPHIBIAN WAS WALKING IN THE DOOR.
TO BE YOUNG IS TO BE MOIST.
DON'T TELL HIRATSUKA-SENSEI THAT, THOUGH.
SHE'D GET SELF-CONSCIOUS.
DROP

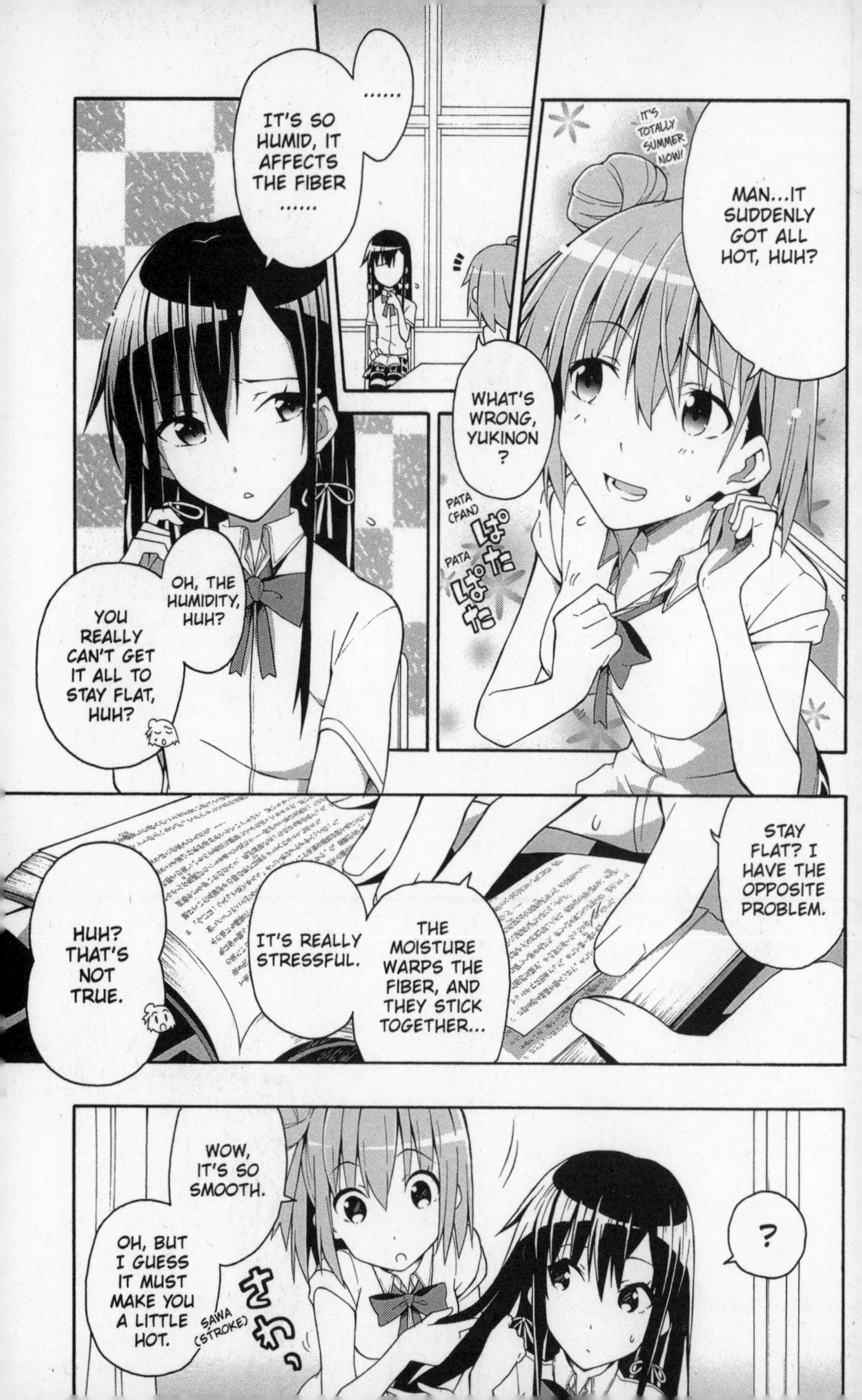
IT'S TOTALLY SUMMER NOW!
MAN...IT SUDDENLY GOT ALL HOT, HUH?
PATA (FAN) ぱた PATA ぱた
WHAT'S WRONG, YUKINON ?
...... IT'S SO HUMID, IT AFFECTS THE FIBER ......
OH, THE HUMIDITY, HUH?
YOU REALLY CAN'T GET IT ALL TO STAY FLAT, HUH?
STAY FLAT? I HAVE THE OPPOSITE PROBLEM.
THE MOISTURE WARPS THE FIBER, AND THEY STICK TOGETHER...
IT'S REALLY STRESSFUL.
HUH? THAT'S NOT TRUE.
?
WOW, IT'S SO SMOOTH.
OH, BUT I GUESS IT MUST MAKE YOU A LITTLE HOT.
SAWA (STROKE) さわっ

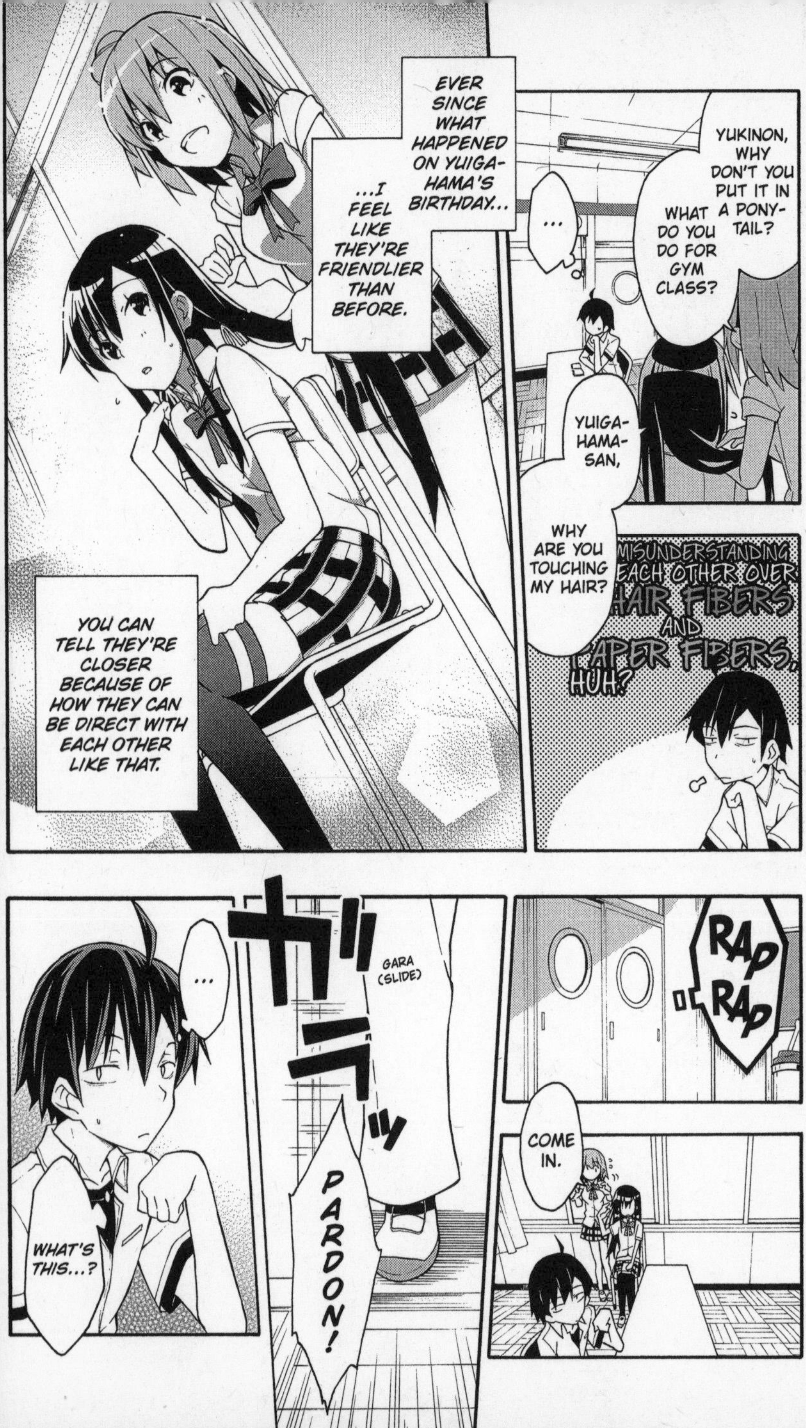
YUKINON, WHY DON'T YOU PUT IT IN A PONY-TAIL?
WHAT DO YOU DO FOR GYM CLASS?
...
YUIGA-HAMA-SAN,
WHY ARE YOU TOUCHING MY HAIR?
MISUNDERSTANDING EACH OTHER OVER HAIR FIBERS AND PAPER FIBERS, HUH?
EVER SINCE WHAT HAPPENED ON YUIGA-HAMA'S BIRTHDAY...
...I FEEL LIKE THEY'RE FRIENDLIER THAN BEFORE.
YOU CAN TELL THEY'RE CLOSER BECAUSE OF HOW THEY CAN BE DIRECT WITH EACH OTHER LIKE THAT.
RAP RAP
COME IN.
GARA (SLIDE)
PARDON!
...
WHAT'S THIS...?

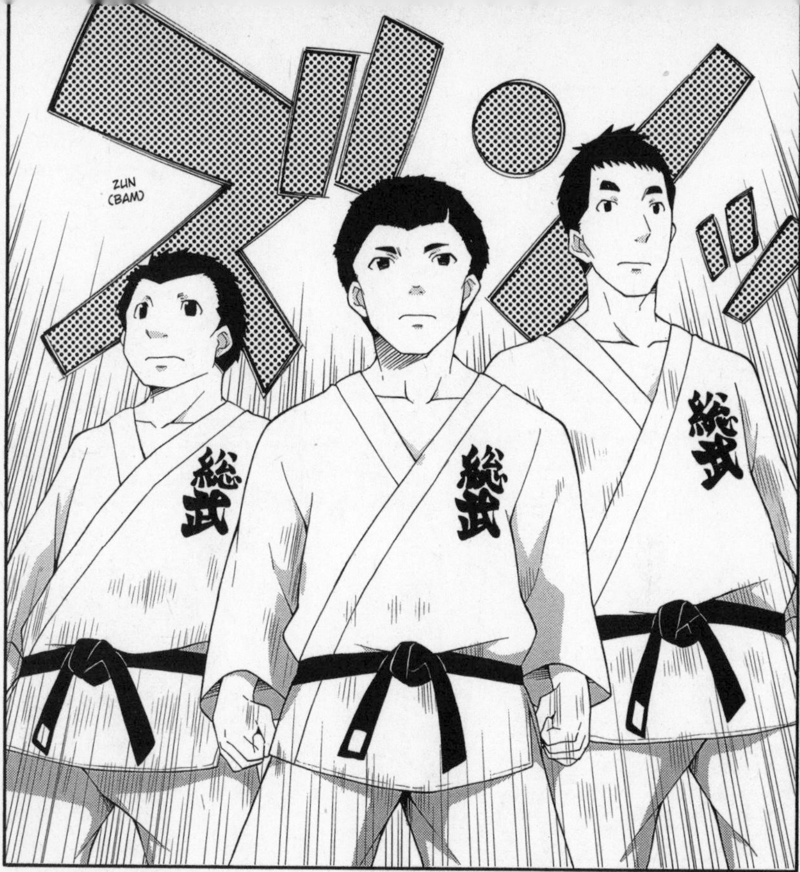
ZUN (BAM)
総武
総武
総武
UNIFORMS: SOUBU

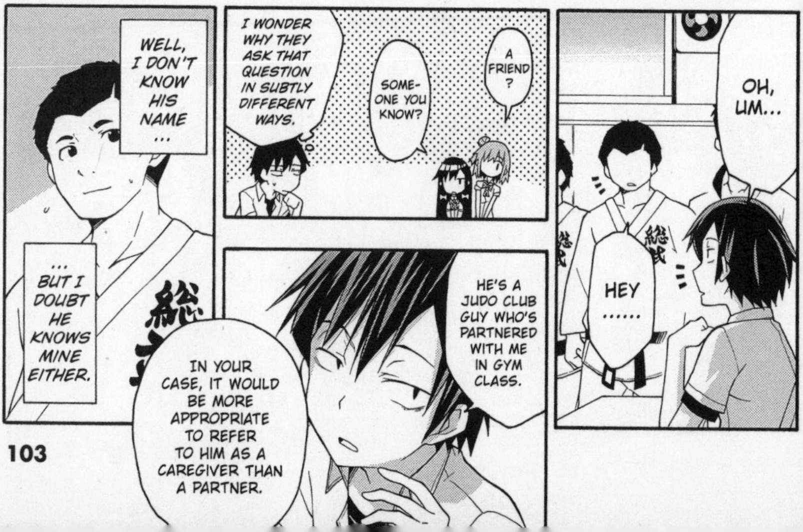
OH, UM...
HEY ......
総武
A FRIEND?
SOME-ONE YOU KNOW?
I WONDER WHY THEY ASK THAT QUESTION IN SUBTLY DIFFERENT WAYS.
HE'S A JUDO CLUB GUY WHO'S PARTNERED WITH ME IN GYM CLASS.
IN YOUR CASE, IT WOULD BE MORE APPROPRIATE TO REFER TO HIM AS A CAREGIVER THAN A PARTNER.
WELL, I DON'T KNOW HIS NAME ...
... BUT I DOUBT HE KNOWS MINE EITHER.

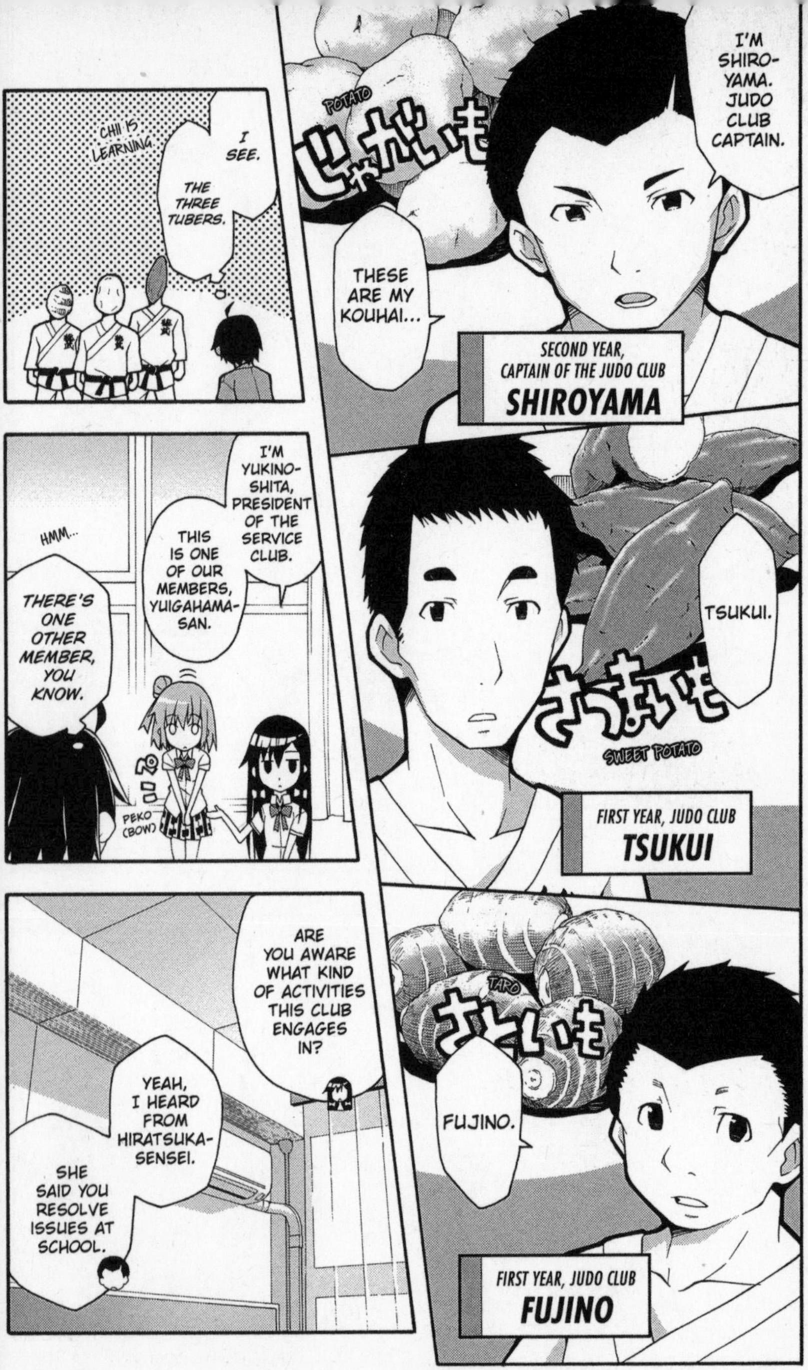

I'M SHIRO-YAMA. JUDO CLUB CAPTAIN.
POTATO
じゃがいも
THESE ARE MY KOUHAI...
SECOND YEAR, CAPTAIN OF THE JUDO CLUB
SHIROYAMA
I SEE.
THE THREE TUBERS.
CHII IS LEARNING.
TSUKUI.
さつまいも
SWEET POTATO
FIRST YEAR, JUDO CLUB
TSUKUI
I'M YUKINO-SHITA, PRESIDENT OF THE SERVICE CLUB.
THIS IS ONE OF OUR MEMBERS, YUIGAHAMA-SAN.
HMM...
THERE'S ONE OTHER MEMBER, YOU KNOW.
PEKO (BOW)
TARO
さといも
FUJINO.
FIRST YEAR, JUDO CLUB
FUJINO
ARE YOU AWARE WHAT KIND OF ACTIVITIES THIS CLUB ENGAGES IN?
YEAH, I HEARD FROM HIRATSUKA-SENSEI.
SHE SAID YOU RESOLVE ISSUES AT SCHOOL.

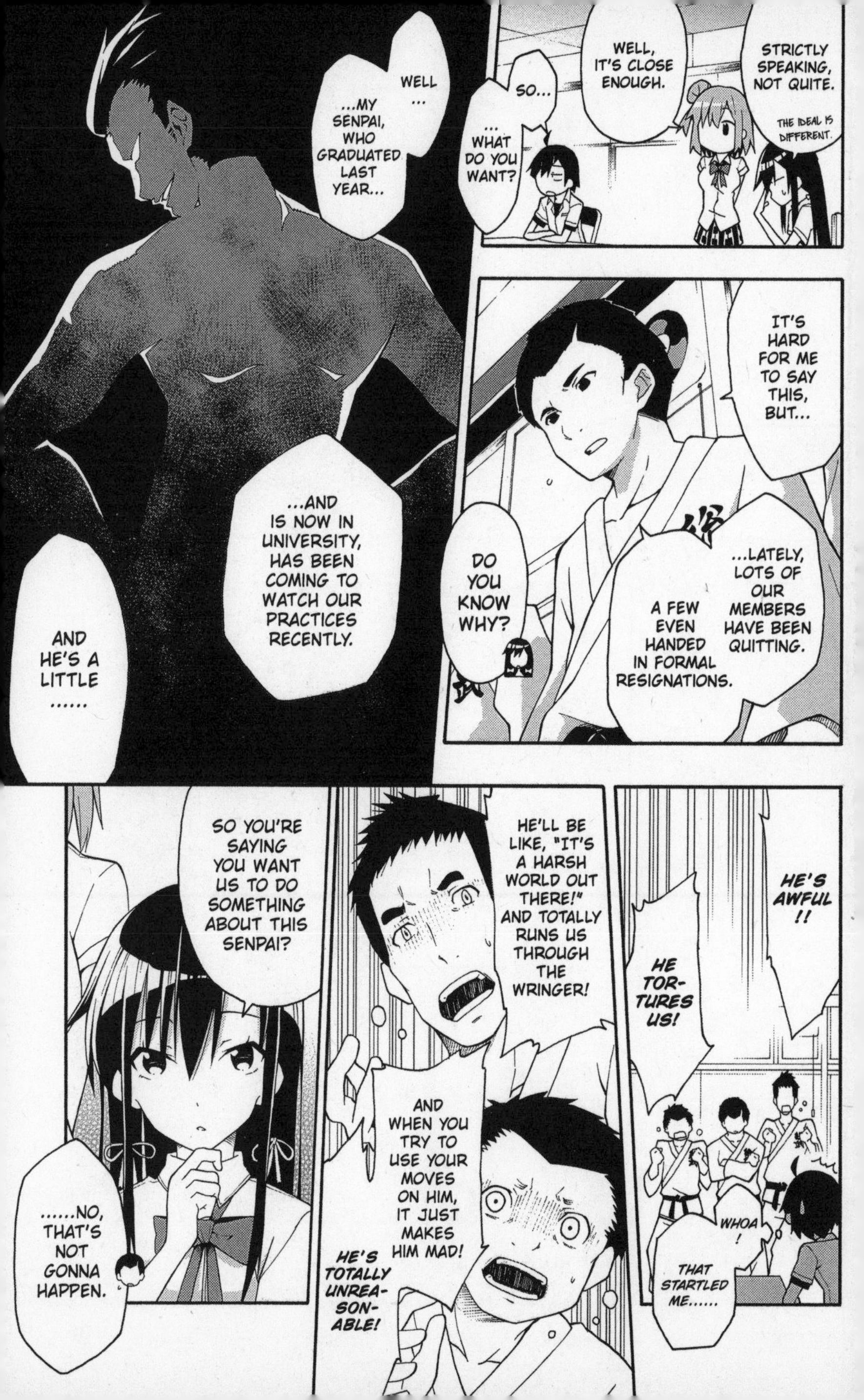
STRICTLY SPEAKING, NOT QUITE.
THE IDEAL IS DIFFERENT.
WELL, IT'S CLOSE ENOUGH.
SO...
...WHAT DO YOU WANT?
IT'S HARD FOR ME TO SAY THIS, BUT...
...LATELY, LOTS OF OUR MEMBERS HAVE BEEN QUITTING.
A FEW EVEN HANDED IN FORMAL RESIGNATIONS.
DO YOU KNOW WHY?
WELL...
...MY SENPAI, WHO GRADUATED LAST YEAR...
...AND IS NOW IN UNIVERSITY, HAS BEEN COMING TO WATCH OUR PRACTICES RECENTLY.
AND HE'S A LITTLE ......
HE'S AWFUL!!
HE TORTURES US!
WHOA!
THAT STARTLED ME......
HE'LL BE LIKE, "IT'S A HARSH WORLD OUT THERE!" AND TOTALLY RUNS US THROUGH THE WRINGER!
AND WHEN YOU TRY TO USE YOUR MOVES ON HIM, IT JUST MAKES HIM MAD!
HE'S TOTALLY UNREA-SON-ABLE!
SO YOU'RE SAYING YOU WANT US TO DO SOMETHING ABOUT THIS SENPAI?
......NO, THAT'S NOT GONNA HAPPEN.

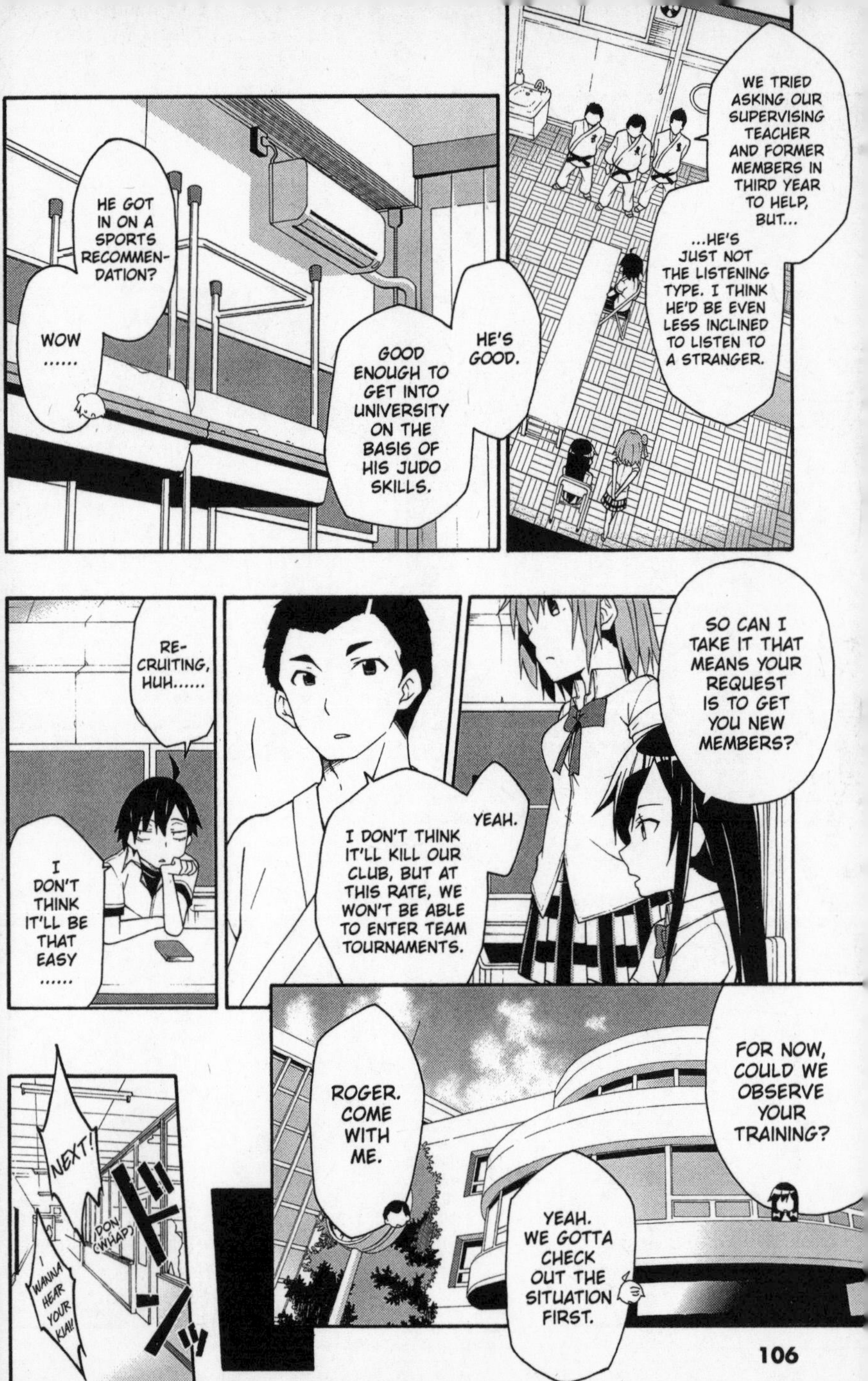
WE TRIED ASKING OUR SUPERVISING TEACHER AND FORMER MEMBERS IN THIRD YEAR TO HELP, BUT...
...HE'S JUST NOT THE LISTENING TYPE. I THINK HE'D BE EVEN LESS INCLINED TO LISTEN TO A STRANGER.
HE'S GOOD.
GOOD ENOUGH TO GET INTO UNIVERSITY ON THE BASIS OF HIS JUDO SKILLS.
HE GOT IN ON A SPORTS RECOMMEN-DATION?
WOW ......
SO CAN I TAKE IT THAT MEANS YOUR REQUEST IS TO GET YOU NEW MEMBERS?
YEAH.
I DON'T THINK IT'LL KILL OUR CLUB, BUT AT THIS RATE, WE WON'T BE ABLE TO ENTER TEAM TOURNAMENTS.
RE-CRUITING, HUH......
I DON'T THINK IT'LL BE THAT EASY ......
FOR NOW, COULD WE OBSERVE YOUR TRAINING?
ROGER. COME WITH ME.
YEAH. WE GOTTA CHECK OUT THE SITUATION FIRST.
NEXT!
DON (WHAP)
I WANNA HEAR YOUR KIAI!

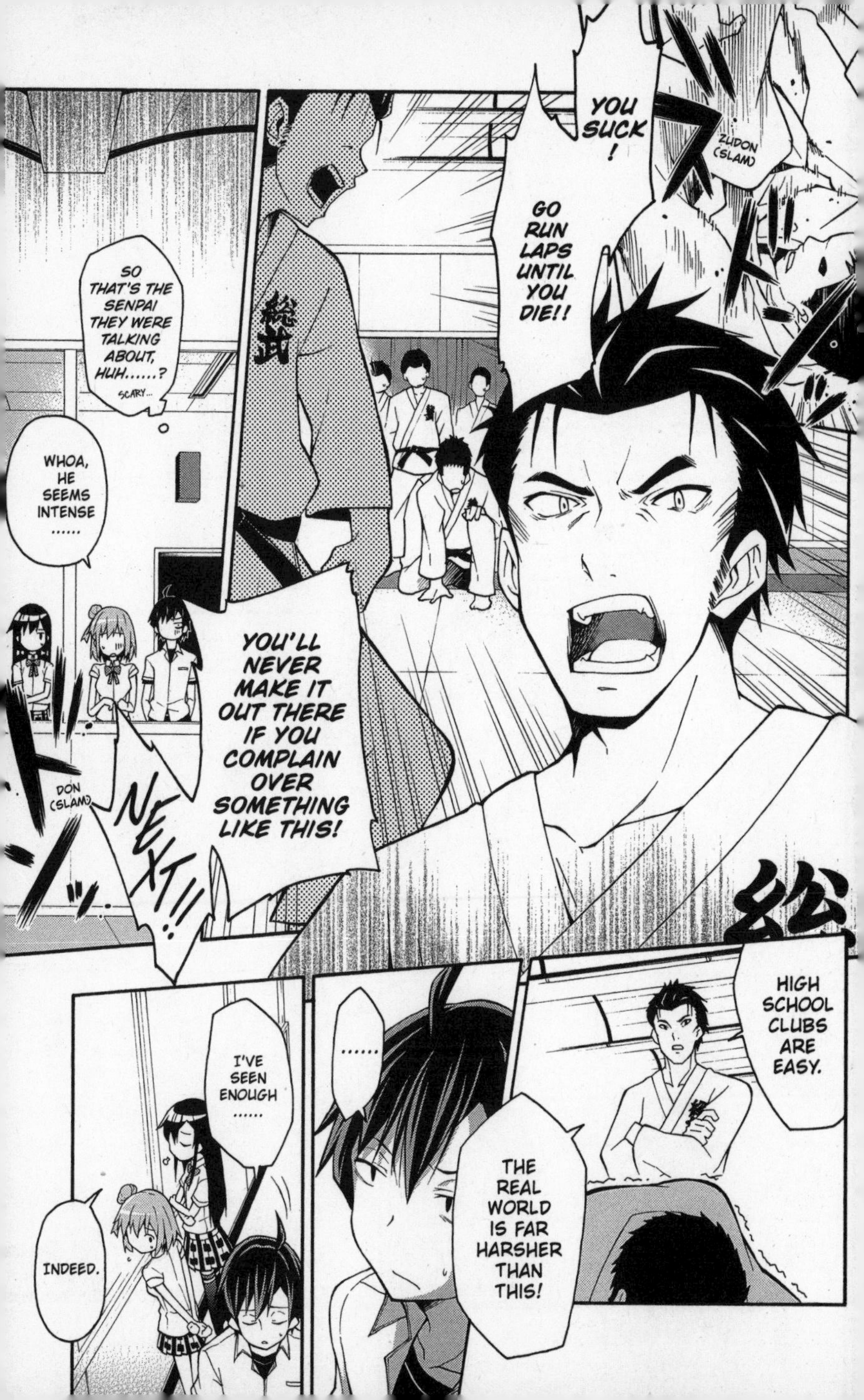
YOU SUCK!
ZUDON (SLAM)
GO RUN LAPS UNTIL YOU DIE!!
YOU'LL NEVER MAKE IT OUT THERE IF YOU COMPLAIN OVER SOMETHING LIKE THIS!
NEXT!!
SO THAT'S THE SENPAI THEY WERE TALKING ABOUT, HUH......?
SCARY...
WHOA, HE SEEMS INTENSE......
DON (SLAM)
HIGH SCHOOL CLUBS ARE EASY.
THE REAL WORLD IS FAR HARSHER THAN THIS!
......
I'VE SEEN ENOUGH......
INDEED.

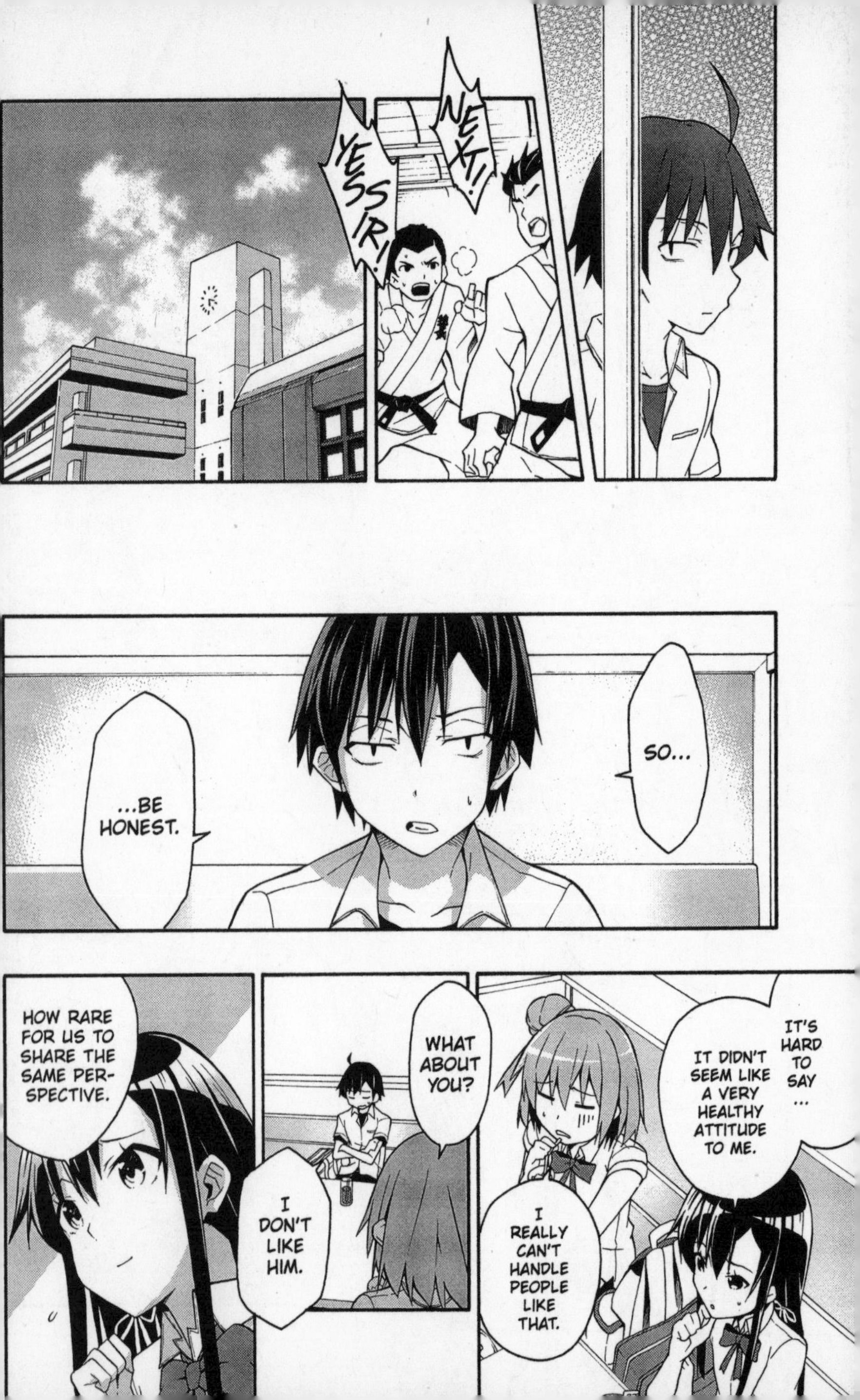
NEXT!!
YESSIR!
SO...
...BE HONEST.
IT'S HARD TO SAY...
IT DIDN'T SEEM LIKE A VERY HEALTHY ATTITUDE TO ME.
I REALLY CAN'T HANDLE PEOPLE LIKE THAT.
WHAT ABOUT YOU?
I DON'T LIKE HIM.
HOW RARE FOR US TO SHARE THE SAME PERSPECTIVE.

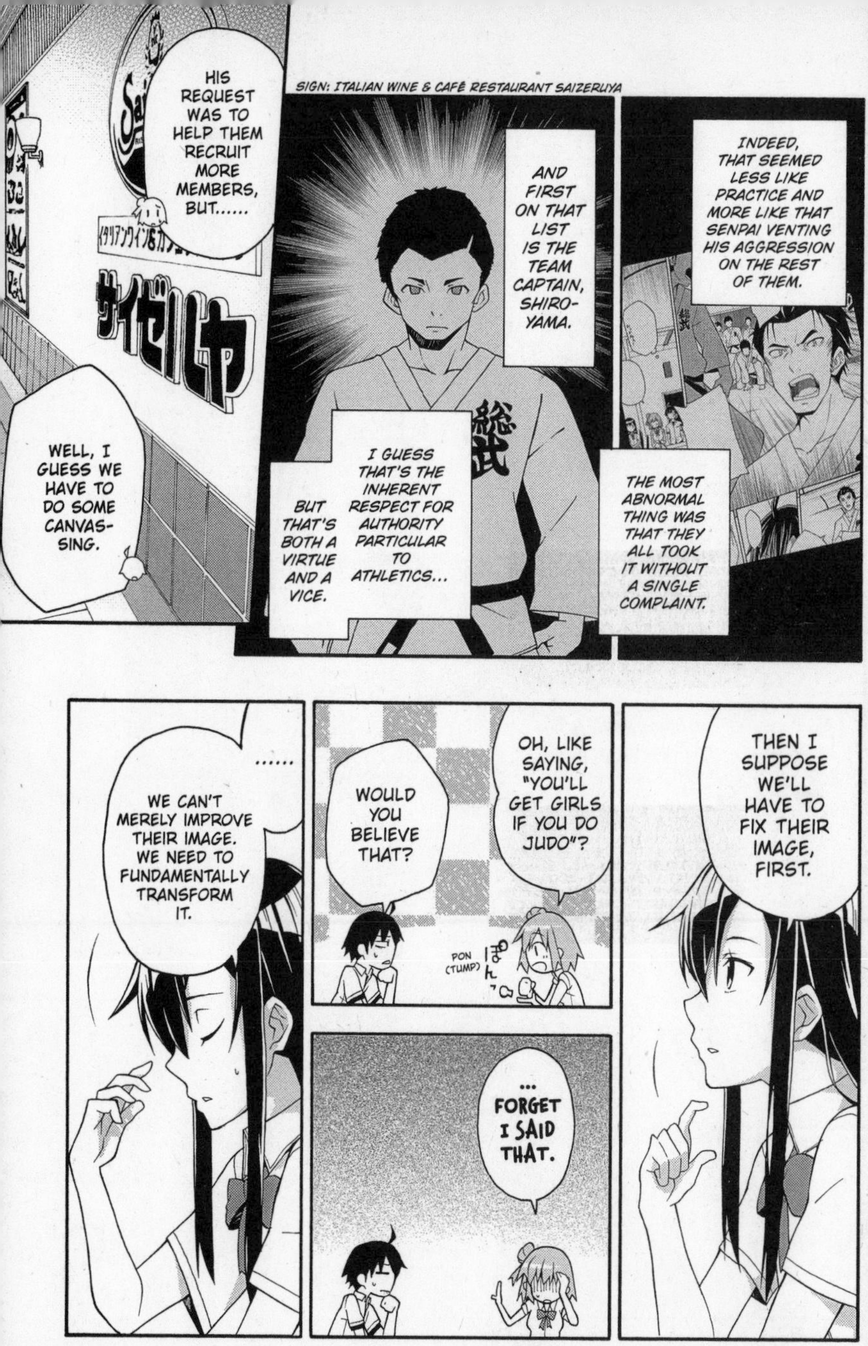
INDEED, THAT SEEMED LESS LIKE PRACTICE AND MORE LIKE THAT SENPAI VENTING HIS AGGRESSION ON THE REST OF THEM.
THE MOST ABNORMAL THING WAS THAT THEY ALL TOOK IT WITHOUT A SINGLE COMPLAINT.
SIGN: ITALIAN WINE & CAFÉ RESTAURANT SAIZERUYA
AND FIRST ON THAT LIST IS THE TEAM CAPTAIN, SHIROYAMA.
I GUESS THAT'S THE INHERENT RESPECT FOR AUTHORITY PARTICULAR TO ATHLETICS...
BUT THAT'S BOTH A VIRTUE AND A VICE.
HIS REQUEST WAS TO HELP THEM RECRUIT MORE MEMBERS, BUT......
サイゼリヤ
WELL, I GUESS WE HAVE TO DO SOME CANVASSING.
THEN I SUPPOSE WE'LL HAVE TO FIX THEIR IMAGE, FIRST.
OH, LIKE SAYING, "YOU'LL GET GIRLS IF YOU DO JUDO"?
WOULD YOU BELIEVE THAT?
PON (TUMP)
... FORGET I SAID THAT.
......
WE CAN'T MERELY IMPROVE THEIR IMAGE. WE NEED TO FUNDAMENTALLY TRANSFORM IT.

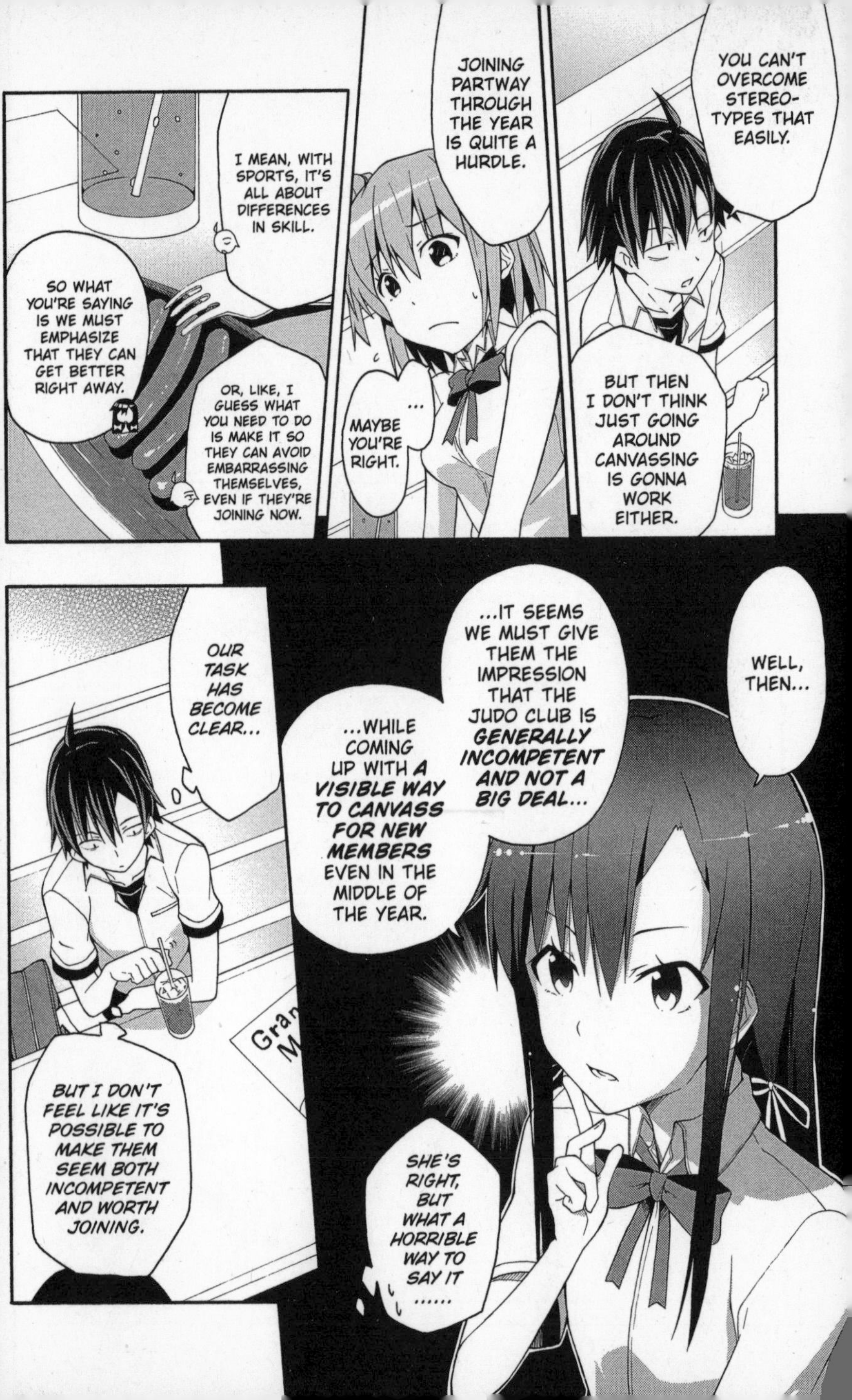
YOU CAN'T OVERCOME STEREO-TYPES THAT EASILY.
BUT THEN I DON'T THINK JUST GOING AROUND CANVASSING IS GONNA WORK EITHER.
JOINING PARTWAY THROUGH THE YEAR IS QUITE A HURDLE.
... MAYBE YOU'RE RIGHT.
I MEAN, WITH SPORTS, IT'S ALL ABOUT DIFFERENCES IN SKILL.
SO WHAT YOU'RE SAYING IS WE MUST EMPHASIZE THAT THEY CAN GET BETTER RIGHT AWAY.
OR, LIKE, I GUESS WHAT YOU NEED TO DO IS MAKE IT SO THEY CAN AVOID EMBARRASSING THEMSELVES, EVEN IF THEY'RE JOINING NOW.
WELL, THEN...
...IT SEEMS WE MUST GIVE THEM THE IMPRESSION THAT THE JUDO CLUB IS GENERALLY INCOMPETENT AND NOT A BIG DEAL...
...WHILE COMING UP WITH A VISIBLE WAY TO CANVASS FOR NEW MEMBERS EVEN IN THE MIDDLE OF THE YEAR.
SHE'S RIGHT, BUT WHAT A HORRIBLE WAY TO SAY IT ......
OUR TASK HAS BECOME CLEAR...
BUT I DON'T FEEL LIKE IT'S POSSIBLE TO MAKE THEM SEEM BOTH INCOMPETENT AND WORTH JOINING.

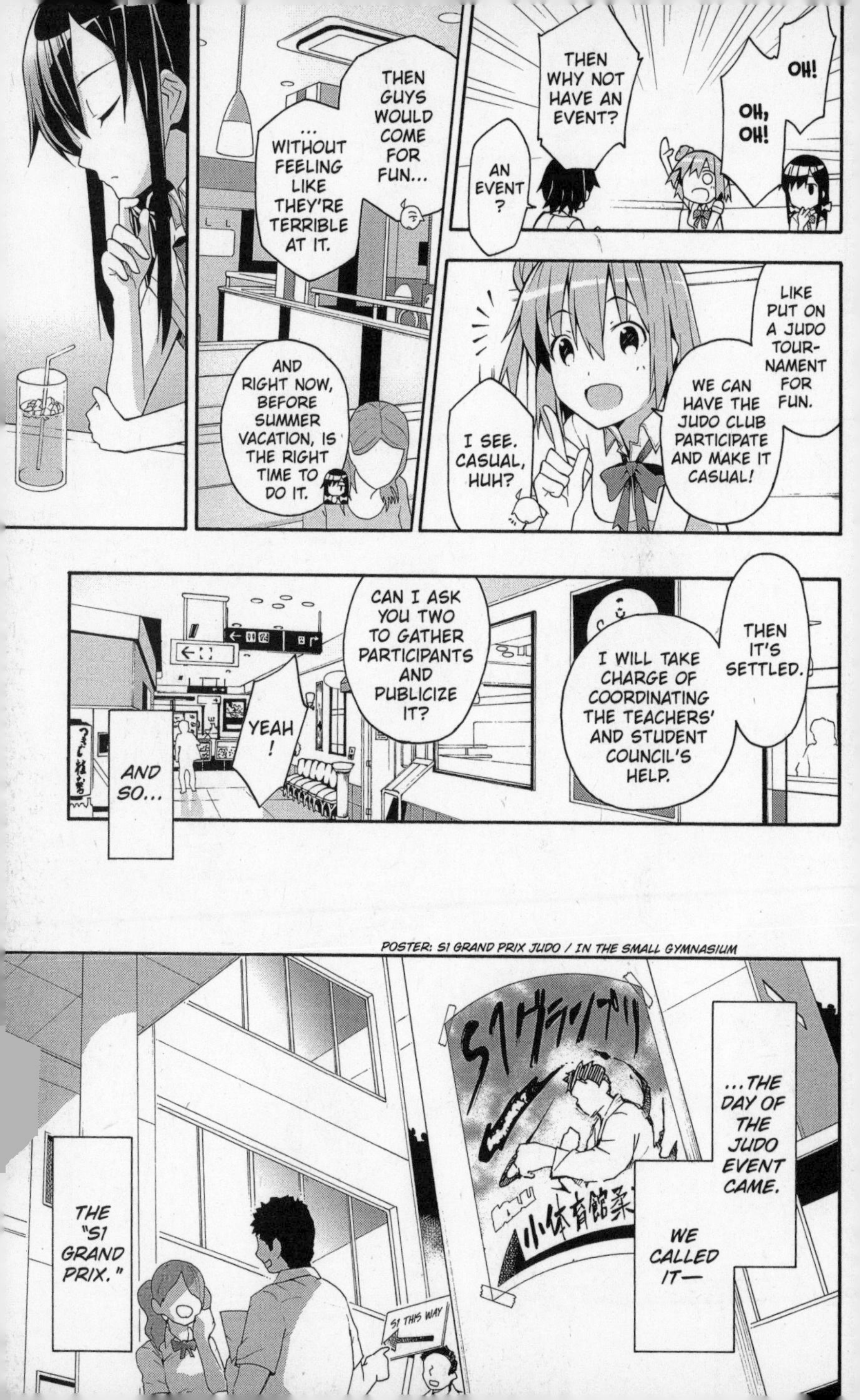
THEN GUYS WOULD COME FOR FUN...
...WITHOUT FEELING LIKE THEY'RE TERRIBLE AT IT.
AND RIGHT NOW, BEFORE SUMMER VACATION, IS THE RIGHT TIME TO DO IT.
THEN WHY NOT HAVE AN EVENT?
AN EVENT?
OH!
OH, OH!
LIKE PUT ON A JUDO TOURNAMENT FOR FUN.
WE CAN HAVE THE JUDO CLUB PARTICIPATE AND MAKE IT CASUAL!
I SEE. CASUAL, HUH?
THEN IT'S SETTLED.
I WILL TAKE CHARGE OF COORDINATING THE TEACHERS' AND STUDENT COUNCIL'S HELP.
CAN I ASK YOU TWO TO GATHER PARTICIPANTS AND PUBLICIZE IT?
YEAH!
AND SO...
POSTER: S1 GRAND PRIX JUDO / IN THE SMALL GYMNASIUM
...THE DAY OF THE JUDO EVENT CAME.
WE CALLED IT—
THE "S1 GRAND PRIX."
S1 THIS WAY

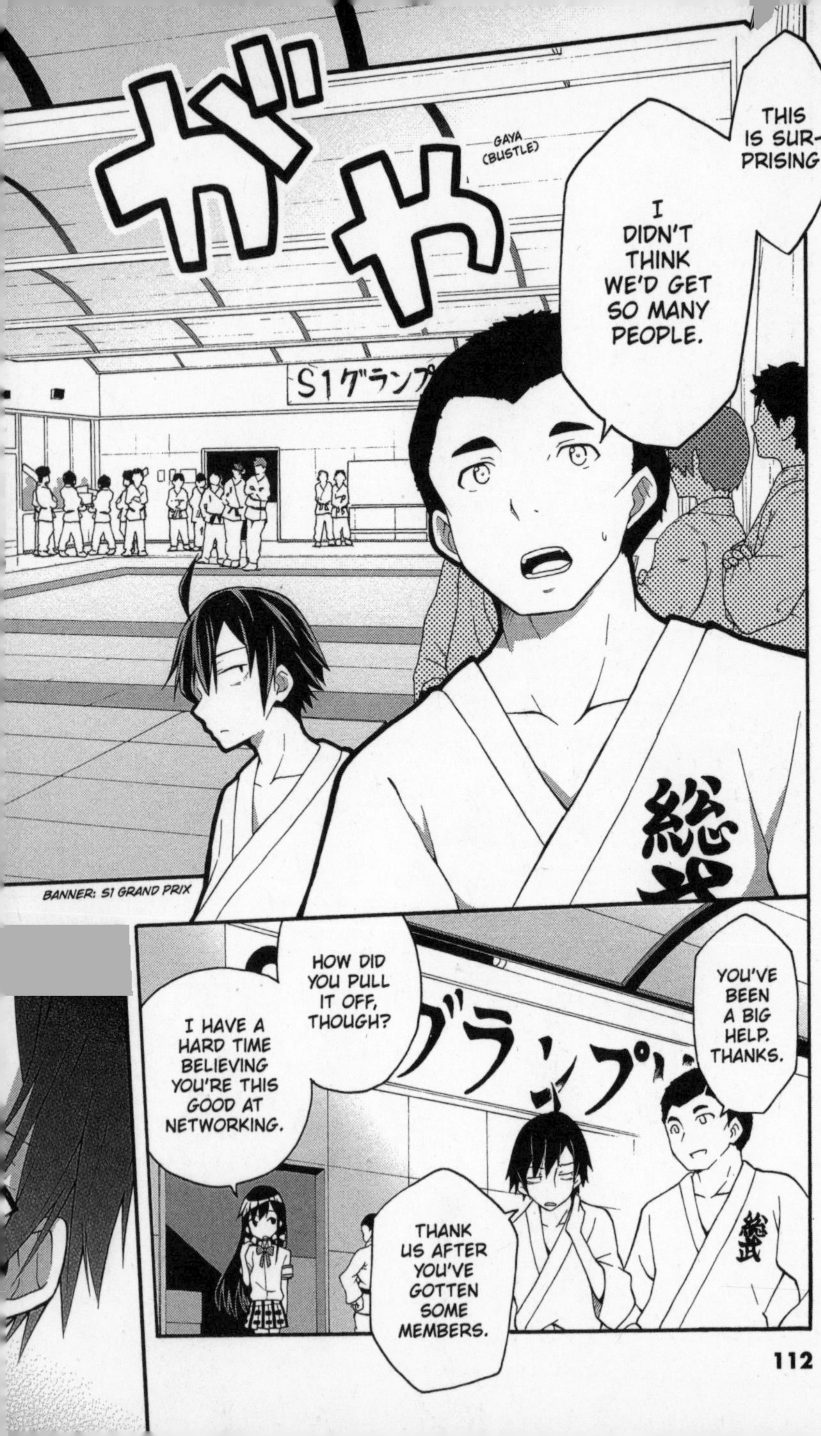
THIS IS SURPRISING.
I DIDN'T THINK WE'D GET SO MANY PEOPLE.
がや
GAYA (BUSTLE)
S1グランプ
BANNER: S1 GRAND PRIX
YOU'VE BEEN A BIG HELP. THANKS.
HOW DID YOU PULL IT OFF, THOUGH?
I HAVE A HARD TIME BELIEVING YOU'RE THIS GOOD AT NETWORKING.
グランプ
THANK US AFTER YOU'VE GOTTEN SOME MEMBERS.

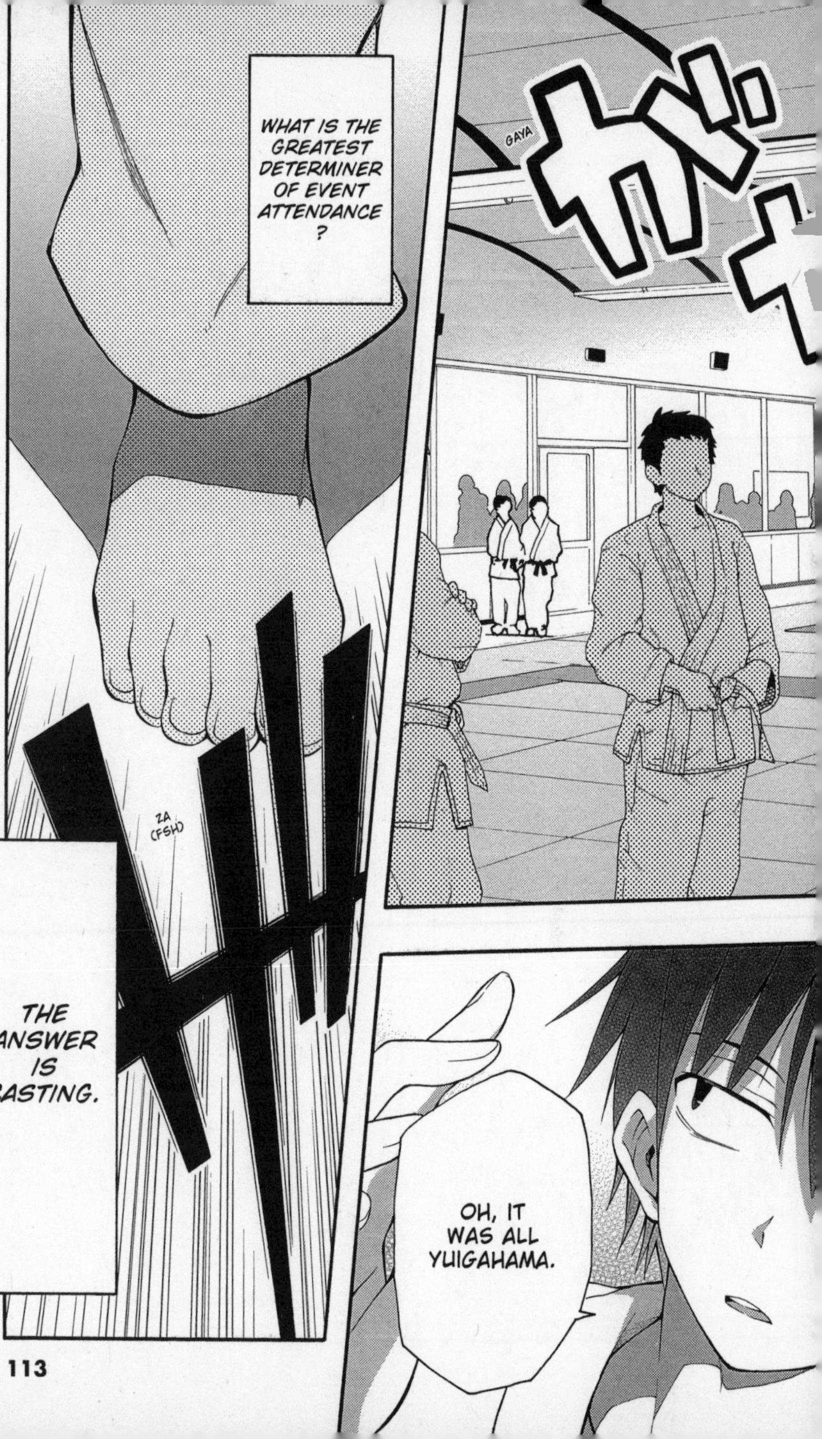
GAYA
OH, IT WAS ALL YUIGAHAMA.
WHAT IS THE GREATEST DETERMINER OF EVENT ATTENDANCE ?
ZA (FSH)
THE ANSWER IS CASTING.

NO, YOU'RE RIGHT ON TIME.

SORRY I'M LATE.

SORRY TO DRAG YOU AWAY FROM YOUR CLUB.

BUT MORE IMPORTANTLY...

HAYATOOOO!!!

HAYATO

...WHY ARE WE ON THE SAME TEAM?

LAST	SECOND	FIRST
HIKI-GAYA	HAYAMA	

DO YOU OBJECT?

PASHA (FLASH)

NI (GRIND)

WELL...... I DO. BUT...

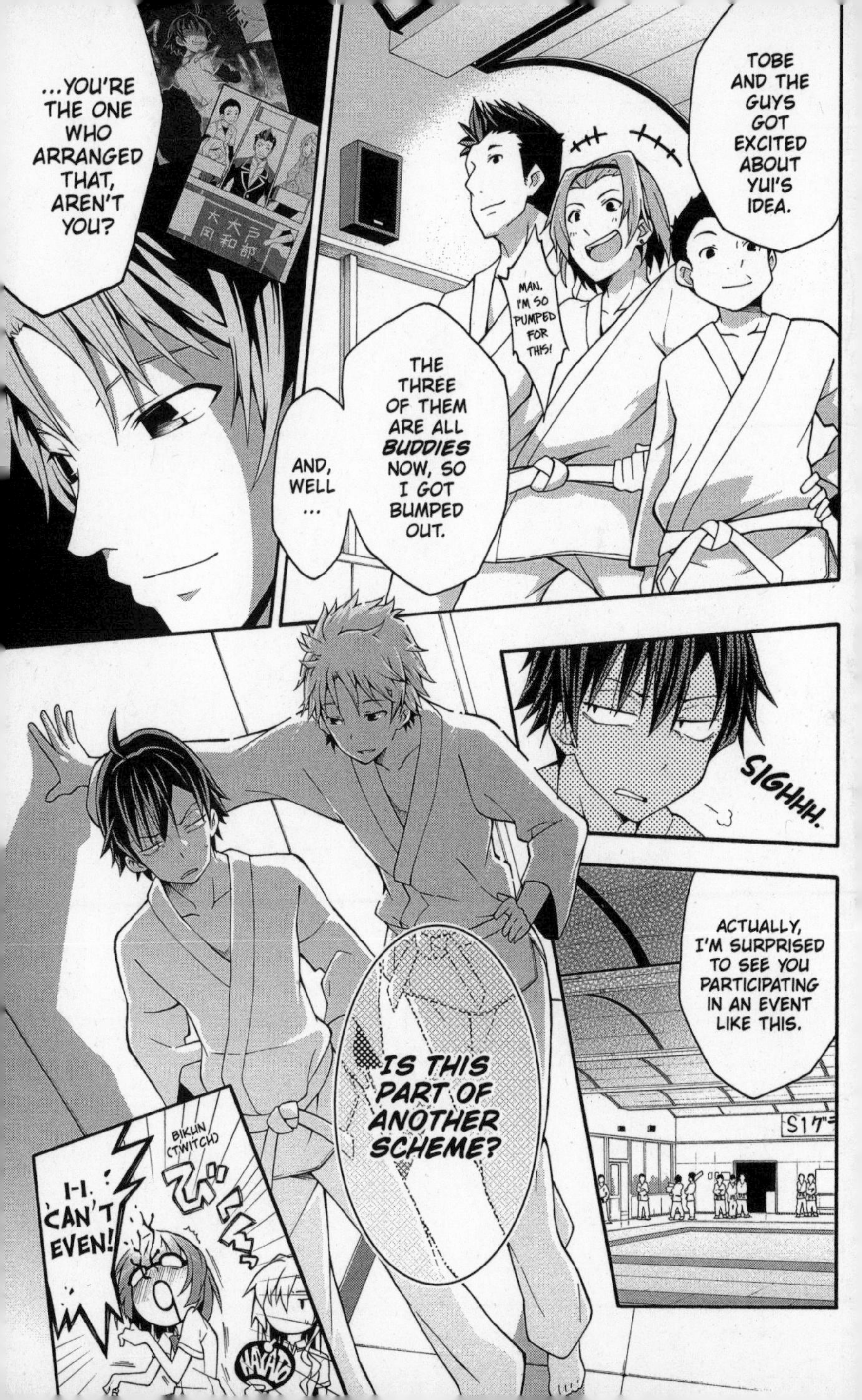

TOBE AND THE GUYS GOT EXCITED ABOUT YUI'S IDEA.
MAN, I'M SO PUMPED FOR THIS!
THE THREE OF THEM ARE ALL *BUDDIES* NOW, SO I GOT BUMPED OUT.
AND, WELL ...
...YOU'RE THE ONE WHO ARRANGED THAT, AREN'T YOU?
SIGHHH.
ACTUALLY, I'M SURPRISED TO SEE YOU PARTICIPATING IN AN EVENT LIKE THIS.
IS THIS PART OF ANOTHER SCHEME?
BIKUN (TWITCH)
I-I CAN'T EVEN!
HAYATO

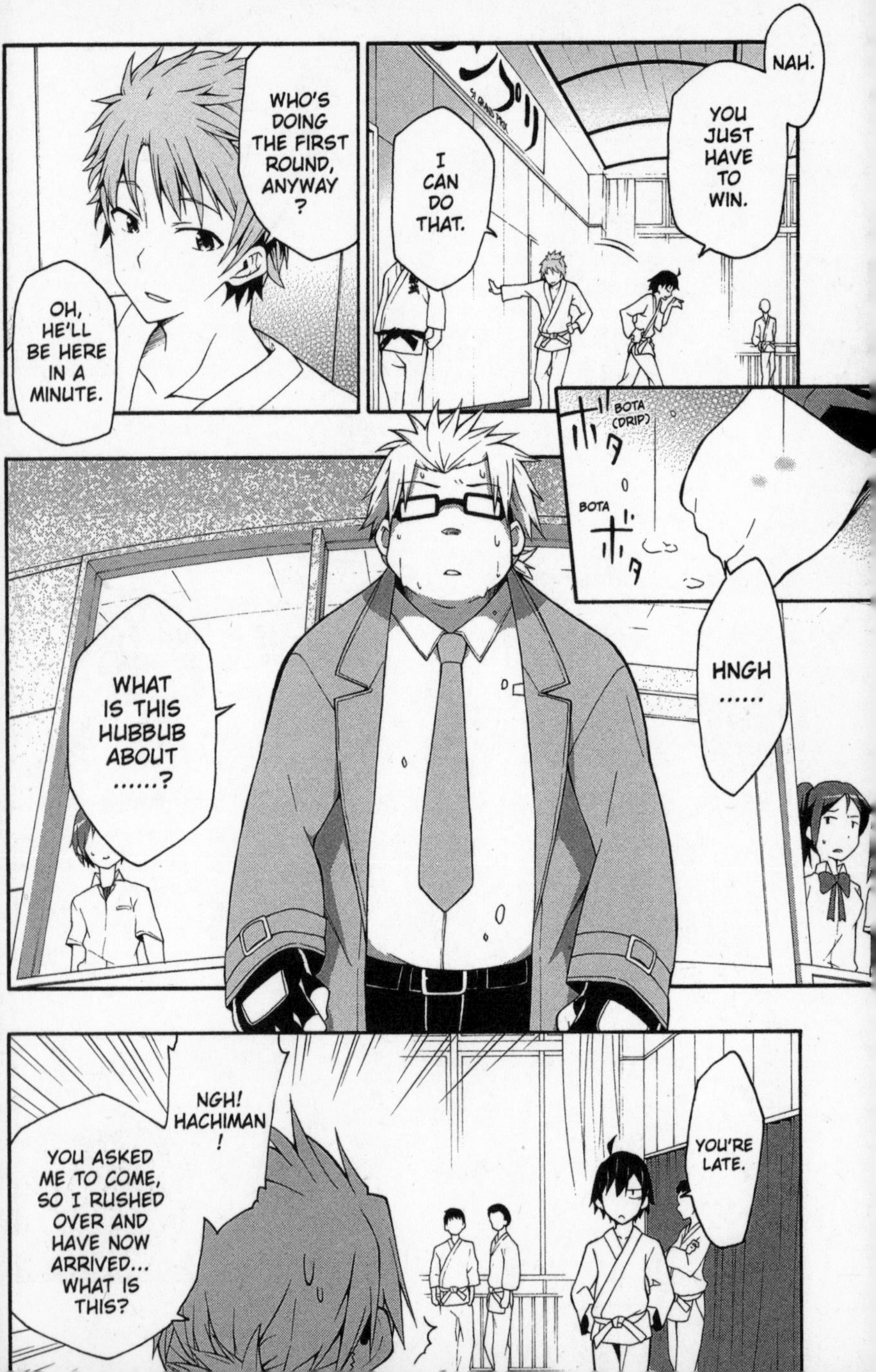
NAH.
YOU JUST HAVE TO WIN.
I CAN DO THAT.
51 GRAND PRIX
WHO'S DOING THE FIRST ROUND, ANYWAY?
OH, HE'LL BE HERE IN A MINUTE.
BOTA (DRIP)
BOTA
HNGH......
WHAT IS THIS HUBBUB ABOUT......?
YOU'RE LATE.
NGH! HACHIMAN!
YOU ASKED ME TO COME, SO I RUSHED OVER AND HAVE NOW ARRIVED... WHAT IS THIS?

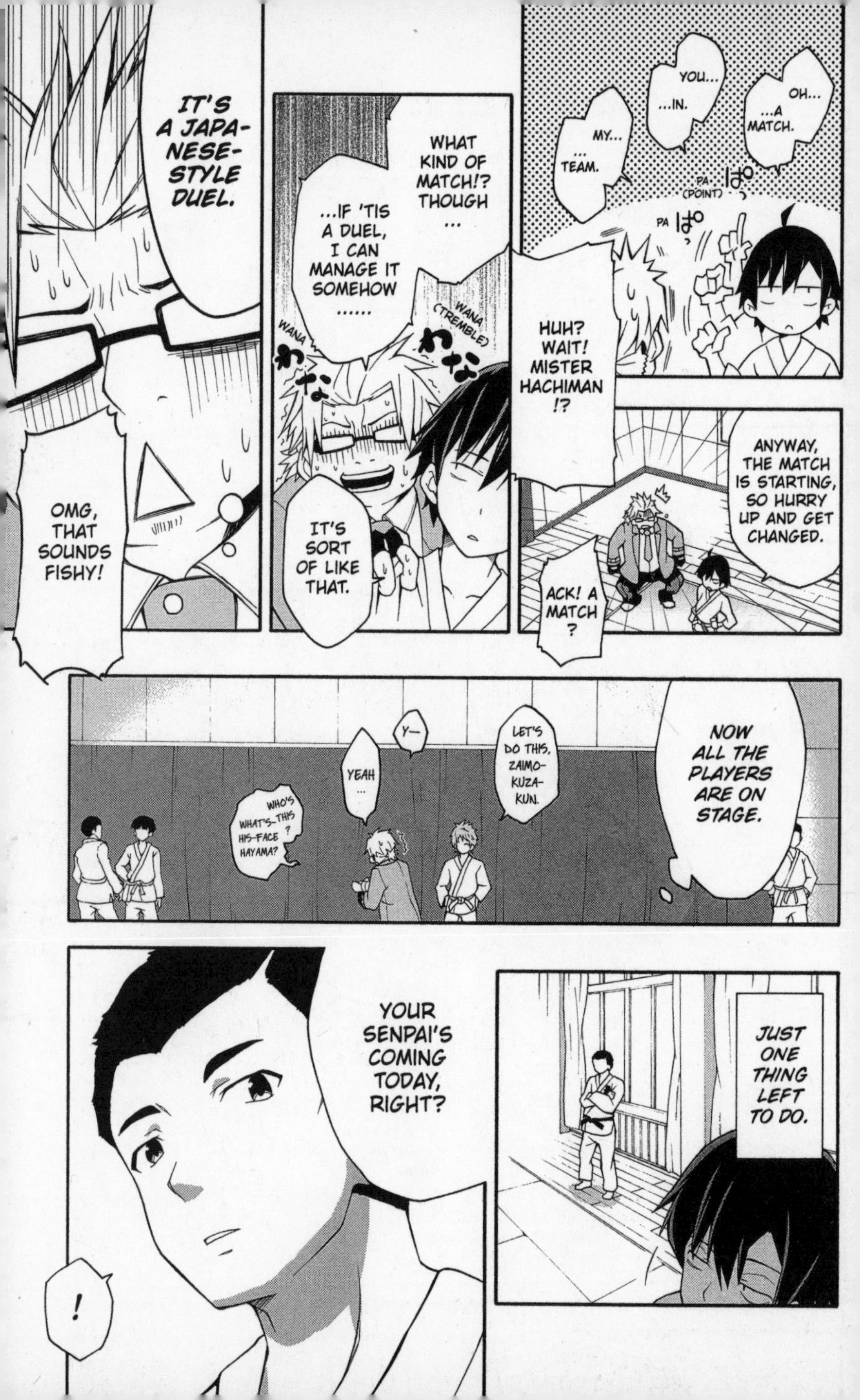
OH... ...A MATCH.
YOU... ...IN.
MY... ... TEAM.
PA (POINT) ぱ
PA ぱ
HUH? WAIT! MISTER HACHIMAN !?
ANYWAY, THE MATCH IS STARTING, SO HURRY UP AND GET CHANGED.
ACK! A MATCH ?
WHAT KIND OF MATCH!? THOUGH ...
...IF 'TIS A DUEL, I CAN MANAGE IT SOMEHOW ......
WANA (TREMBLE) わな
WANA わな
IT'S SORT OF LIKE THAT.
IT'S A JAPANESE-STYLE DUEL.
OMG, THAT SOUNDS FISHY!
NOW ALL THE PLAYERS ARE ON STAGE.
LET'S DO THIS, ZAIMOKUZA-KUN.
Y—
YEAH ...
WHO'S WHAT'S-THIS-HIS-FACE HAYAMA?
JUST ONE THING LEFT TO DO.
YOUR SENPAI'S COMING TODAY, RIGHT?
!

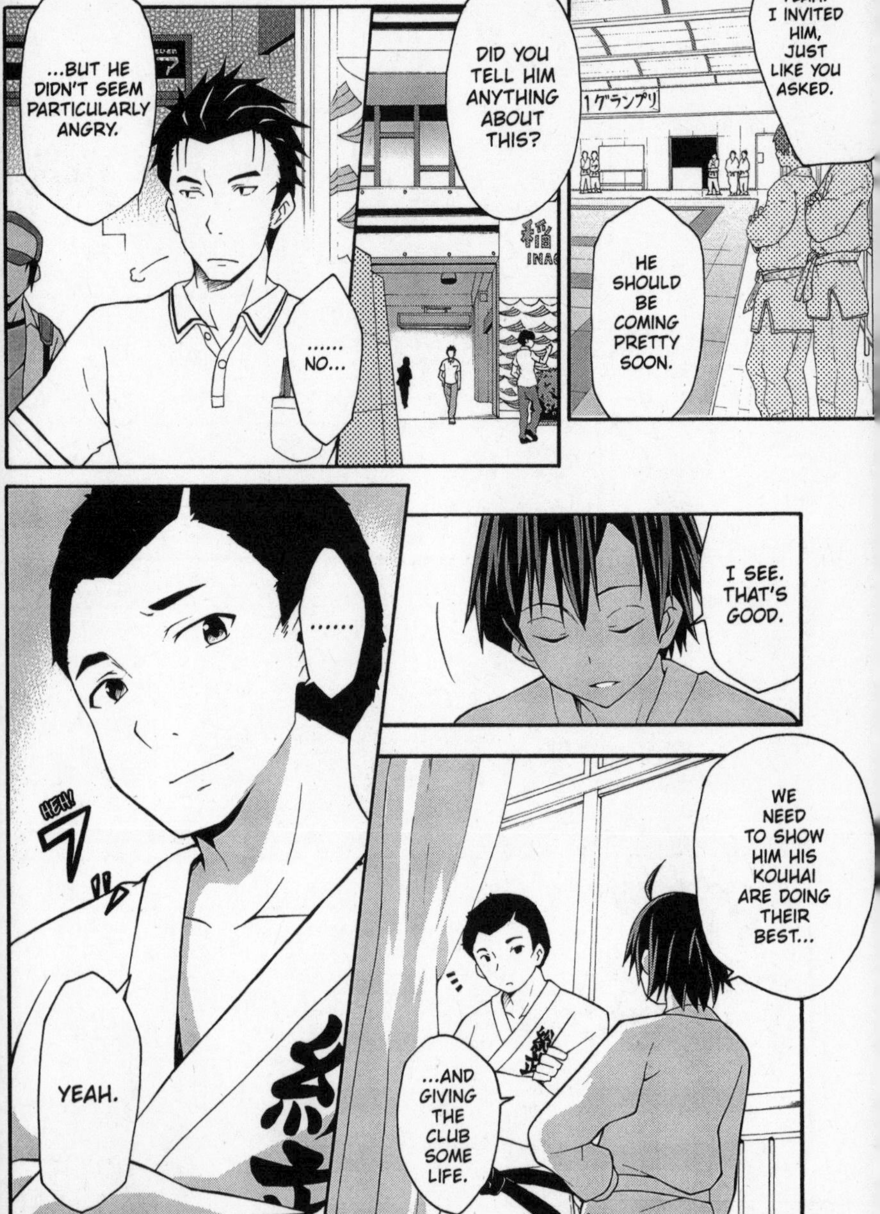
YEAH. I INVITED HIM, JUST LIKE YOU ASKED.
HE SHOULD BE COMING PRETTY SOON.
DID YOU TELL HIM ANYTHING ABOUT THIS?
......NO...
...BUT HE DIDN'T SEEM PARTICULARLY ANGRY.
I SEE. THAT'S GOOD.
WE NEED TO SHOW HIM HIS KOUHAI ARE DOING THEIR BEST...
...AND GIVING THE CLUB SOME LIFE.
......
HEH!
YEAH.

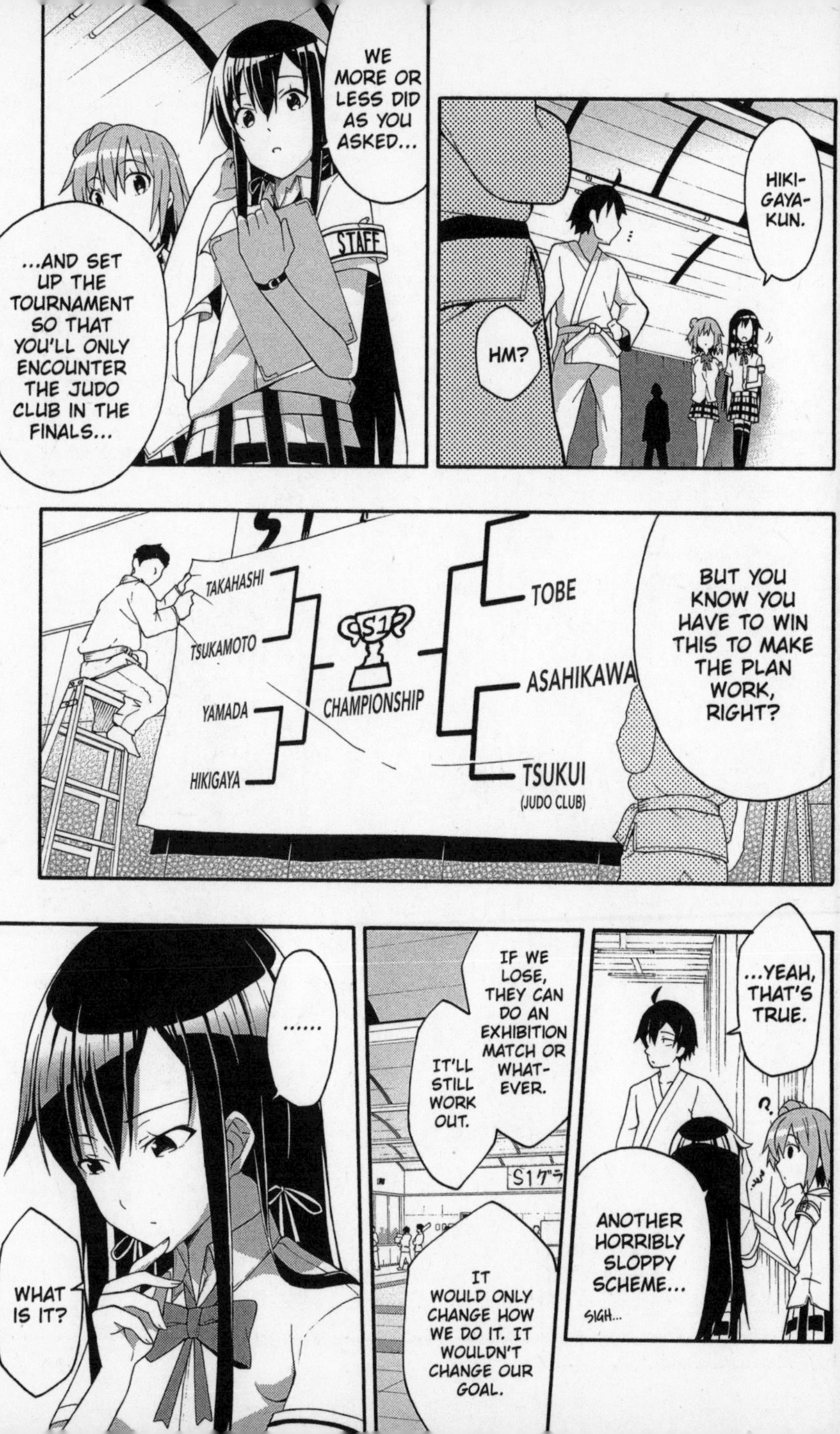
HIKI-GAYA-KUN.
HM?
WE MORE OR LESS DID AS YOU ASKED...
STAFF
...AND SET UP THE TOURNAMENT SO THAT YOU'LL ONLY ENCOUNTER THE JUDO CLUB IN THE FINALS...
BUT YOU KNOW YOU HAVE TO WIN THIS TO MAKE THE PLAN WORK, RIGHT?
TOBE
ASAHIKAWA
TSUKUI
(JUDO CLUB)
S1
CHAMPIONSHIP
TAKAHASHI
TSUKAMOTO
YAMADA
HIKIGAYA
...YEAH, THAT'S TRUE.
ANOTHER HORRIBLY SLOPPY SCHEME...
SIGH...
IF WE LOSE, THEY CAN DO AN EXHIBITION MATCH OR WHAT-EVER.
IT'LL STILL WORK OUT.
S1グラ
IT WOULD ONLY CHANGE HOW WE DO IT. IT WOULDN'T CHANGE OUR GOAL.
......
WHAT IS IT?

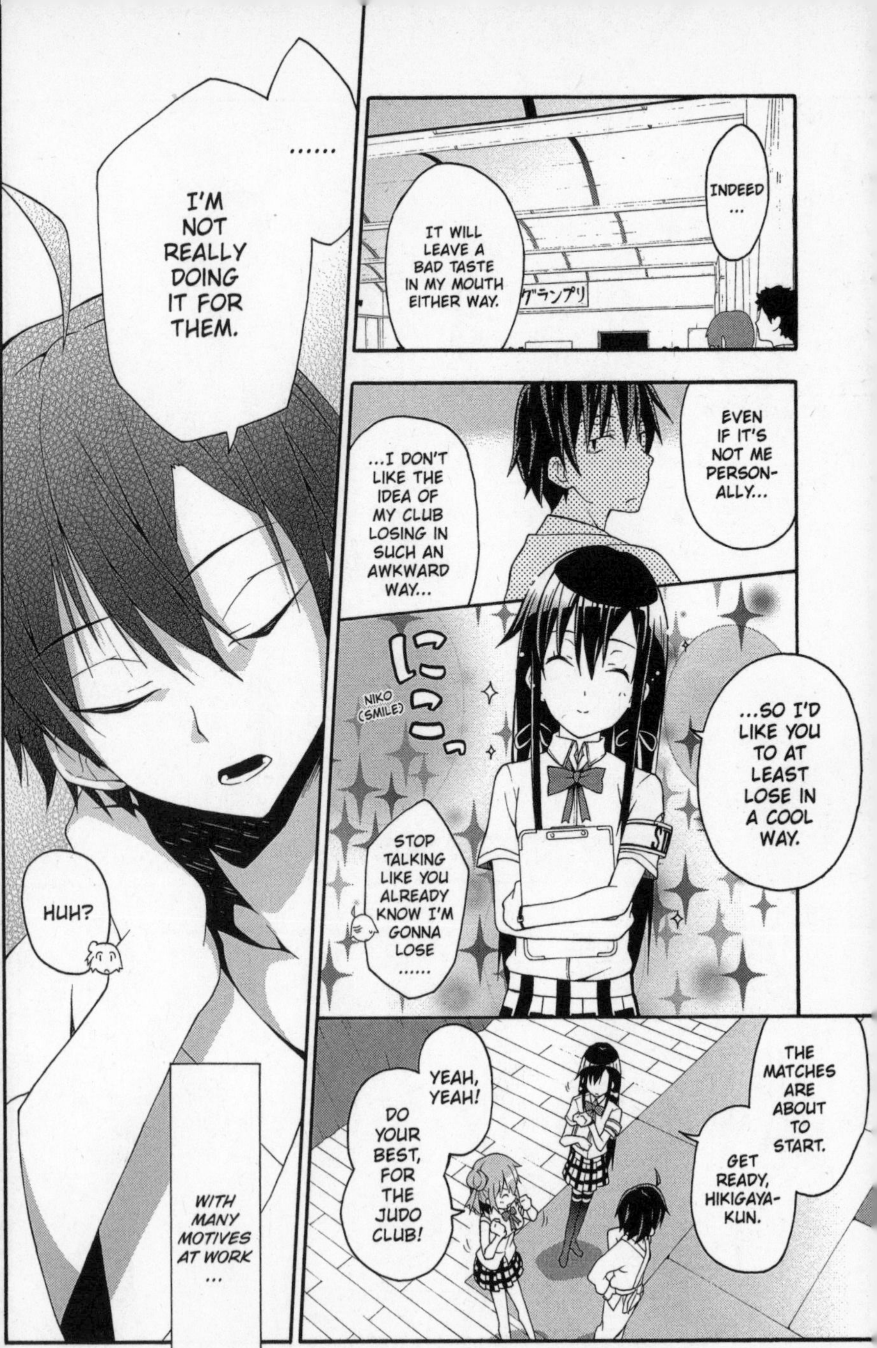
INDEED ...
IT WILL LEAVE A BAD TASTE IN MY MOUTH EITHER WAY.
グランプリ
EVEN IF IT'S NOT ME PERSONALLY...
...I DON'T LIKE THE IDEA OF MY CLUB LOSING IN SUCH AN AWKWARD WAY...
...SO I'D LIKE YOU TO AT LEAST LOSE IN A COOL WAY.
NIKO (SMILE)
STOP TALKING LIKE YOU ALREADY KNOW I'M GONNA LOSE ......
THE MATCHES ARE ABOUT TO START.
GET READY, HIKIGAYA-KUN.
YEAH, YEAH!
DO YOUR BEST, FOR THE JUDO CLUB!
......
I'M NOT REALLY DOING IT FOR THEM.
HUH?
WITH MANY MOTIVES AT WORK ...

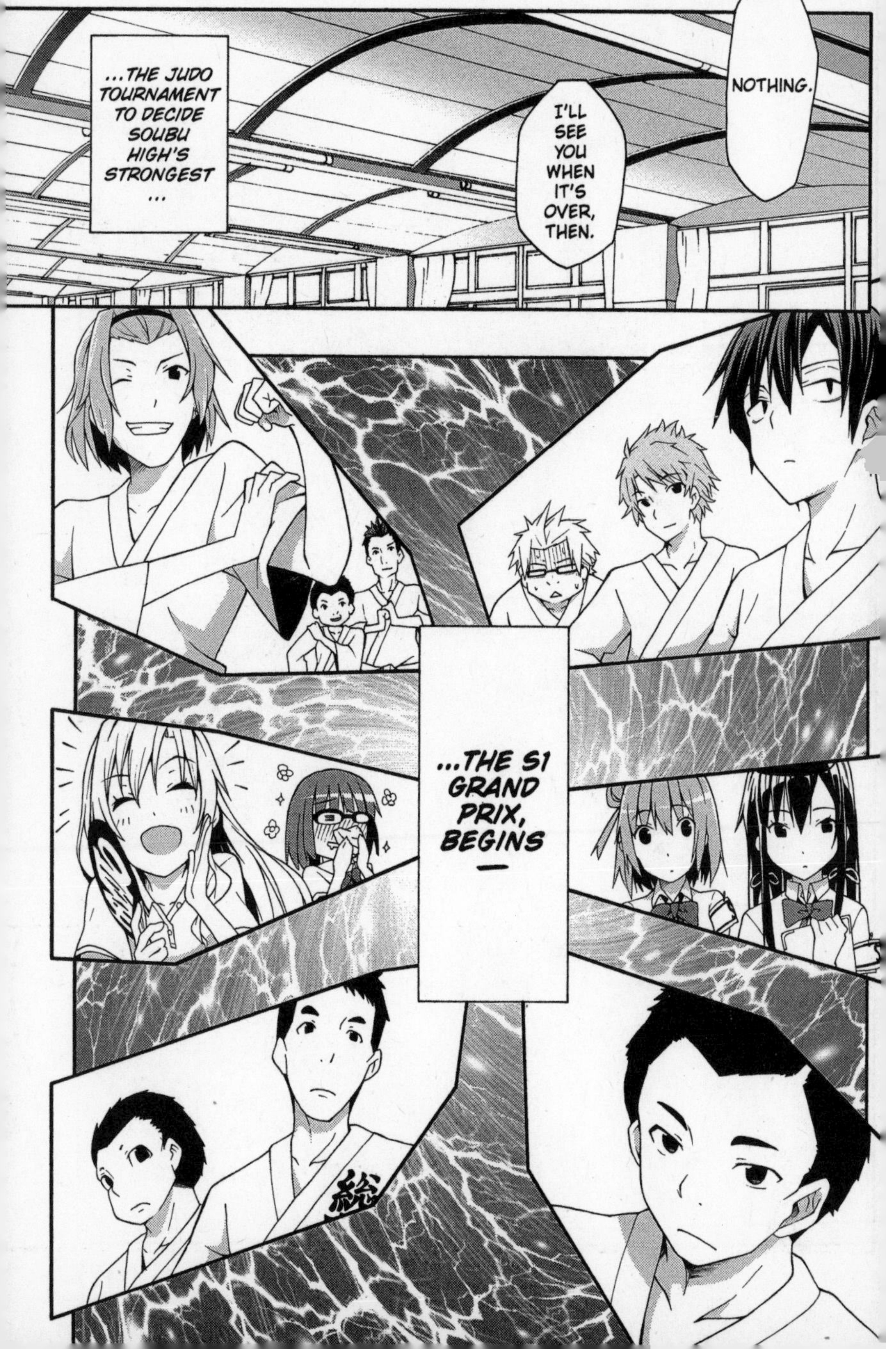
NOTHING.
I'LL SEE YOU WHEN IT'S OVER, THEN.
...THE JUDO TOURNAMENT TO DECIDE SOUBU HIGH'S STRONGEST ...
...THE S1 GRAND PRIX, BEGINS —

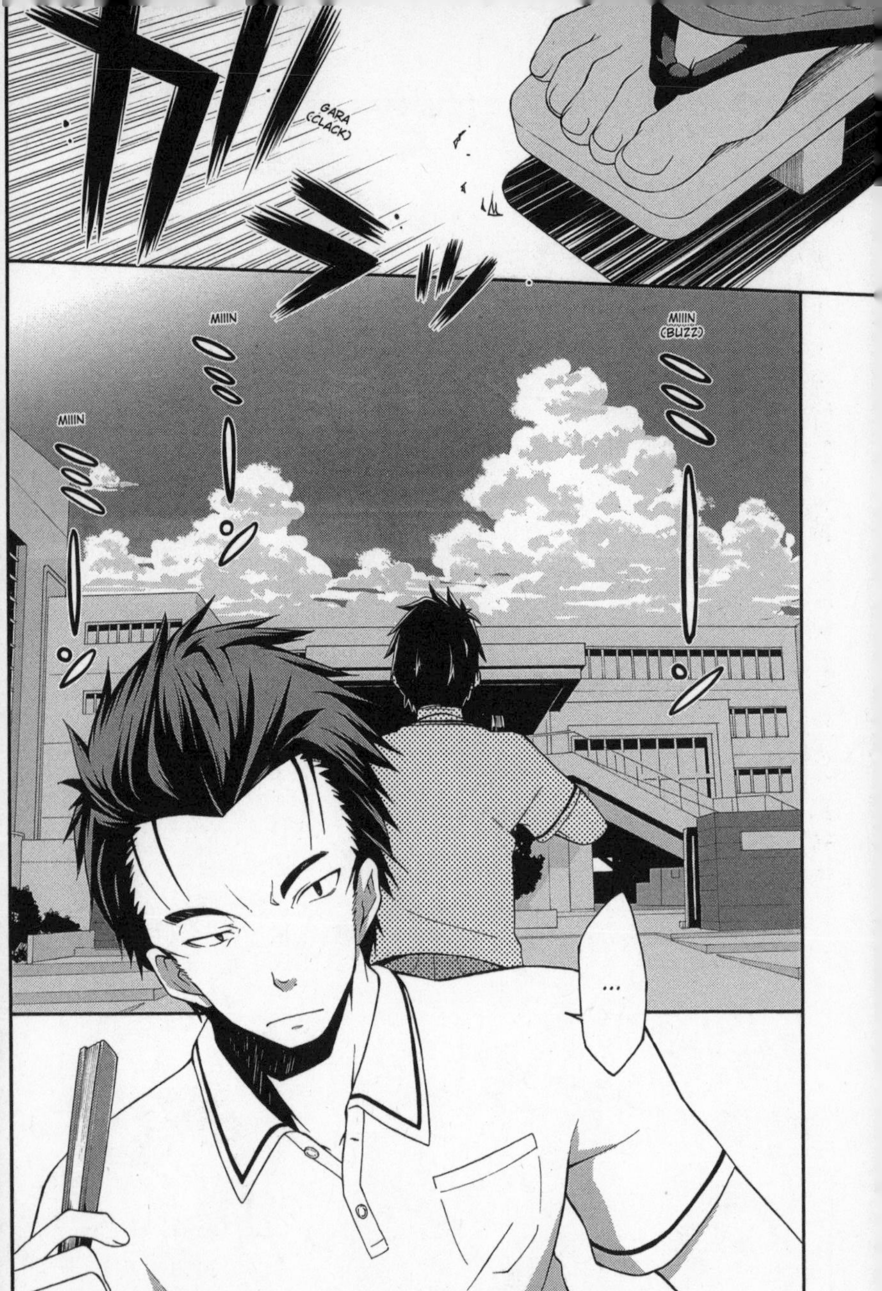
GARA
(CLACK)
MIIN
(BUZZ)
MIIN
MIIN
...

CHAPTER 22 ... THEY HAVE YET TO KNOW OF A PLACE THEY SHOULD GO BACK TO. (PART TWO)

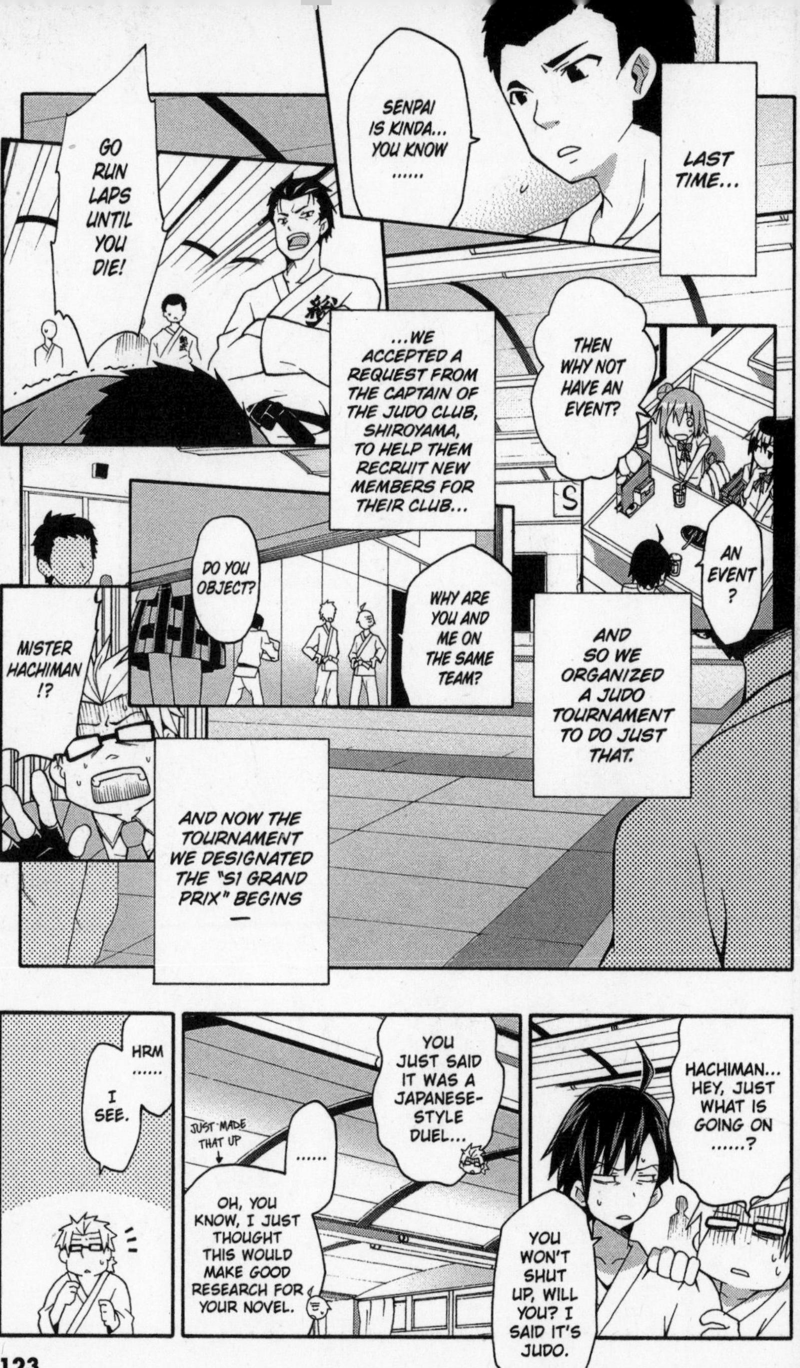
LAST TIME...
SENPAI IS KINDA... YOU KNOW ......
GO RUN LAPS UNTIL YOU DIE!
THEN WHY NOT HAVE AN EVENT?
AN EVENT?
...WE ACCEPTED A REQUEST FROM THE CAPTAIN OF THE JUDO CLUB, SHIROYAMA, TO HELP THEM RECRUIT NEW MEMBERS FOR THEIR CLUB...
AND SO WE ORGANIZED A JUDO TOURNAMENT TO DO JUST THAT.
WHY ARE YOU AND ME ON THE SAME TEAM?
DO YOU OBJECT?
MISTER HACHIMAN!?
AND NOW THE TOURNAMENT WE DESIGNATED THE "S1 GRAND PRIX" BEGINS —
HACHIMAN... HEY, JUST WHAT IS GOING ON ......?
YOU WON'T SHUT UP, WILL YOU? I SAID IT'S JUDO.
YOU JUST SAID IT WAS A JAPANESE-STYLE DUEL...
......
JUST MADE THAT UP
OH, YOU KNOW, I JUST THOUGHT THIS WOULD MAKE GOOD RESEARCH FOR YOUR NOVEL.
HRM ...... I SEE.

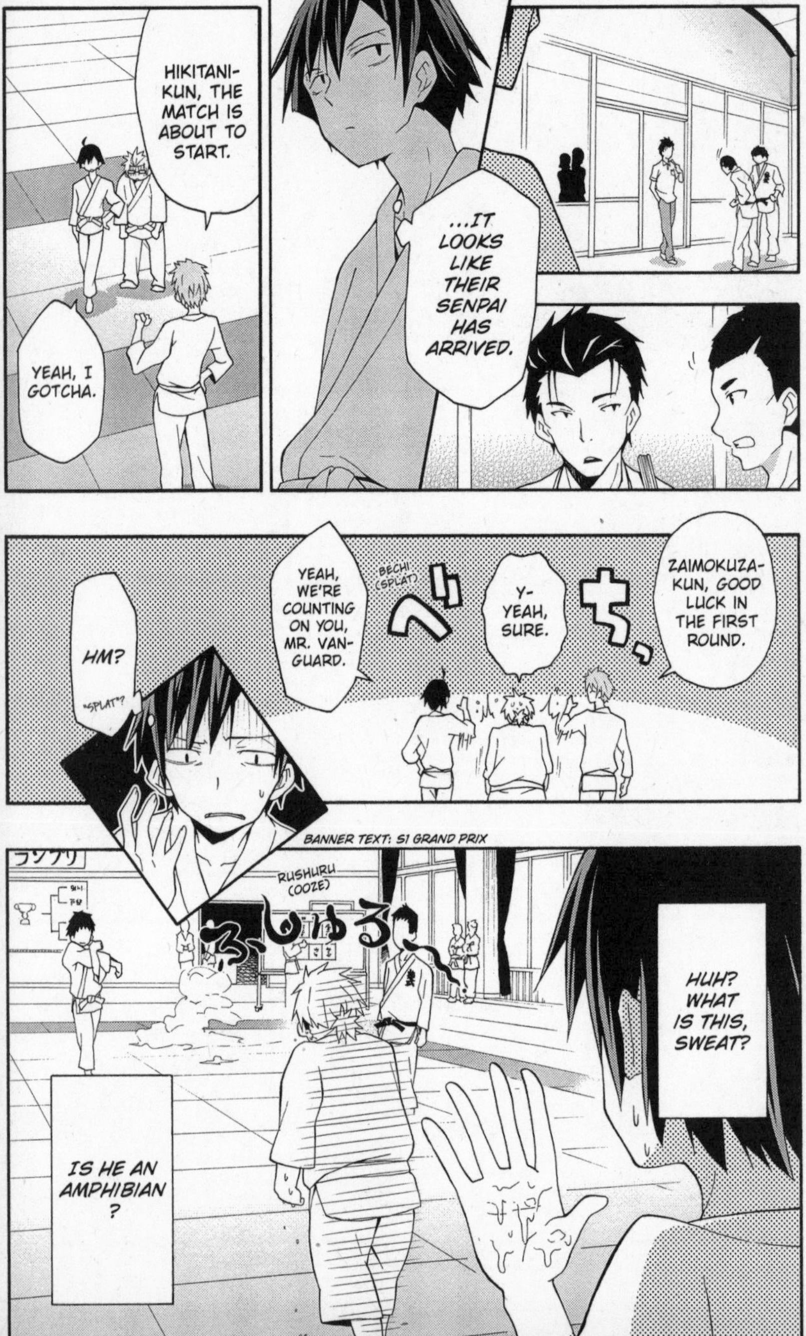
...IT LOOKS LIKE THEIR SENPAI HAS ARRIVED.
HIKITANI-KUN, THE MATCH IS ABOUT TO START.
YEAH, I GOTCHA.
ZAIMOKUZA-KUN, GOOD LUCK IN THE FIRST ROUND.
Y-YEAH, SURE.
BECHI (SPLAT)
YEAH, WE'RE COUNTING ON YOU, MR. VANGUARD.
HM?
"SPLAT"?
BANNER TEXT: S1 GRAND PRIX
HUH? WHAT IS THIS, SWEAT?
RUSHURU (OOZE)
IS HE AN AMPHIBIAN?

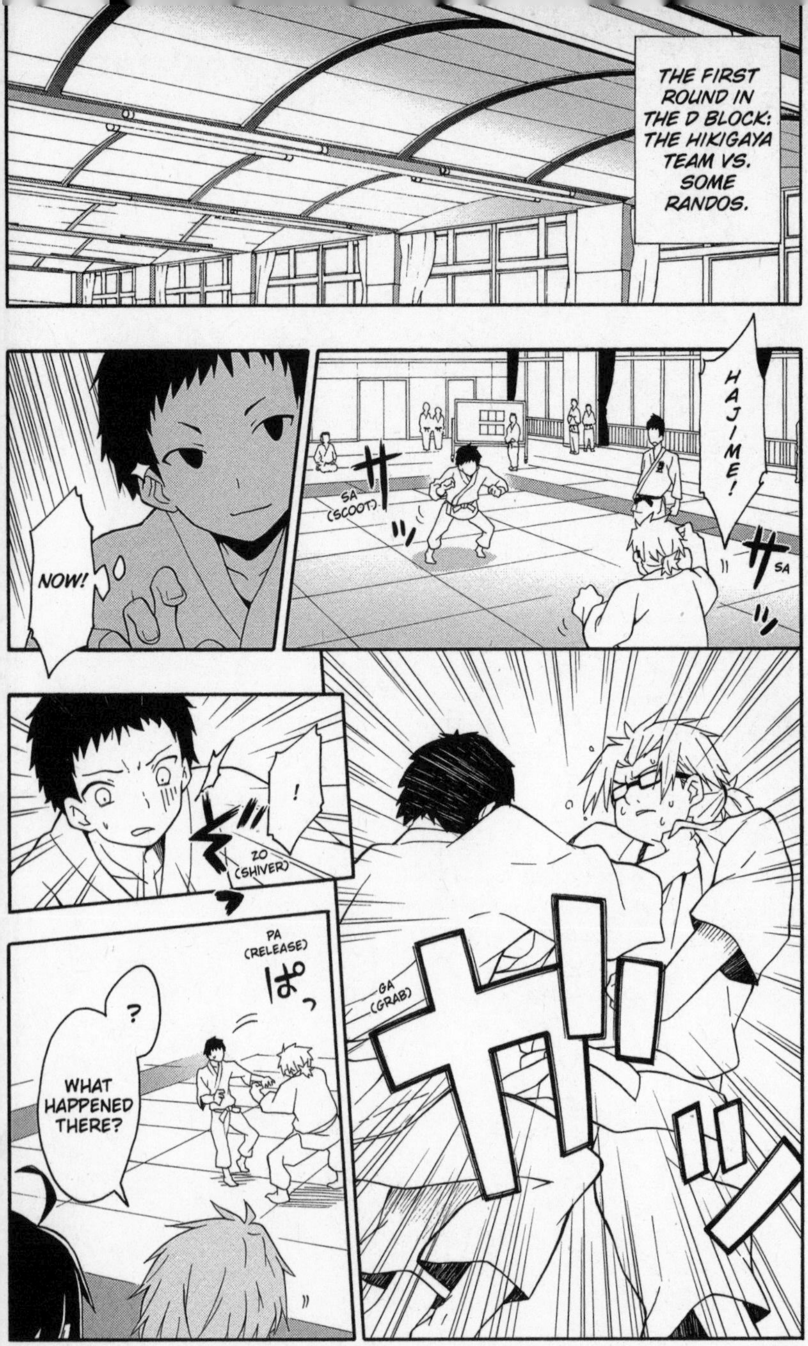

THE FIRST ROUND IN THE D BLOCK: THE HIKIGAYA TEAM VS. SOME RANDOS.
HAJIME!
SA
SA (SCOOT)
NOW!
GA (GRAB)
!
ZO (SHIVER)
PA (RELEASE)
ぱっ
?
WHAT HAPPENED THERE?

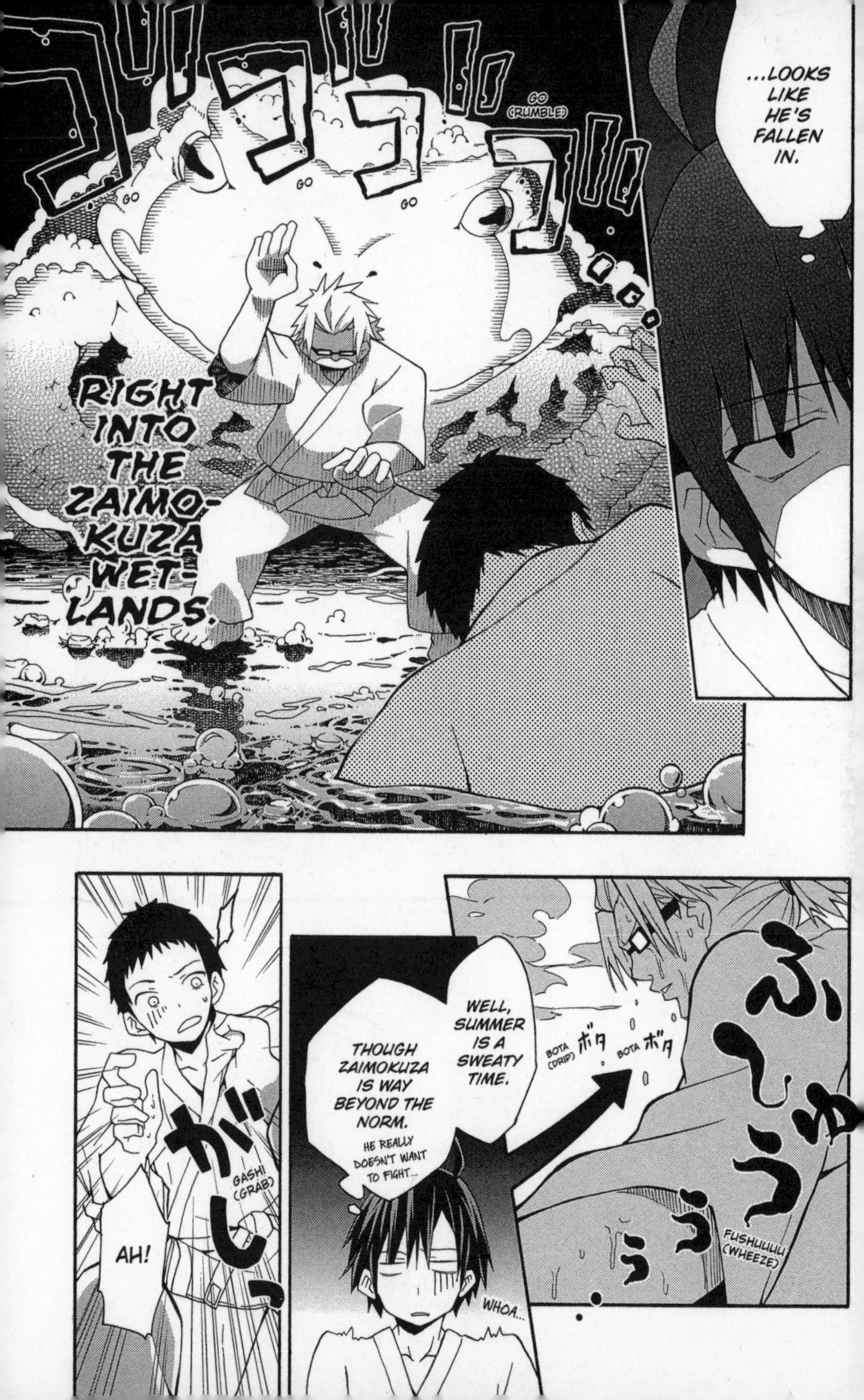
...LOOKS LIKE HE'S FALLEN IN.
GO (RUMBLE)
GO
GO
GO
GO
RIGHT INTO THE ZAIMOKUZA WETLANDS.
BOTA (DRIP) ボタ
BOTA ボタ
FUSHUUUU (WHEEZE)
WELL, SUMMER IS A SWEATY TIME.
THOUGH ZAIMOKUZA IS WAY BEYOND THE NORM.
HE REALLY DOESN'T WANT TO FIGHT...
WHOA...
GASHI (GRAB)
AH!

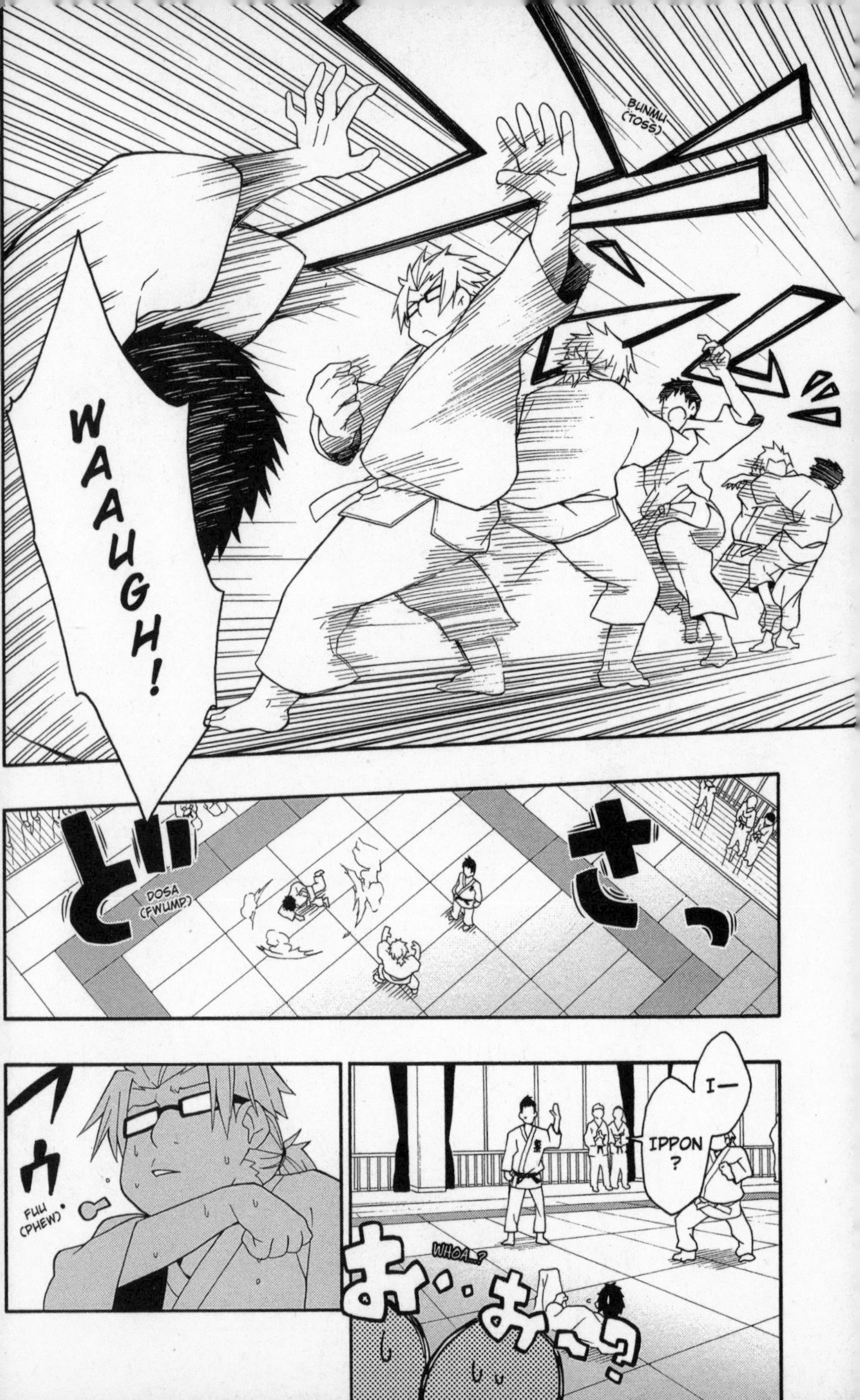

BUNMU (TOSS)
WAAUGH!
どさっ
DOSA (FWUMP)
I—
IPPON ?
WHOA...?
FUU (PHEW)

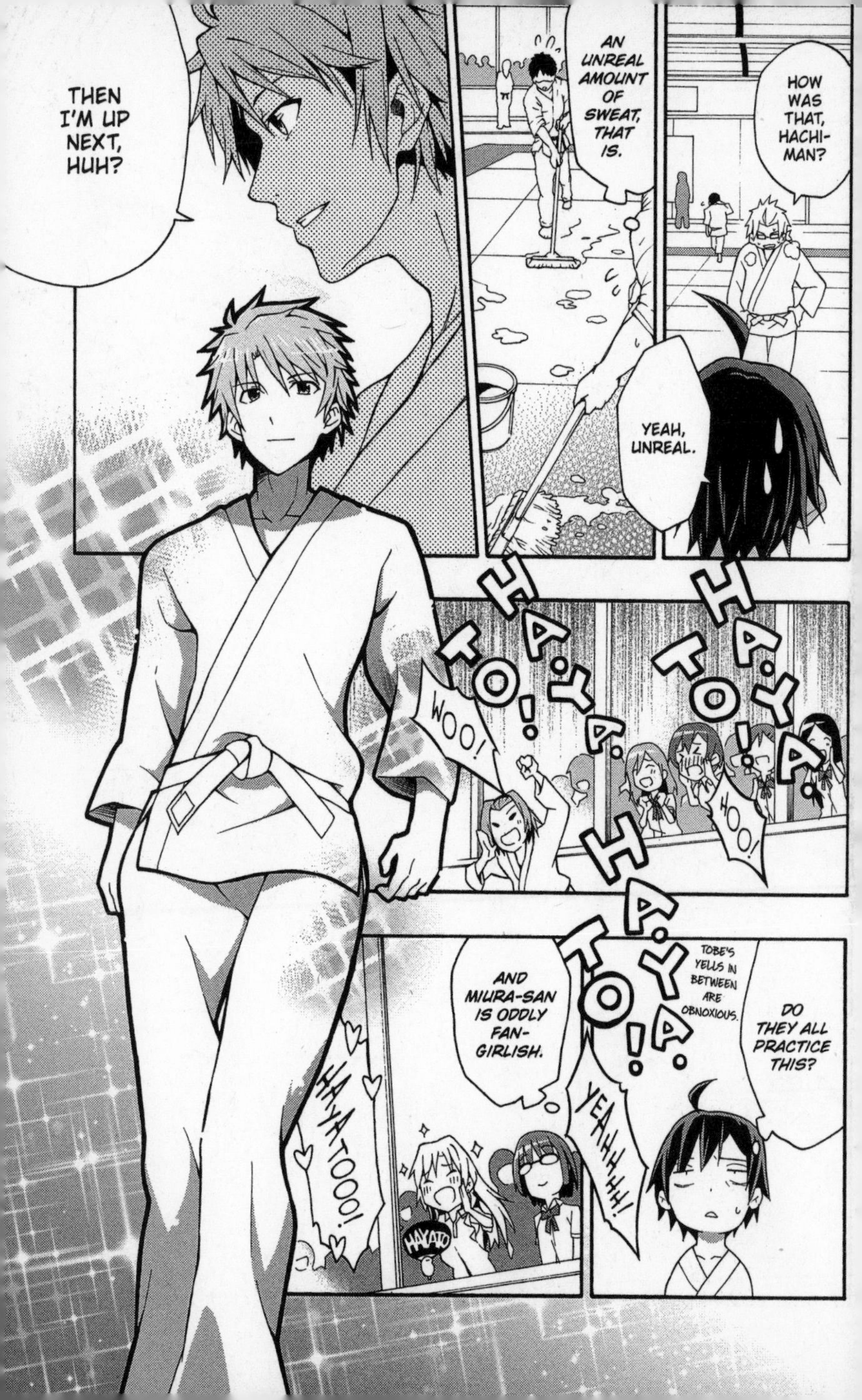
HOW WAS THAT, HACHI-MAN?
AN UNREAL AMOUNT OF SWEAT, THAT IS.
YEAH, UNREAL.
THEN I'M UP NEXT, HUH?
HA-YA-TO!
HA-YA-TO!
WOO!
HOO!
HA-YA-TO!
DO THEY ALL PRACTICE THIS?
TOBE'S YELLS IN BETWEEN ARE OBNOXIOUS.
AND MIURA-SAN IS ODDLY FAN-GIRLISH.
YEAHHHH!
HAYATOOO!
HAYATO

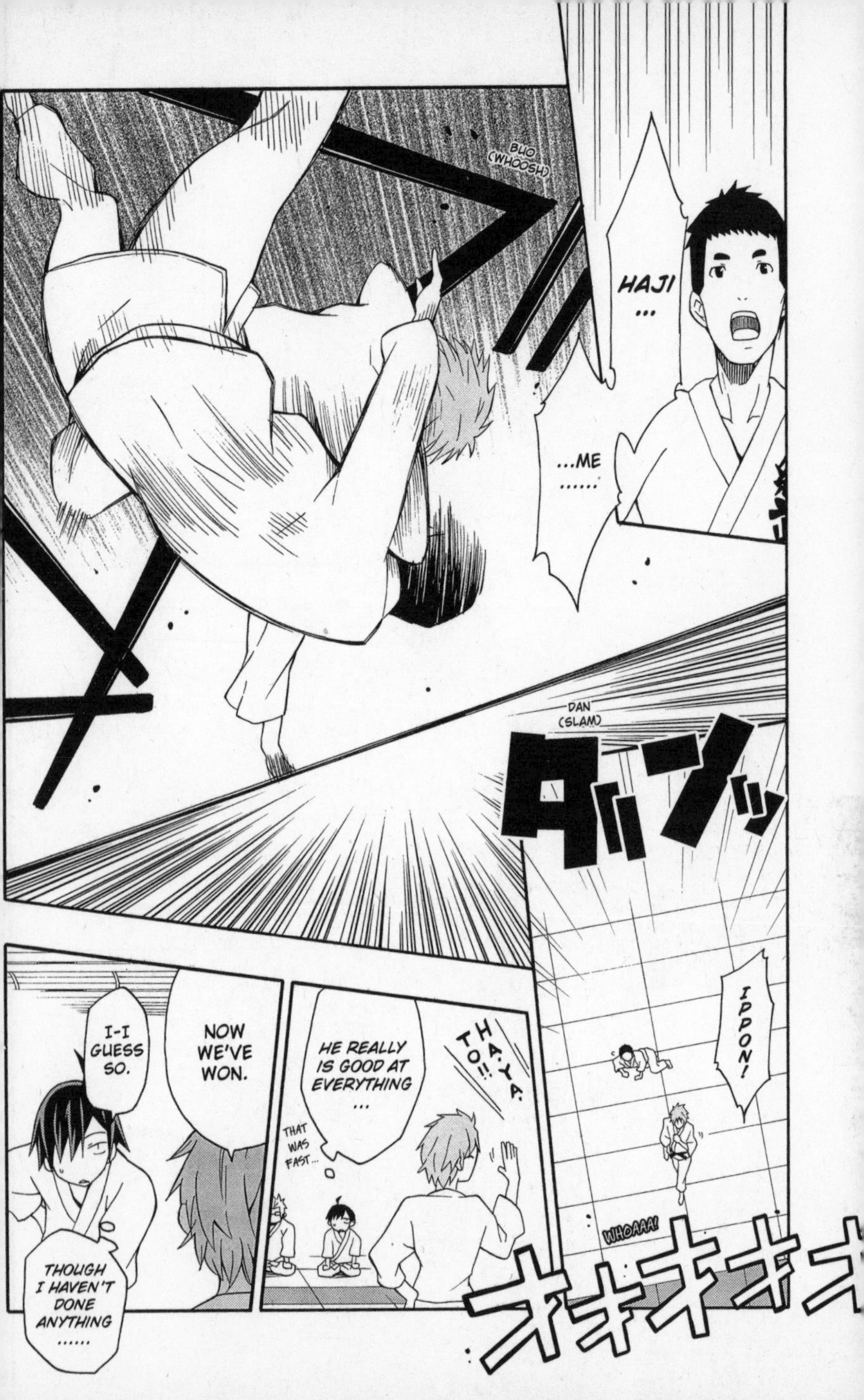
HAJI ...
...ME ......
BUO (WHOOSH)
DAN (SLAM)
IPPON!
WHOAAA!
THA-YA-TO!!
HE REALLY IS GOOD AT EVERYTHING ...
THAT WAS FAST...
NOW WE'VE WON.
I-I GUESS SO.
THOUGH I HAVEN'T DONE ANYTHING ......

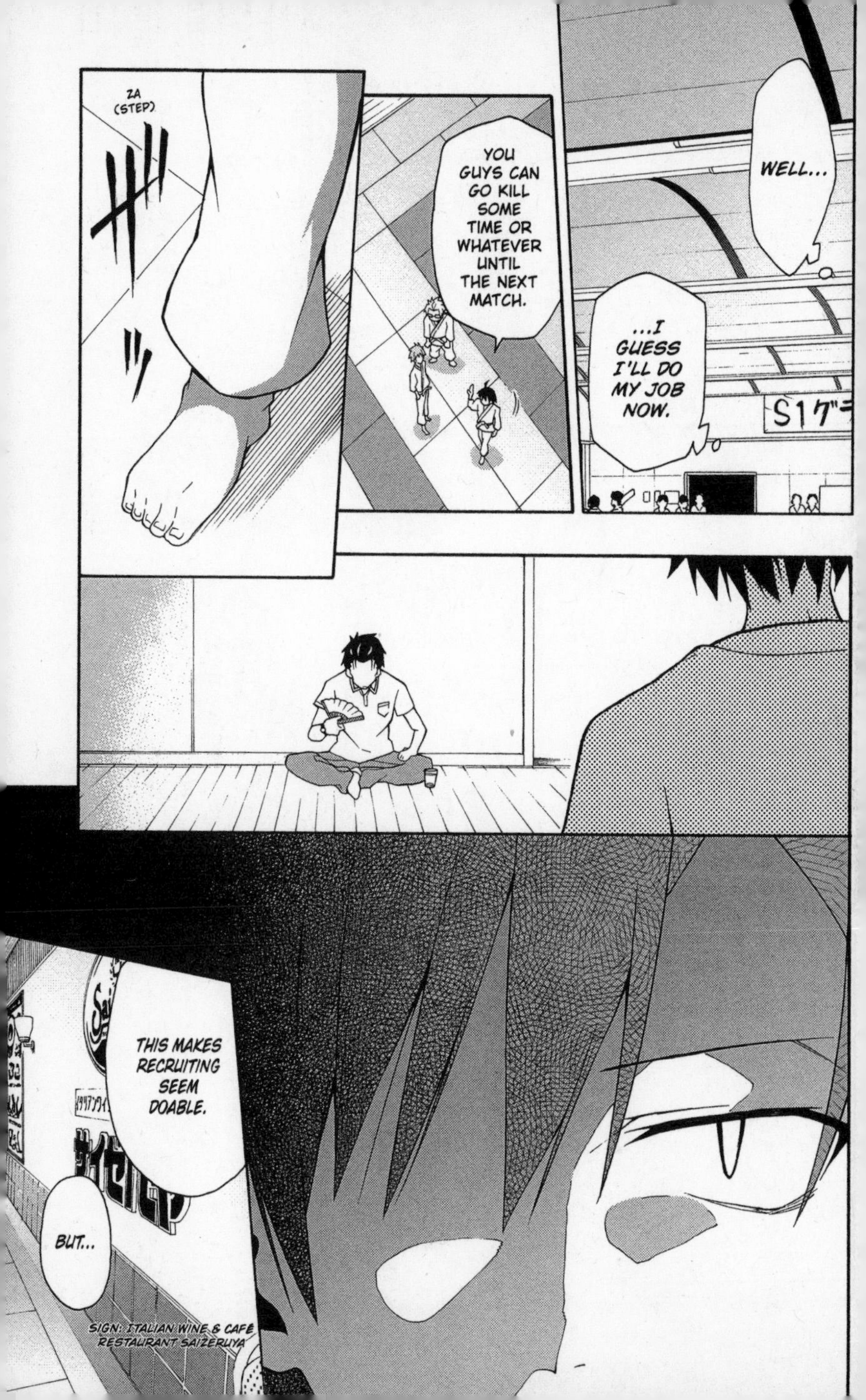
WELL...
...I GUESS I'LL DO MY JOB NOW.
S1グ
YOU GUYS CAN GO KILL SOME TIME OR WHATEVER UNTIL THE NEXT MATCH.
ZA (STEP)
THIS MAKES RECRUITING SEEM DOABLE.
BUT...
SIGN: ITALIAN WINE & CAFE RESTAURANT SAIZERUYA

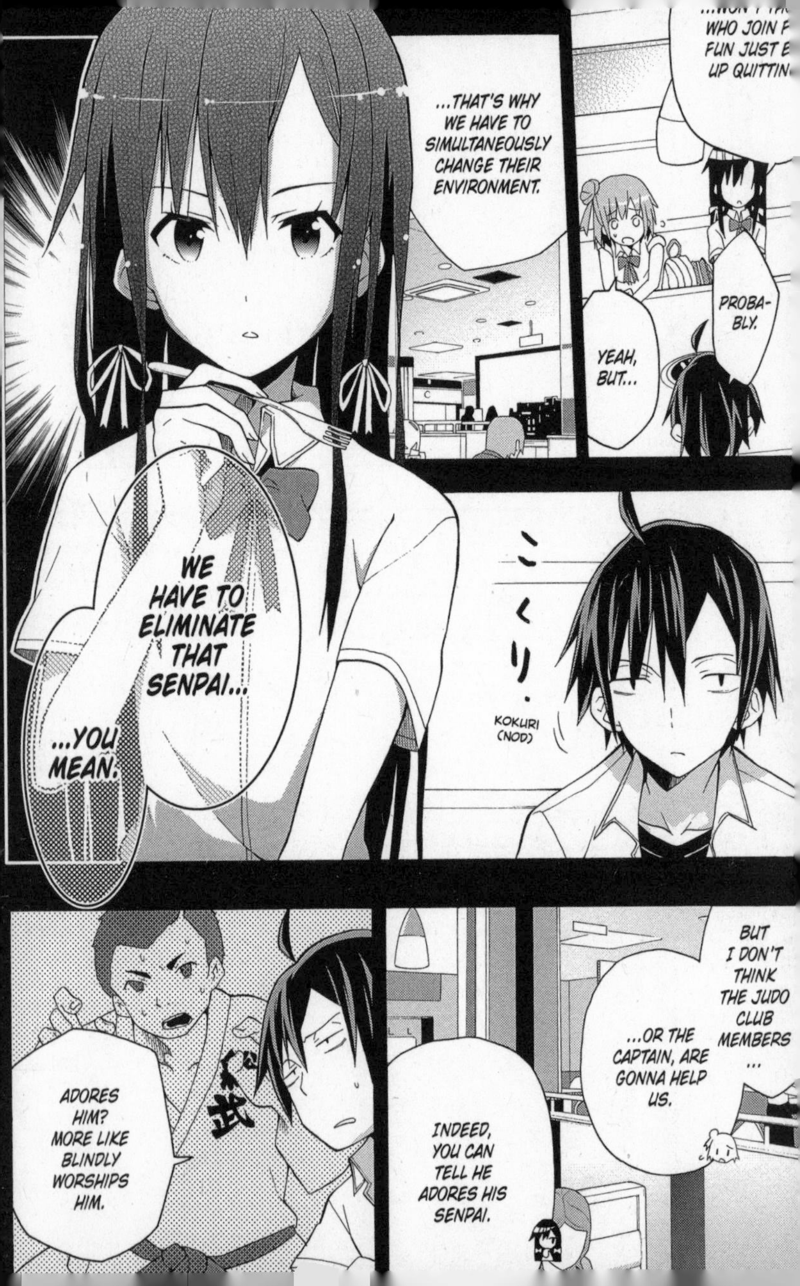
WHO JOIN F FUN JUST E UP QUITTIN
PROBABLY.
YEAH, BUT...
...THAT'S WHY WE HAVE TO SIMULTANEOUSLY CHANGE THEIR ENVIRONMENT.
WE HAVE TO ELIMINATE THAT SENPAI...
...YOU MEAN.
こくり
KOKURI (NOD)
BUT I DON'T THINK THE JUDO CLUB MEMBERS ...
...OR THE CAPTAIN, ARE GONNA HELP US.
INDEED, YOU CAN TELL HE ADORES HIS SENPAI.
ADORES HIM? MORE LIKE BLINDLY WORSHIPS HIM.

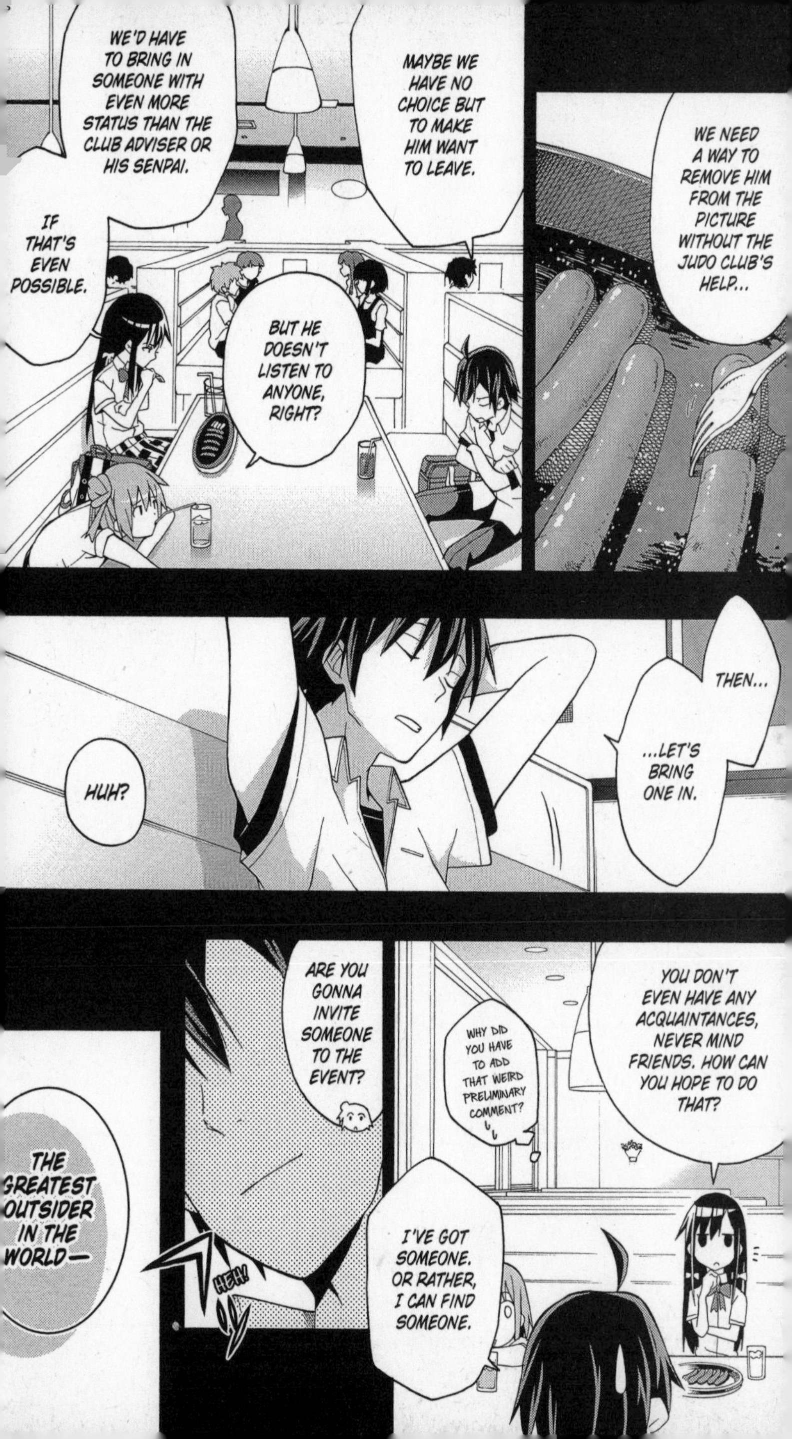
WE NEED A WAY TO REMOVE HIM FROM THE PICTURE WITHOUT THE JUDO CLUB'S HELP...
MAYBE WE HAVE NO CHOICE BUT TO MAKE HIM WANT TO LEAVE.
WE'D HAVE TO BRING IN SOMEONE WITH EVEN MORE STATUS THAN THE CLUB ADVISER OR HIS SENPAI.
IF THAT'S EVEN POSSIBLE.
BUT HE DOESN'T LISTEN TO ANYONE, RIGHT?
THEN...
...LET'S BRING ONE IN.
HUH?
YOU DON'T EVEN HAVE ANY ACQUAINTANCES, NEVER MIND FRIENDS. HOW CAN YOU HOPE TO DO THAT?
WHY DID YOU HAVE TO ADD THAT WEIRD PRELIMINARY COMMENT?
I'VE GOT SOMEONE. OR RATHER, I CAN FIND SOMEONE.
ARE YOU GONNA INVITE SOMEONE TO THE EVENT?
HEH!
THE GREATEST OUTSIDER IN THE WORLD—

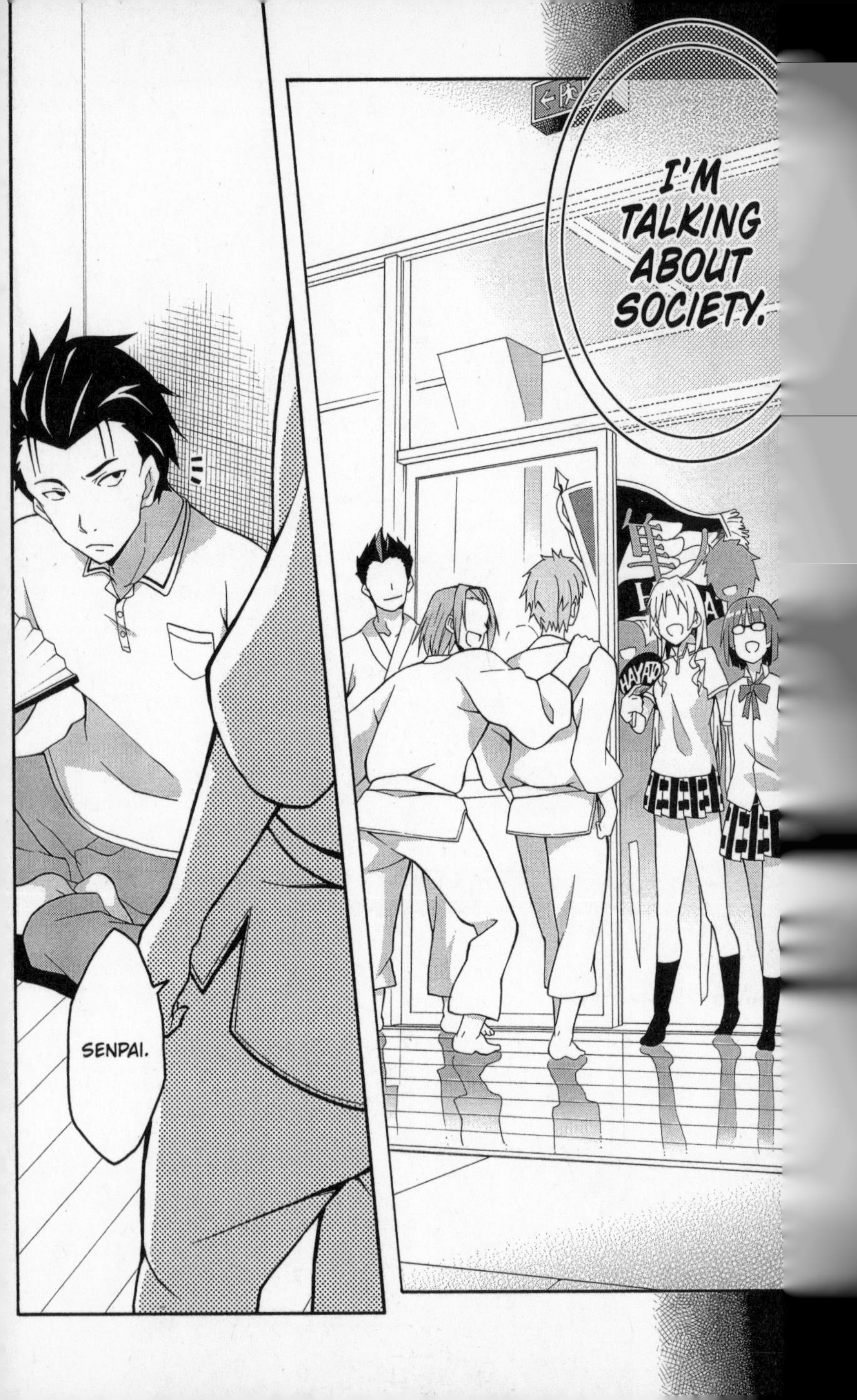
I'M TALKING ABOUT SOCIETY.
HAYATO
SENPAI.

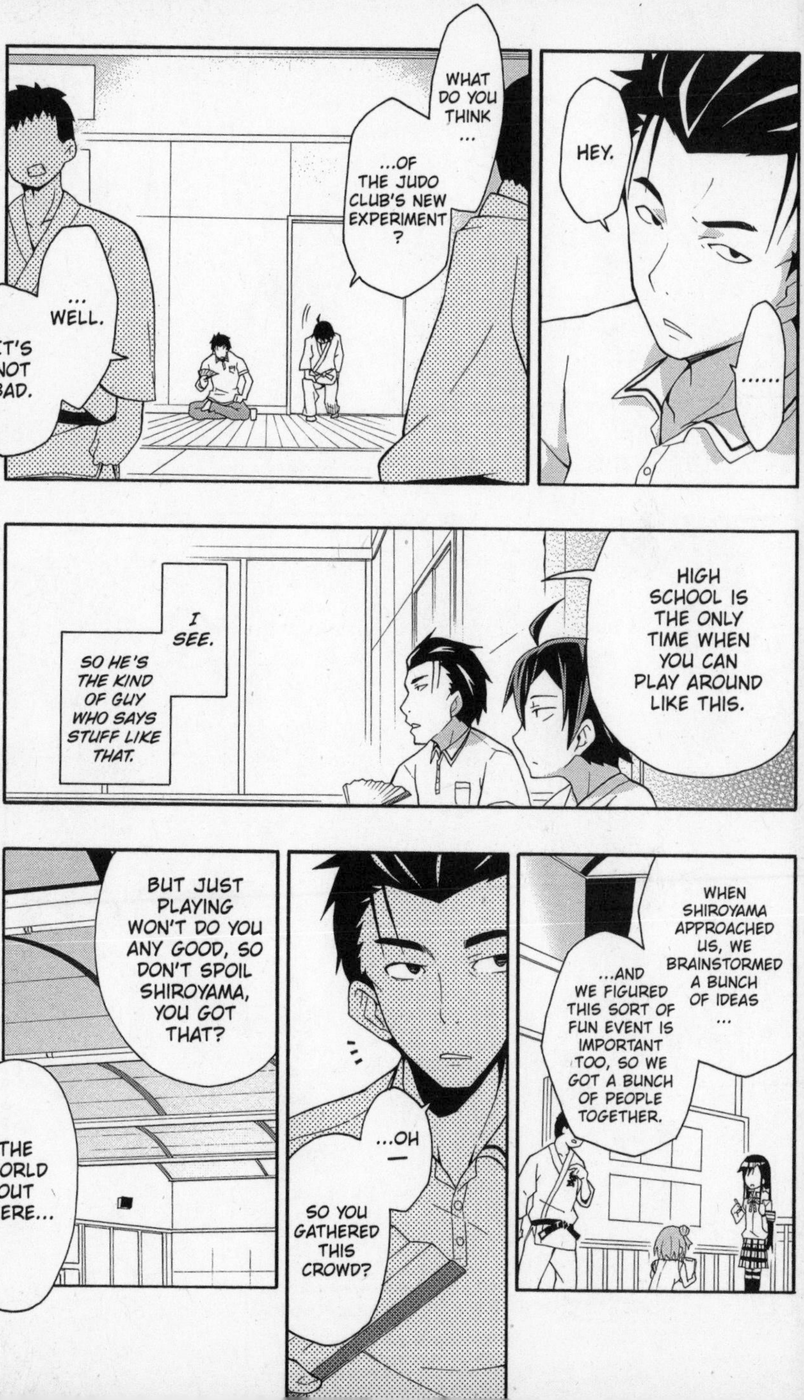
HEY.
......
WHAT DO YOU THINK ...
...OF THE JUDO CLUB'S NEW EXPERIMENT?
... WELL.
IT'S NOT BAD.
HIGH SCHOOL IS THE ONLY TIME WHEN YOU CAN PLAY AROUND LIKE THIS.
I SEE.
SO HE'S THE KIND OF GUY WHO SAYS STUFF LIKE THAT.
WHEN SHIROYAMA APPROACHED US, WE BRAINSTORMED A BUNCH OF IDEAS ...
...AND WE FIGURED THIS SORT OF FUN EVENT IS IMPORTANT TOO, SO WE GOT A BUNCH OF PEOPLE TOGETHER.
...OH—
SO YOU GATHERED THIS CROWD?
BUT JUST PLAYING WON'T DO YOU ANY GOOD, SO DON'T SPOIL SHIROYAMA, YOU GOT THAT?
THE WORLD OUT THERE...

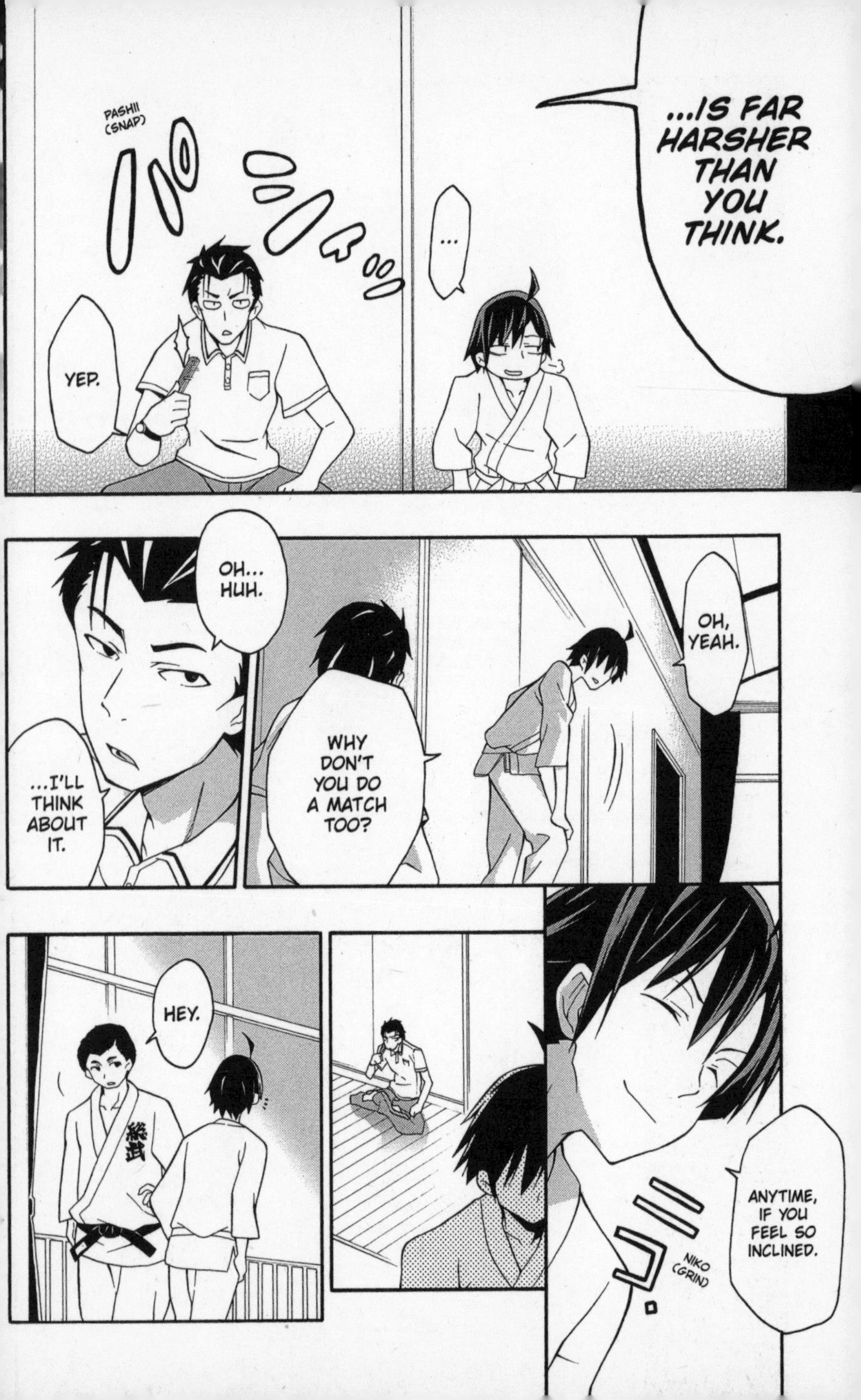
...IS FAR HARSHER THAN YOU THINK.
...
PASHII (SNAP)
YEP.
OH, YEAH.
WHY DON'T YOU DO A MATCH TOO?
OH... HUH.
...I'LL THINK ABOUT IT.
ANYTIME, IF YOU FEEL SO INCLINED.
NIKO (GRIN)
HEY.

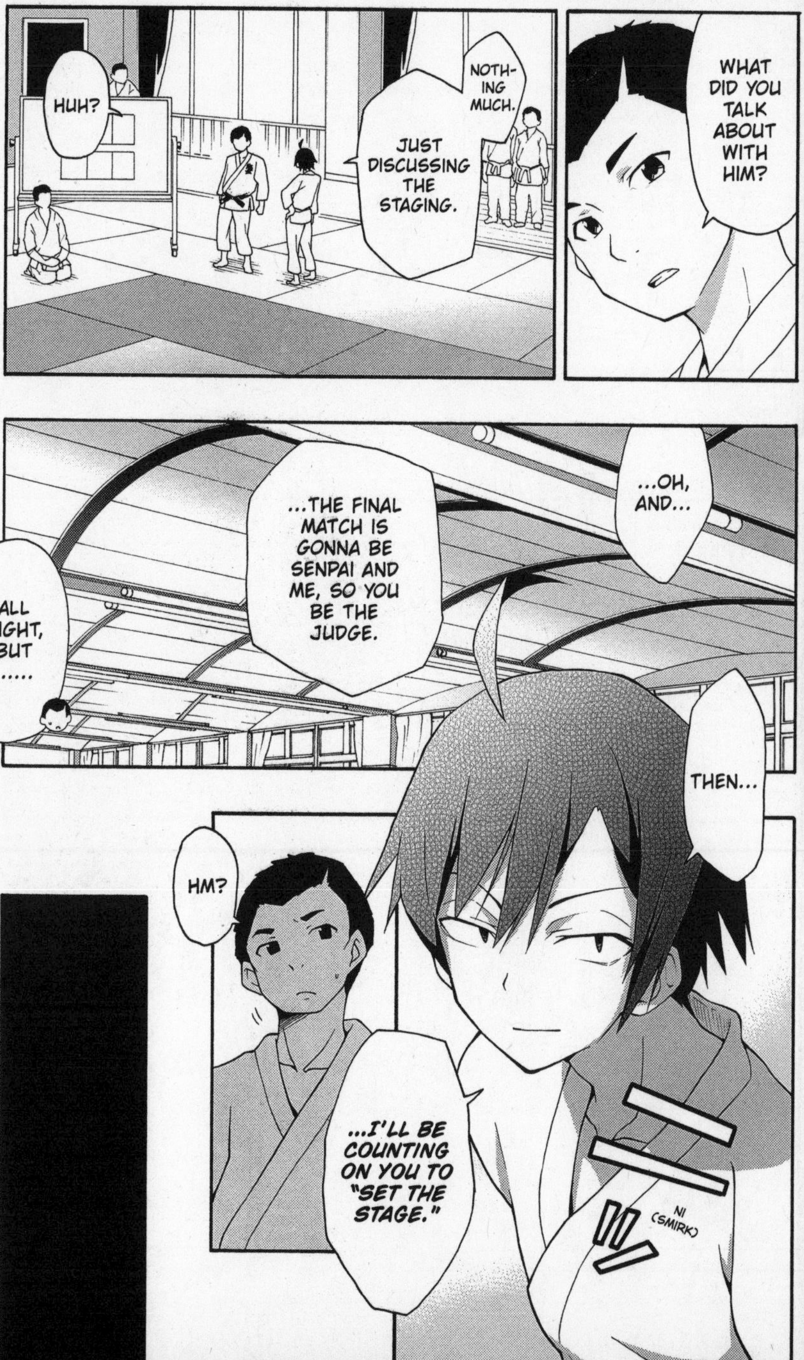
WHAT DID YOU TALK ABOUT WITH HIM?
NOTH-ING MUCH.
JUST DISCUSSING THE STAGING.
HUH?
...OH, AND...
...THE FINAL MATCH IS GONNA BE SENPAI AND ME, SO YOU BE THE JUDGE.
ALL RIGHT, BUT ......
THEN...
HM?
...I'LL BE COUNTING ON YOU TO "SET THE STAGE."
NI (SMIRK)

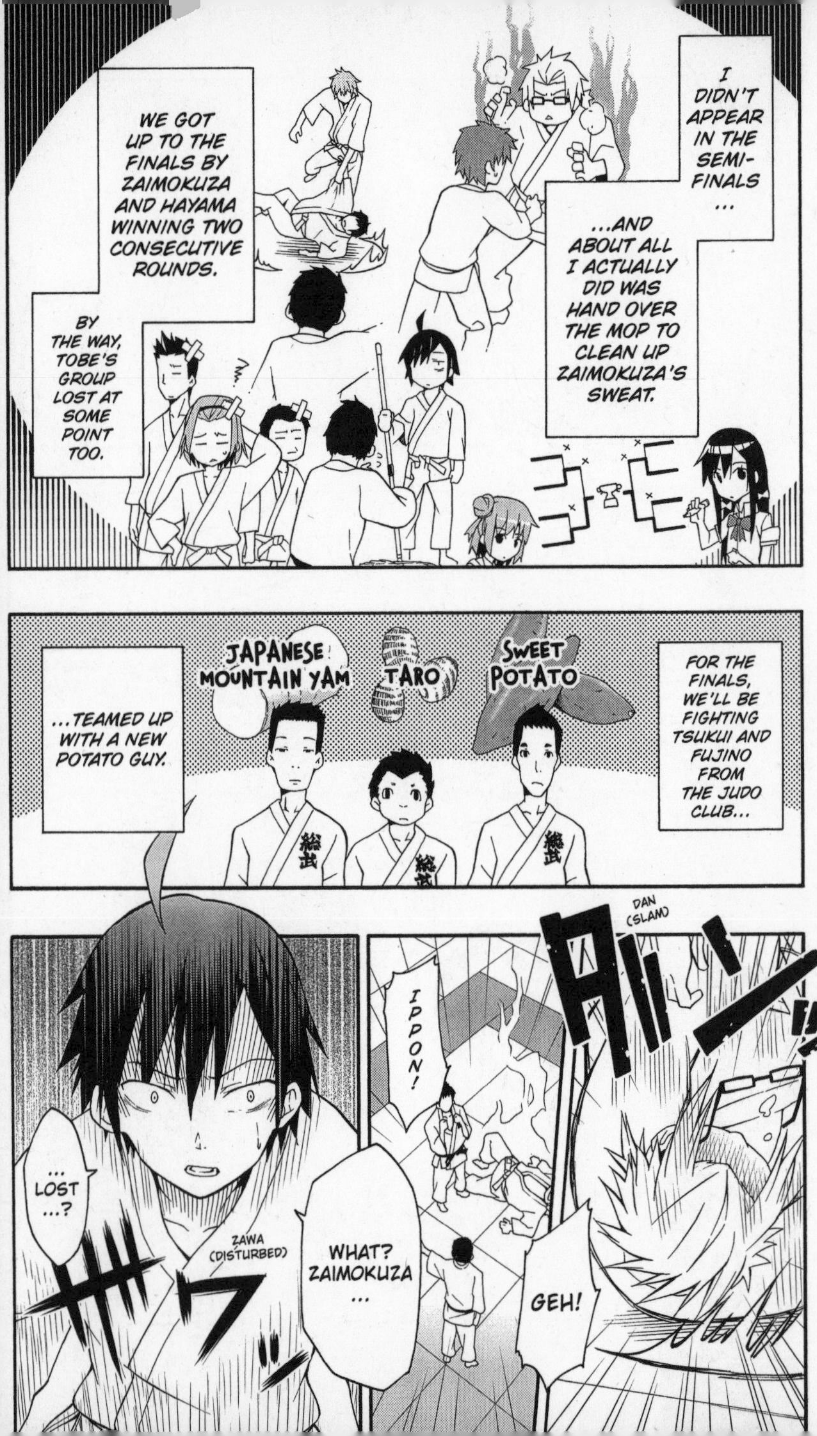
I DIDN'T APPEAR IN THE SEMI-FINALS...
...AND ABOUT ALL I ACTUALLY DID WAS HAND OVER THE MOP TO CLEAN UP ZAIMOKUZA'S SWEAT.
WE GOT UP TO THE FINALS BY ZAIMOKUZA AND HAYAMA WINNING TWO CONSECUTIVE ROUNDS.
BY THE WAY, TOBE'S GROUP LOST AT SOME POINT TOO.
FOR THE FINALS, WE'LL BE FIGHTING TSUKUI AND FUJINO FROM THE JUDO CLUB...
SWEET POTATO
TARO
JAPANESE MOUNTAIN YAM
...TEAMED UP WITH A NEW POTATO GUY.
総武
総武
総武
DAN (SLAM)
IPPON!
GEH!
WHAT? ZAIMOKUZA...
ZAWA (DISTURBED)
...LOST...?

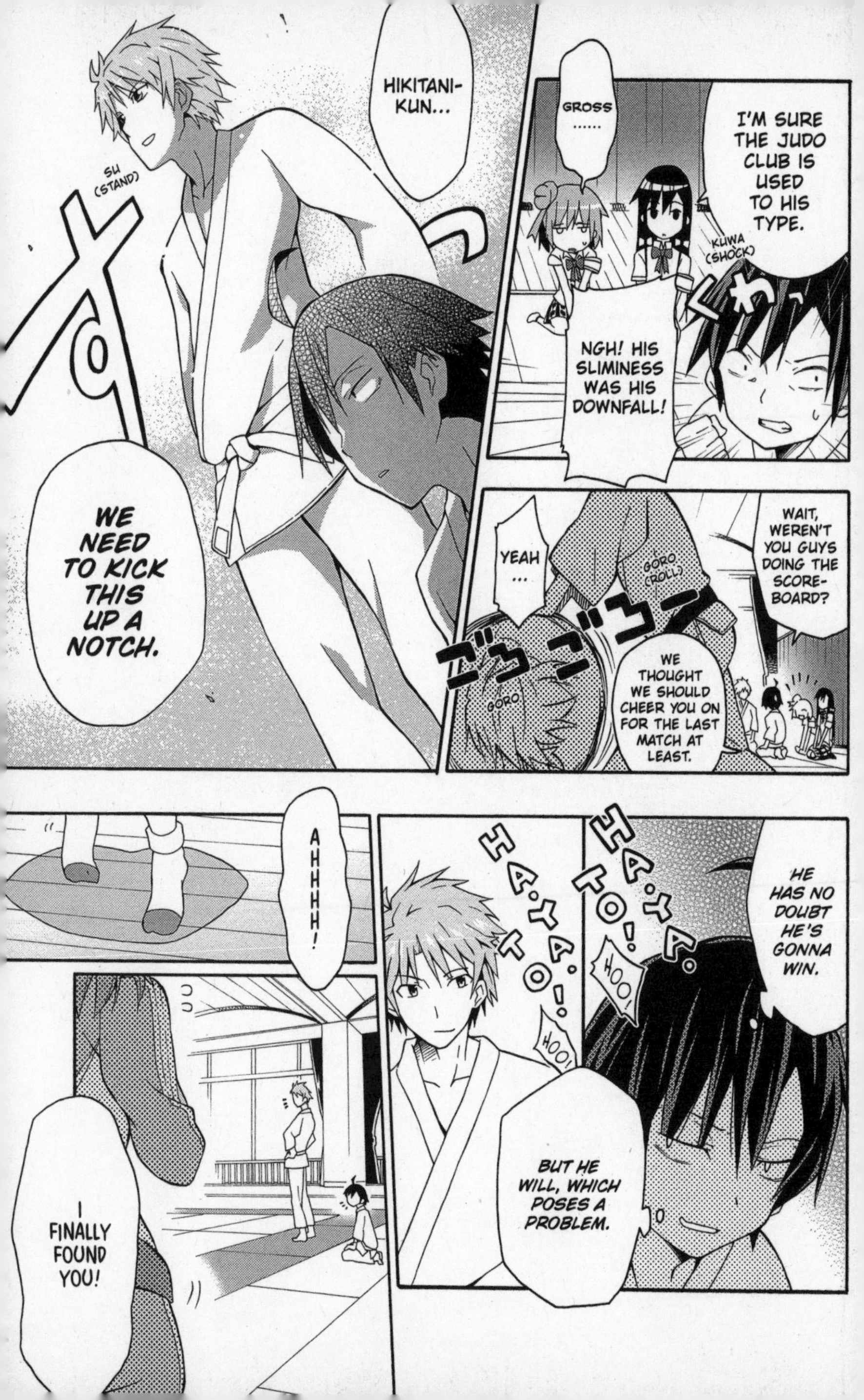
I'M SURE THE JUDO CLUB IS USED TO HIS TYPE.
KUWA (SHOCK)
GROSS ......
NGH! HIS SLIMINESS WAS HIS DOWNFALL!
WAIT, WEREN'T YOU GUYS DOING THE SCORE-BOARD?
YEAH ...
GORO (ROLL)
GORO
WE THOUGHT WE SHOULD CHEER YOU ON FOR THE LAST MATCH AT LEAST.
HIKITANI-KUN...
SU (STAND)
WE NEED TO KICK THIS UP A NOTCH.
HA-YA-TO!
HA-YA-TO!
HOO!
HOO!
HE HAS NO DOUBT HE'S GONNA WIN.
BUT HE WILL, WHICH POSES A PROBLEM.
AHHHH!
I FINALLY FOUND YOU!

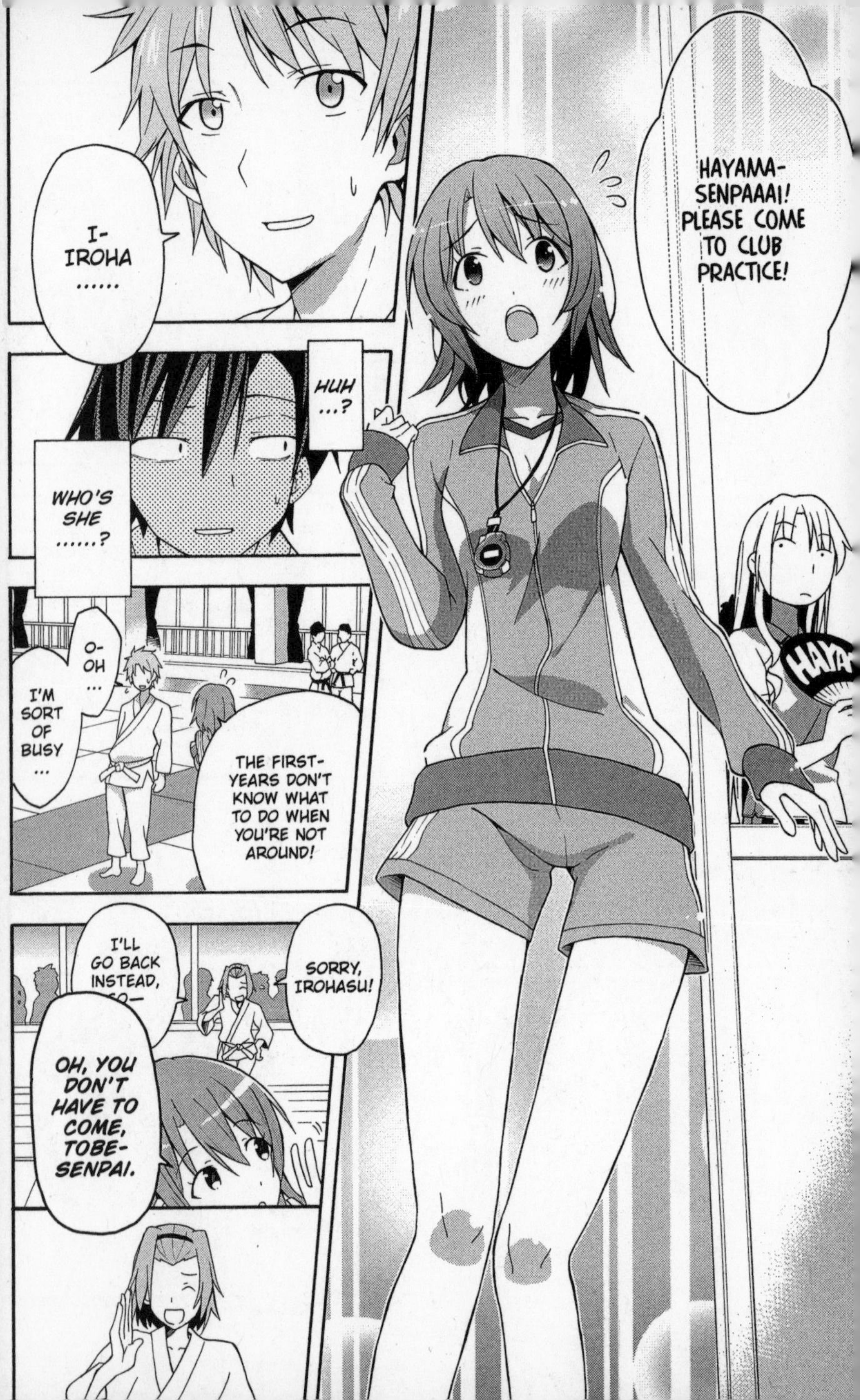

HAYAMA-SENPAAAI! PLEASE COME TO CLUB PRACTICE!
I- IROHA ......
HUH ...?
WHO'S SHE ......?
O-OH ... I'M SORT OF BUSY ...
THE FIRST-YEARS DON'T KNOW WHAT TO DO WHEN YOU'RE NOT AROUND!
SORRY, IROHASU!
I'LL GO BACK INSTEAD, SO—
OH, YOU DON'T HAVE TO COME, TOBE-SENPAI.

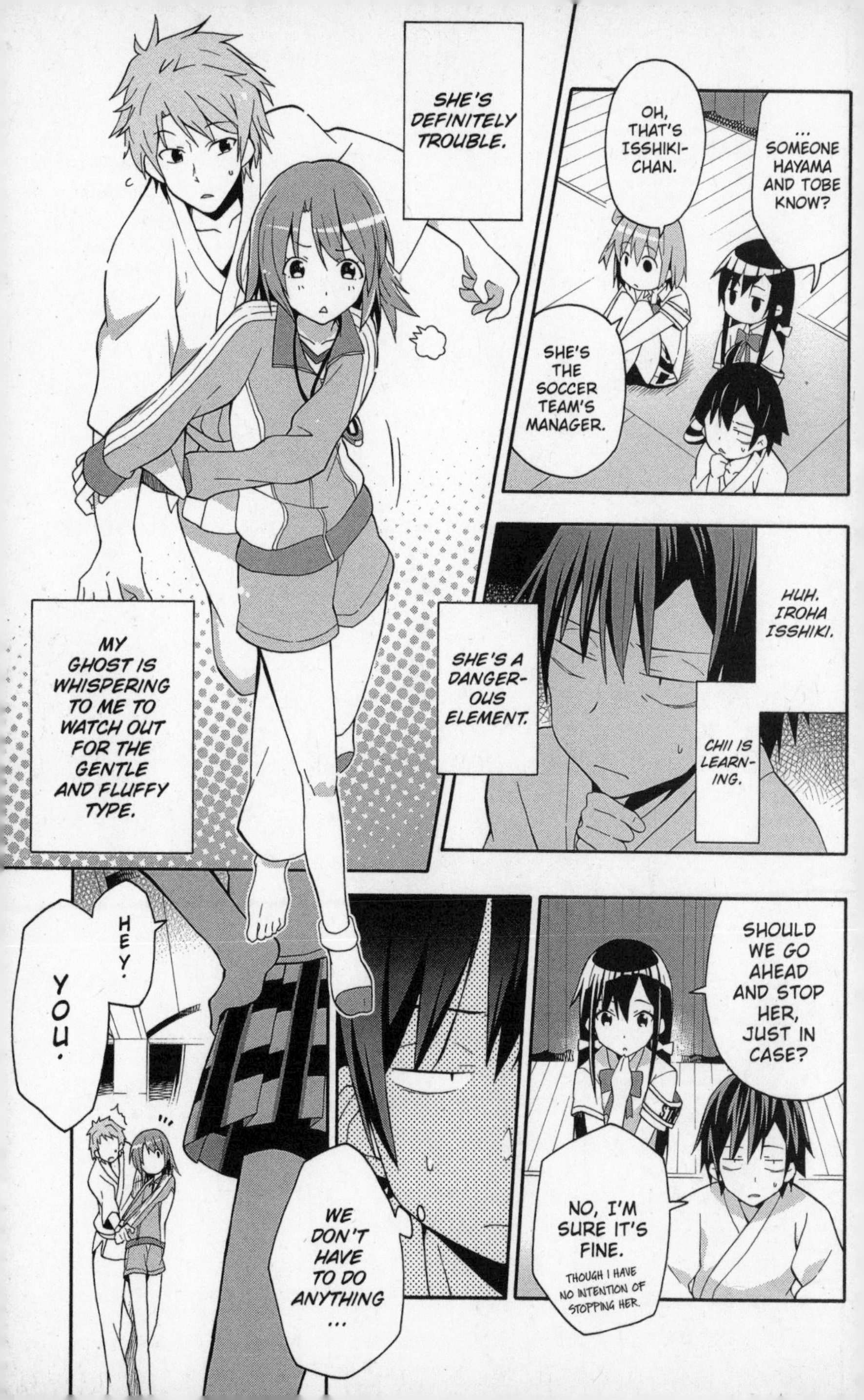

... SOMEONE HAYAMA AND TOBE KNOW?
OH, THAT'S ISSHIKI-CHAN.
SHE'S THE SOCCER TEAM'S MANAGER.
HUH. IROHA ISSHIKI.
SHE'S A DANGER-OUS ELEMENT.
CHII IS LEARN-ING.
SHE'S DEFINITELY TROUBLE.
MY GHOST IS WHISPERING TO ME TO WATCH OUT FOR THE GENTLE AND FLUFFY TYPE.
SHOULD WE GO AHEAD AND STOP HER, JUST IN CASE?
NO, I'M SURE IT'S FINE.
THOUGH I HAVE NO INTENTION OF STOPPING HER.
WE DON'T HAVE TO DO ANYTHING ...
HEY.
YOU.

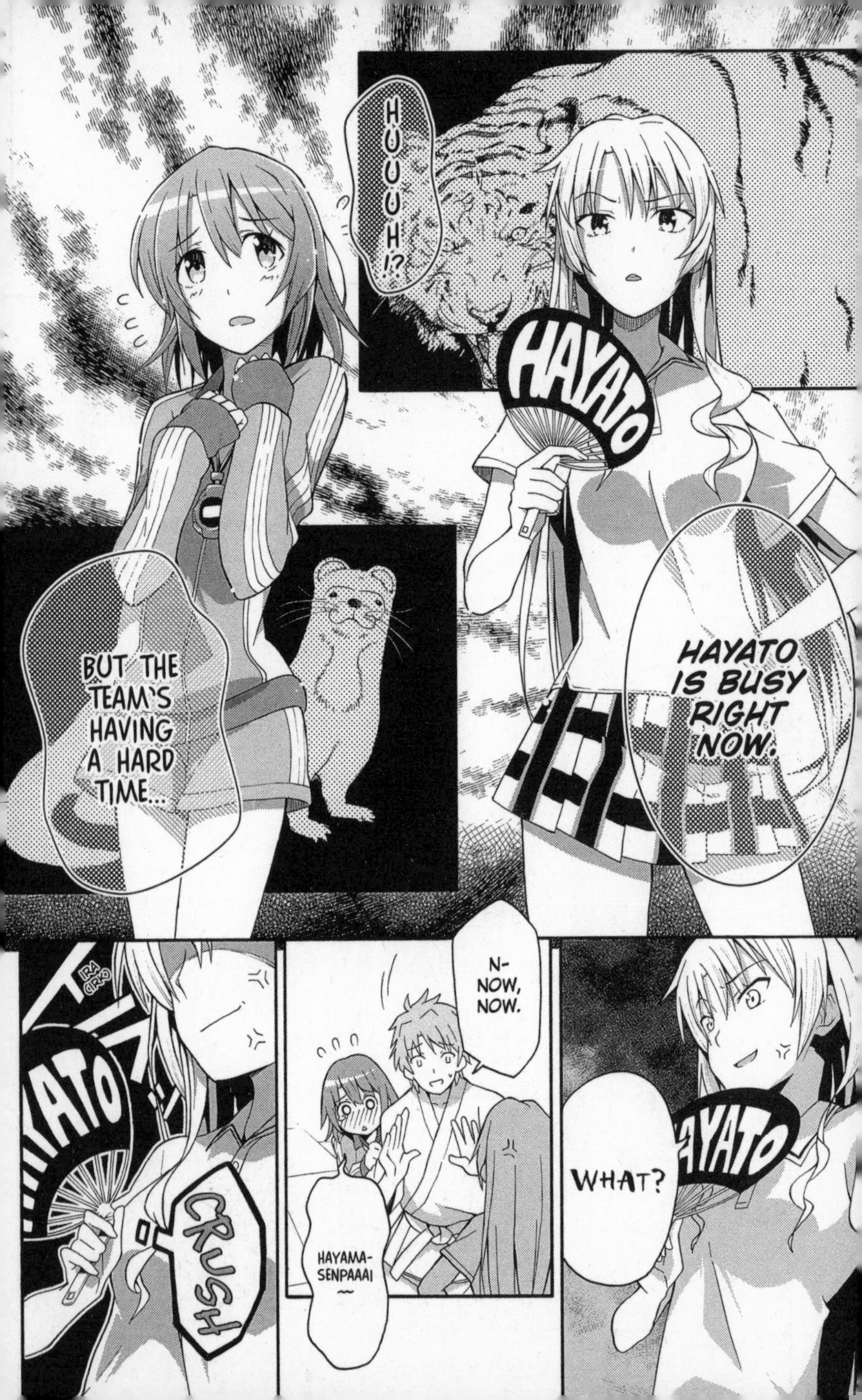

HUUUH!?
HAYATO
HAYATO IS BUSY RIGHT NOW.
BUT THE TEAM'S HAVING A HARD TIME...
HAYATO
WHAT?
N- NOW, NOW.
HAYAMA-SENPAAAI ~
IRA IRA
HAYATO
CRUSH

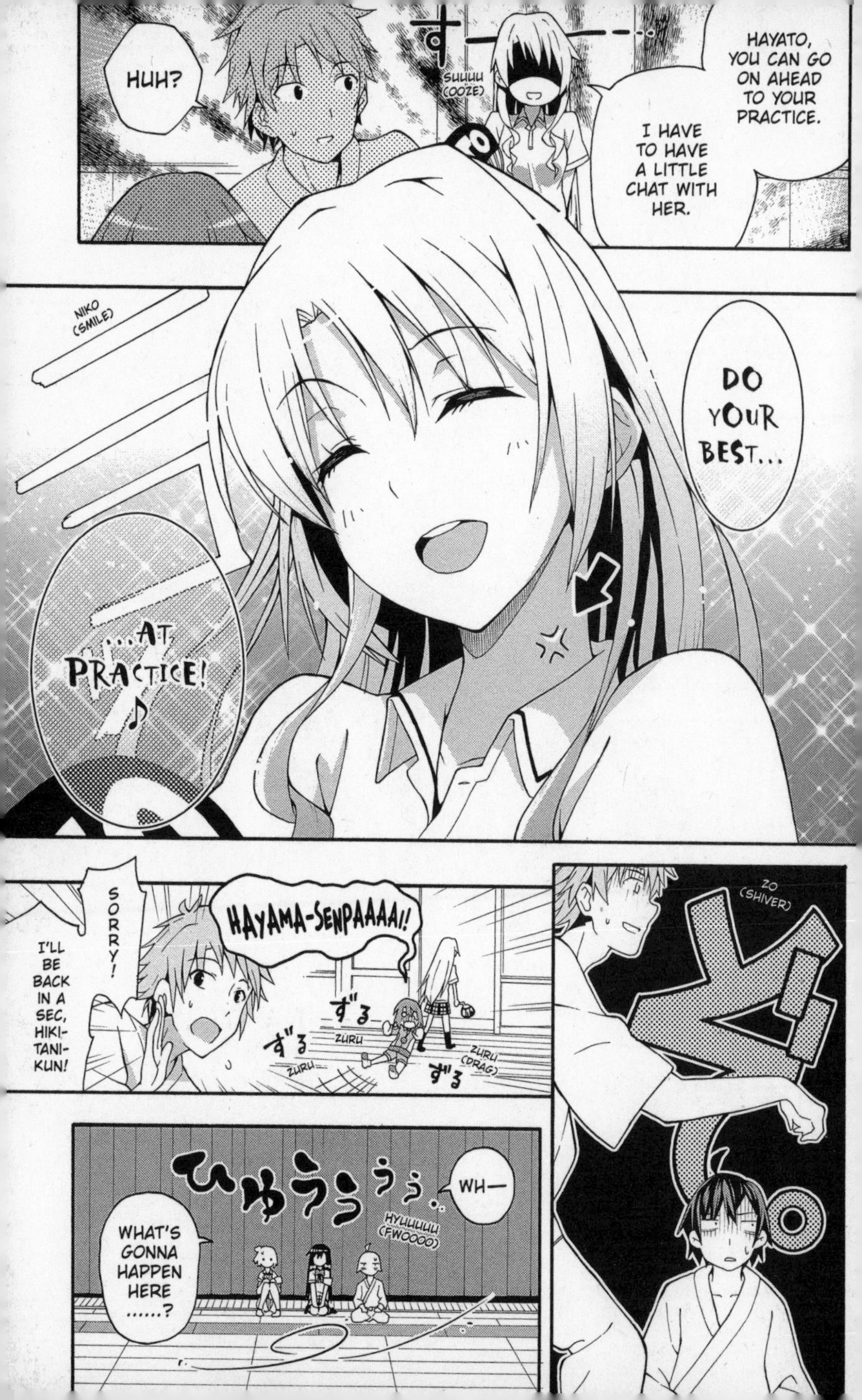
HAYATO, YOU CAN GO ON AHEAD TO YOUR PRACTICE.
I HAVE TO HAVE A LITTLE CHAT WITH HER.
すー
SUUUU (OOZE)
HUH?
DO YOUR BEST...
NIKO (SMILE)
...AT PRACTICE! ♪
ZO (SHIVER)
HAYAMA-SENPAAAAI!!
ずる
ZURU (DRAG)
ずる
ZURU
ずる
ZURU
SORRY!
I'LL BE BACK IN A SEC, HIKITANI-KUN!
WH—
ひゅうううう
HYUUUUU (FWOOOO)
WHAT'S GONNA HAPPEN HERE ......?

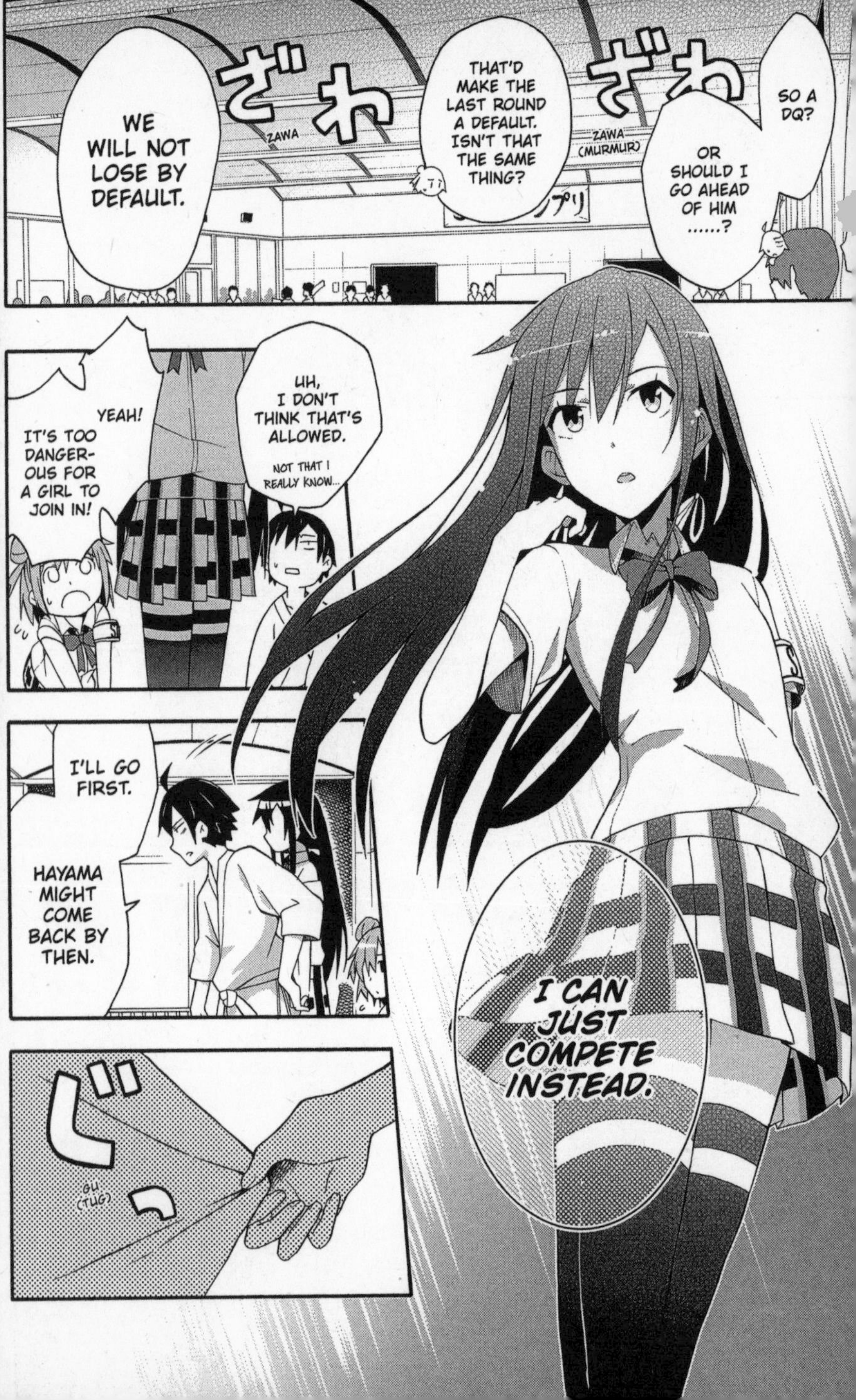
SO A DQ?
OR SHOULD I GO AHEAD OF HIM ......?
ざわ
ZAWA (MURMUR)
THAT'D MAKE THE LAST ROUND A DEFAULT. ISN'T THAT THE SAME THING?
ざわ
ZAWA
WE WILL NOT LOSE BY DEFAULT.
I CAN JUST COMPETE INSTEAD.
UH, I DON'T THINK THAT'S ALLOWED.
NOT THAT I REALLY KNOW...
YEAH! IT'S TOO DANGER-OUS FOR A GIRL TO JOIN IN!
I'LL GO FIRST.
HAYAMA MIGHT COME BACK BY THEN.
GU (TUG)

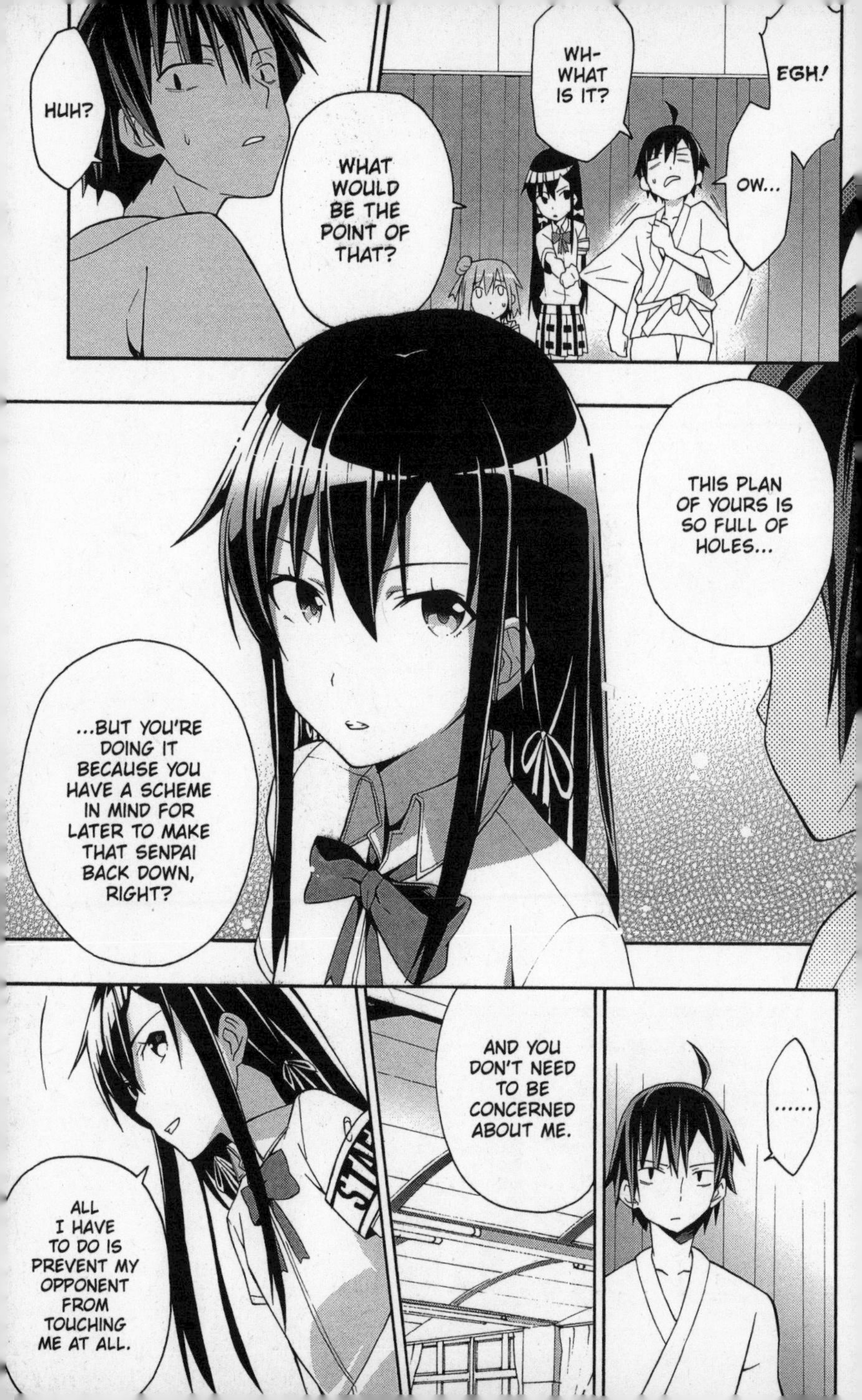
EGH!
WH- WHAT IS IT?
OW...
WHAT WOULD BE THE POINT OF THAT?
HUH?
THIS PLAN OF YOURS IS SO FULL OF HOLES...
...BUT YOU'RE DOING IT BECAUSE YOU HAVE A SCHEME IN MIND FOR LATER TO MAKE THAT SENPAI BACK DOWN, RIGHT?
......
AND YOU DON'T NEED TO BE CONCERNED ABOUT ME.
ALL I HAVE TO DO IS PREVENT MY OPPONENT FROM TOUCHING ME AT ALL.

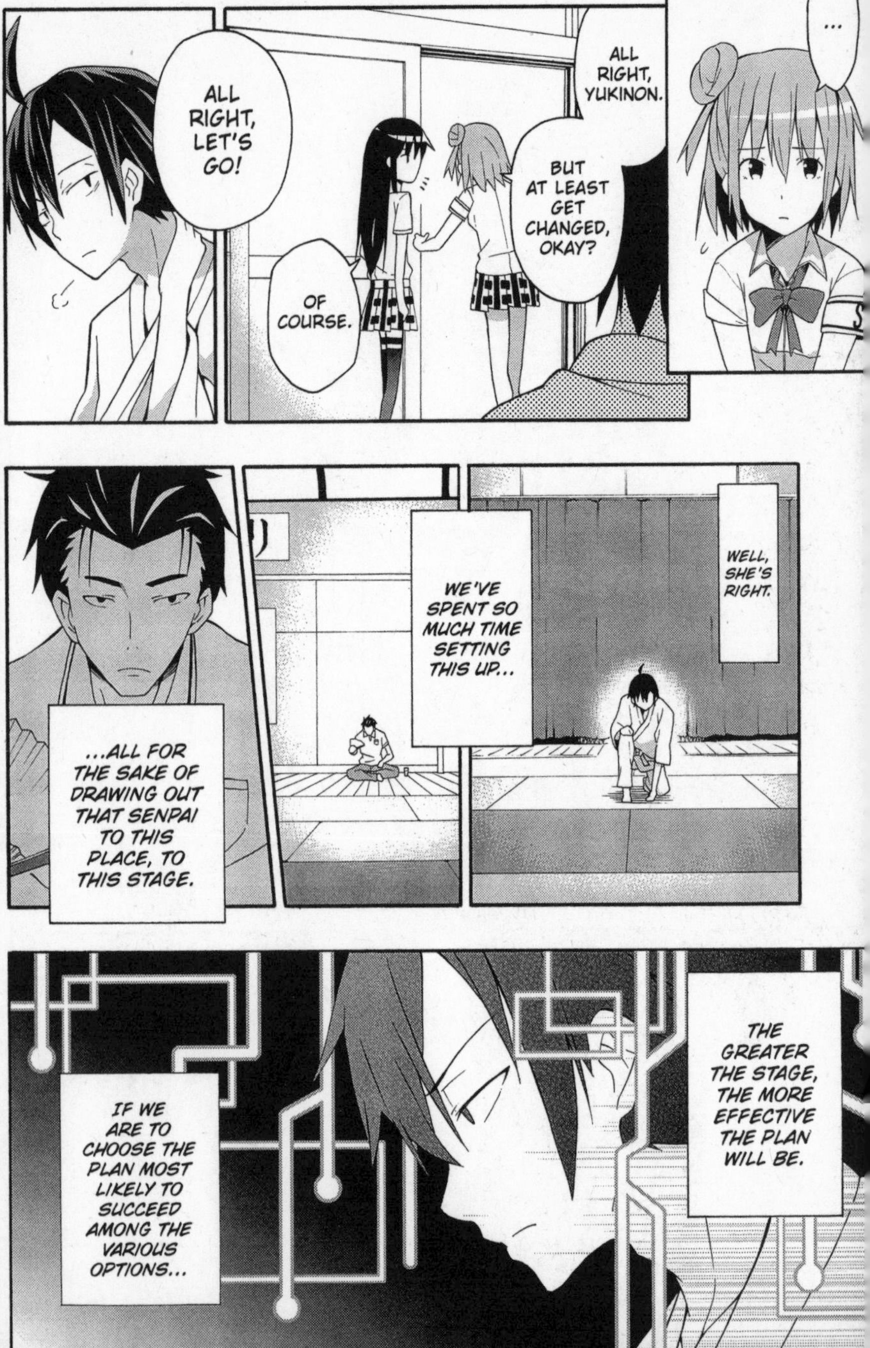
...
ALL RIGHT, YUKINON.
BUT AT LEAST GET CHANGED, OKAY?
OF COURSE.
ALL RIGHT, LET'S GO!
WELL, SHE'S RIGHT.
WE'VE SPENT SO MUCH TIME SETTING THIS UP...
...ALL FOR THE SAKE OF DRAWING OUT THAT SENPAI TO THIS PLACE, TO THIS STAGE.
THE GREATER THE STAGE, THE MORE EFFECTIVE THE PLAN WILL BE.
IF WE ARE TO CHOOSE THE PLAN MOST LIKELY TO SUCCEED AMONG THE VARIOUS OPTIONS...

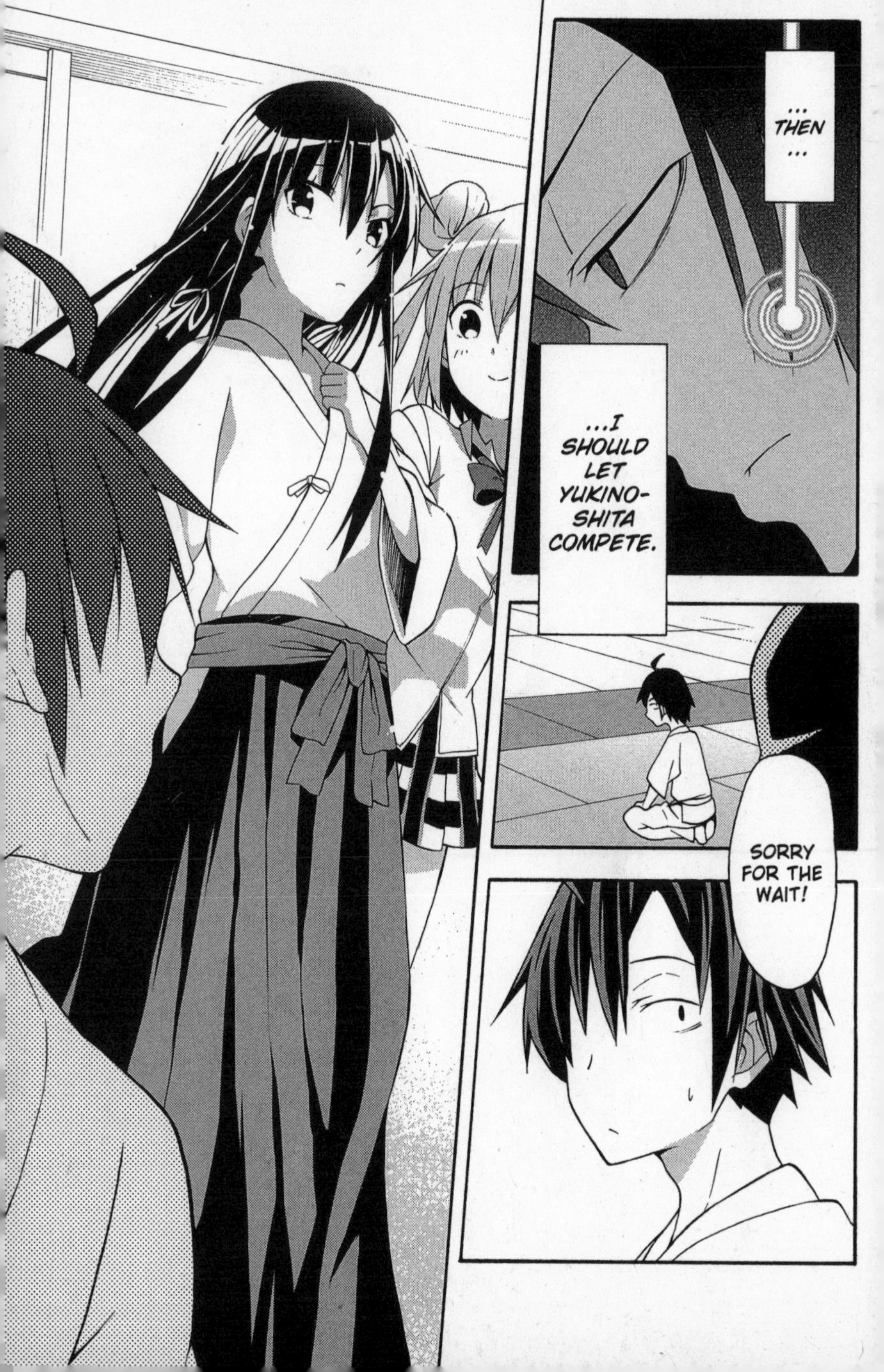
...THEN...
...I SHOULD LET YUKINO-SHITA COMPETE.
...SORRY FOR THE WAIT!

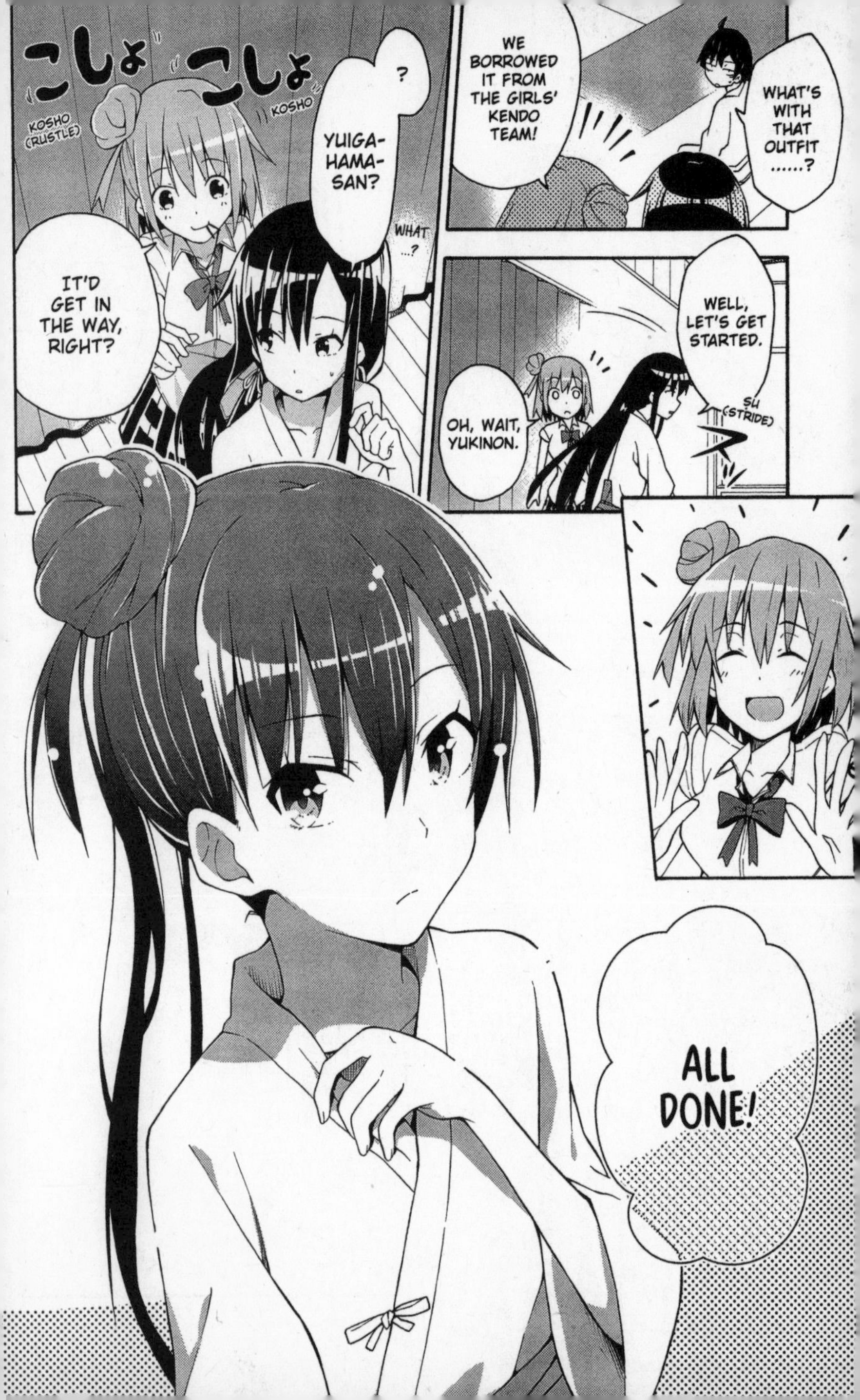
WHAT'S WITH THAT OUTFIT ......?
WE BORROWED IT FROM THE GIRLS' KENDO TEAM!
WELL, LET'S GET STARTED.
SU (STRIDE)
OH, WAIT, YUKINON.
?
YUIGA-HAMA-SAN?
WHAT ...?
こしょ こしょ
KOSHO
KOSHO (RUSTLE)
IT'D GET IN THE WAY, RIGHT?
ALL DONE!

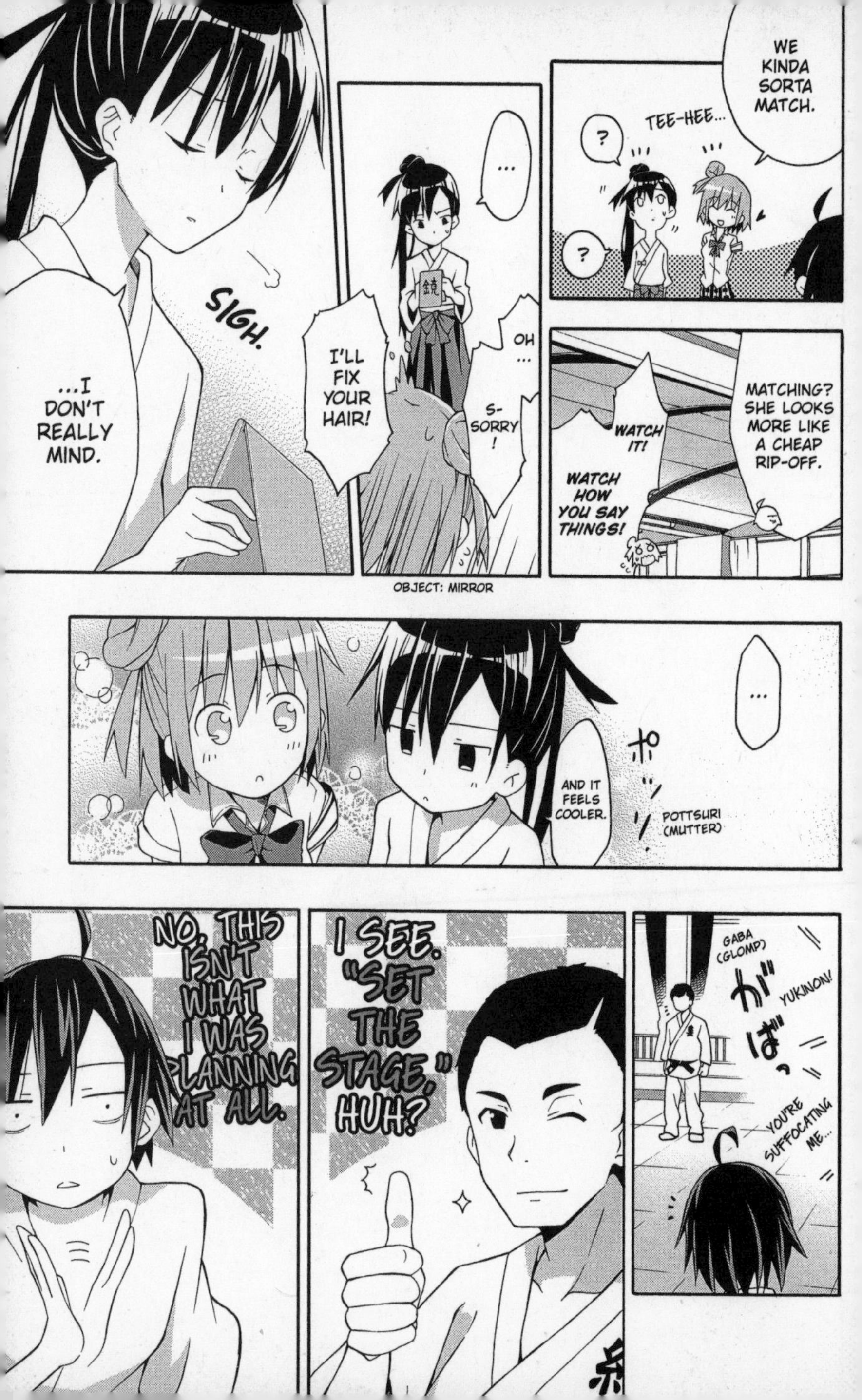
WE KINDA SORTA MATCH.
TEE-HEE...
?
?
MATCHING? SHE LOOKS MORE LIKE A CHEAP RIP-OFF.
WATCH IT!
WATCH HOW YOU SAY THINGS!
...
OH...
S-SORRY!
I'LL FIX YOUR HAIR!
SIGH.
...I DON'T REALLY MIND.
OBJECT: MIRROR
...
ポッ
POTTSURI (MUTTER)
AND IT FEELS COOLER.
GABA (GLOMP)
がばっ
YUKINON!
YOU'RE SUFFOCATING ME...
I SEE. "SET THE STAGE," HUH?
NO, THIS ISN'T WHAT I WAS PLANNING AT ALL.

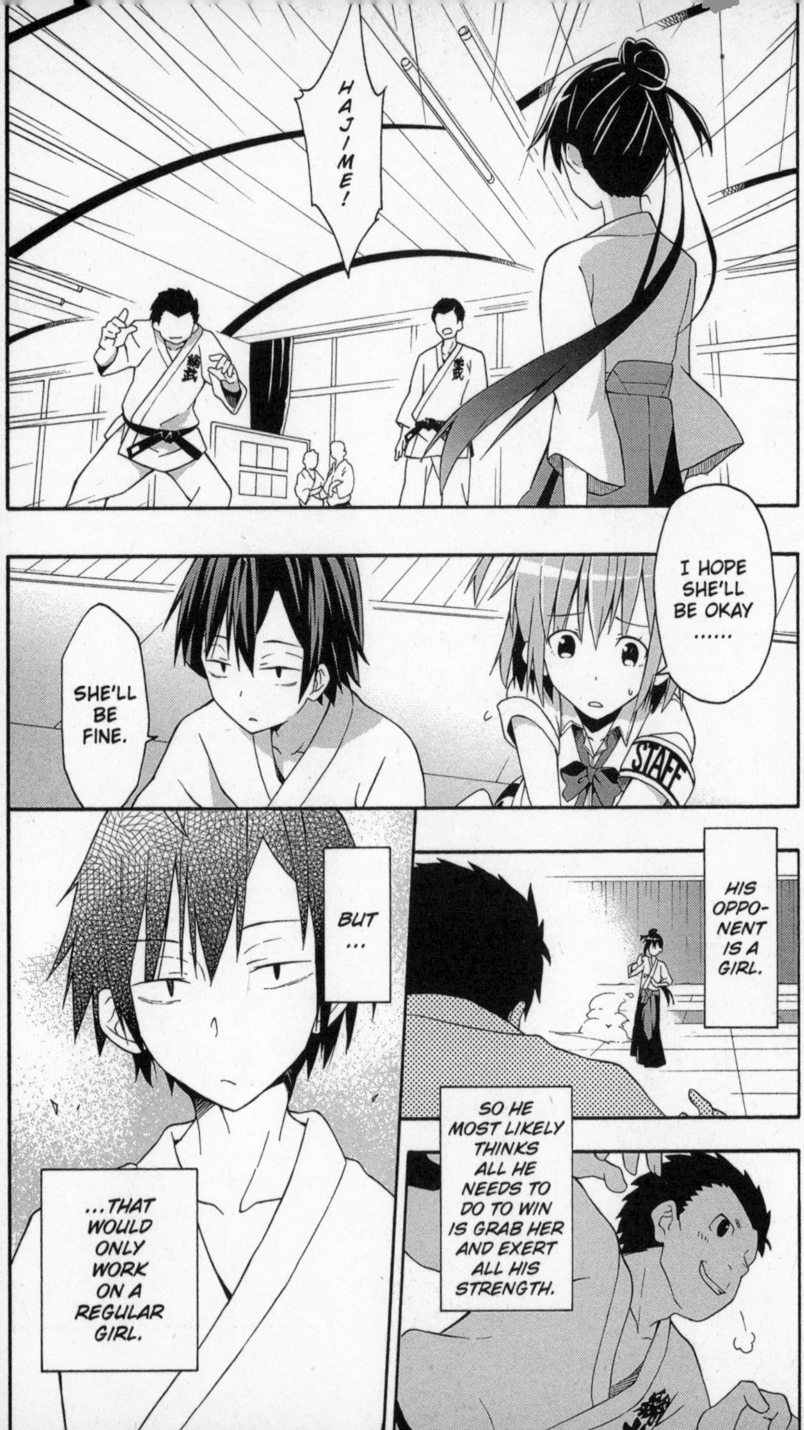
HAJIME!
I HOPE SHE'LL BE OKAY ......
SHE'LL BE FINE.
HIS OPPONENT IS A GIRL.
SO HE MOST LIKELY THINKS ALL HE NEEDS TO DO TO WIN IS GRAB HER AND EXERT ALL HIS STRENGTH.
BUT ...
...THAT WOULD ONLY WORK ON A REGULAR GIRL.

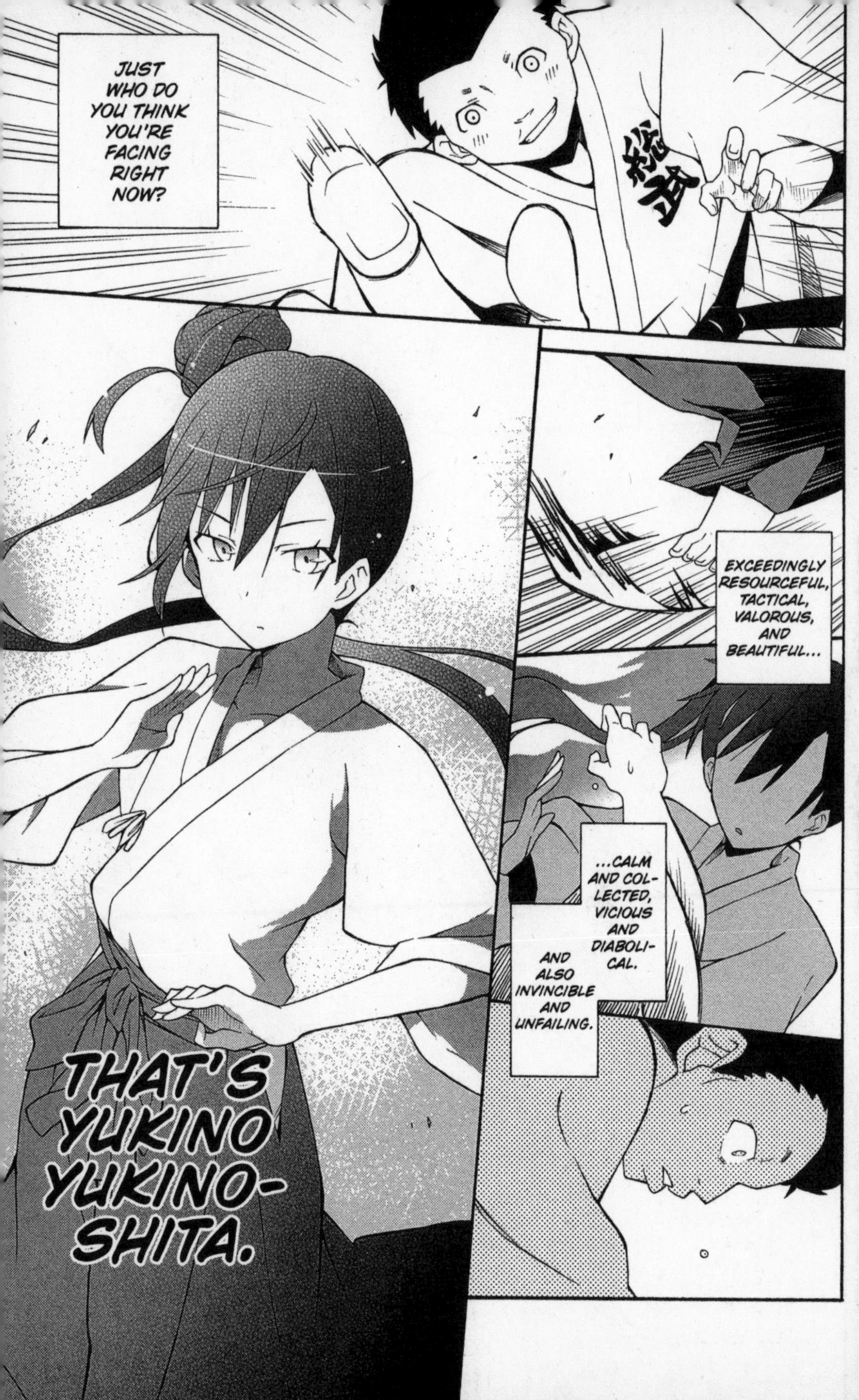
JUST WHO DO YOU THINK YOU'RE FACING RIGHT NOW?
EXCEEDINGLY RESOURCEFUL, TACTICAL, VALOROUS, AND BEAUTIFUL...
...CALM AND COLLECTED, VICIOUS AND DIABOLICAL.
AND ALSO INVINCIBLE AND UNFAILING.
THAT'S YUKINO YUKINOSHITA.

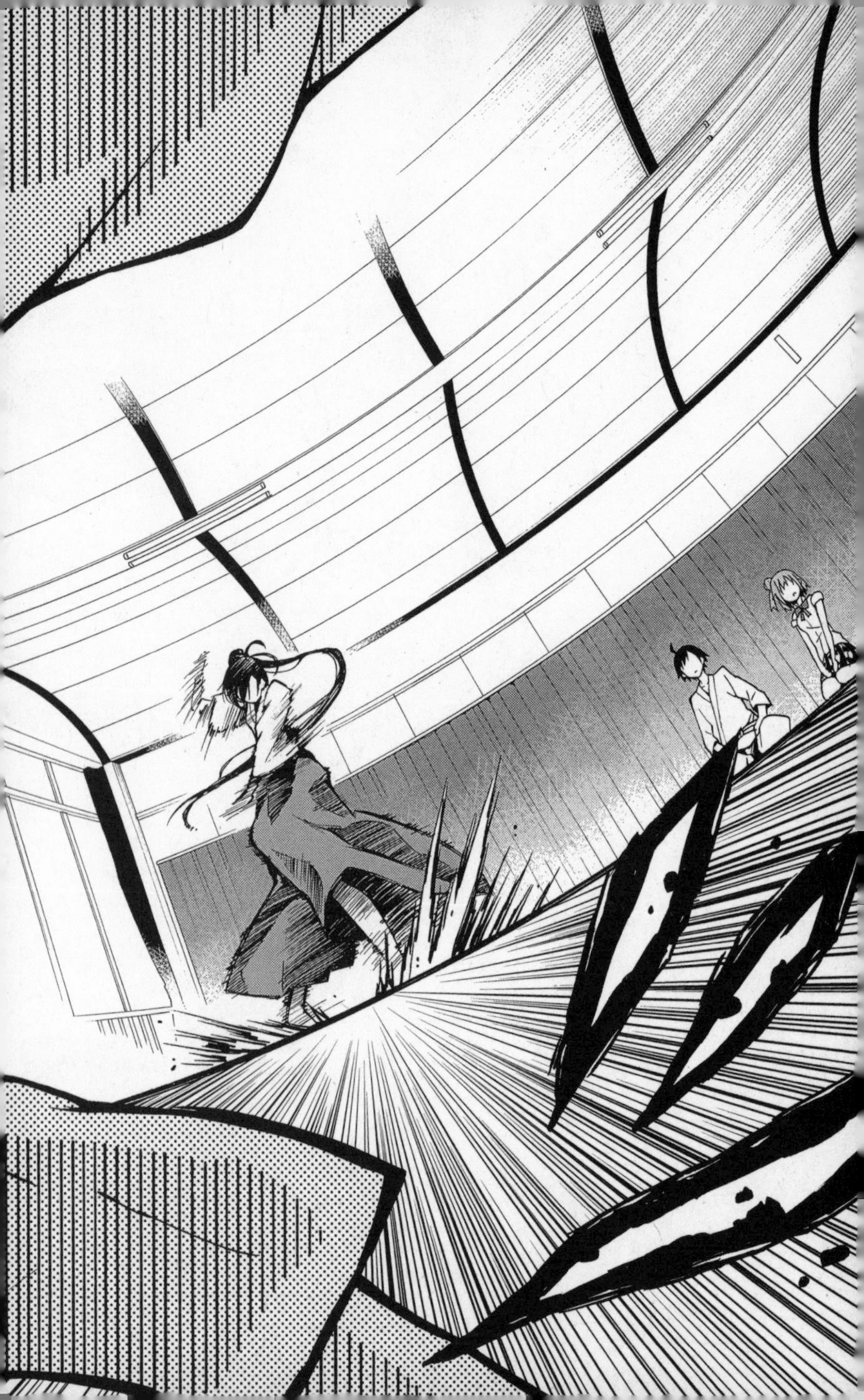

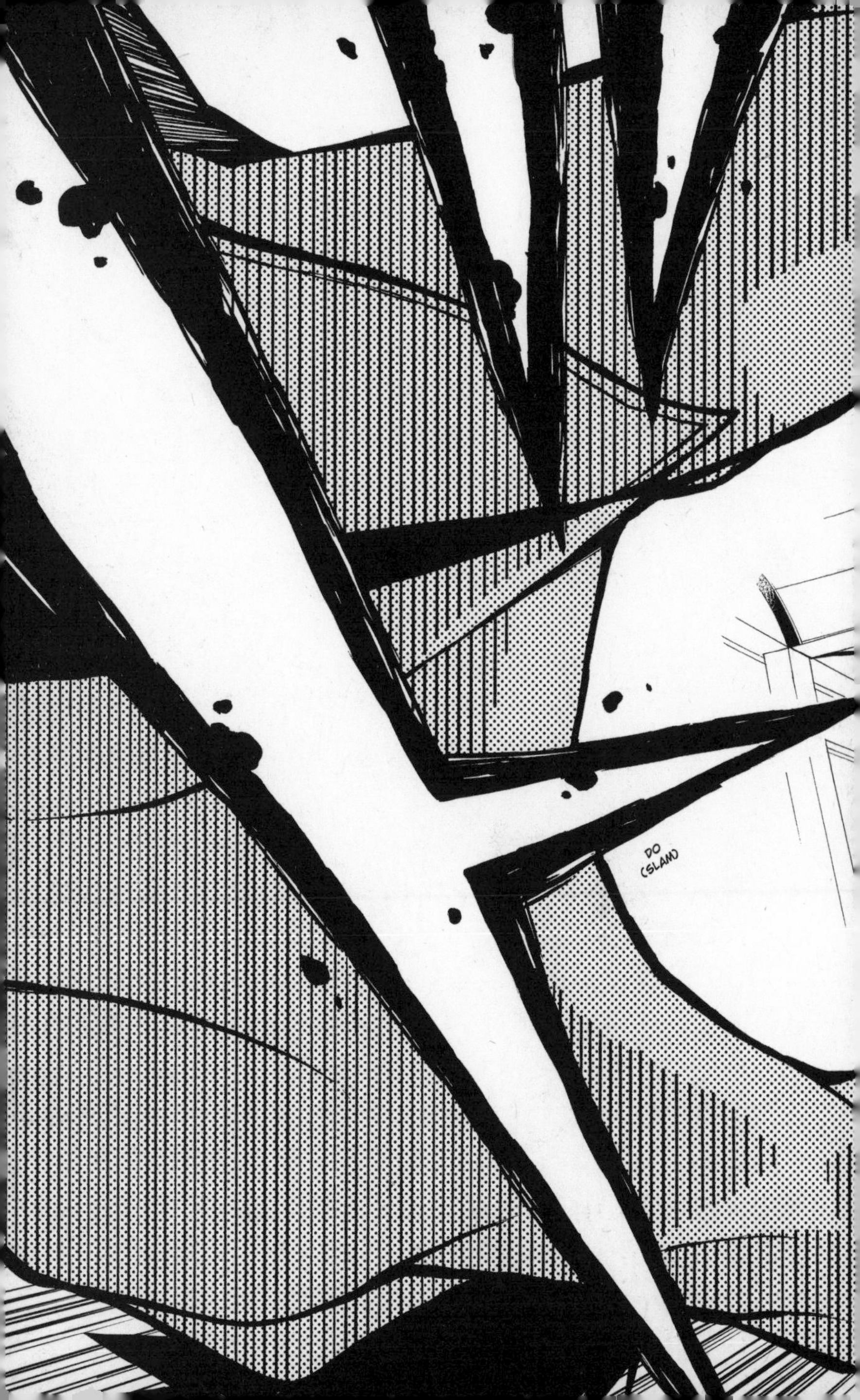
DO
(SLAM)

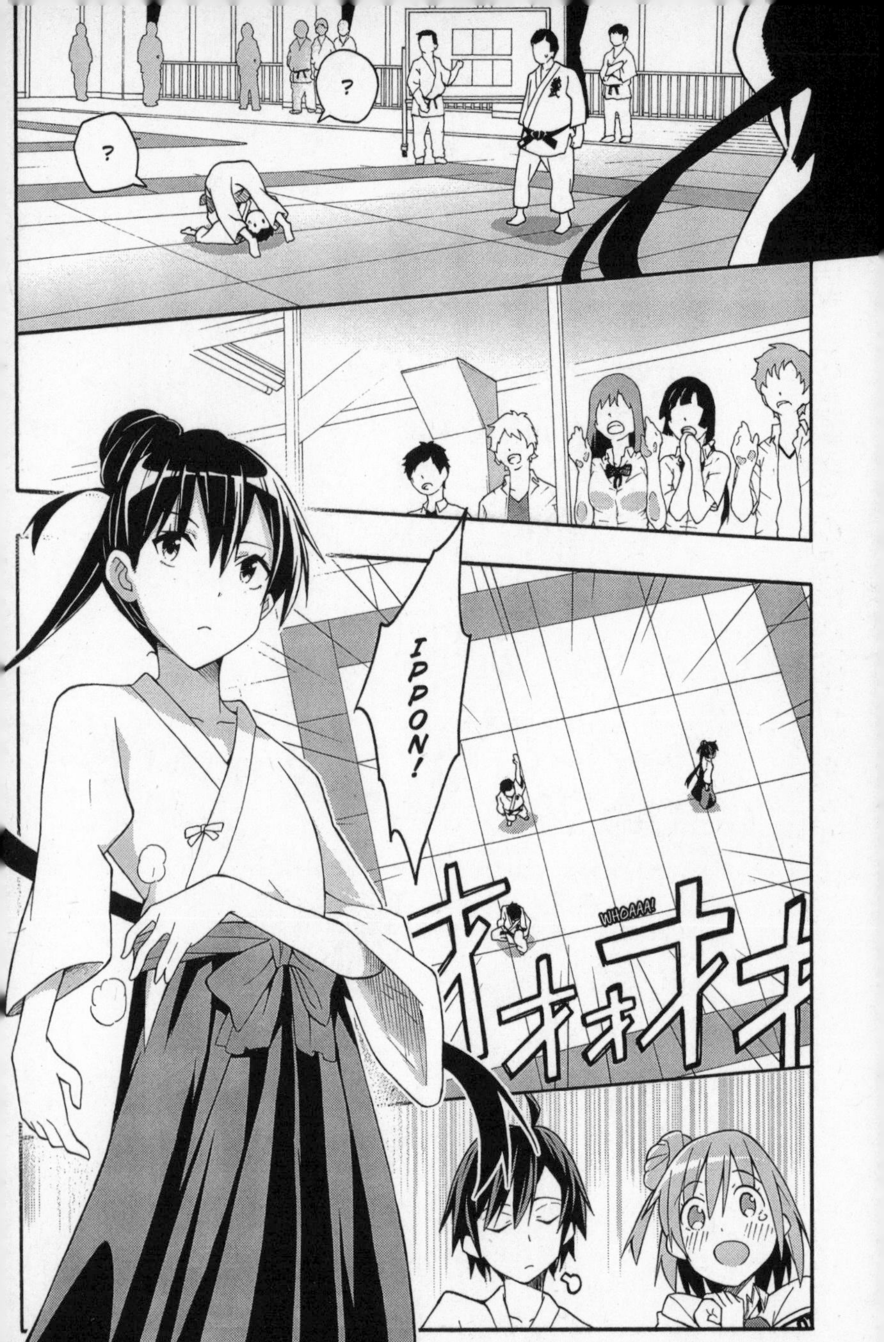
?
?
IPPON!
オォォオオ
WHOAAA!

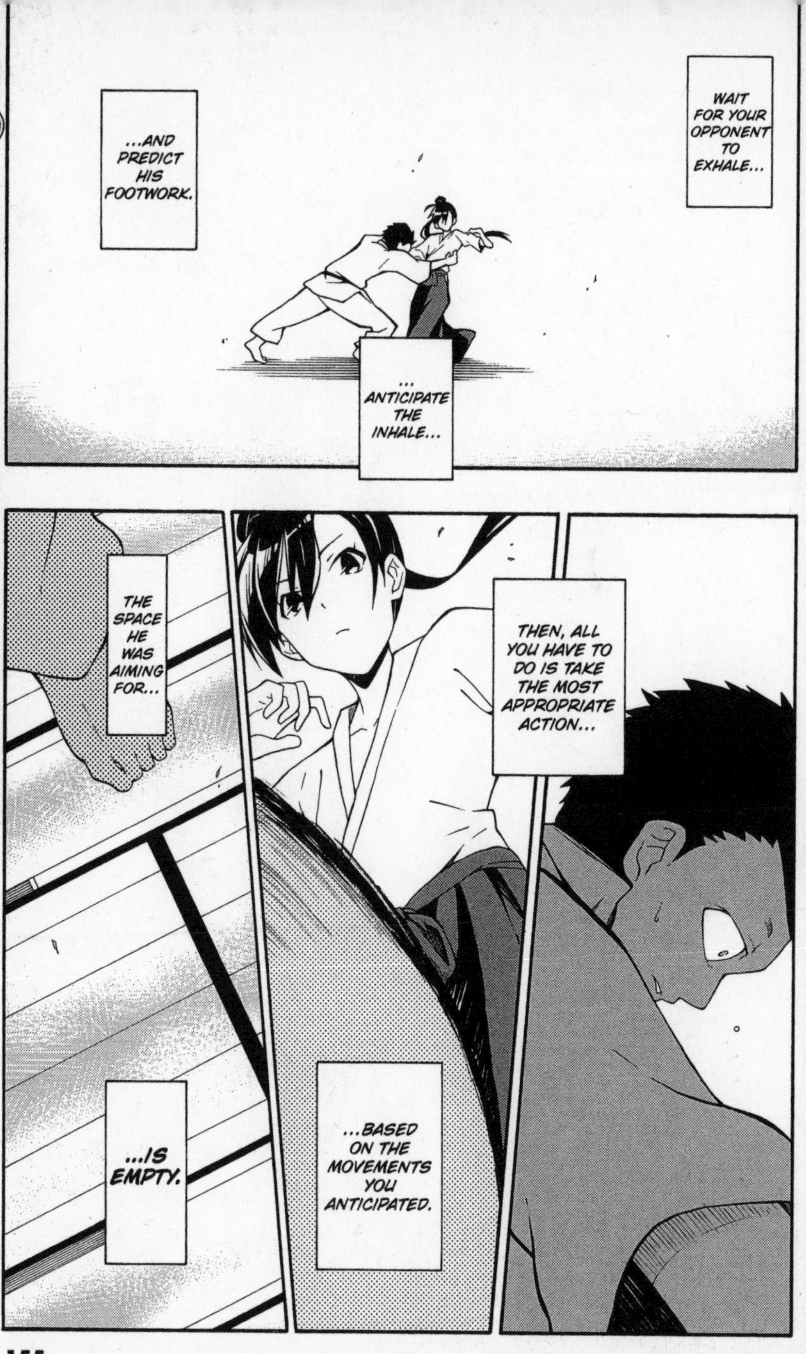
WAIT FOR YOUR OPPONENT TO EXHALE...
...AND PREDICT HIS FOOTWORK.
...ANTICIPATE THE INHALE...
THEN, ALL YOU HAVE TO DO IS TAKE THE MOST APPROPRIATE ACTION...
...BASED ON THE MOVEMENTS YOU ANTICIPATED.
THE SPACE HE WAS AIMING FOR...
...IS EMPTY.

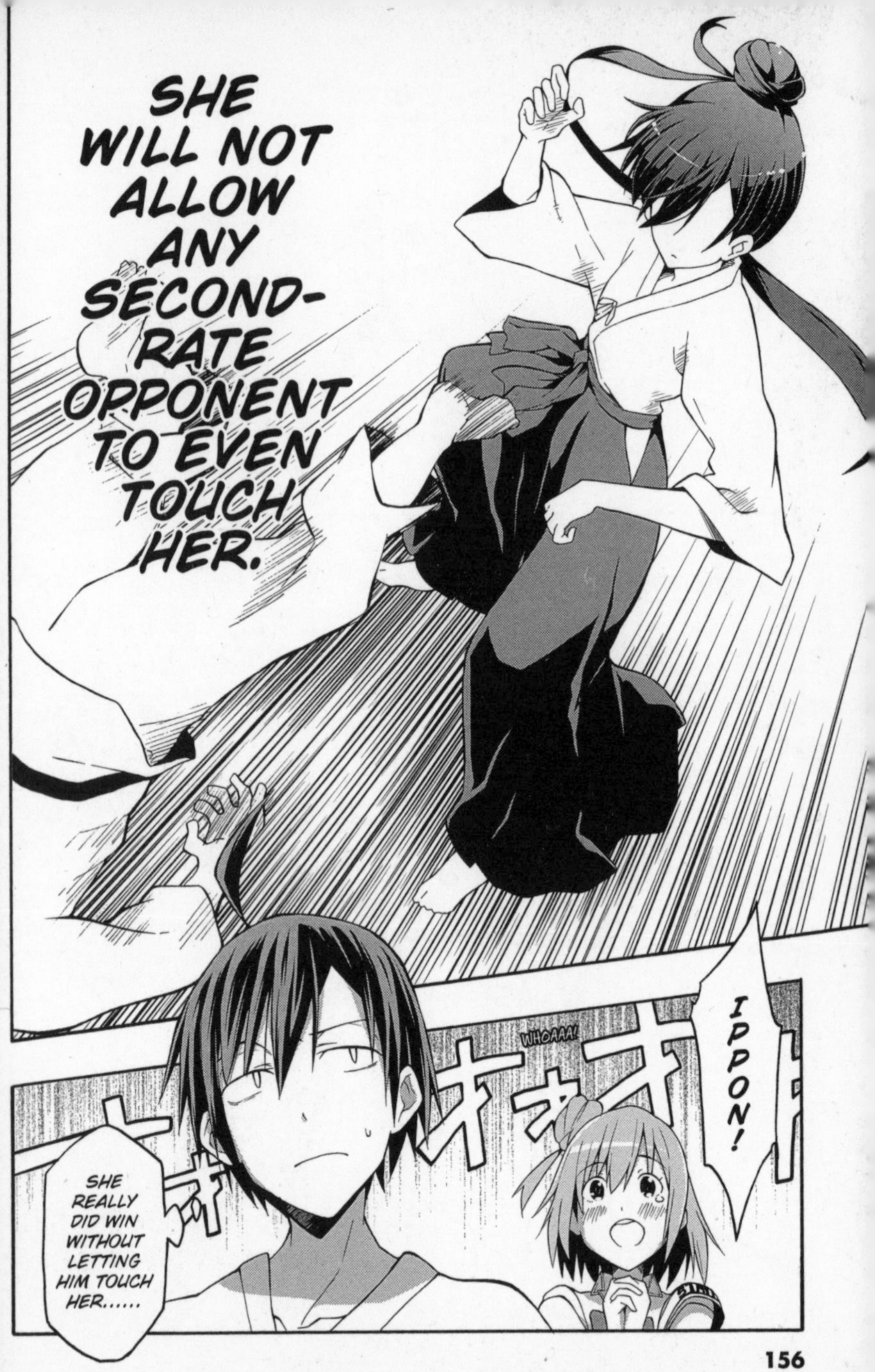
SHE WILL NOT ALLOW ANY SECOND-RATE OPPONENT TO EVEN TOUCH HER.
IPPON!
WHOAAA!
SHE REALLY DID WIN WITHOUT LETTING HIM TOUCH HER......

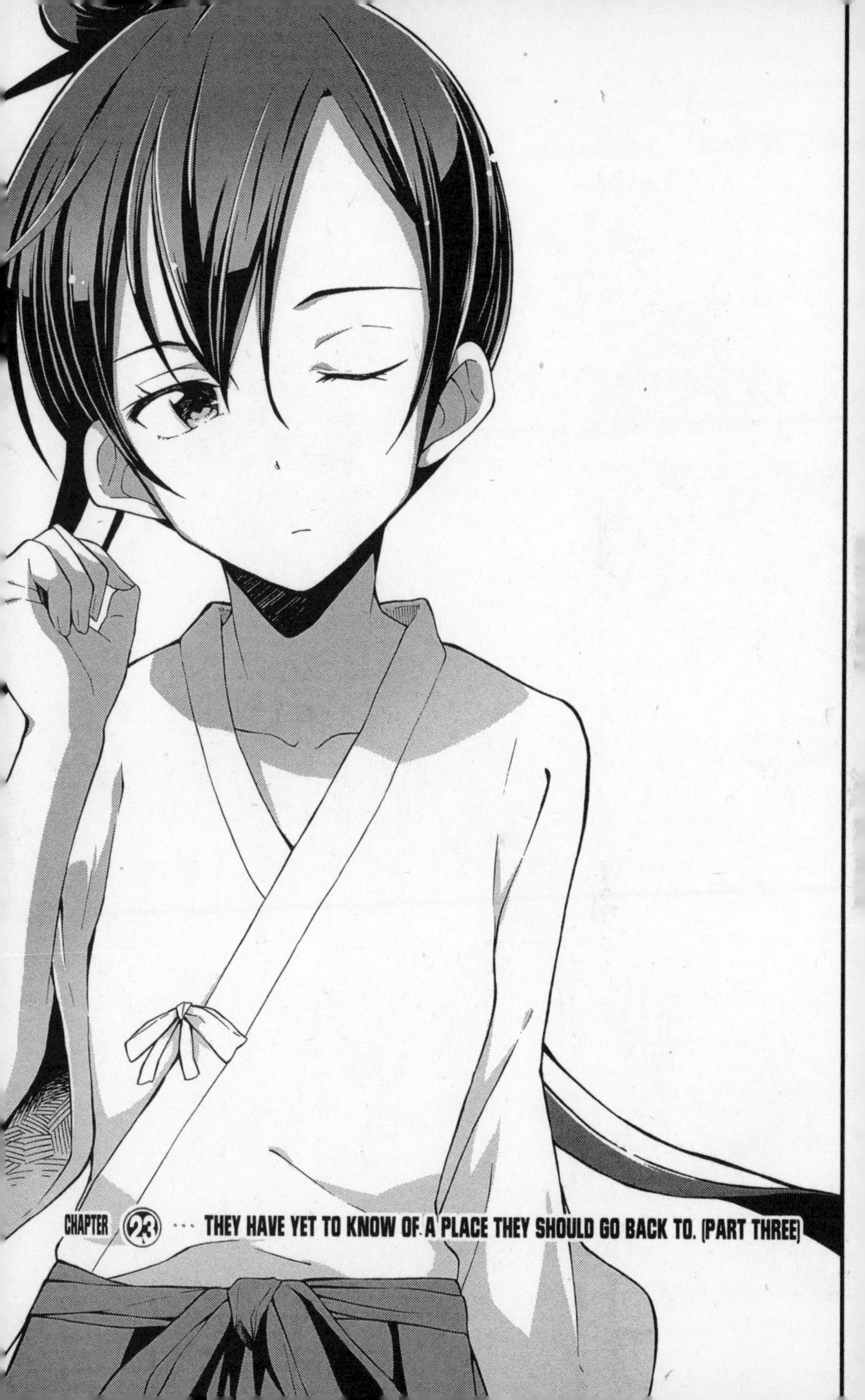
CHAPTER 23 … THEY HAVE YET TO KNOW OF A PLACE THEY SHOULD GO BACK TO. (PART THREE)

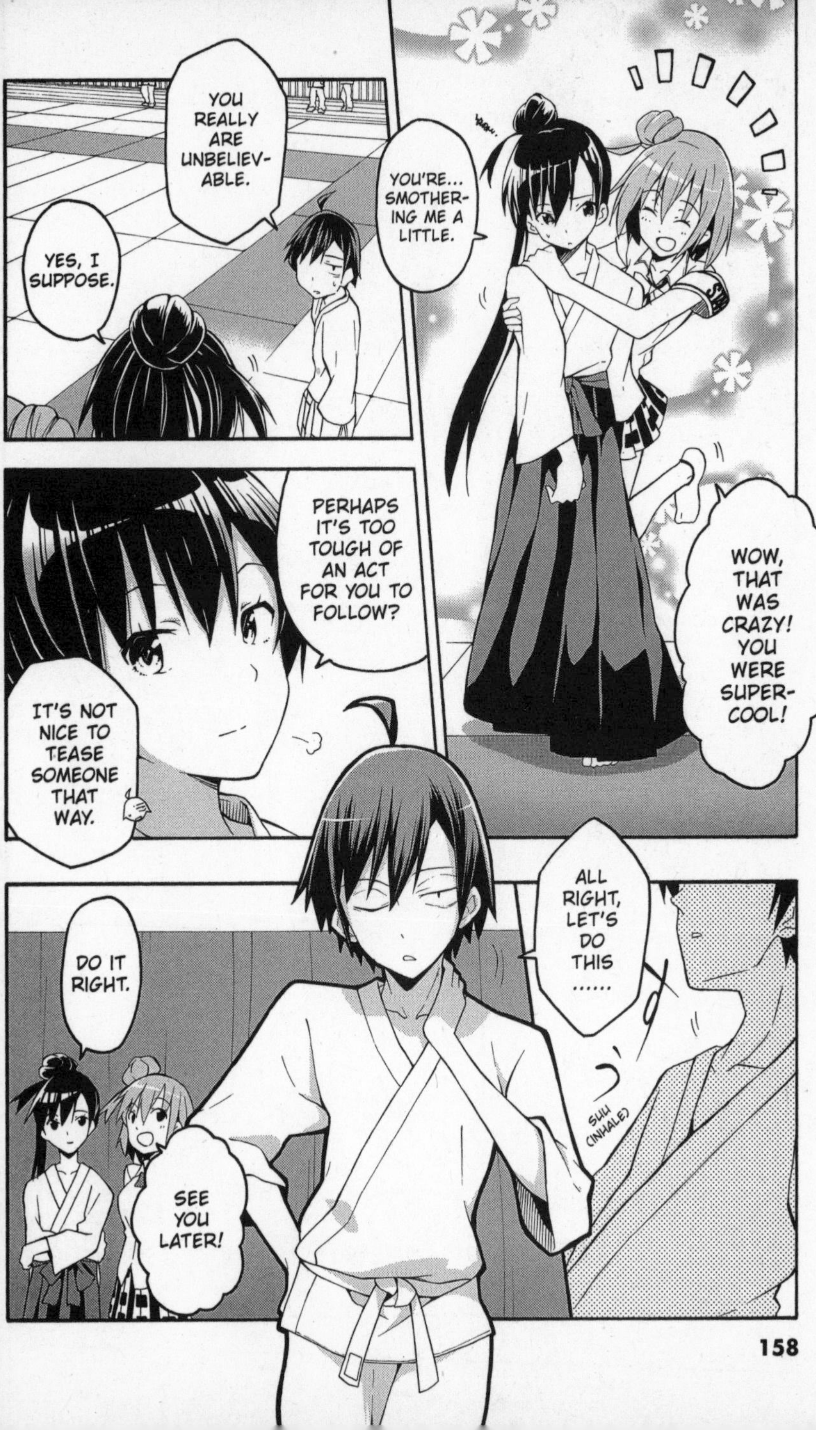
WOW, THAT WAS CRAZY! YOU WERE SUPER-COOL!
YOU'RE... SMOTHERING ME A LITTLE.
YOU REALLY ARE UNBELIEV-ABLE.
YES, I SUPPOSE.
PERHAPS IT'S TOO TOUGH OF AN ACT FOR YOU TO FOLLOW?
IT'S NOT NICE TO TEASE SOMEONE THAT WAY.
ALL RIGHT, LET'S DO THIS......
SUU (INHALE)
DO IT RIGHT.
SEE YOU LATER!

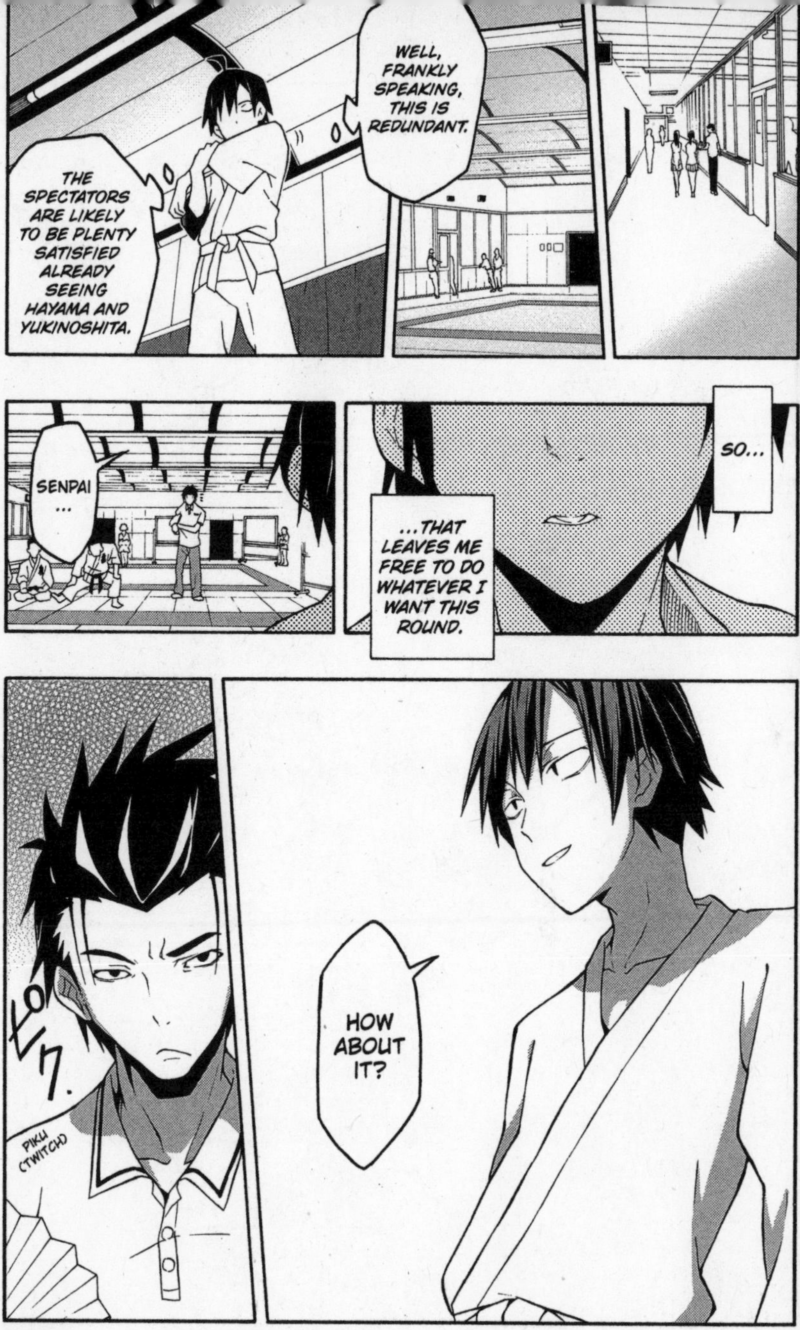
WELL, FRANKLY SPEAKING, THIS IS REDUNDANT.
THE SPECTATORS ARE LIKELY TO BE PLENTY SATISFIED ALREADY SEEING HAYAMA AND YUKINOSHITA.
SO...
...THAT LEAVES ME FREE TO DO WHATEVER I WANT THIS ROUND.
SENPAI ...
HOW ABOUT IT?
PIKU (TWITCH)

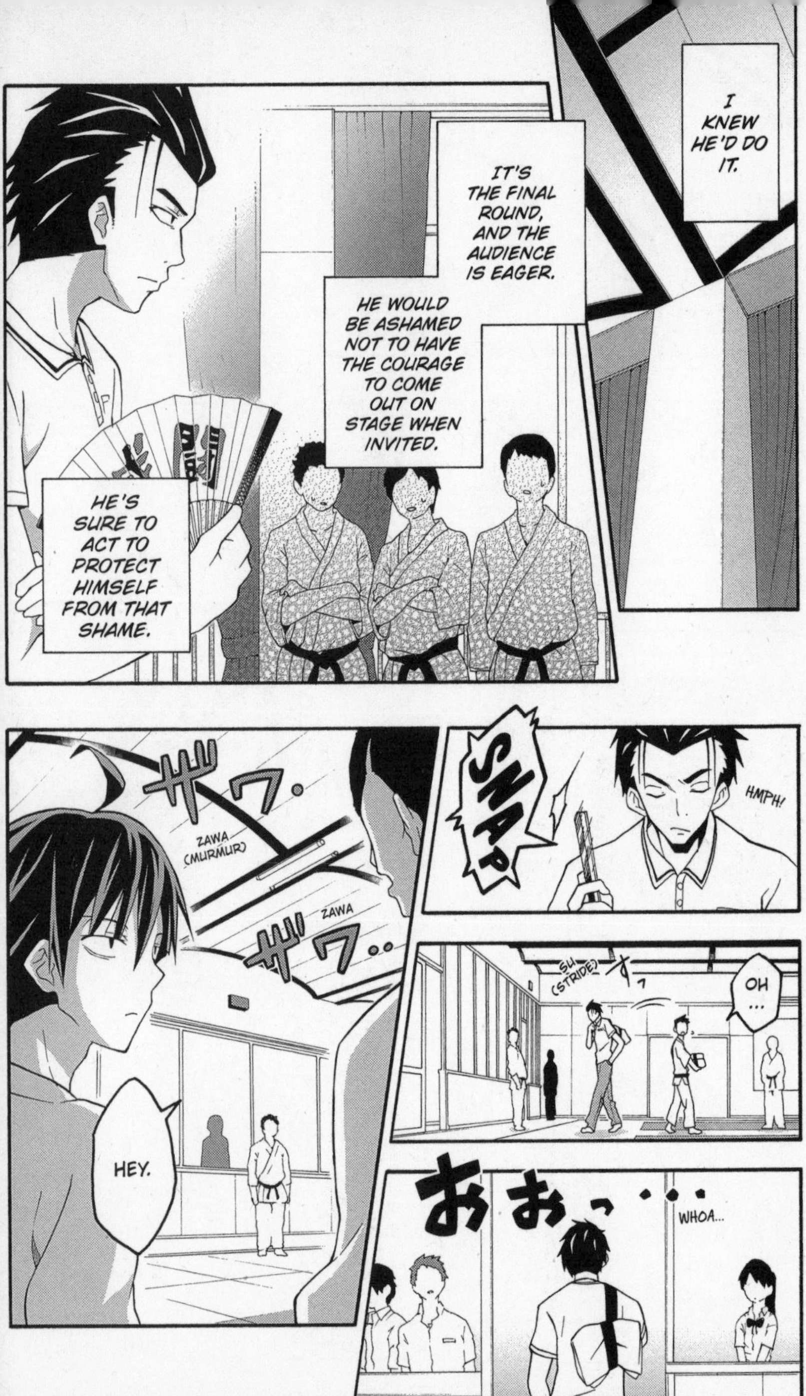
I KNEW HE'D DO IT.
IT'S THE FINAL ROUND, AND THE AUDIENCE IS EAGER.
HE WOULD BE ASHAMED NOT TO HAVE THE COURAGE TO COME OUT ON STAGE WHEN INVITED.
HE'S SURE TO ACT TO PROTECT HIMSELF FROM THAT SHAME.
SNAP
HMPH!
OH ...
すっ
SU (STRIDE)
おおっ・・・
WHOA...
ザワ・
ZAWA (MURMUR)
ザワ‥
ZAWA
HEY.

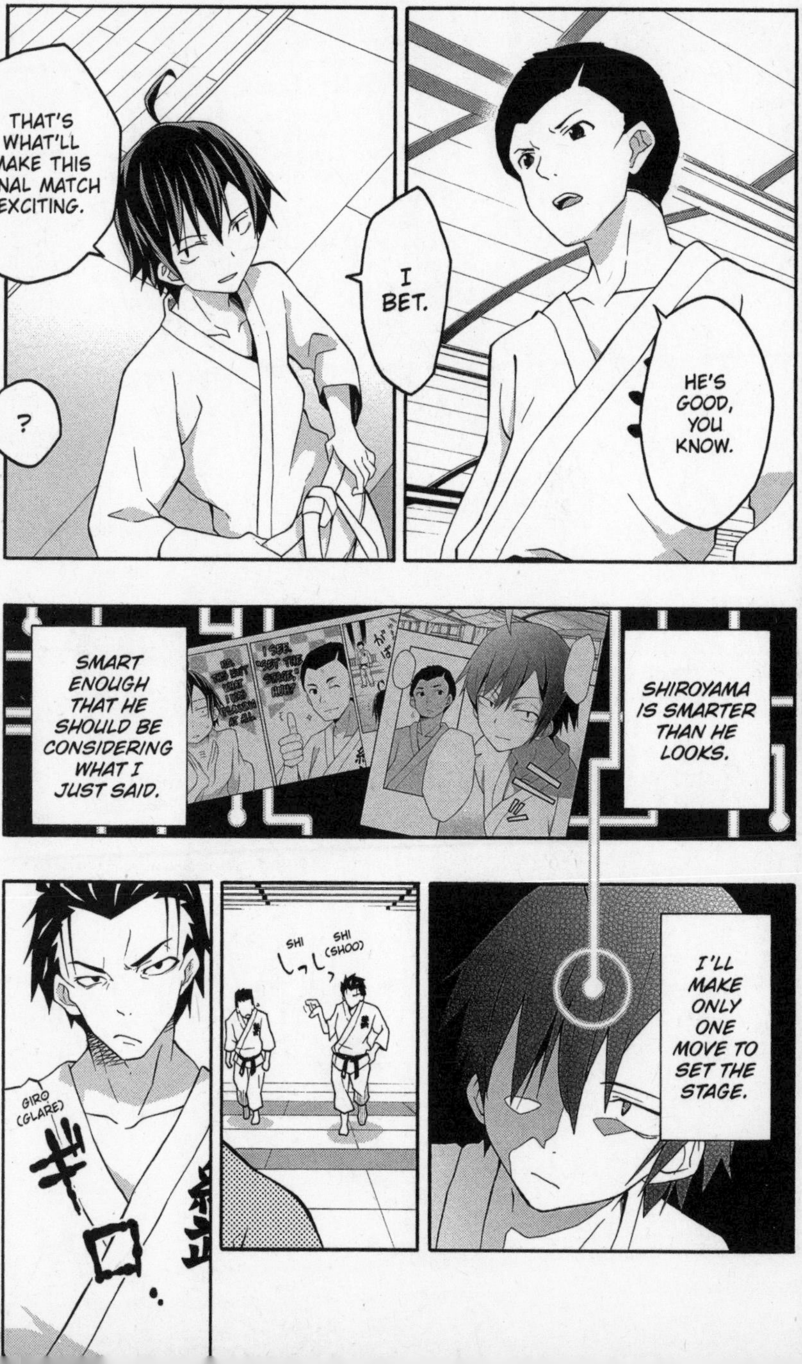
HE'S GOOD, YOU KNOW.
I BET.
THAT'S WHAT'LL MAKE THIS FINAL MATCH EXCITING.
?
SHIROYAMA IS SMARTER THAN HE LOOKS.
SMART ENOUGH THAT HE SHOULD BE CONSIDERING WHAT I JUST SAID.
I'LL MAKE ONLY ONE MOVE TO SET THE STAGE.
SHI SHI (SHOO)
GIRO (GLARE)

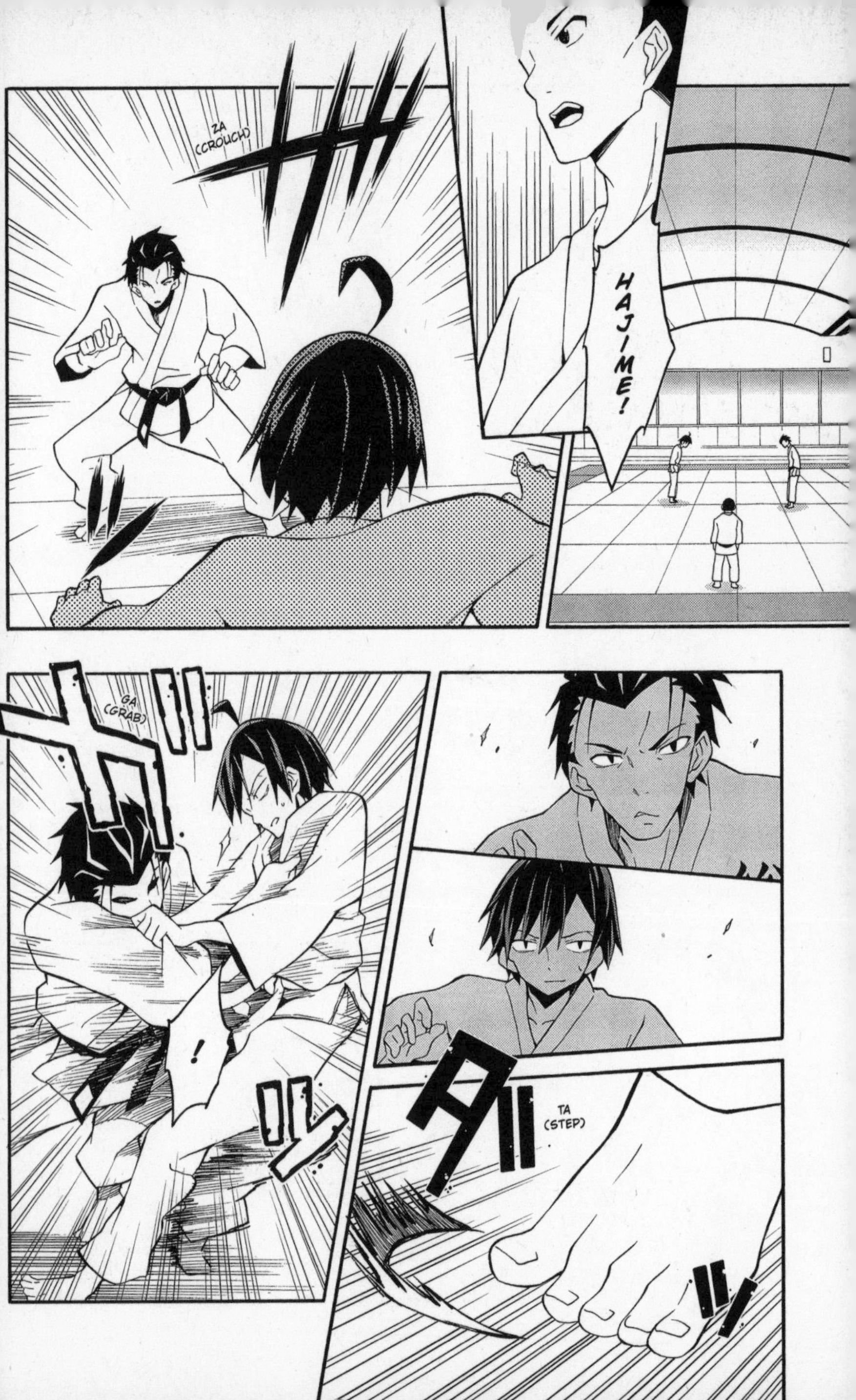
HAJIME!
ZA
(CROUCH)
TA
(STEP)
GA
(GRAB)
!

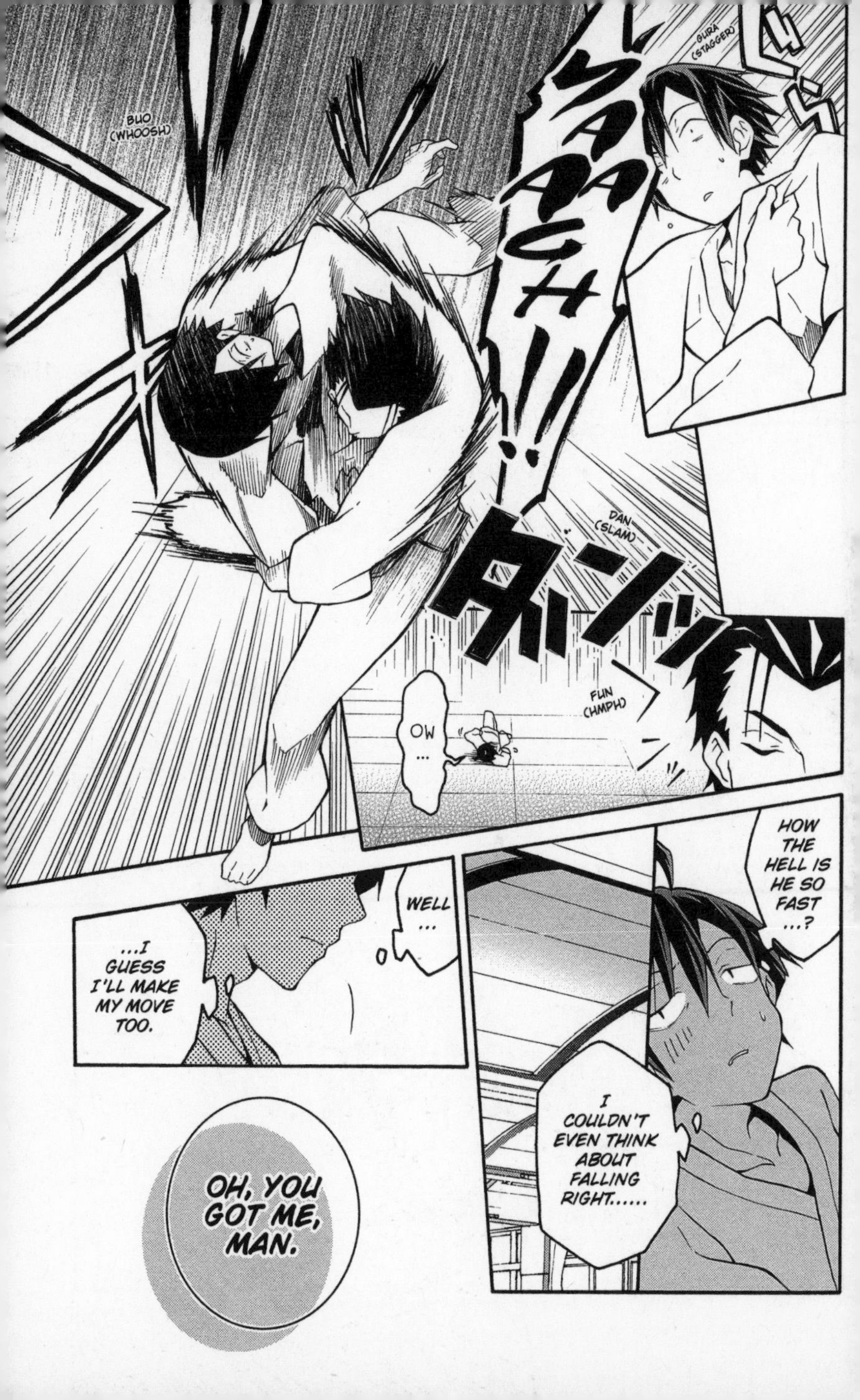
GURA (STAGGER)
WAAAGH!!
BUO (WHOOSH)
DAN (SLAM)
FUN (HMPH)
OW...
HOW THE HELL IS HE SO FAST...?
I COULDN'T EVEN THINK ABOUT FALLING RIGHT......
WELL...
...I GUESS I'LL MAKE MY MOVE TOO.
OH, YOU GOT ME, MAN.

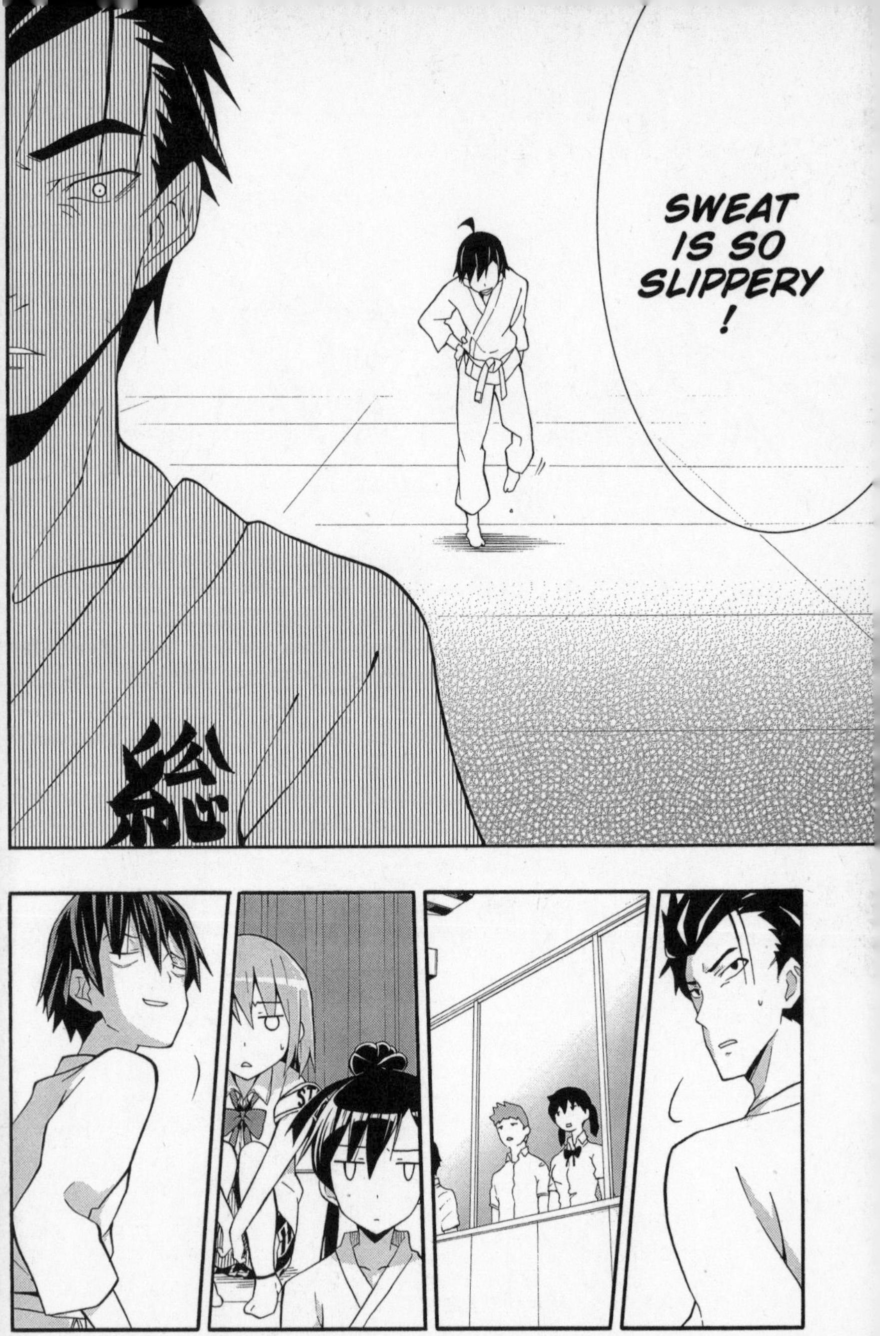
SWEAT IS SO SLIPPERY!
総

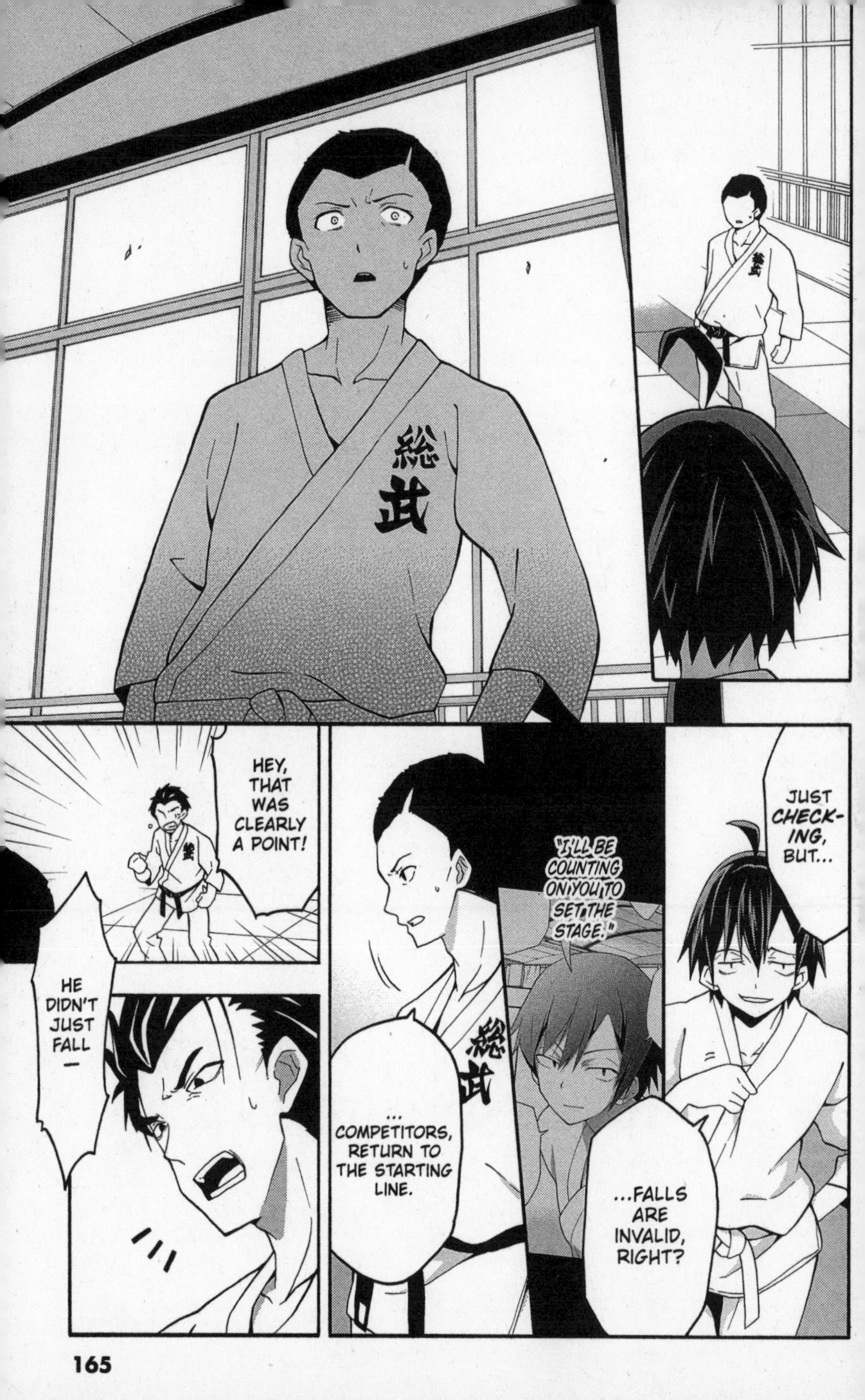
JUST CHECKING, BUT...
"I'LL BE COUNTING ON YOU TO SET THE STAGE."
...FALLS ARE INVALID, RIGHT?
...COMPETITORS, RETURN TO THE STARTING LINE.
HEY, THAT WAS CLEARLY A POINT!
HE DIDN'T JUST FALL—

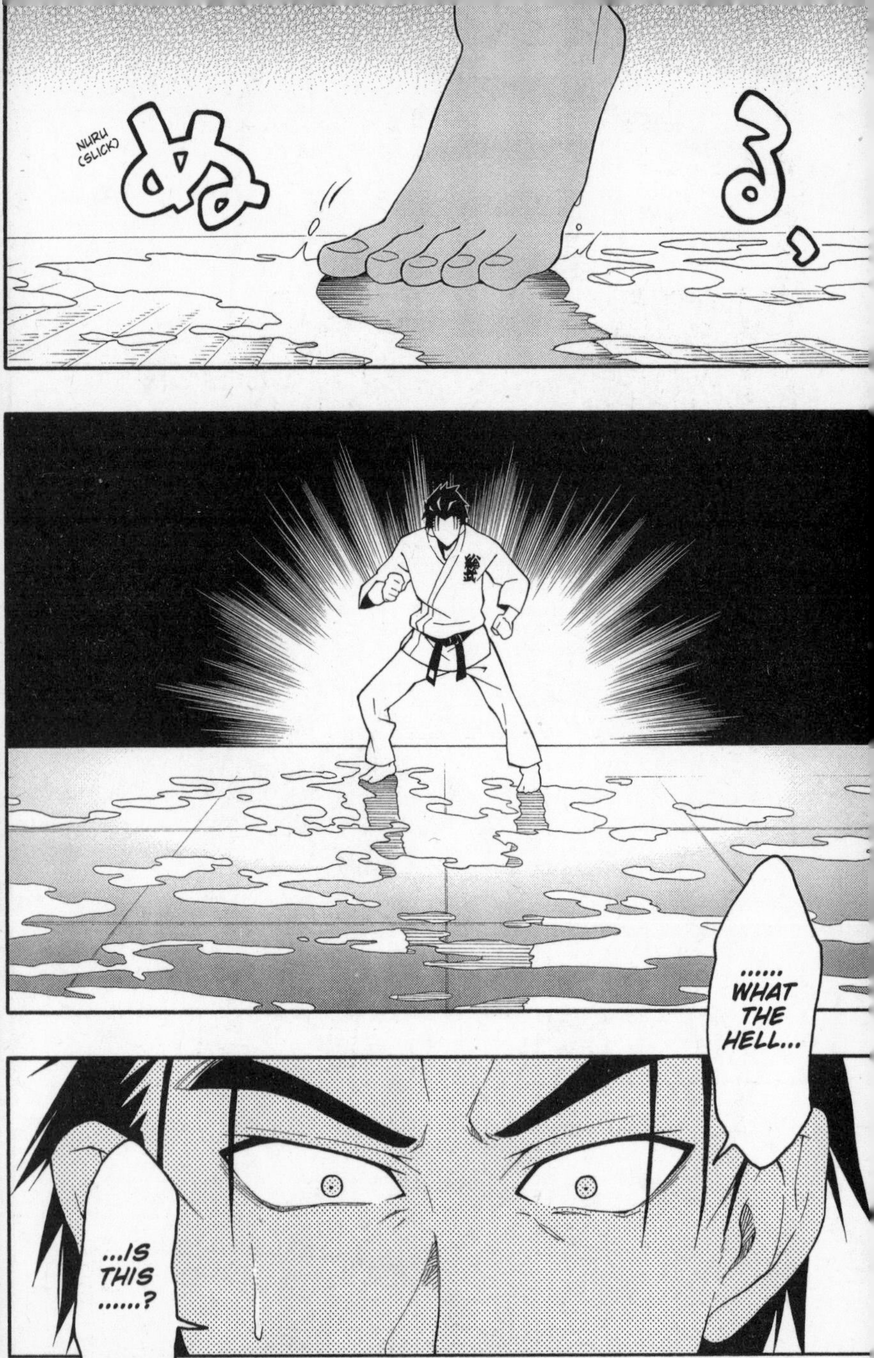
ぬる、
NURU (SLICK)
......WHAT THE HELL...
...IS THIS ......?

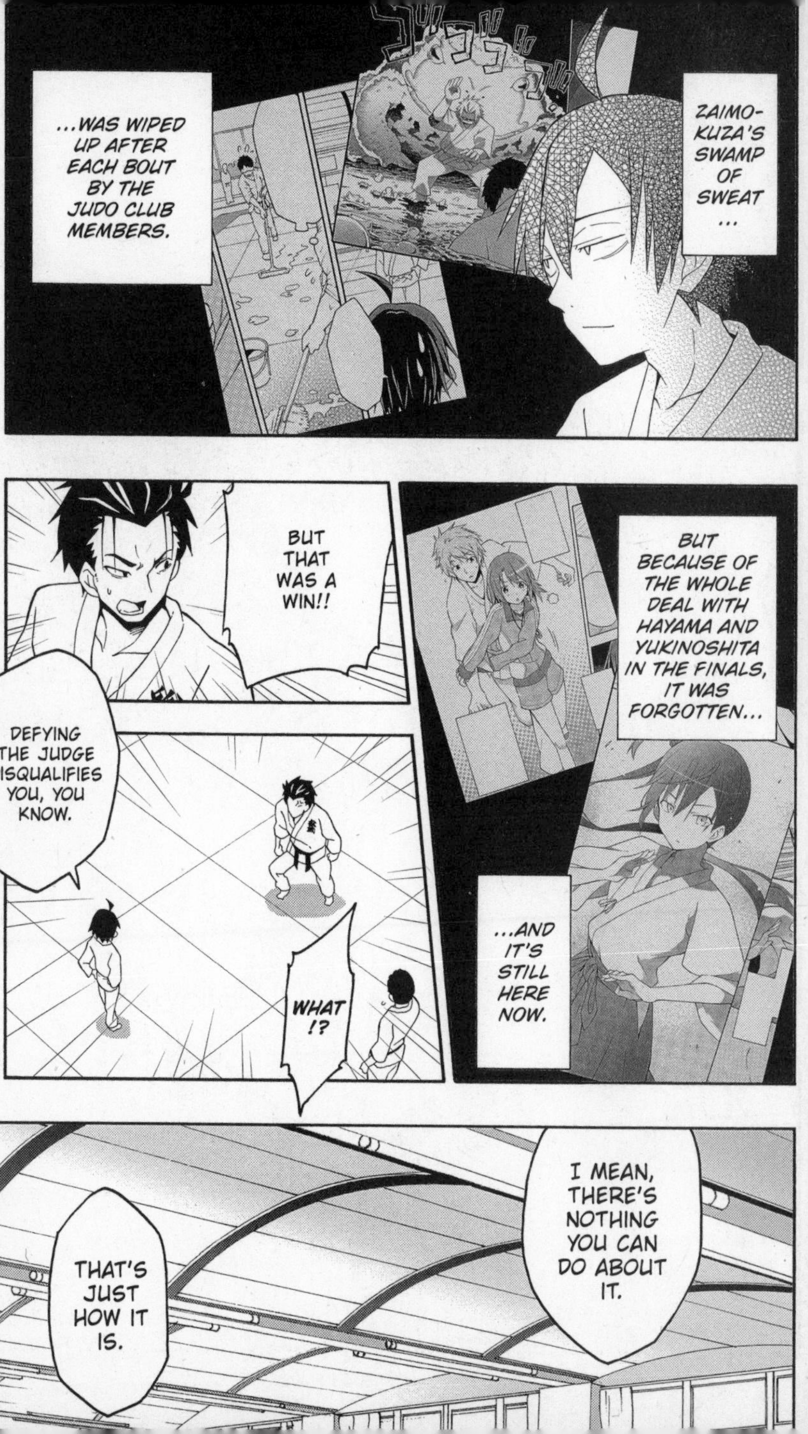
ZAIMOKUZA'S SWAMP OF SWEAT...
...WAS WIPED UP AFTER EACH BOUT BY THE JUDO CLUB MEMBERS.
BUT BECAUSE OF THE WHOLE DEAL WITH HAYAMA AND YUKINOSHITA IN THE FINALS, IT WAS FORGOTTEN...
...AND IT'S STILL HERE NOW.
BUT THAT WAS A WIN!!
DEFYING THE JUDGE DISQUALIFIES YOU, YOU KNOW.
WHAT!?
I MEAN, THERE'S NOTHING YOU CAN DO ABOUT IT.
THAT'S JUST HOW IT IS.

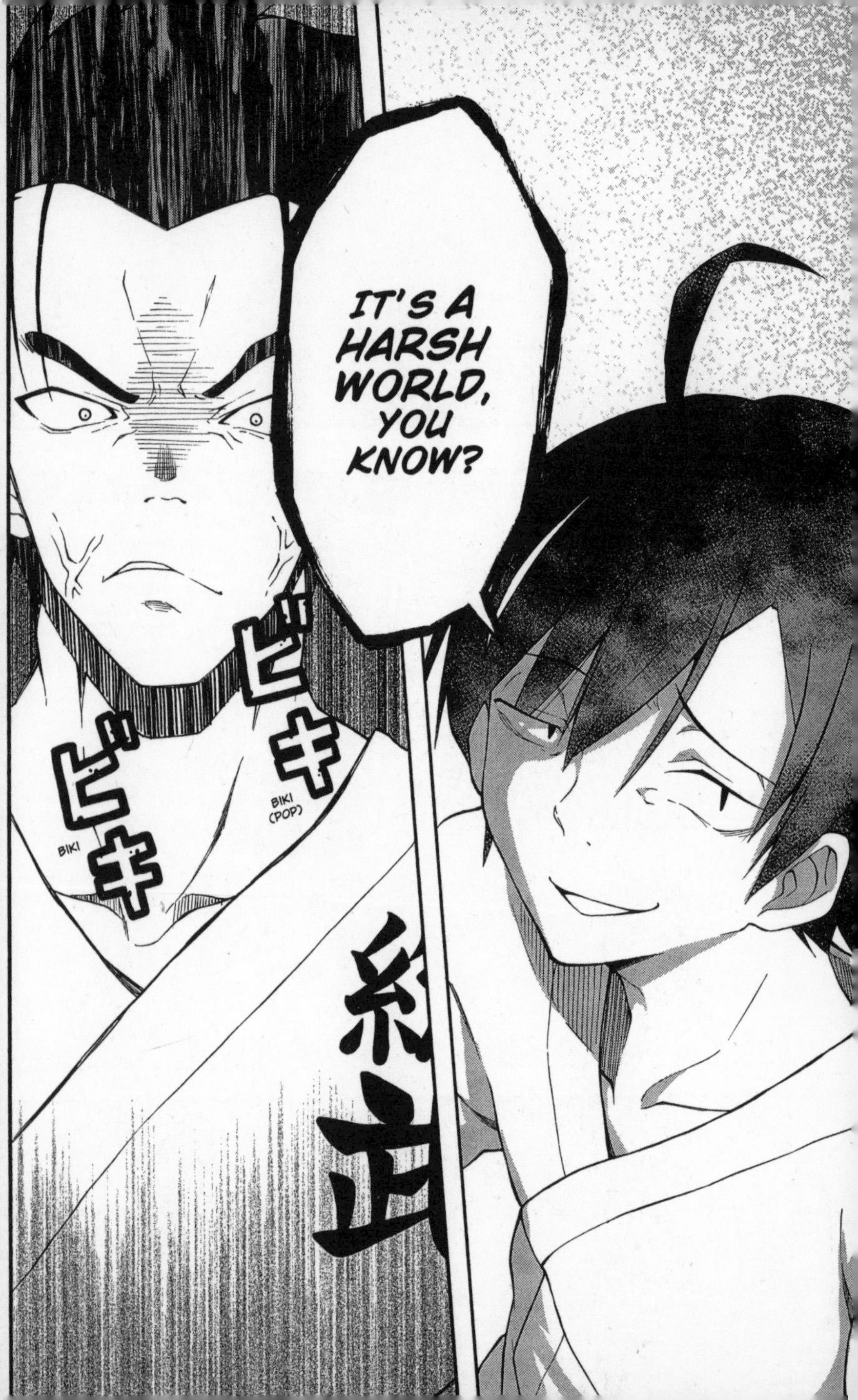
IT'S A HARSH WORLD, YOU KNOW?
ビキ
BIKI (POP)
ビキ
BIKI

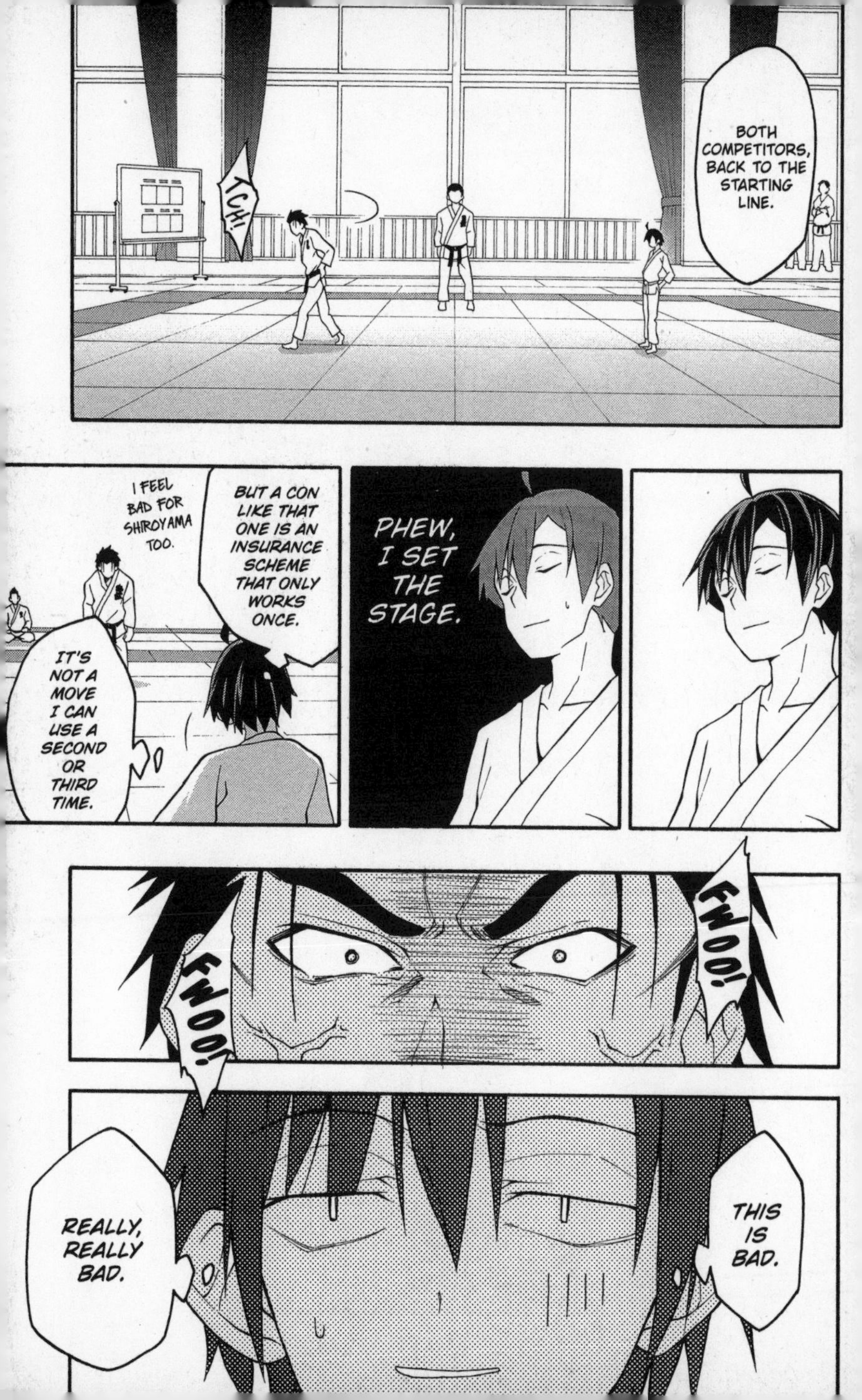
BOTH COMPETITORS, BACK TO THE STARTING LINE.
TCH!
PHEW, I SET THE STAGE.
BUT A CON LIKE THAT ONE IS AN INSURANCE SCHEME THAT ONLY WORKS ONCE.
I FEEL BAD FOR SHIROYAMA TOO.
IT'S NOT A MOVE I CAN USE A SECOND OR THIRD TIME.
FWOO!
FWOO!
THIS IS BAD.
REALLY, REALLY BAD.

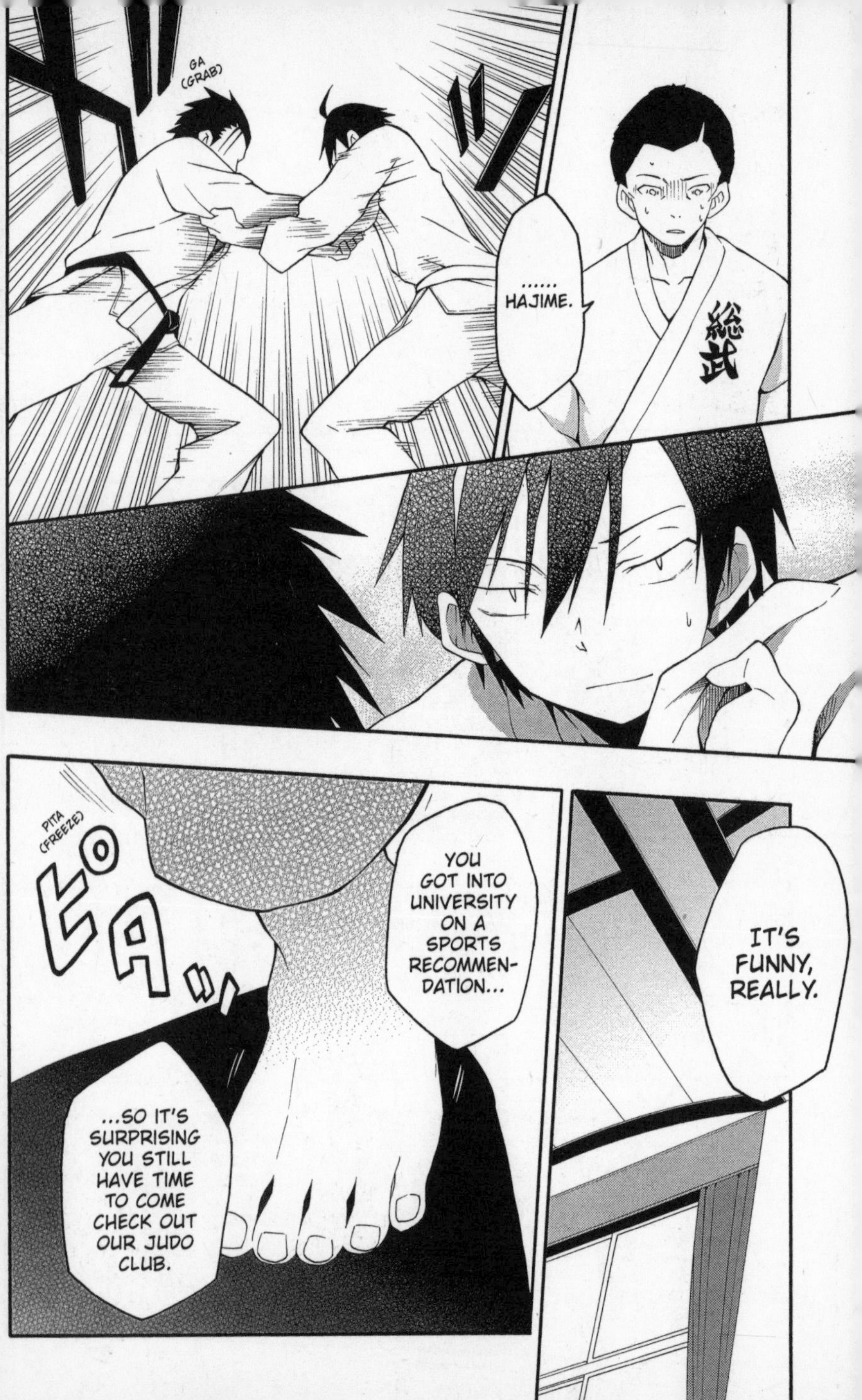
......HAJIME.
GA (GRAB)
IT'S FUNNY, REALLY.
YOU GOT INTO UNIVERSITY ON A SPORTS RECOMMENDATION...
PITA (FREEZE)
...SO IT'S SURPRISING YOU STILL HAVE TIME TO COME CHECK OUT OUR JUDO CLUB.

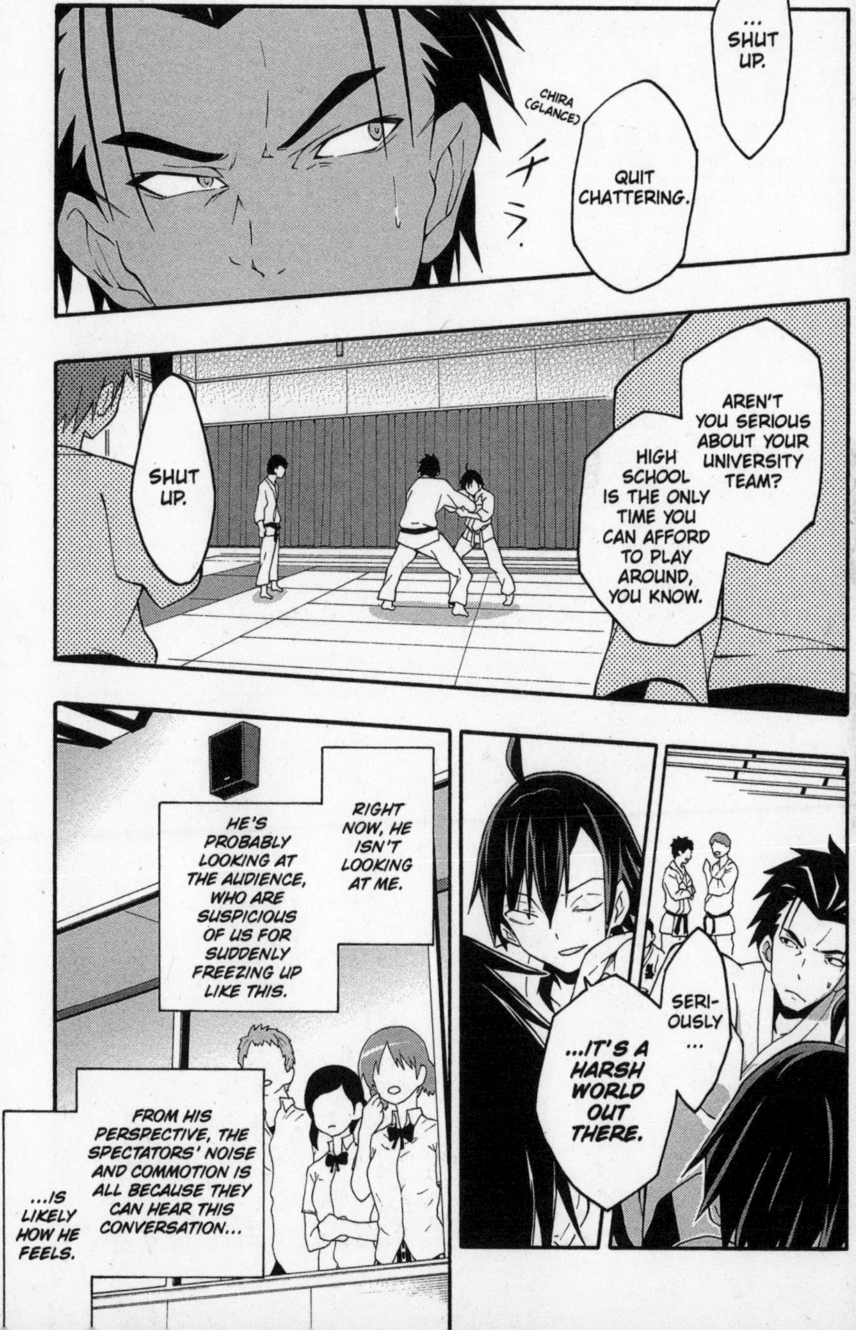
...SHUT UP.
QUIT CHATTERING.
CHIRA (GLANCE)
AREN'T YOU SERIOUS ABOUT YOUR UNIVERSITY TEAM?
HIGH SCHOOL IS THE ONLY TIME YOU CAN AFFORD TO PLAY AROUND, YOU KNOW.
SHUT UP.
SERI-OUSLY...
...IT'S A HARSH WORLD OUT THERE.
RIGHT NOW, HE ISN'T LOOKING AT ME.
HE'S PROBABLY LOOKING AT THE AUDIENCE, WHO ARE SUSPICIOUS OF US FOR SUDDENLY FREEZING UP LIKE THIS.
FROM HIS PERSPECTIVE, THE SPECTATORS' NOISE AND COMMOTION IS ALL BECAUSE THEY CAN HEAR THIS CONVERSATION...
...IS LIKELY HOW HE FEELS.

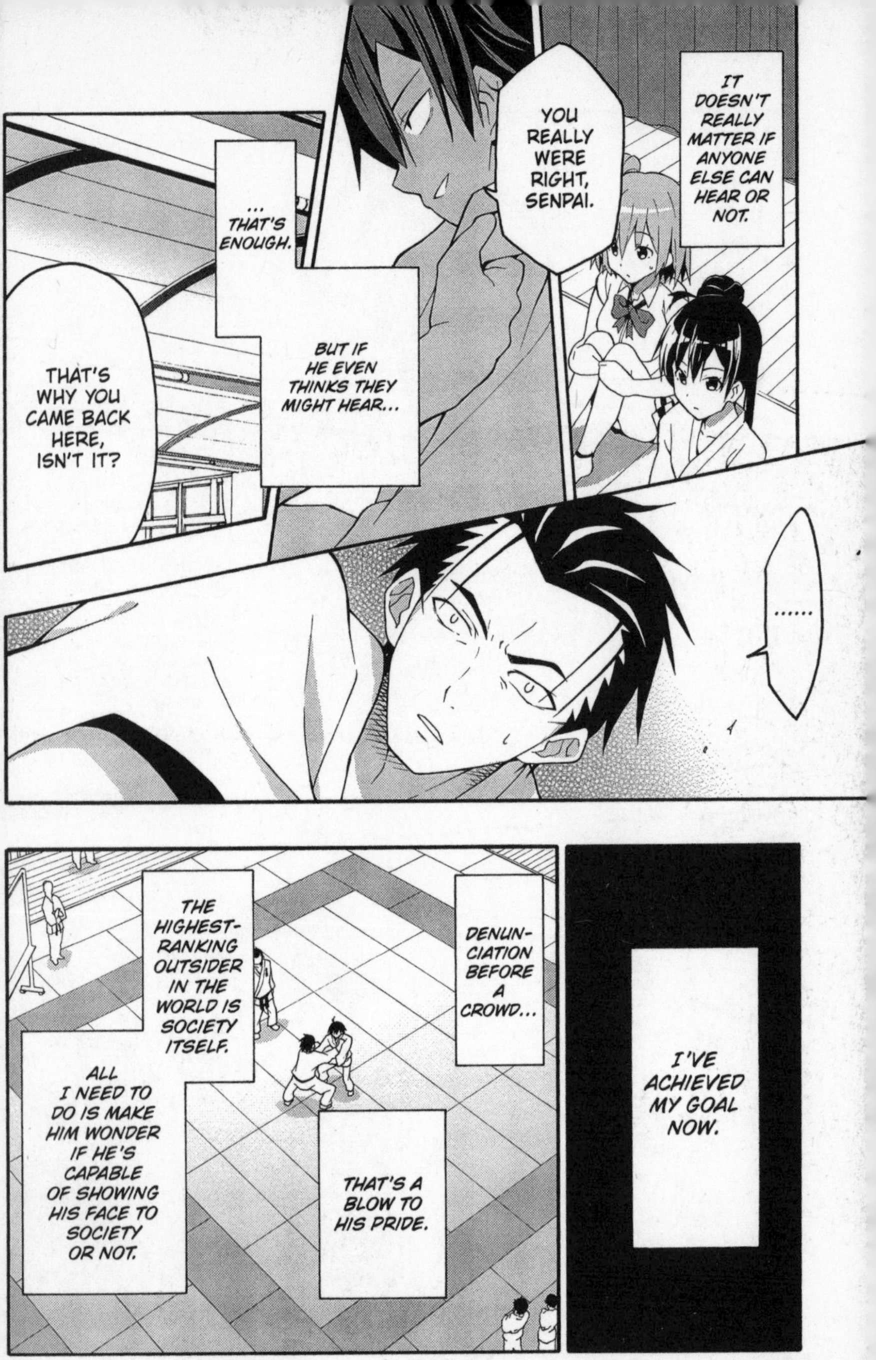
IT DOESN'T REALLY MATTER IF ANYONE ELSE CAN HEAR OR NOT.
YOU REALLY WERE RIGHT, SENPAI.
... THAT'S ENOUGH.
BUT IF HE EVEN THINKS THEY MIGHT HEAR...
THAT'S WHY YOU CAME BACK HERE, ISN'T IT?
......
I'VE ACHIEVED MY GOAL NOW.
DENUN-CIATION BEFORE A CROWD...
THAT'S A BLOW TO HIS PRIDE.
THE HIGHEST-RANKING OUTSIDER IN THE WORLD IS SOCIETY ITSELF.
ALL I NEED TO DO IS MAKE HIM WONDER IF HE'S CAPABLE OF SHOWING HIS FACE TO SOCIETY OR NOT.

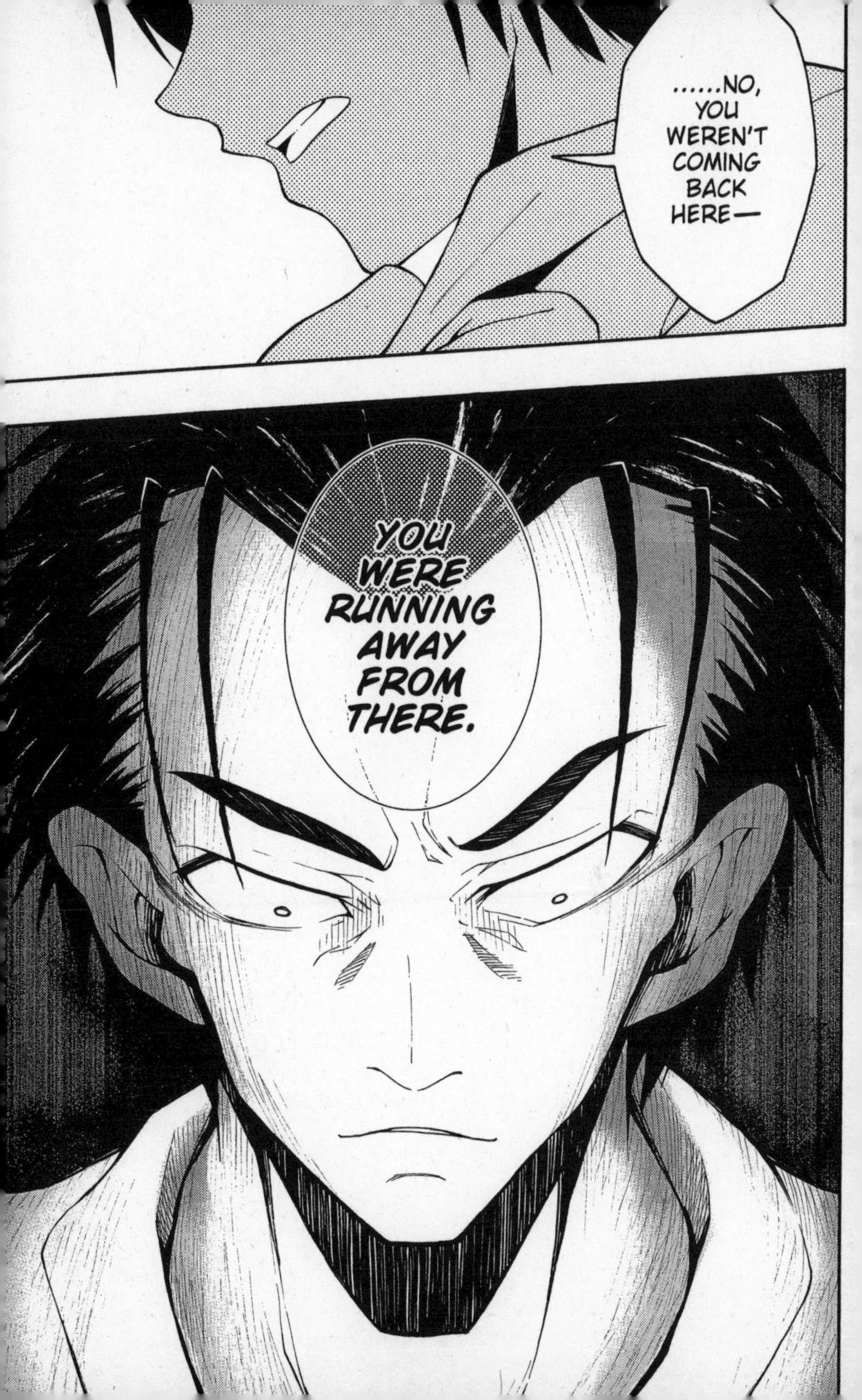
......NO, YOU WEREN'T COMING BACK HERE—
YOU WERE RUNNING AWAY FROM THERE.

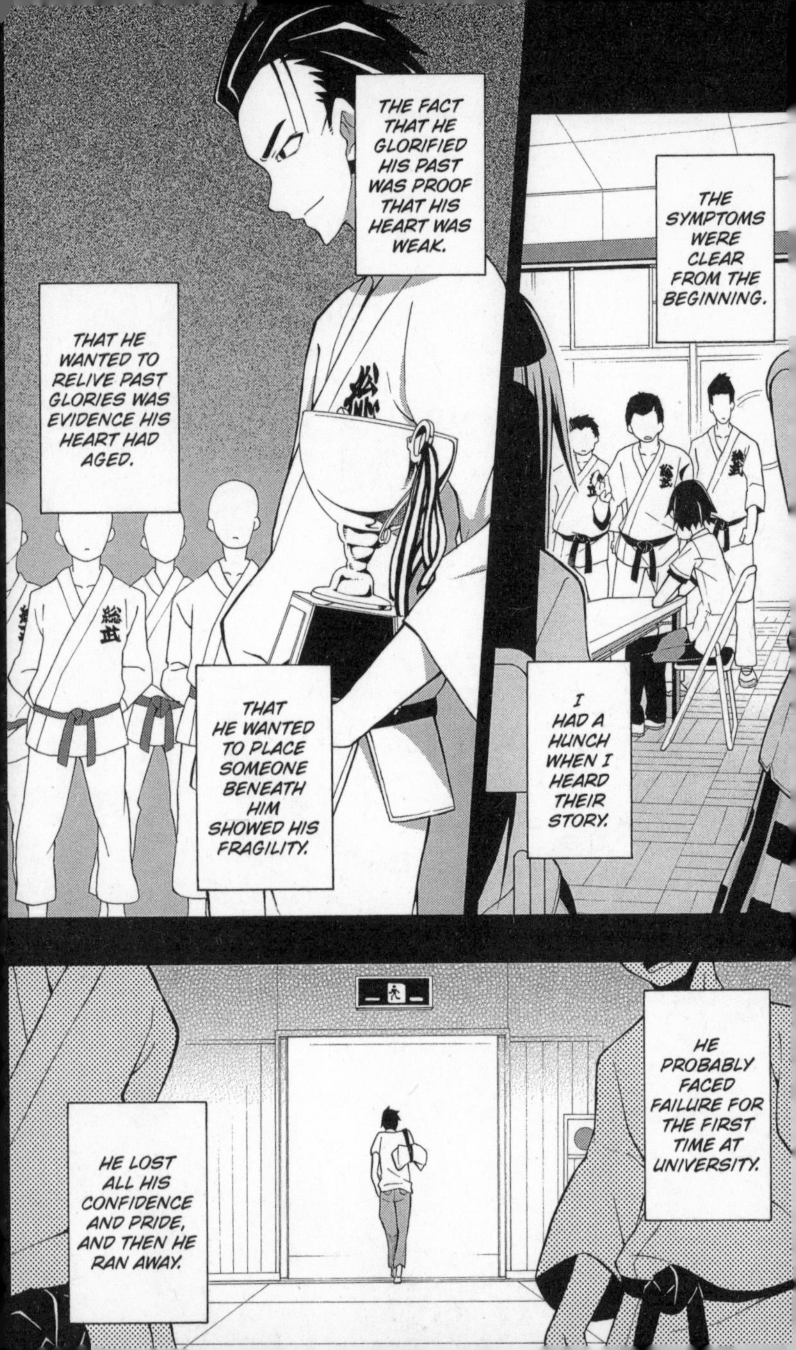
THE SYMPTOMS WERE CLEAR FROM THE BEGINNING.
I HAD A HUNCH WHEN I HEARD THEIR STORY.
THE FACT THAT HE GLORIFIED HIS PAST WAS PROOF THAT HIS HEART WAS WEAK.
THAT HE WANTED TO RELIVE PAST GLORIES WAS EVIDENCE HIS HEART HAD AGED.
THAT HE WANTED TO PLACE SOMEONE BENEATH HIM SHOWED HIS FRAGILITY.
HE PROBABLY FACED FAILURE FOR THE FIRST TIME AT UNIVERSITY.
HE LOST ALL HIS CONFIDENCE AND PRIDE, AND THEN HE RAN AWAY.

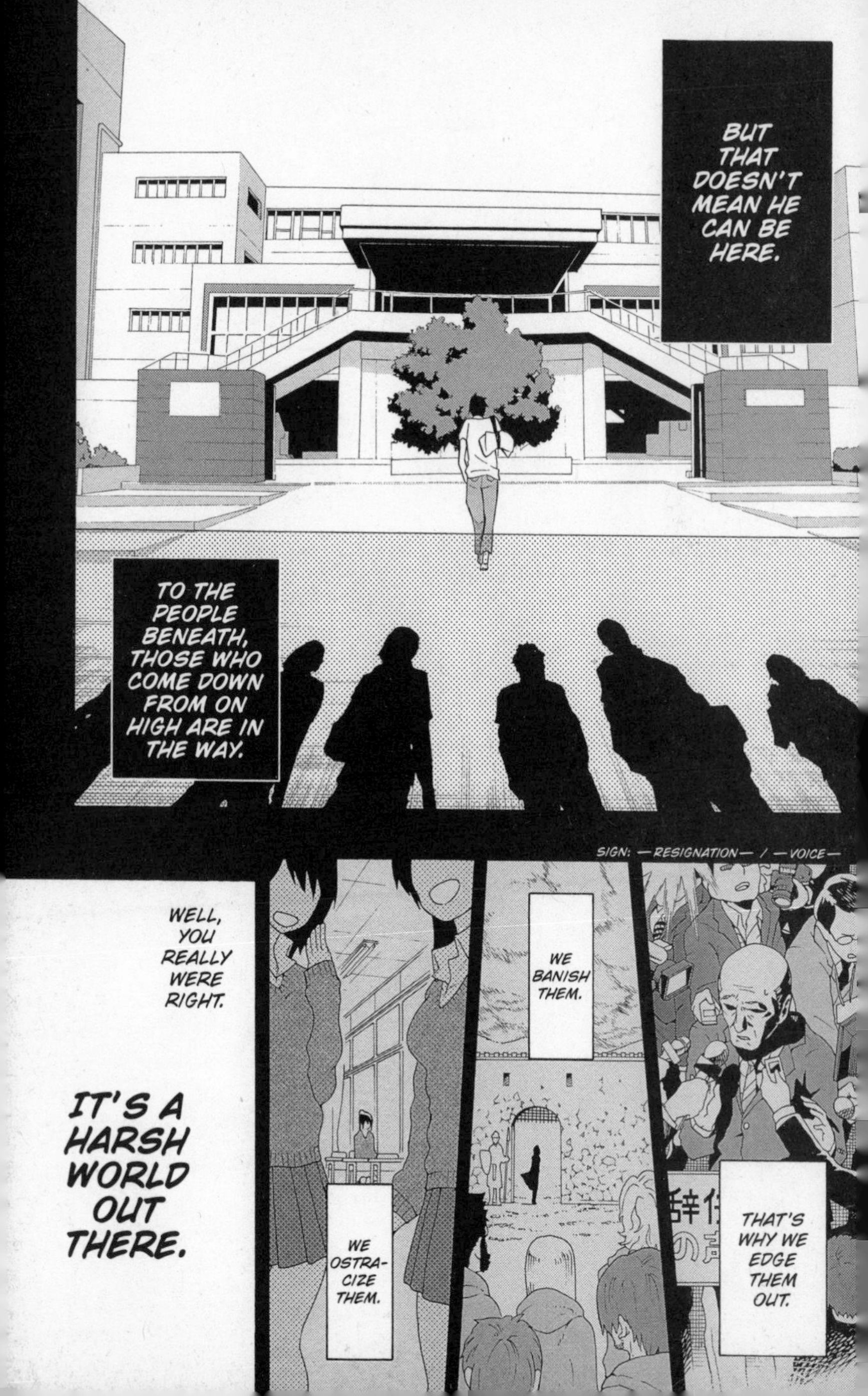
BUT THAT DOESN'T MEAN HE CAN BE HERE.
TO THE PEOPLE BENEATH, THOSE WHO COME DOWN FROM ON HIGH ARE IN THE WAY.
SIGN: —RESIGNATION— / —VOICE—
THAT'S WHY WE EDGE THEM OUT.
WE BANISH THEM.
WE OSTRA-CIZE THEM.
WELL, YOU REALLY WERE RIGHT.
IT'S A HARSH WORLD OUT THERE.

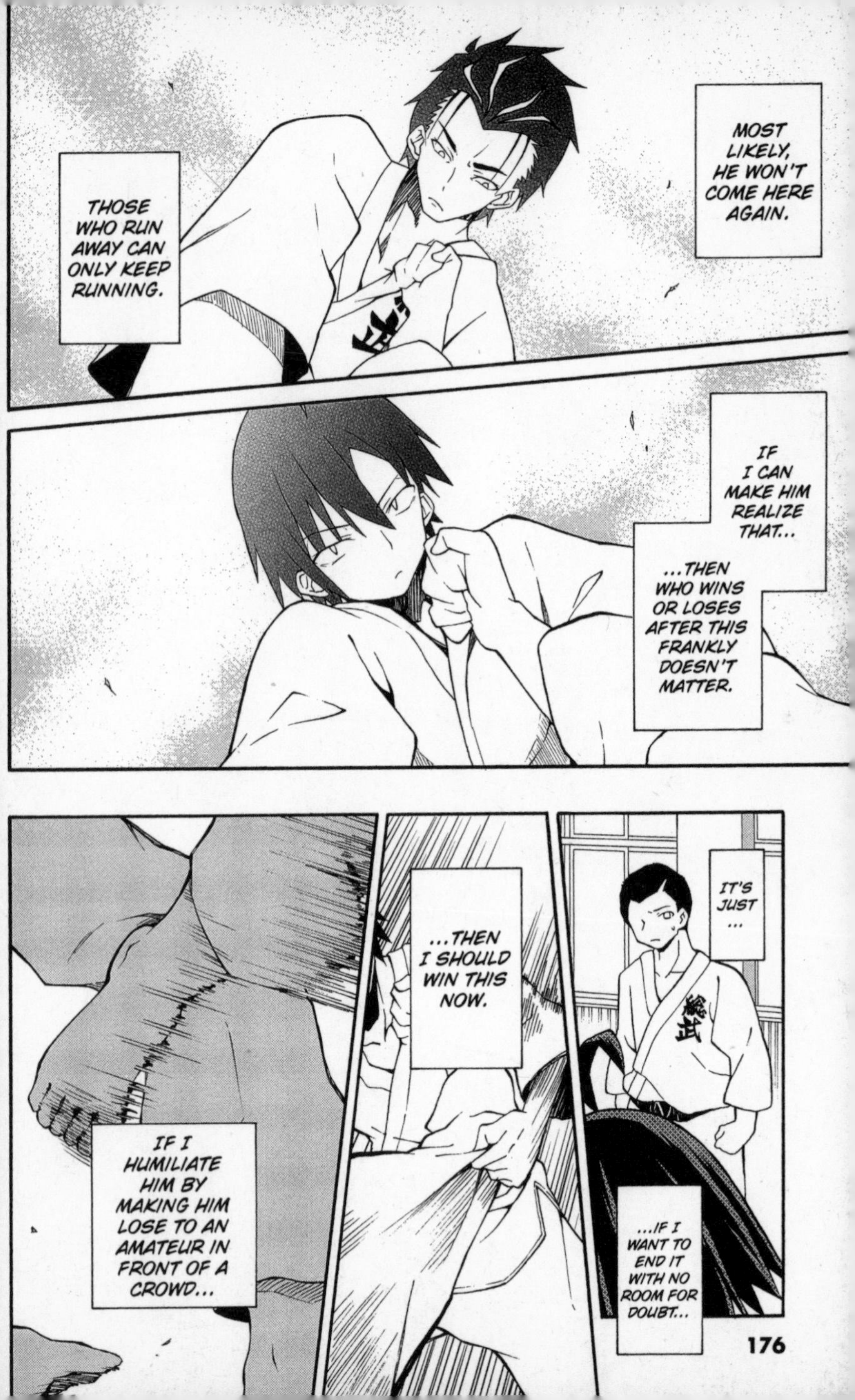
MOST LIKELY, HE WON'T COME HERE AGAIN.
THOSE WHO RUN AWAY CAN ONLY KEEP RUNNING.
IF I CAN MAKE HIM REALIZE THAT...
...THEN WHO WINS OR LOSES AFTER THIS FRANKLY DOESN'T MATTER.
IT'S JUST ...
...IF I WANT TO END IT WITH NO ROOM FOR DOUBT...
...THEN I SHOULD WIN THIS NOW.
IF I HUMILIATE HIM BY MAKING HIM LOSE TO AN AMATEUR IN FRONT OF A CROWD...

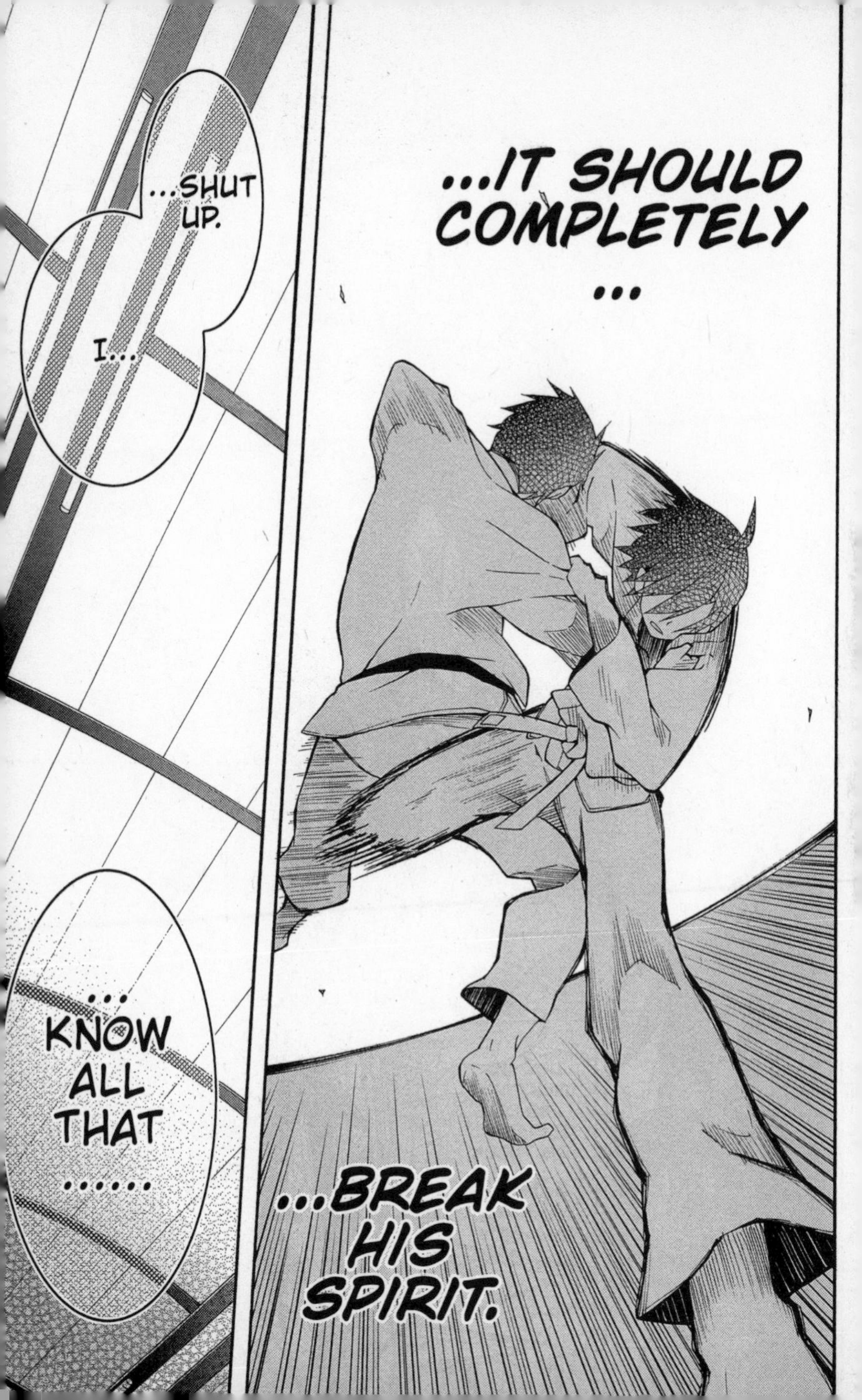
...IT SHOULD COMPLETELY ...
...BREAK HIS SPIRIT.
...SHUT UP.
I...
...KNOW ALL THAT ......

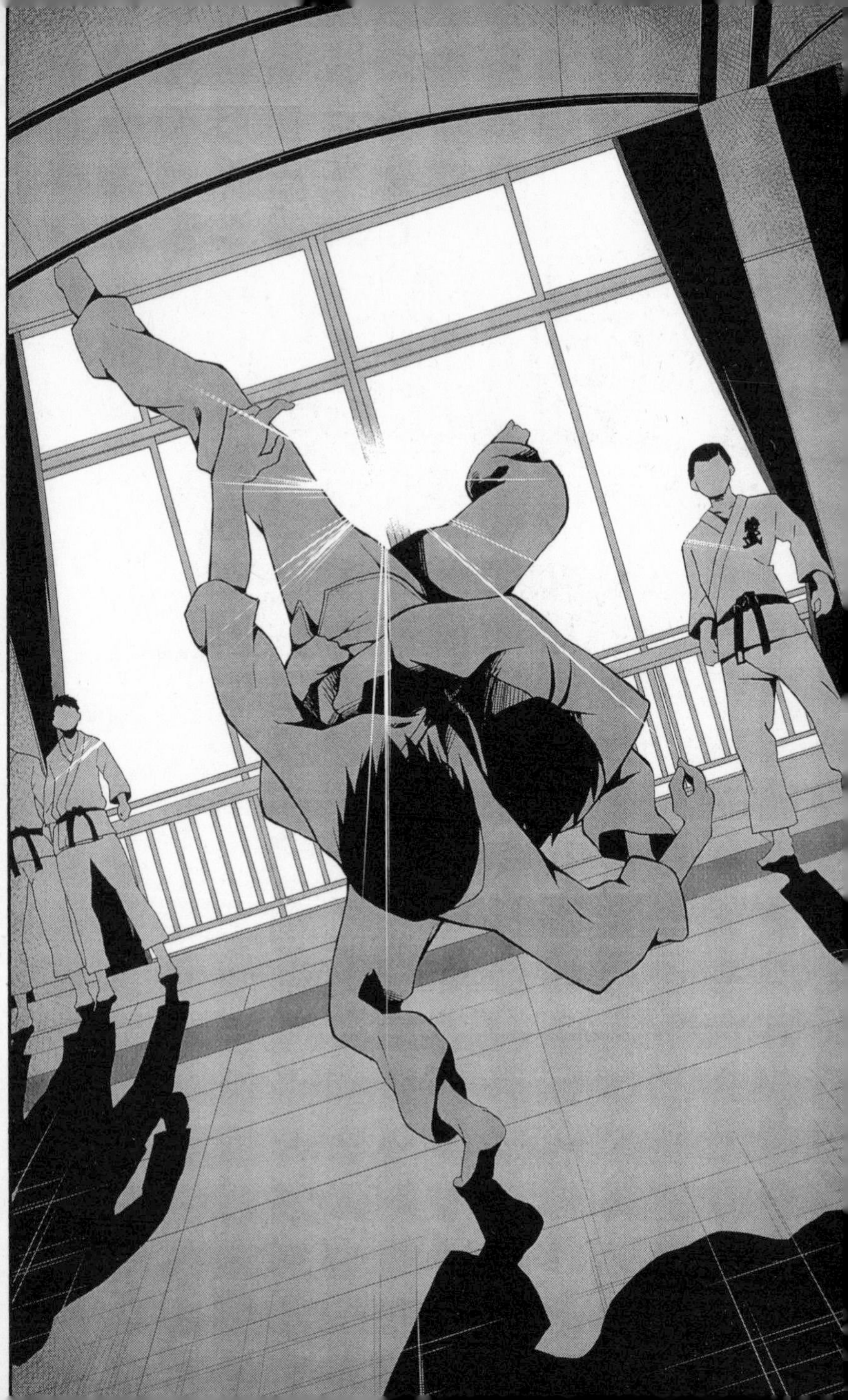

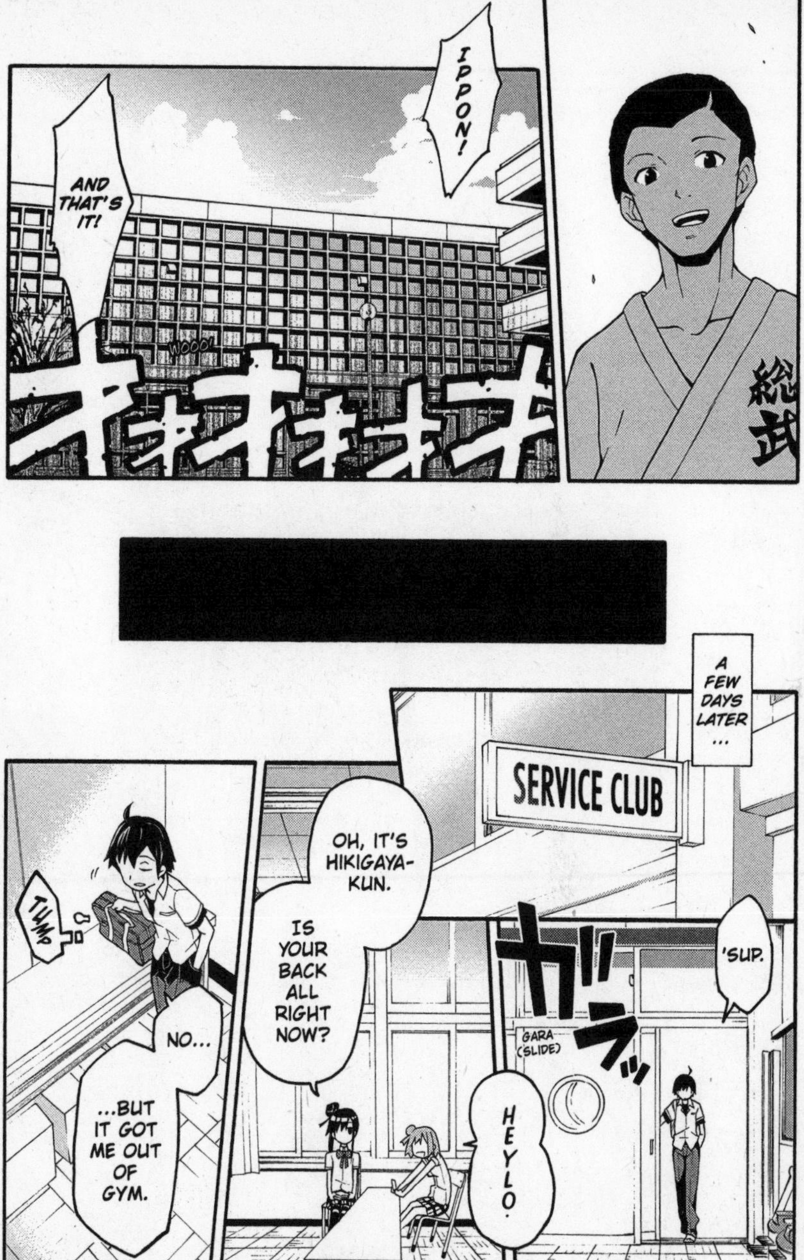
IPPON!
AND THAT'S IT!
WOOO!
A FEW DAYS LATER...
SERVICE CLUB
'SUP.
GARA (SLIDE)
HEYLO.
OH, IT'S HIKIGAYA-KUN.
IS YOUR BACK ALL RIGHT NOW?
THUMP
NO...
...BUT IT GOT ME OUT OF GYM.

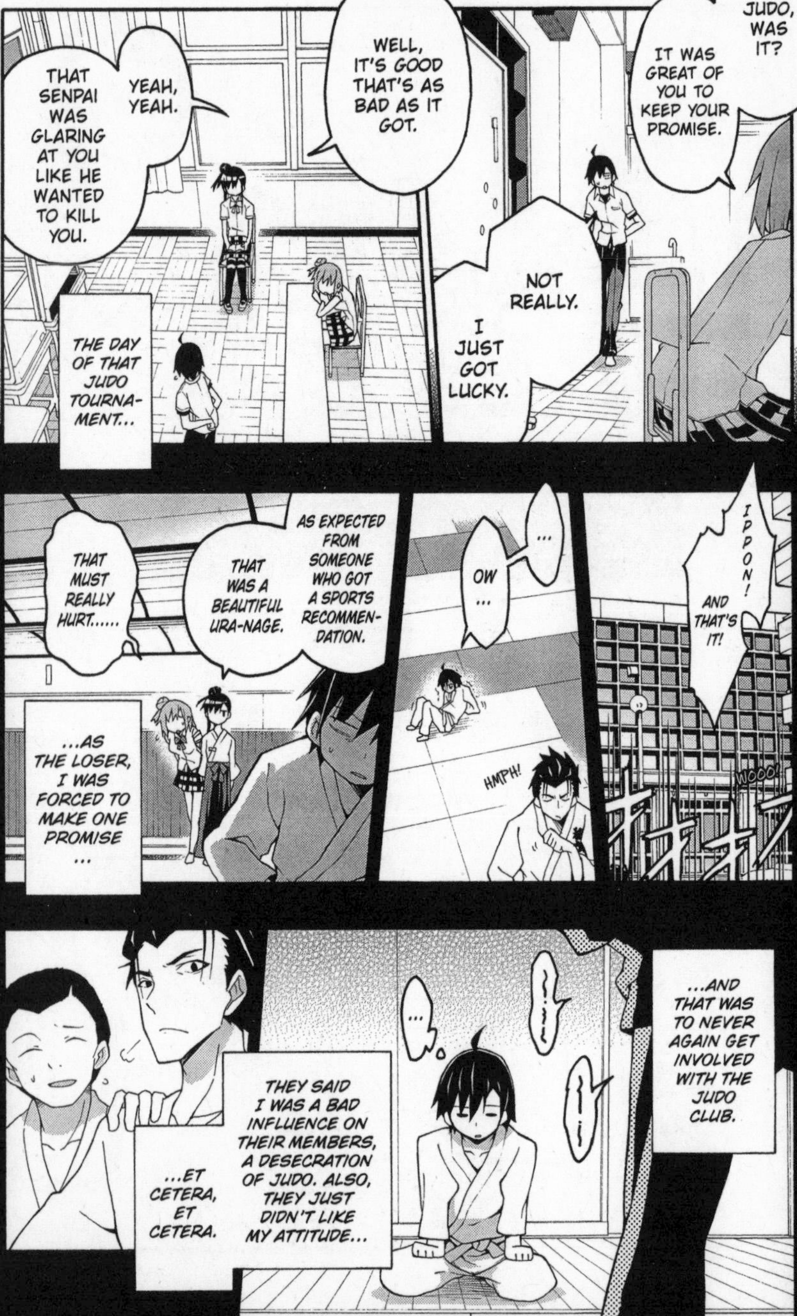
JUDO, WAS IT?
IT WAS GREAT OF YOU TO KEEP YOUR PROMISE.
NOT REALLY.
I JUST GOT LUCKY.
WELL, IT'S GOOD THAT'S AS BAD AS IT GOT.
YEAH, YEAH.
THAT SENPAI WAS GLARING AT YOU LIKE HE WANTED TO KILL YOU.
THE DAY OF THAT JUDO TOURNAMENT...
IPPON!
AND THAT'S IT!
WOOO!
...
OW...
HMPH!
AS EXPECTED FROM SOMEONE WHO GOT A SPORTS RECOMMENDATION.
THAT WAS A BEAUTIFUL URA-NAGE.
THAT MUST REALLY HURT......
...AS THE LOSER, I WAS FORCED TO MAKE ONE PROMISE...
...AND THAT WAS TO NEVER AGAIN GET INVOLVED WITH THE JUDO CLUB.
...
THEY SAID I WAS A BAD INFLUENCE ON THEIR MEMBERS, A DESECRATION OF JUDO. ALSO, THEY JUST DIDN'T LIKE MY ATTITUDE...
...ET CETERA, ET CETERA.

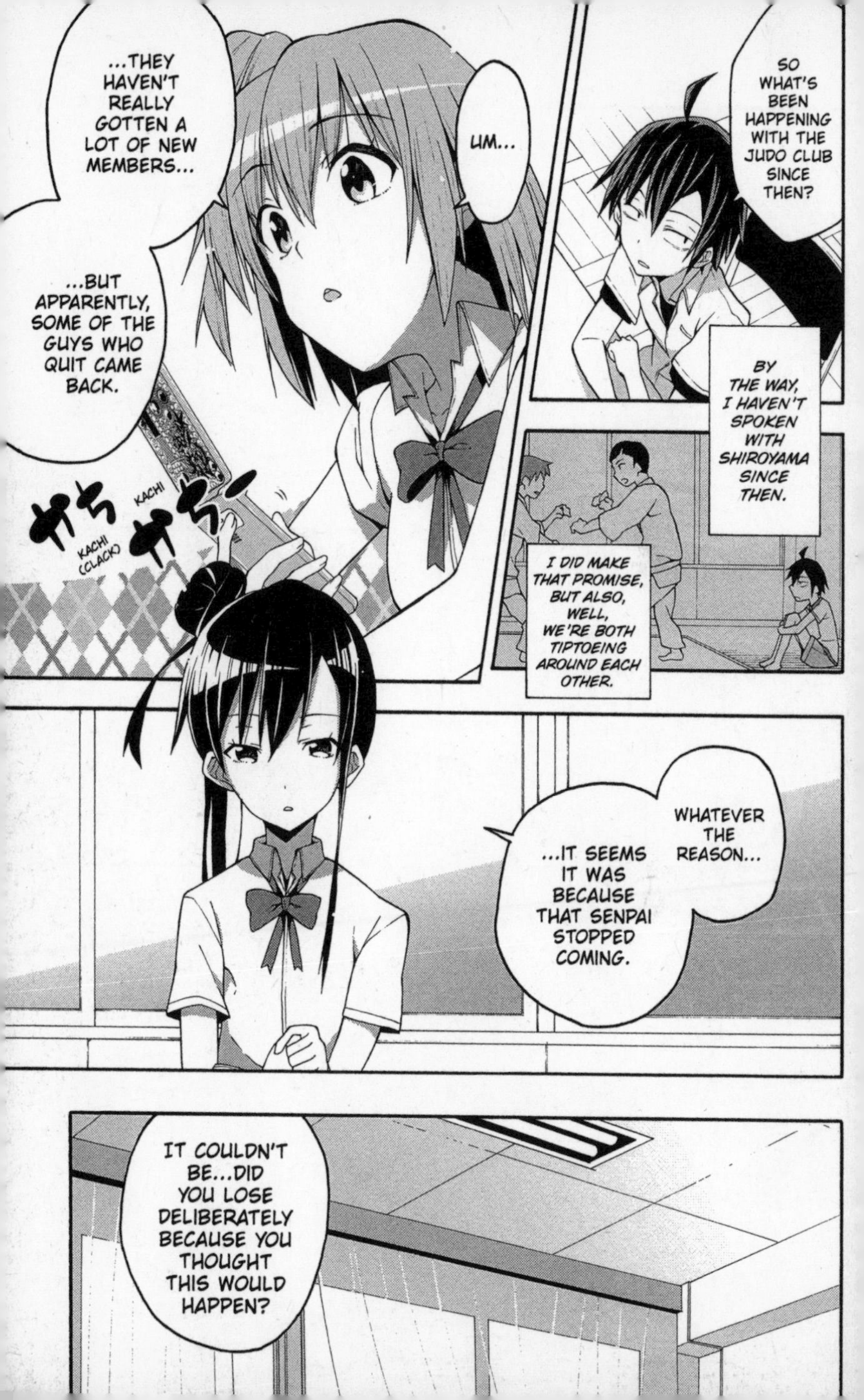
SO WHAT'S BEEN HAPPENING WITH THE JUDO CLUB SINCE THEN?
BY THE WAY, I HAVEN'T SPOKEN WITH SHIROYAMA SINCE THEN.
I DID MAKE THAT PROMISE, BUT ALSO, WELL, WE'RE BOTH TIPTOEING AROUND EACH OTHER.
UM...
...THEY HAVEN'T REALLY GOTTEN A LOT OF NEW MEMBERS...
...BUT APPARENTLY, SOME OF THE GUYS WHO QUIT CAME BACK.
KACHI
KACHI (CLACK)
WHATEVER THE REASON...
...IT SEEMS IT WAS BECAUSE THAT SENPAI STOPPED COMING.
IT COULDN'T BE...DID YOU LOSE DELIBERATELY BECAUSE YOU THOUGHT THIS WOULD HAPPEN?

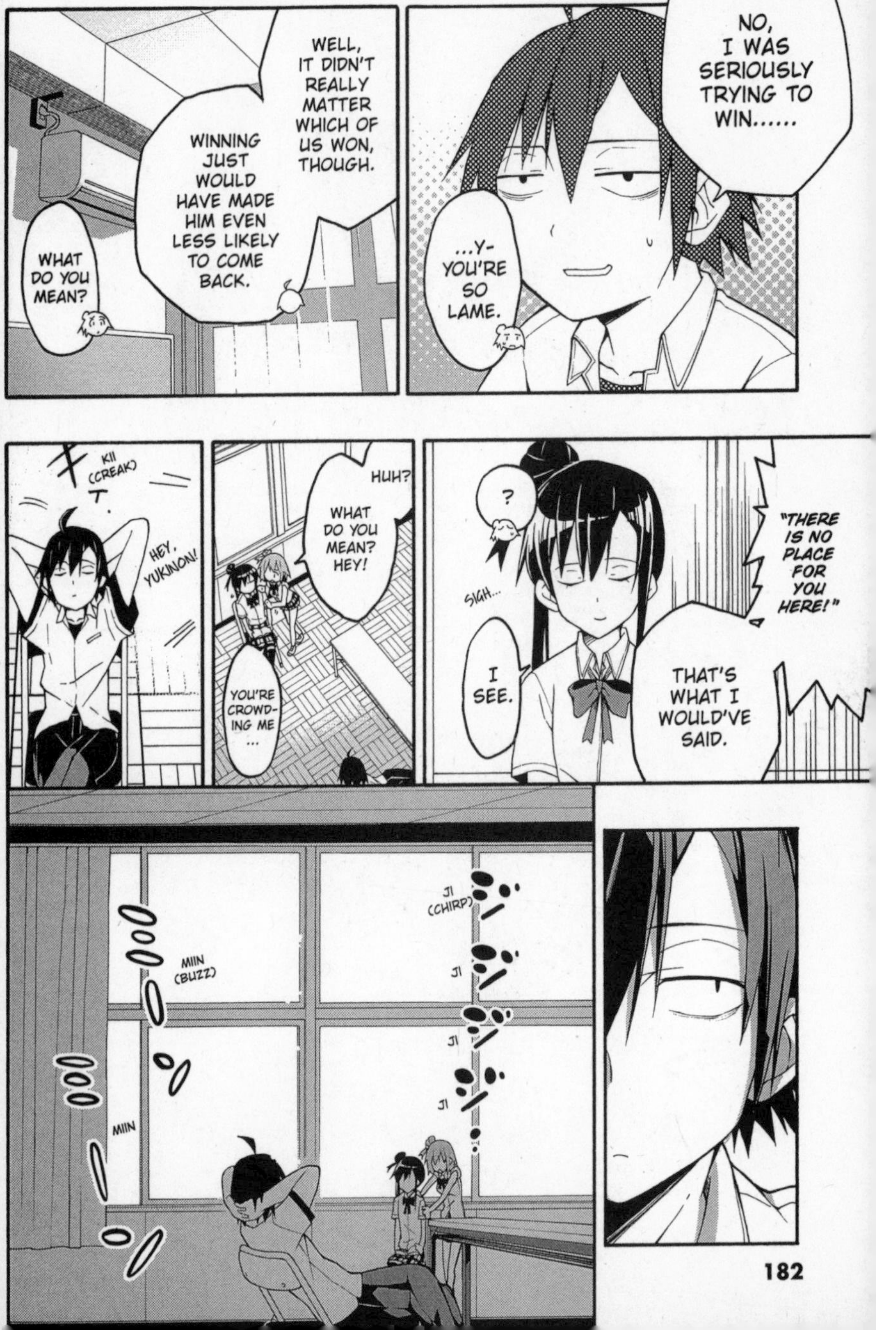
NO, I WAS SERIOUSLY TRYING TO WIN......
...Y-YOU'RE SO LAME.
WELL, IT DIDN'T REALLY MATTER WHICH OF US WON, THOUGH.
WINNING JUST WOULD HAVE MADE HIM EVEN LESS LIKELY TO COME BACK.
WHAT DO YOU MEAN?
"THERE IS NO PLACE FOR YOU HERE!"
THAT'S WHAT I WOULD'VE SAID.
?
SIGH...
I SEE.
HUH?
WHAT DO YOU MEAN? HEY!
YOU'RE CROWDING ME ...
KII (CREAK)
HEY, YUKINON!
JI (CHIRP)
JI
JI
JI
MIIN (BUZZ)
MIIN

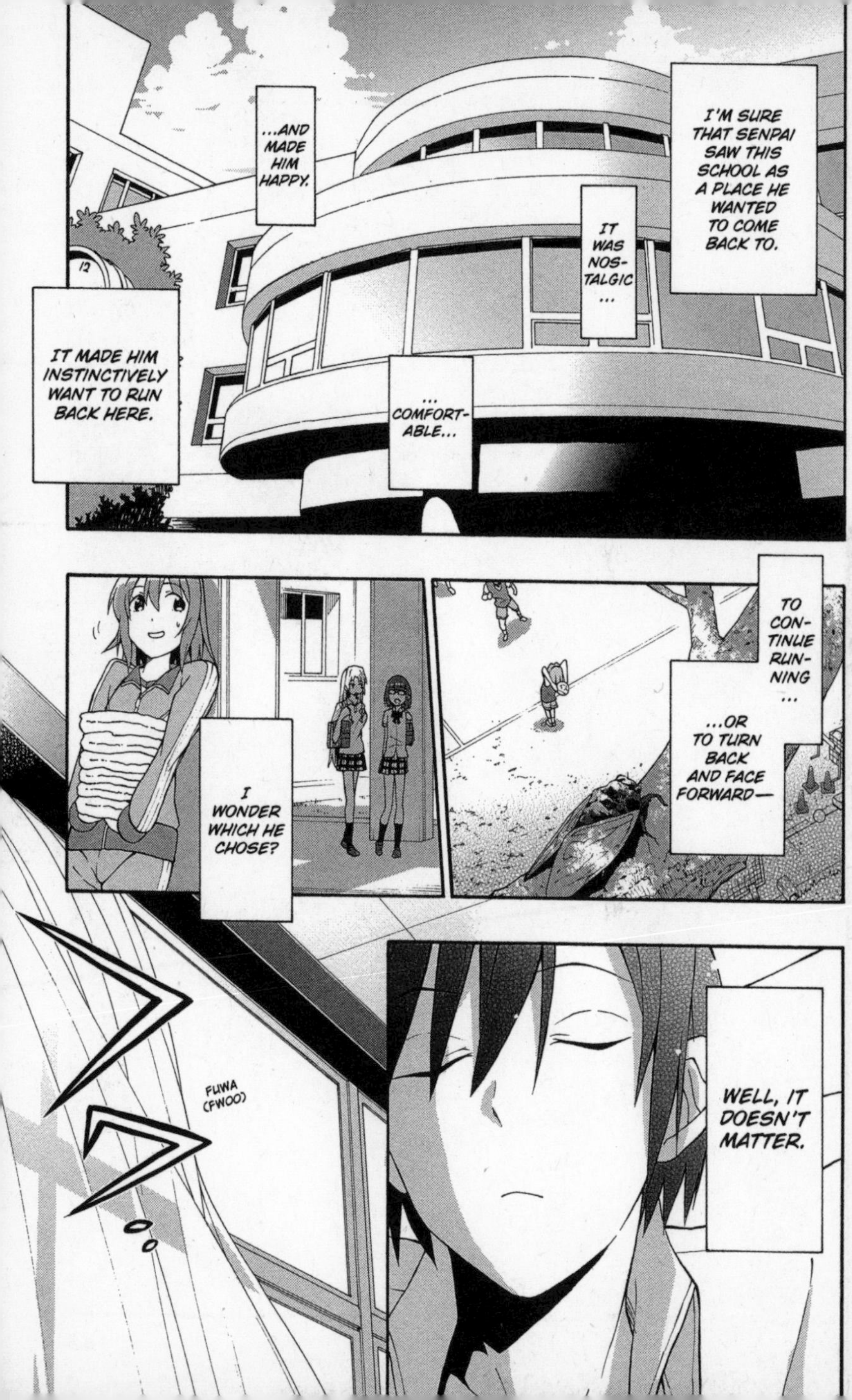
I'M SURE THAT SENPAI SAW THIS SCHOOL AS A PLACE HE WANTED TO COME BACK TO.
IT WAS NOS-TALGIC...
...COMFORT-ABLE...
...AND MADE HIM HAPPY.
IT MADE HIM INSTINCTIVELY WANT TO RUN BACK HERE.
TO CON-TINUE RUN-NING...
...OR TO TURN BACK AND FACE FORWARD—
I WONDER WHICH HE CHOSE?
WELL, IT DOESN'T MATTER.
FUWA (FWOO)

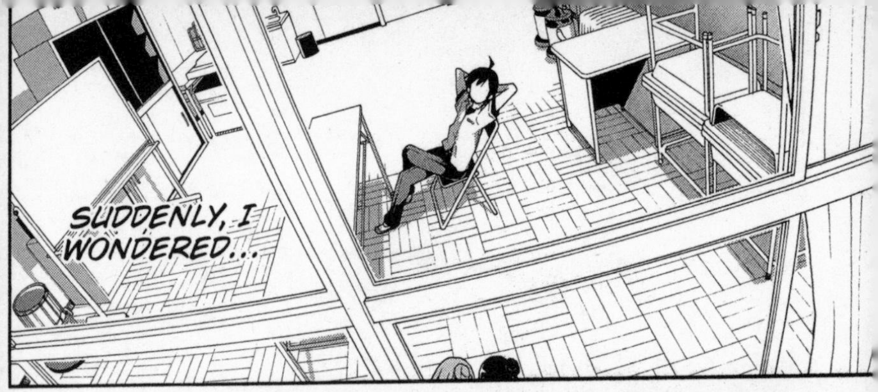
SUDDENLY, I WONDERED...

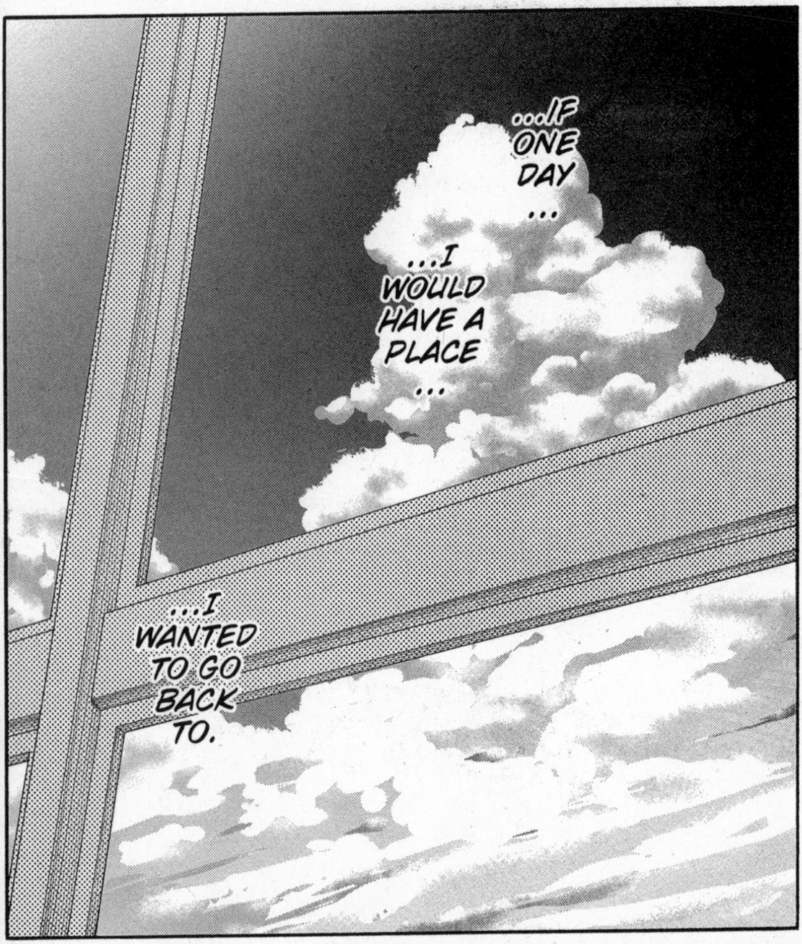
...IF ONE DAY ...
...I WOULD HAVE A PLACE ...
...I WANTED TO GO BACK TO.

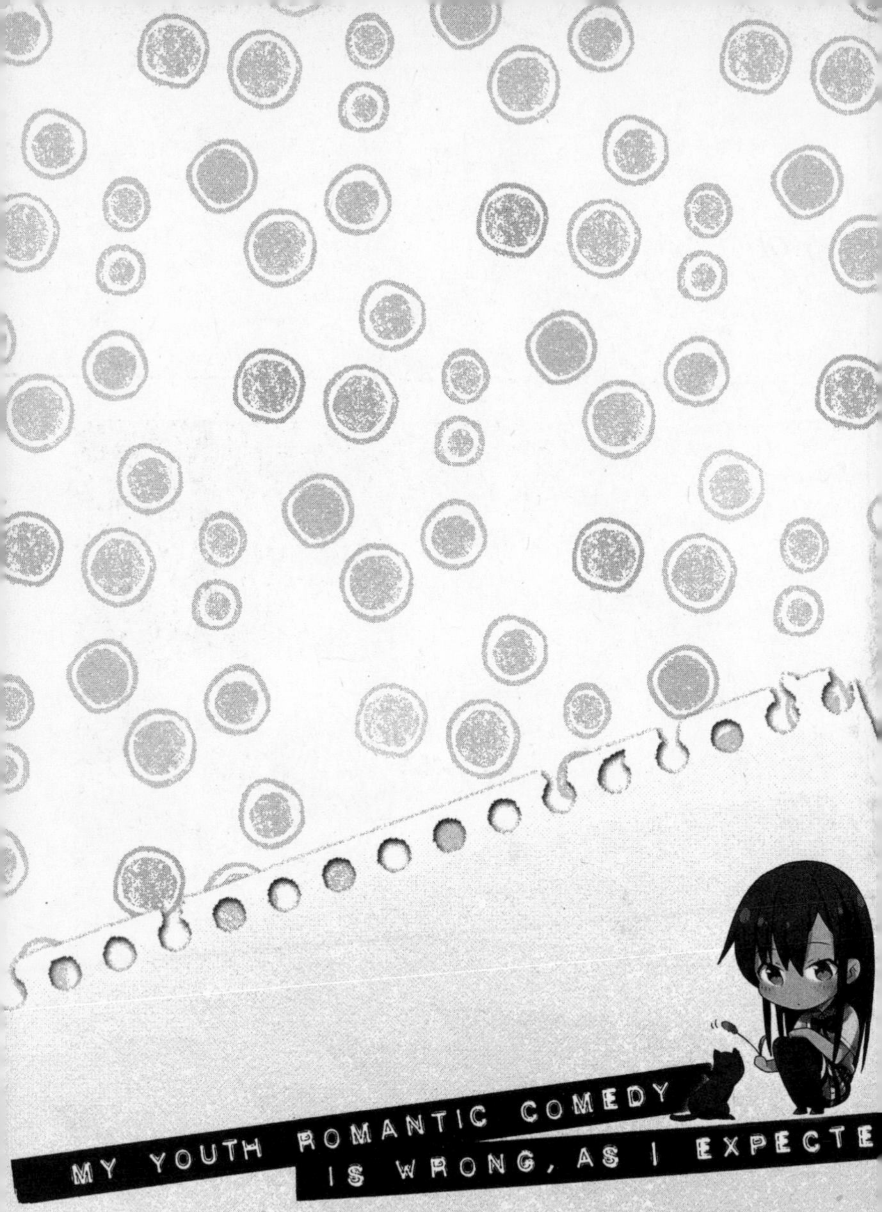
MY YOUTH ROMANTIC COMEDY
IS WRONG, AS I EXPECTE

…To Be Continued

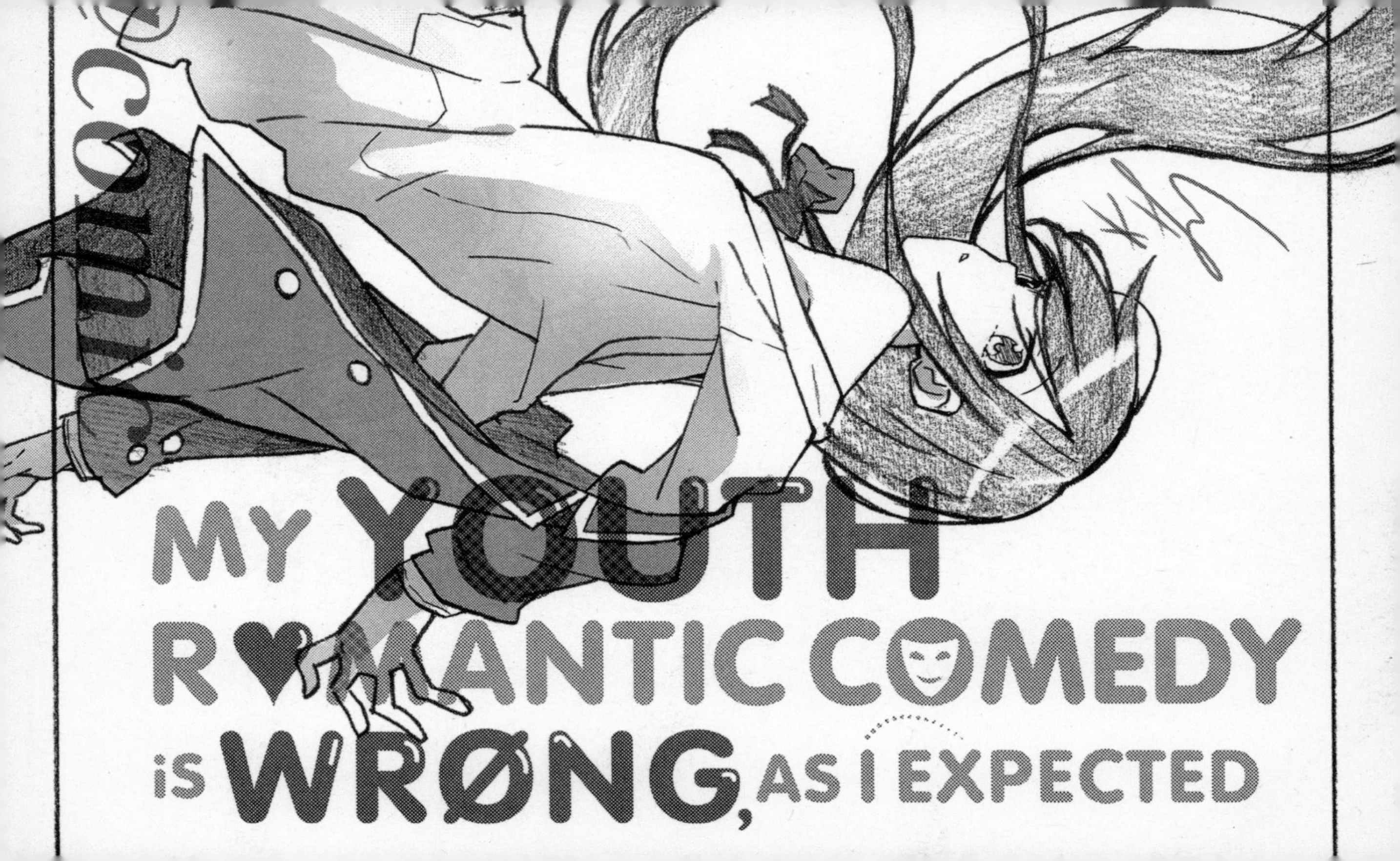
MY YOUTH
R♥MANTIC COMEDY
iS WRØNG, AS I EXPECTED

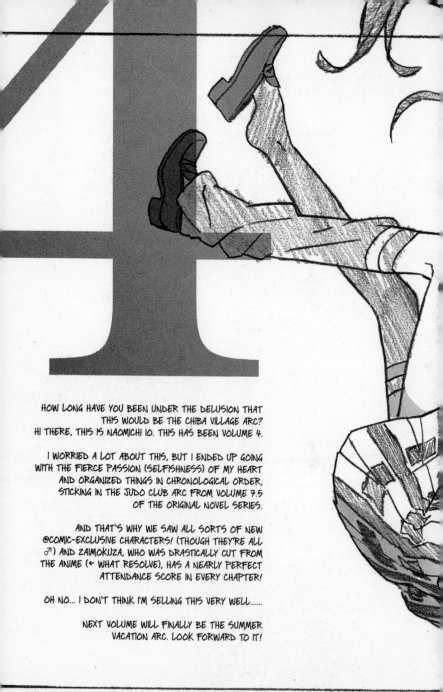

HOW LONG HAVE YOU BEEN UNDER THE DELUSION THAT
THIS WOULD BE THE CHIBA VILLAGE ARC?
HI THERE, THIS IS NAOMICHI IO. THIS HAS BEEN VOLUME 4.

I WORRIED A LOT ABOUT THIS, BUT I ENDED UP GOING
WITH THE FIERCE PASSION (SELFISHNESS) OF MY HEART
AND ORGANIZED THINGS IN CHRONOLOGICAL ORDER,
STICKING IN THE JUDO CLUB ARC FROM VOLUME 7.5
OF THE ORIGINAL NOVEL SERIES.

AND THAT'S WHY WE SAW ALL SORTS OF NEW
@COMIC-EXCLUSIVE CHARACTERS! (THOUGH THEY'RE ALL
♂) AND ZAIMOKUZA, WHO WAS DRASTICALLY CUT FROM
THE ANIME (← WHAT RESOLVE), HAS A NEARLY PERFECT
ATTENDANCE SCORE IN EVERY CHAPTER!

OH NO... I DON'T THINK I'M SELLING THIS VERY WELL......

NEXT VOLUME WILL FINALLY BE THE SUMMER
VACATION ARC. LOOK FORWARD TO IT!

THANKS: WATARU WATARI-SENSEI, PONKAN⑧-SENSEI, THE EDITORIAL DEPARTMENT AT GAGAGA PUBLISHING, THE MONTHLY SUNDAY GX EDITORIAL DEPARTMENT, CHIBA CITY LOCATION SERVICES.
SPECIAL THANKS: YAMADA-KUN, TAKAHASHI-KUN, MATSUNAGA-KUN, KOUTAROU TAKADA-SENSEI, AKKI, MITSUKI, AND YOU, THE READER.

TRANSLATION NOTES

Page 1
Hachiemon is a play on the titular character from the manga and anime *Doraemon*, which is about a robot cat from the future who can pull advanced inventions from his front pocket.

Gian (as in "giant") is a large and dim-witted bully in *Doraemon*. In the English language version of the anime, he's called "Big G."

Page 4
Zaimokuza's pose in panel one is the "Gendou Ikari pose" from the anime *Neon Genesis Evangelion*. Gendou is the mysterious and cunning father of the protagonist, Shinji, who heads an organization to protect the Earth from enigmatic creatures called "Angels."

Page 6
A *fujoshi* is a fangirl of male-male relationships in fiction, media, and sometimes even real life. *Fujoshi* literally means "rotten girl."

Page 9
"Quiver like a bowstring's pulse" is a line from the main theme of the Japanese animated film *Princess Mononoke*. The shadows below Zaimokuza's eyes are an imitation of the warpaint worn by San, a girl who was raised by wolves in the film.

"Silence, boy!" is a line from Moro, the god of the wolves in *Princess Mononoke*. The sound effect **Moroo**, plus the **wolf face in the background**, are references to Moro as well.

Page 13
The **U.G. Club** is the *Yuugi-bu* ("Gameplay Club") in the Japanese version, referring to the fact that the members are serious gamers and to the manga series / card game phenomenon *Yu-Gi-Oh!*

Page 20
The card game **Millionaire** is known as *Daifugou* ("Great Millionaire"). In English, it's also known as "President."

Page 23
"Trap card, open!" is also from the manga series *Yu-Gi-Oh!* Trap cards are specific cards that can only be triggered due to an opponent's action.

Page 26
Yakyuuken ("baseball fist") originally meant entertainment through singing and performing while playing rock-paper-scissors with a group at a drinking party, but variety TV shows have popularized the idea that it's basically just strip rock-paper-scissors. **Mahjong** is a board game similar to rummy played with tiles that is Chinese in origin but has unique rules in its Japanese variant. *Yakyuuken* and strip mahjong video games were mainstays of Japanese arcades in previous decades, so the fact that Hachiman believes stripping is common in mahjong shows that he thinks of these games primarily in terms of video games.

Page 56
"Infinity Slash," along with the eight of clubs in the background, are references to the "Endless Eight" arc of the light novel series *The Melancholy of Haruhi Suzumiya*. The characters are forced to repeat the same eight days for almost an eternity.

Page 58
End of Genesis, Revolution Type-D is a play on the one-time pop music duo of T.M. Revolution and Daisuke Asakura. In anime, T.M. Revolution is known for singing songs from series such as *Rurouni Kenshin* and *Mobile Suit Gundam SEED*. Asakura was the composer for anime such as *Gravitation*.

Page 101–102
In the Japanese version, rather than a confusion between **hair fiber and paper fiber**, the misunderstanding comes from the fact that the words for hair and paper are pronounced the same way: *kami*.

Page 104
"Chii is learning" became an internet meme due to how often the robot girl says that line in the CLAMP manga and anime series *Chobits*. It's something you say whenever you learn something new, especially new words.

Page 115
In the Japanese version, Hina's exclamation "I-I can't even!" is *"G-gusai!"* ("R-rotten!") because she's a *fujoshi*, or "rotten girl."

Page 117
The use of the word **"duel"** here is specifically from *Yu-Gi-Oh!* As established, Zaimokuza is familiar with the series, and Hachiman is trying to use the ambiguity of the word to convince him.

"OMG, that sounds fishy!" involves the phrase *desushi osushi* in Japanese, a sentence-ending particle popularized by players of the MMORPG *Final Fantasy XI*. It combines the verbal tic *desushi* with a popular in-game item, *osushi*.

Page 126
Hajime means "begin" and is the standard way to announce the start of a match in judo.

Page 128
Ippon is Japanese for "one point" and is the highest score an individual action can earn in judo. A partial or half point is known as *waza-ari*.

TRANSLATION NOTES (CONTINUED)

Page 141
A **manager** in Japanese school sports team is less a supervisor of the team and more of an assistant who handles clerical, administrative, and scouting duties. They handle a variety of miscellaneous tasks, such as cleaning uniforms, keeping track of equipment, recording team stats, and researching other teams.

"My ghost is whispering" refers to the manga and anime franchise *Ghost in the Shell*. In it, the main heroine Motoko Kusanagi has a cybernetic body. What makes her human is her soul, or "ghost."

Inside Front Cover
"Sword Master" in the Japanese version is the designated pronunciation, but the kanji characters literally mean "Master Swordsman General."

Supreme King Number 8 is based on the fact that the *Hachi* in Hachiman means "eight."

Inside Back Cover
Zaimokuza's outfit is reminiscent of Edward Elric's from *Fullmetal Alchemist*, and the **ouroboros symbol** behind Zaimokuza is also very similar to the iconic mark in the same show.

Infinity Blade Field is a blatant ripoff of Unlimited Blade Works, a special technique from the visual novel *Fate/Stay Night* and its related spin-offs. Unlimited Blade Works allows the user to create and bring forth a seemingly endless array of mythical weapons from throughout history.

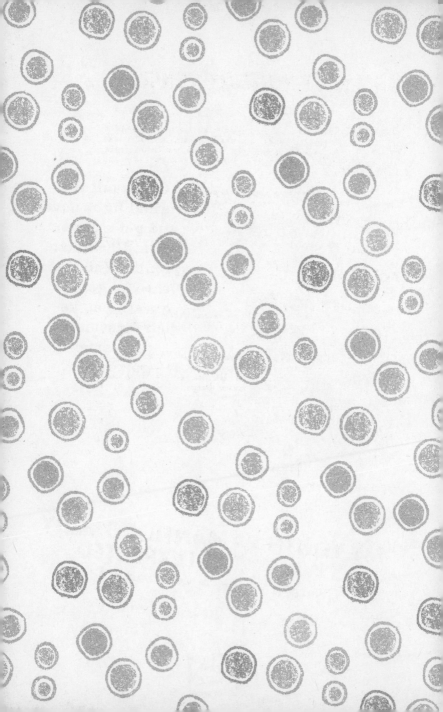

MY **YOUTH**
R♥MANTIC C☺MEDY
is **WRØNG,** AS I EXPECTED
@ *comic*

MY YOUTH ROMANTIC COMEDY IS WRONG, AS I EXPECTED @COMIC ④

Original Story: Wataru Watari
Art: Naomichi Io
Character Design: Ponkan⑧
ORIGINAL COVER DESIGN/Hiroyuki KAWASOME (Graphio)

Translation: Jennifer Ward

Lettering: Bianca Pistillo

This book is a work of fiction. Names, characters, places, and incidents are the product of the author's imagination or are used fictitiously. Any resemblance to actual events, locales, or persons, living or dead, is coincidental.

YAHARI ORE NO SEISHUN LOVE COME WA MACHIGATTEIRU.
@COMIC Vol. 4 by Wataru WATARI, Naomichi IO, PONKAN⑧
© 2013 Wataru WATARI, Naomichi IO, PONKAN⑧
All rights reserved.
Original Japanese edition published by SHOGAKUKAN.
English translation rights arranged with SHOGAKUKAN through Tuttle-Mori Agency, Inc., Tokyo.

English translation © 2017 by Yen Press, LLC

Yen Press
1290 Avenue of the Americas
New York, NY 10104

Visit us at yenpress.com
facebook.com/yenpress
twitter.com/yenpress
yenpress.tumblr.com
instagram.com/yenpress

First Yen Press Edition: March 2017

Yen Press is an imprint of Yen Press, LLC.
The Yen Press name and logo are trademarks of Yen Press, LLC.

The publisher is not responsible for websites (or their content) that are not owned by the publisher.

Library of Congress Control Number: 2016931004

ISBN: 978-0-316-31812-9

10 9 8 7 6 5 4 3 2 1

BVG

Printed in the United States of America